CORPS COMPETENCY?

MODERN WAR STUDIES

William Thomas Allison
General Editor

Raymond Callahan
Heather Marie Stur
Allan R. Millett
Carol Reardon
David R. Stone
Samuel J. Watson
Jacqueline E. Whitt
James H. Willbanks
Series Editors

Theodore A. Wilson
General Editor Emeritus

CORPS COMPETENCY?

III Marine Amphibious Force

Headquarters in Vietnam

Michael F. Morris

UNIVERSITY PRESS OF KANSAS

© 2024 by the University Press of Kansas
All rights reserved

Published by the University Press of Kansas (Lawrence, Kansas 66045), which was
organized by the Kansas Board of Regents and is operated and funded by Emporia
State University, Fort Hays State University, Kansas State University, Pittsburg State
University, the University of Kansas, and Wichita State University.

Library of Congress Cataloging-in-Publication Data

Names: Morris, Michael F., 1963– author.
Title: Corps competency? : III Marine Amphibious Force Headquarters in
  Vietnam / Michael F. Morris.
Other titles: III Marine Amphibious Force Headquarters in Vietnam
Description: Lawrence : University Press of Kansas, [2024] | Series: Modern
  war studies | Includes bibliographical references and index.
Identifiers: LCCN 2024003041 (print) | LCCN 2024003042 (ebook)
  ISBN 9780700636938 (cloth)
  ISBN 9780700636945 (ebook)
Subjects: LCSH: United States. Marine Corps. Amphibious Force, III. |
  United States. Marine Corps. Combined Action Program—History. | United
  States. Marine Corps—History—Vietnam War, 1961–1975. |
  Counterinsurgency—Vietnam—History—20th century. | Combined operations
  (Military science)—History—20th century.
Classification: LCC DS558.4 .M67 2024 (print) | LCC DS558.4 (ebook) | DDC
  959.704/342—dc23/eng/20240207
LC record available at https://lccn.loc.gov/2024003041.
LC ebook record available at https://lccn.loc.gov/2024003042.

British Library Cataloguing-in-Publication Data is available.

To my mother, Eloise,
who taught me early on the joy of a good book.

Contents

Photo gallery follows page 143.

Illustrations

Acknowledgments

There are many people to whom I owe a debt of gratitude for their valuable help on this project. I would like to begin with a special thanks to my dissertation committee chair at Texas A&M University, Dr. Brian Linn, and the other members of that group, including Dr. Jasen Castillo, Dr. Elizabeth Cobbs, Dr. Olga Dror, and Dr. Lorien Foote, for their guidance and support throughout the research and writing process. There could not have been a finer or more professional dissertation committee. I am proud to call all of these scholars friends as well as mentors.

Thanks also go to my fellow graduate students and other history department faculty and staff for making my time at the university such a wonderful experience. My cohort's Summer Writing Project and the members of A&M's War & Society Working Group made learning the historian's craft especially productive and enjoyable.

Research would be impossible without the assistance of the professional archivists, librarians, historians, and staff who guide our forays into their Aladdin's Cave of treasures. I owe a special debt of gratitude to the following men and women for their patience, support, and expertise in helping a novice researcher access their collections:

Army Center of Military History: Andrew Birtle, Tom Crecca, Shane Makowicki, Kate Richards, Erik Villard

Army Command and Staff College Ike Skelton Combined Arms Research Library: Elizabeth Dubuisson

Army Heritage and Education Center: Richard Baker, Rodney Foytik, Mike Lynch, Adria Olmi, James Scudieri, Mark Viney

Library of the Marine Corps: Greg Cina

Lyndon B. Johnson Presidential Library: Jenna de Graffenried, John Wilson

Marine Corps History Division and Archive: Fred Allison, Annette Amerman, Steve Coode, Jim Ginther, Yvette House, John Lyles, Alyson Mazzone, Ed Nevgloski, Charlie Niemeyer, Tyler Reed, Paul Weber

National Museum of the Marine Corps: Lin Ezell, Robin Mooney
NARA II: Marie Carpenti, Stan Fanaras, Martin Gedra,
    Alicia Henneberry, Russell Hill, Michael Knight, Nate Patch,
    Eric Van Slander
Naval Academy Nimitz Library: David D'Onofrio
Naval History and Heritage Command: Joe Gordon,
    John Sherwood, Laura Waayers
Naval Institute Library and Archive: Janis Jorgensen
Naval War College Library: Dennis Zambrotta
Navy Seabee Museum: Amber DelaCruz
Texas A&M Cushing Library: Jennifer Reibenspies,
    Vaprrenon Severs, Leslie Winter
Texas A&M Research Library: Joel Kitchens, Laura Sare
Texas Tech University Vietnam Center & Archive:
    Stephen Maxner, Amy Mondt, Sheon Montgomery

The following sources furnished generous financial assistance for research:

Albritton Center for Grand Strategy, Texas A&M University
    (Research Grant)
Texas A&M University Glasscock Center for Humanities
    (Graduate Research Fellowship)
History Department, Texas A&M University (Research and
    Travel Grants)
Marine Corps Heritage Foundation (Shepherd Dissertation
    Fellowship)
Office of Graduate and Professional Studies, Texas A&M
    University (Travel Grant)
Society for Military History (Allen R. Millett Dissertation
    Research Fellowship)
Vietnam Center & Archive, Texas Tech University (Travel Grant)

Vietnam historians Merle Pribbenow, Mark Moyar, and Jim Will-banks were gracious in sharing their time, expertise, advice, and materials to further my own research. Dr. Willbanks provided a complete digital copy of his own invaluable archive of records and publications collected over a lifetime of study in the field.

A special thanks is also due to my many colleagues, friends, and mentors at Marine Corps University who inspired me to pursue doctoral studies. Especially important among this group were Dr. Don Bittner,

Dr. Sandy Cochran, Dr. Rich DiNardo, Dr. Paul Gelpi, Dr. Bill Gordon, Dr. Bruce Gudmundsson, Dr. Chris Harmon, Dr. Rebecca Johnson, Dr. Wray Johnson, Dr. James Lacey, Dr. Doug McKenna, Dr. Brad Meyer, Dr. Williamson Murray, Dr. Charlie Neimeyer, Dr. Gordon Rudd, Dr. Eric Shibuya, Dr. Doug Streusand, Dr. Craig Swanson, Dr. Paolo Tripodi, Dr. Jerre Wilson, and Dr. Bradford Wineman. Professor Wray Johnson provided a thorough critique of the draft manuscript; his insight and advice improved the final product in many ways.

Dr. Tom Marks of National Defense University introduced me to new ideas on counterinsurgency when I studied under him twenty years ago. In the same influential category, but teaching at the Army War College, is my friend and mentor Professor Len Fullenkamp, an inspirational teacher, strategist, and staff-ride expert who has shared sage counsel since I studied under him in Carlisle's Advanced Strategic Arts Program in academic year 2005. Managing Editor Kelly Chrisman Jacques and the team at the University Press of Kansas have been patient and professional with a first-time author.

Finally, my deepest appreciation is owed to my wife, Sue, who lived and loved the A&M journey with me every step of the way. There is no one prouder of the university and what it means to be an Aggie. She continues to support my teaching, research, and writing pursuits now that we are back at Marine Corps University in Quantico, Virginia. I am grateful beyond words for her love and encouragement.

All the family, friends, colleagues, teachers, and mentors mentioned above aided, contributed to, and inspired what is best about this work. I alone am responsible for any remaining mistakes or shortcomings.

Acronyms and Abbreviations

ARVN	Army of the Republic of Vietnam
C2	command and control
CAP	Combined Action Platoon
CB	Construction Battalion ("Seabee")
CG	commanding general
CIA	Central Intelligence Agency
CORDS	Civil Operations and Revolutionary DevelopmentSupport
DMZ	Demilitarized Zone
FLC	Force Logistics Command
FLSG	Force Logistics Support Group
FMFPAC	Fleet Marine Force, Pacific
G-1	Staff code for Administrative section
G-2	Staff code for Intelligence section
G-3	Staff code for Operations section
G-4	Staff code for Logistics section
G-5	Staff code for Plans section (became Civil Affairs section in 1965)
HES	Hamlet Evaluation System
HQMC	Headquarters Marine Corps
JGS	[Vietnamese] Joint General Staff
KIA	killed in action
MAB	Marine Amphibious Brigade
MACV	Military Assistance Command, Vietnam
MAF/III MAF	Marine Amphibious Force/III Marine Amphibious Force
MAGTF	Marine Air-Ground Task Force
MAW	Marine Aircraft Wing
MEB	Marine Expeditionary Brigade
MEC	Marine Expeditionary Corps
MEF	Marine Expeditionary Force
MR	Military Region
NCO	noncommissioned officer

NMCB	Naval Mobile Construction Battalion
NSA	Naval Support Activity
NVA	North Vietnamese Army
POW	prisoner of war
PSDF	People's Self Defense Force
RLT	Regimental Landing Team
ROK	Republic of Korea
RVN	Republic of Vietnam (South Vietnam)
RVNAF	Republic of Vietnam Armed Forces
SEER	System for Evaluating the Effectiveness of Republic of Vietnam Armed Forces
SNCO	staff noncommissioned officer
SVN	South Vietnam
USMC	United States Marine Corps
VC	Vietcong
VCI	Vietcong infrastructure
WWI/WWII	World War I/World War II

Introduction

Waging War in I Corps

The Vietnam War continues to engage, divide, and traumatize the American public. The central paradox of the struggle endures: How did the world's strongest nation fail to secure the Republic of Vietnam's (RVN, or South Vietnam) freedom? In this book I address that vexing question by focusing on the senior Marine headquarters in the conflict's most dangerous region. The South Vietnamese called it I Corps (pronounced "EYE-core"), a geographical zone covering the northern five provinces of South Vietnam. This area featured the bloodiest fighting against the North Vietnamese Army (NVA), the Vietcong's (VC, the South Vietnamese communist movement and its military arm) strongest infrastructure, the disputed border with North Vietnam, key portions of the Ho Chi Minh Trail, and the important political and economic prizes of Hue and Da Nang. This sector was also the site of the first major American military operation (Operation STARLITE), the Battles of Hue City and Khe Sanh during the 1968 Tet Offensive, and a key military innovation known as the Combined Action Platoon (CAP), which later was cited as a counterinsurgency technique that could have won the war if applied more widely.

Despite the region's importance, our understanding of the conflict in I Corps remains patchy. The contest there has been broken into largely unconnected categories of analysis: the "grunt's eye" view, individual battles, specific units, debates over competing military strategies, and the influence of policymaking in Washington, DC, and Saigon. The result is that, a half-century later, historians know comparatively little about the overall gestalt of the war in this pivotal five-province region.

In this book I unify this fragmented narrative by approaching the regional conflict through the lens of III Marine Amphibious Force

(III MAF), the primary US tactical command in I Corps from 1965 to 1970.[1] Focusing on the American headquarters responsible for waging war in this sector offers a coherence missing in piecemeal accounts of particular actions. I will investigate several questions largely over-looked in the Vietnam War's historiography. These include: What role did III MAF headquarters play? How did that corps-level command element conceptualize, organize, implement, support, and evaluate operations? How did the Marines adapt to the challenges they faced? In short, how did the American military wage war in the most critical region of the most controversial twentieth-century conflict?

As to that last question, the answer is: poorly. I argue that III MAF was unprepared for the scope and scale of the conflict it encountered in I Corps, that it failed in its three most important tasks, and that the United States Marine Corps learned little from its longest and bloodiest experience of corps-level command. Tacitus observed that victory is claimed by many fathers, while defeat is typically an or-phan.[2] In Vietnam, failure had many fathers. The reasons for the MAF's troubles were legion. Some flowed from national policy and theater strategy that were beyond a regional headquarters' ability to alter. Some were self-inflicted. But one factor loomed large: Marines placed little emphasis on corps-level command. The service had dis-banded its corps headquarters after World War II (WWII). On the ground in Vietnam, the MAF acted more as an administrative than a warfighting command. After the war ended, senior Marines did not evaluate III MAF's effectiveness. An institutional culture that stressed operations at the regimental level and below led inevitably to mediocre corps-level command. Marine officers hungered to lead companies and battalions—higher realms were "echelons above reality"—and figured that junior-level training had imparted all they needed to know about tactics. Vietnam's school of hard knocks taught otherwise, proving the crucial role of the corps and what happens when such a large unit is not handled well. What follows unpacks those conclusions and shows why the house the Marines helped construct did not stand.

My interest in this topic commenced many years ago. As a Marine officer commissioned in 1985, I grew up in the Corps under staff non-commissioned officers (SNCOs) as well as field grade and flag rank officers who learned their trade in Vietnam. In my first fifteen years of service I learned tribal wisdom about the conflict from them, as well as from brief coverage of the war in various military schools. Most of the instruction focused on small unit actions and individual heroics in iconic battles such as Hue City and Khe Sanh. But for the most part, the Marine Corps had moved on from the memories of this most distasteful war.

In April 2000, my curiosity was piqued when I first visited Vietnam on a staff ride studying key locales, including the former Demilitarized Zone (DMZ), Da Nang, Ho Chi Minh City, and the Mekong Delta. Our group of staff college students walked the ground of Operation STARLITE, the first major clash between US and VC forces, accompanied by veterans from both sides telling us their experiences. Since then I have been back to Vietnam five times, leading delegations of field grade officers and historians to wartime sites from Dien Bien Phu and Hanoi in the North to Khe Sanh, Hue City, and Ap Bac in the South. As the associate dean for warfighting at the Marine Corps Staff College in 2006, I created a counterinsurgency planning exercise using a scenario based on Jeffrey Race's *War Comes to Long An*.[3] Later, as the director of the School of Advanced Warfighting (SAW) at Marine Corps University, I led a graduate seminar based on that book. It challenged my thinking on counterinsurgency more than any other single work because it argues that, contrary to doctrine, political work can and should precede establishment of a secure environment. Faculty at the School of Advanced Warfighting also taught a series of seminars on the war (with classes held in Virginia, followed by on-the-ground instruction in Vietnam) that prepared students for visits to the locations of the events they had studied. Despite this intermittent academic and professional exposure to our nation's most divisive foreign war, one overarching question remained unclear: How and to what effect had III MAF directed the I Corps actions we studied? This work answers that question.

A corps is the echelon of command between division and field army and represents a seldom-studied and undervalued aspect of military operations. Napoleon originated the idea of packaging a few divisions into formations that could fight independently for a time yet also combine with other corps to form a field army for decisive battles. In the American Civil War, both the Union and the Confederacy fielded corps. In World War I (WWI), the United States Army employed multiple corps, but they fought for a period of only three months in 1918. All the major combatants in WWII organized their divisions into corps. The US Army again employed corps in Korea. US Military Assistance Command, Vietnam (MACV) fielded three corps-level headquarters. Two of these (I and II Field Forces) were US Army commands. The Marine Corps sourced the third such command and the first to deploy: III MAF.

In combat, a corps-level headquarters serves like an orchestra conductor, directing and coordinating diverse combat, logistic, administrative, and other resources toward a strategic goal. The forces a corps employs typically range between forty thousand and one hundred thousand troops, with the corps headquarters supervising two or more divisions. Additional corps-level troops include smaller battalion- and brigade-size units that provide specialized capabilities like artillery, engineering, communications, military police, intelligence, civil affairs, and motor transport. These units either serve directly under the corps headquarters to conduct their discrete functions or get assigned to reinforce the divisions' combat power.

The Marine Corps has directed corps-level combat operations less than a dozen times: eight campaigns in WWII, Vietnam, the Gulf War, and the Iraq War. The experience in Vietnam, where it fielded a naval corps-level command operating ashore, represented the longest and most costly of those campaigns. In 1968 III MAF became the largest combat formation ever fielded by the Marine Corps. In Vietnam, the MAF managed a multitude of functions, balancing the complicated political and military goals of senior American and South Vietnamese leaders and those of its own combat units. It operated within a complex web of command relationships that linked allied, service, higher, adjacent, and supporting headquarters. For those seeking lessons, a case study of I Corps provides insights into the influence of education, training, and doctrine on command proficiency, how organizations adapt during war, and the constraints of campaigning within a theater headquarters' operational construct.

In twentieth-century military history, scholarly treatments of corps-level operations and headquarters are scarce. Books on regiments, divisions, and armies abound, but a focus on the echelon that connects divisions with armies remains relatively rare. WWI studies offer some of the best analysis of what corps do in combat. Works in this vein include Timothy Travers's *How the War Was Won*, Robin Prior and Trevor Wilson's *Command on the Western Front*, Simon Robbins's *British Generalship on the Western Front*, and Andy Simpson's excellent *Directing Operations: British Corps Command on the Western Front, 1914–1918*.[4] Corps-level assessments from WWII include Harold Winton's evaluation titled *Corps Commanders of the Bulge*, Douglas Delaney's study of British and Canadian corps commanders, Nathan Prefor's *Patton's Ghost Corps*, and Michael Reynolds's two-volume study of Germany's 1st SS Panzer Corps.[5] Beyond these pivotal works, anyone interested in learning more about the corps level of command is left primarily with reminisces by former commanders. The latter genre includes memoirs by generals such as Bernard Montgomery and William Slim for the British army; Hermann Balck, Erich von Manstein, F. W. von Mellenthin, and Erhard Raus for the German army; and J. Lawton Collins, Lucian Truscott, and Matthew Ridgeway for the US Army.[6] For the Korean conflict, several studies of X Corps provide useful insights.[7] In the Vietnam War literature, studies that focus on corps commands are even more scarce. Much has been written on the war in South Vietnam, but no work interprets those events based on the actions of the senior Vietnamese or American commands responsible for protecting Saigon's four administrative and military regions.[8]

American corps in Vietnam were unlike their World War I/II and Korean predecessors. They not only held tactical responsibilities but also exercised civil-military nation-building and host-nation security force development roles. This, combined with the stationary and long-term nature of the conflict, caused corps staffs to grow in size and capability. Corps-level troop units also grew in capacity. By 1968 the standard US Army corps included battalion- to brigade-size air defense, artillery, aviation, civil affairs, engineering, intelligence, logistic, medical, military police, signal, and transport units.[9] The Marine Corps, however, did not similarly expand the size and capacity of its force-level units. That service placed little emphasis on corps-level doctrine, organization, education, and training ever since it disbanded its two amphibious corps in 1946. Instead Marine commanders and staff officers focused on operations conducted below the division level. The limited attention paid to corps-level responsibilities led to an unnecessarily steep learning curve for III MAF in I Corps.

Corps-level concerns mattered in Vietnam because that echelon of command translated the edicts of MACV and the Vietnamese Joint General Staff (JGS) into action on the ground. The MAF, and its US Army counterparts in II and III Corps, bore responsibility for conducting the multipronged strategy that would secure South Vietnam's future. As the corps closest to North Vietnam, III MAF faced the most dangerous conventional threat throughout the war.[10] If the allied strategy was to succeed, the MAF had to show that it could work even under the most challenging conditions. In the strategic sense, III MAF's area of responsibility served as Saigon's proverbial canary in the coal mine.

This story sits uncomfortably within the larger historiography of the Vietnam War, which is divided into two intellectually hostile camps. The so-called orthodox school holds that the conflict was unnecessary, immoral, and unwinnable. So-called revisionists, by contrast, counter that the war was a key component of Cold War strategy, a just and even noble endeavor, and could have preserved an independent, noncommunist South Vietnam had different ways and means been employed.[11] My analysis does not directly engage that overarching debate, which has obfuscated more than illuminated the story of the war, beyond three observations that undermine my confidence in the orthodox view. First, all wars are unnecessary, so long as at least one side is willing to endure the consequences that flow from choosing not to fight. Second, my research has revealed no evidence of command-sanctioned atrocities or war crimes in I Corps, with the exception of the assassinations and mass killings (e.g., Hue in 1968) undertaken as a matter of policy by communist forces. Finally, it is illogical to argue that alternate ways and means could not lead to a different outcome.

Within the revisionist ranks, a similar long-standing debate between "big war" and "small war" advocates has also shed more heat than light. The big war school, best represented by the work of Harry G. Summers, Jr., contends that pacification was a distraction from the critical task of defeating the North Vietnamese Army.[12] Small war supporters, led by scholars like Andrew F. Krepinevich, Jr., counter that destroying South Vietnam's insurgency represented the more important mission.[13] The works of Lewis Sorley, a well-known supporter of the counterinsurgency camp, further argued that General William C. Westmoreland overemphasized large unit operations, an error that General Creighton Abrams, his successor, quickly and usefully rectified in 1968.[14] Some scholarship published in the twenty-first century has argued for more continuity than change under the two generals' respective commands.[15] My study of the conflict within I Corps reveals a more nuanced and even counterintuitive interpretation of the standard big war–versus–small war dispute.

The analysis that follows illuminates aspects of the revisionist debate, just not in a quest to settle which style of fighting was most necessary or effective. The communist foe in I Corps was hybrid by design, comprising both conventional and irregular components. The allies' response, by necessity, was hybrid too. With that idea in mind, this work covers the regional conflict by examining how the Marine Corps between WWII and Vietnam prepared its senior tactical headquarters, how III MAF understood its enemy in Vietnam, how it managed the war in I Corps, why it made the operational choices it did, what happened as a result, and why those outcomes matter. It also considers some of the options the MAF chose not to employ and what the service learned from III MAF's experiences.

My goal is to make several contributions to the historiography of the Vietnam War. This book provide the first composite analysis of the war in I Corps through the eyes of the corps-level Marine headquarters. There is no comparable study of *how* the war was fought at the corps level in any of South Vietnam's four regions. I also present a narrative of the origins and evolution of III MAF in addition to case studies of its most important combat and state-building functions. Through a close study of III MAF planning and operations, I will explore some of the little-known roads untaken by American strategists, from political warfare to establishing a fortified line along the border. I also investigate the frictions III MAF experienced with General Westmoreland's senior headquarters in Saigon and how those conflicts foreshadowed subsequent doctrinal development including functional headquarters (Joint Force Air and Land Component Commanders).

The ensuing story tells how this little-known and somewhat maligned naval headquarters commanded and coordinated field army–size Marine, US Army, and Army of the Republic of Vietnam (ARVN; pronounced "AR-vin") forces across a large region against a determined foe. The resulting insights provide not only a deeper understanding of the war in Vietnam's I Corps but also a better appreciation for what current and future corps headquarters must do to prepare for and conduct operations in a hybrid (conventional and irregular) war environment. As such, this book should interest national security professionals of all stripes today. This group includes soldiers who craft conventional and counterinsurgency campaigns and also policymakers and security studies scholars who seek a better understanding of how corps headquarters conduct combat and nation-building operations, how they prepare for those tasks, and how they adjust their actions in stride.

The primary sources for this story come from official Marine Corps records, including III MAF's monthly command chronologies, the monthly operational summaries prepared by the Fleet Marine Force, Pacific (FMFPAC) headquarters, intelligence summaries, combat and pacification plans, operation orders and after-action reports, personal papers of key leaders, message traffic, senior leader memoirs, oral histories by participants, and studies generated by Marine staffs in Da Nang, Honolulu, and Washington, DC. Records at the National Archives, US Army Center of Military History, Washington Navy Yard,

LBJ Library, Texas Tech University Vietnam Center and Archive, US Army Heritage and Education Center, Library of the Marine Corps, Fort Leavenworth Research Library, US Navy Seabee Museum, and Naval Institute archive and library complemented those found at the Marine Corps archive.

Official records of III MAF's actions are thorough. Some fifty-five thousand pages of documents reside in the Marine Corps archive, but they are not as extensive as the records from the MACV or division/ wing levels. The fact that fewer corps-level staff studies, plans, and orders were saved underscores the observation that Marines viewed the MAF as less important than the divisions and smaller units that were closer to the fighting. Of the more than five thousand Marine oral histories from Vietnam, less than 2 percent feature conversations with MAF staff, and many of those focus on interviewees' command tours. Even the MAF commanders' taped speeches, conferences, briefings, and interviews paid little attention to corps-level doctrine, organization, training, or functions. The relative paucity of evidence in comparison to other echelons of command and other topics illustrates the lack of emphasis on the MAF's role and efficiency.

The research method I employed did not compare III MAF's experience to other American or Vietnamese corps (US Army corps were known as Field Forces in Vietnam), partly because the techniques the six other allied corps-level HQs operating in South Vietnam employed, and even their outcomes, were more alike than different. Instead it analyzes how the Marine command organized, conducted, and assessed its operations through the lens of the MAF's primary staff and warfighting functions. Reliance on official documents and oral histories risks echoing the party line as told by participants reporting their own performances. To guard against that problem, I have read such records against the grain, probing for the omissions, inconsistencies, and lapses in logic that sometimes reveal as much as do intentional observations. My interpretations challenge several of the established narratives on key issues of the war within I Corps. Three examples drawn from the MAF's three main tasks—conventional combat, pacification operations, and training/advising ARVN—illustrate the point.

First, in the realm of conventional combat, Westmoreland viewed the Marines as reluctant warriors in the quest to destroy communist conventional formations. Yet the Marines had their own proud heritage of regular combat derived from iconic battles such as Belleau Wood, Iwo Jima, and Inchon. From the beginning of their time in I Corps Marines employed amphibious, air assault, and combined arms techniques to battle main force VC and NVA units when and where they found them. Their aggressive offensive tactics, however, achieved Pyrrhic victories at a cost even the USMC Commandant deemed unsustainable by 1967. Meanwhile, III MAF's first two commanders did not complete the defensive barrier system that MACV had directed them to construct in late 1966. My analysis concludes that this decision (accepted in the literature as common sense) represented a missed opportunity to test a key component of an alternate theater strategy.

Second, standard assessments by small war aficionados laud the Marines for their pacification emphasis in I Corps, especially the creation of Combined Action Platoons to improve village security. The successes of the CAP program indeed merit recognition, but I argue they did not include achievement of CAP's primary task, which was to eliminate the VC shadow government. Instead CAP's security operations—along with the blizzard of allied small unit sweeps, patrols, and ambushes conducted by regular infantry squads, platoons, and companies—gradually reduced the guerrilla threat in I Corps. Over time, attrition proved a more effective method in the small wars campaign than it did against the NVA. But the Vietcong infrastructure (VCI)—that is, the shadow government the guerrillas protected and expanded—remained surprisingly resilient. Political warfare, another facet of counterinsurgency seldom addressed, constituted another weak point of III MAF's small wars campaign.

Finally, too little attention has been paid to ARVN in the conflict's broader literature. Developing ARVN was the MAF's third essential task in I Corps. The lack of South Vietnamese records after the war leaves scholars largely dependent on American sources. Despite this constraint, important research on ARVN remains to be done. The I Corps story, for example, undermines the common narrative that ARVN was militarily hopeless. ARVN's I Corps fielded the best units within the South Vietnamese army even though its troops endured socioeconomic conditions even worse than those found in the three more southerly regions. Consistently ranked among Saigon's top divisions and regiments, I Corps' forces routinely met VC and NVA opponents on equal terms, often defeating them even without large amounts of American assistance. In this work I consider how III MAF missed opportunities to make its Vietnamese counterpart headquarters even more capable.

My research reveals four reasons for III MAF's inability to win the war in I Corps. First, a competent and determined enemy comprising NVA and VC regulars, guerrillas, and cadre conducted a complex form of hybrid warfare that the MAF never mastered. Second, Marine doctrine, organization, training, and experience undermined aspects of the headquarters' effectiveness as a corps-level command. Third, the MAF failed to accomplish its essential tasks: preventing the NVA from operating inside I Corps, destroying the insurgency's shadow government, and preparing ARVN's I Corps to protect the region independently. Finally, III MAF succeeded tactically but failed operationally—that is to say, it won many battles but never crafted a campaign that accomplished the three tasks listed above. By evaluating the MAF's experience in I Corps and analyzing each of its warfighting functions, my text substantiates each claim and indicates how these factors contributed to III MAF's ultimate failure.

This book is organized as follows: the prologue argues that the Marine Corps had not prepared its largest tactical headquarters for the conflict that III MAF encountered in Vietnam. It examines the service's limited experience with corps-level operations in the Central Pacific campaigns of WWII where the III and V Amphibious Corps played an important albeit rarely acknowledged role. After 1945, Marine schools and exercises devoted minimal attention to corps-level operations. By the early 1960s the Marine Air-Ground Task Force (MAGTF) model emerged in service doctrine. The largest of the MAGTFs, the Marine Expeditionary Corps (MEC), was the organization most suited to the challenges encountered in 1965, yet this doctrinal command element was not employed in I Corps. Instead the smaller Marine Expeditionary Force (MEF) assumed the task of directing what would eventually become a field army–size force.

Chapter 1 provides historical context by tracing the course of the war in I Corps between 1965 and 1971. It identifies the major allied and communist offensives and counteroffensives, including both conventional and counterinsurgency initiatives. This narrative highlights the characteristics of a hybrid war and how difficult it was for South Vietnamese security forces and their American and Korean counterparts to address the dual regular-irregular threats and the simultaneous political and military challenges they entailed. The chapter argues that the first three years of the war were primarily a US Marine production, with III MAF free to employ its preferred strategy even when its emphasis on pacification conflicted with Westmoreland's search-and-destroy priorities. After the 1968 Tet Offensive, a more joint environment marked the final half of III MAF's tenure. Supplementing the chronological overview, a pattern analysis illustrates the conflict's shifting contours. The second section's vignettes show how the MAF failed to act as a tactical warfighting headquarters, accomplish its three primary tasks, and craft campaigns that supported essential military and political strategies.

The rest of the text examines how III MAF executed its primary warfighting functions: command and control (C2), intelligence, operations, logistics, and plans. Chapter 2 analyzes the MAF headquarters' C2 system, which was the most important of the five functions because it integrated the effects of the other four. The text assesses command and staff actions, the way the headquarters organized the force to accomplish its mission, and the roles that senior officer leadership and doctrine played in two organizational mistakes that resulted in III MAF losing control in 1968 of the ground war in its most threatened sector as well as control of its strike and reconnaissance aircraft. In the subsequent literature on the war, the former case received less attention than the latter, but both illustrate why corps-level commands require savvy leadership and sound staff processes to maximize the MAF's operational effectiveness. Most accounts avoid discussion of service friction. Yet the quiet removal of General Robert E. Cushman, Jr.'s control over the ground war in northern I Corps remains the biggest Army–Marine conflict since the USMC's Lieutenant General Holland "Howlin' Mad" Smith relieved the US Army's Major General Ralph Smith on Saipan in 1944.

In Chapter 3, case studies illustrate how the MAF understood its regular and unconventional foes in I Corps, the extent to which the headquarters anticipated the Tet Offensive, and how intelligence supported pacification operations following Tet. A final section assesses the tension between conventional and irregular threats, arguing that senior Marine leaders emphasized the insurgency, with baleful consequences. Meanwhile, both III MAF and ARVN's I Corps became accustomed to large NVA formations residing permanently within the region. While many analysts have praised the Marine Corps for its counterinsurgency focus, they generally omit two key points underscored here: The pacification emphasis did not include a strong intelligence effort on the shadow government, and the MAF's conclusion that the insurgency represented the most dangerous threat turned out to be inaccurate.

Chapter 4 addresses operational aspects of III MAF's campaign. It breaks the multitude of responsibilities inherent in the complex I Corps mission into three major categories: advising and training ARVN; pacification duties; and conventional combat operations. It analyzes how the MAF's operational responses fared against its communist foes. The chapter clarifies that, to achieve a sustainable peace in I Corps, any two of the three primary tasks—building ARVN up while keeping the VC down and the NVA out—had to be accomplished. This did not happen.

Logistics made possible the extensive operations chronicled in I Corps. Chapter 4 demonstrates what a narrow margin pertained in manpower management, facility construction (especially ports and roads), supply inventories, equipment repair, and medical support. The MAF's organic logistic command expanded threefold during the war. A United States Navy logistics command, more than twice the size of its Marine counterpart, further reinforced the effort. Without navy and (later) army theater logistics support, III MAF would not have been able to function. Its confused organizational design for logistics incorporated a mix of units from its own forces as well as similar commands from I MEF in California. Despite its ad hoc organization and just-in-time development, this naval logistics construct worked surprisingly well in what was a large but static zone of operations.

While the logisticians proceeded by trial and error, Marine planners struggled even more throughout the six-year campaign. Chapter 6 details several examples that emphasize the point. III MAF's Plans section was small and lacked influence within the headquarters. Early on, it developed products that undermined Westmoreland's confidence in the command's competence. Planners at Marine Forces Pacific and Headquarters Marine Corps (HQMC) failed to help with a plan addressing one of the biggest problems III MAF faced: determining how many troops were required in I Corps to win the war. A bad assumption scuttled that 1966 plan. Planners in Da Nang spent much of the following year changing specifications for the DMZ barrier that Generals Lewis W. Walt and Cushman did not want to build. Eventually the latter managed to derail the project entirely. Finally, the 1969 combined campaign plan for I Corps highlighted how easy it was to identify valid objectives while failing to explain the actions that would obtain those goals. Plans mattered because they were blueprints for action, and the MAF's operational struggles reflected its planning woes.

Chapter 7 summarizes the findings for each of III MAF's command functions and draws implications from them. It assesses the senior Marine headquarters' performance, concluding that it was not effective in the long run because the campaign in I Corps did not establish the conditions necessary to achieve the intended political goal. This outcome followed inevitably the MAF's failure to solve its two primary operational problems: uprooting VC infrastructure and preventing NVA incursions. Many impressive tactical innovations emerged from

III MAF's efforts in Vietnam, but the adjustments required to resolve those two threats proved elusive. In its first wartime trial, MAGTF doctrine contributed to combined arms synergy that led to many local victories. But it also undermined III MAF's focus on traditional large unit doctrinal precepts as well as the need to support the region's growing allied forces with Marine aviation. Corps-level command in I Corps taxed the MAF headquarters, one that was not built or trained to control so many subordinate, division-size ground, aviation, and logistic commands. In the end III MAF managed to keep at bay, but not defeat, the region's lethal hybrid threats.

The epilogue tells the story of what the Marine Corps learned from III MAF's experience in Vietnam. Like its US Army counterpart, the USMC evinced little interest in pondering what the longest and bloodiest war in its history might mean for future conflicts, especially regarding corps-level operations. Few doctrinal, organizational, or training refinements followed. Instead the Marine Corps reemphasized smaller unit amphibious operations, developed a new role on Europe's northern flank, and trained to project rapid response forces to the Middle East. Consequently, twenty years later, during the Gulf War, the I MEF headquarters that directed corps-level operations encountered many of the same doctrinal, organizational, and training challenges that III MAF had experienced in I Corps, without the benefit of lessons learned.

Corps-level combat command has been an important but uncommon event in Marine Corps history. The service has employed such headquarters in war twelve of the last eighty years. Half of that experience took place in I Corps. What follows is the story of a naval expeditionary headquarters evolving under the combined pressure of a determined enemy, a harsh environment, and competing ideas on how best to win the war. An inspirational as well as cautionary tale, it is a piece of Marine Corps history too long untold.

Prologue

Marines and Corps-Level Command, 1941–1965

The United States Marine Corps had little experience with corps-level command prior to the Vietnam War. In the preceding quarter-century, five factors shaped Marines' preparation for corps warfighting responsibilities. These include: institutional memory from World War II; new Marine Air-Ground Task Force doctrine; the organizational transition from Pacific War amphibious corps to Cold War Marine Expeditionary Forces; the focus of interwar Marine schools; and the service's pre-Vietnam training regimens. Collectively, these influences shaped III Marine Amphibious Force's readiness for the challenges it would face in Southeast Asia.

Corps-Level Experience

The Marine Corps fielded no corps-level combat formations until World War II. In the conflicts between the American Revolution and World War I, Marines served in shipboard detachments, led brief incursions ashore, and occasionally augmented US Army forces in more extended campaigns. Prior to 1918, the Corps never employed a unit larger than three thousand men in combat. During World War I, a single brigade (the 4th of Belleau Wood fame) was the largest Marine ground force that saw action. Marine officers commanded five army brigades and two divisions, but no Marine commanded a corps, and few garnered staff experience at that level. Between the world wars the Marine Corps provided small units, up to the size of a brigade, for guard and small wars duties in China, Hispaniola, and Nicaragua.[1]

During WWII the Corps expanded to field 458,000 troops in six divisions and five air wings.[2] To command these new formations, Marine leaders in 1942 established two corps-level headquarters: III and

V Amphibious Corps.³ They controlled combat operations in the Solomon Islands, Bougainville–Treasury Islands, Gilbert Islands, the Marshalls, the Marianas, Palau, Iwo Jima, and Okinawa.⁴

Together the two commands conducted more than a dozen major operations in the Pacific, all of which involved amphibious landings. Most featured assaults against prepared defenses, but island geography and enemy dispositions prevented wide-ranging maneuver ashore. Early objectives rarely demanded more than one division, but as the war progressed and enemy defenses stiffened, multi-division assaults became the norm. Offensive operations exceeded ninety days only once. After seizing an island, Marine assault forces handed over the hard-earned ground to designated (usually army) occupation forces. After the war V Corps served as an occupation headquarters in Japan, while III Corps assisted in the demobilization of Japanese troops in northern China. Both units deactivated in 1946.⁵

Since only a single Marine division fought in Korea, no corps-level Marine headquarters participated in that conflict.⁶ Initially the 1st Marine Division fought under the US Army's X Corps, commanded by Major General Ned Almond. This proved an unhappy relationship, as senior army and Marine leaders disagreed on tactics. Later in the war the Marine division served under I Corps, and several Marine officers gained experience working on a corps-level staff in Korea. In the 1958 Lebanon intervention, the Marines employed a small brigade working for an army headquarters.⁷ During the 1962 Cuban Missile Crisis, II MEF briefly deployed its own East Coast division, a ten-thousand-man West Coast brigade, and four hundred Marine aircraft for potential attacks on Soviet nuclear weapon sites in Cuba. The 1965 incursion in the Dominican Republic featured a small Marine brigade headquarters controlling just four battalions and four aircraft squadrons.⁸ Thus, when III MAF entered Vietnam in May 1965, two decades had passed since a Marine headquarters had fought at the corps level.

Corps-Level Doctrine

Notwithstanding the lack of recent combat experience above the division level, Cold War–era Marines did think and write about how they intended to employ a corps headquarters when the next opportunity arose. During WWII the Marine Corps relied on army doctrine for large unit ground combat other than amphibious operations.⁹ Despite III and V Amphibious Corps' accomplishments in the Pacific War,

Headquarters Marine Corps published no service guidance on corps-level operations before 1965. Instead a new organizational doctrine emerged that applied to Marine formations at multiple levels of command, including corps. This concept, the Marine Air-Ground Task Force, stipulated that Marines would customarily operate as a team featuring four components: command, ground combat, aviation, and combat service support.[10]

The Marine Corps never fought as a MAGTF (pronounced "MAG-taff") in World War II or Korea because Marine aviation worked under navy, army, or air force command in those conflicts. Senior Marine commanders sought a doctrinal and organizational fix to remedy this perceived deficiency. In the early 1960s the scalable MAGTF model became the service's operational standard. Two Marine Corps orders released in 1962 introduced and codified the new canon's organizational precepts.[11] A primary purpose of this doctrine was to ensure that in future wars Marine aircraft would be controlled by Marine commanders.

In addition to its new organizational doctrine, the Corps also updated its guidance on staff functions. The Marine *Command and Staff Action* manual, modeled after similar army directives, addressed the duties of primary staff officers—administrative (G-1), intelligence (G-2), operations (G-3), and logistics (G-4)—and special staff officers including adjutant, artillery, engineer, legal, and others. Updated in 1965, the principles outlined in this text guided the staff work that III MAF performed in Vietnam.[12] The Marines thus arrived in I Corps armed with corps-level staff and fighting concepts based on long-standing US Army doctrine in addition to a unique MAGTF organizational model that departed from the archetypal army corps in important ways.

Corps-Level Organization

In the Pacific War, Marine and army corps organized similarly. Equivalent missions conducted on comparable terrain against the same foe drove both services to nearly identical organizational solutions. Since tactical units rotated in and out based on the next objective, it was the changing list of assigned divisions as well as its allocated corps-level troops that determined a Marine or army corps' combat power. As landward extensions of a fighting fleet, III and V Amphibious Corps developed a standard collection of organic commands to complement their assigned infantry divisions. This corps-level structure included headquarters, medical, motor transport, construction, signal, armor, antiarmor, amphibian tractor, and artillery units.[13]

After the war, the two services took different paths with their corps-level formations. In 1965 army doctrine envisioned a corps fielding up to four infantry and armor divisions, an engineer brigade, an armored cavalry regiment, a tank regiment, four artillery groups, an air defense group, a helicopter battalion, a chemical battalion, and a civil affairs company.[14] Marine Expeditionary Forces lacked the army's corps-level engineers, cavalry, armor, artillery, air defense, chemical, and civil affairs units. Unlike their amphibious corps predecessors, MEFs commanded only a single division but retained an organic air wing. The new doctrine declared Marine aviation an essential component of every MAGTF.[15] Marines argued that separating aircraft from their associated ground and logistics forces debilitated the service's combined arms teams. This position led to contentious interservice disputes over control of Marine airplanes in Vietnam.

Senior Marine leaders did not view MEFs as corps-level commands because they were not intended to direct multiple divisions, as traditional corps doctrine required. To address this organizational shortfall, Marines planned, but did not establish, a Marine Expeditionary Corps designed to control two or three divisions and one or more air wings.[16] MAGTF doctrine acknowledged the need for a command post capable of supervising multiple divisions, but the Marines fielded no permanent headquarters to perform the mission. The Marine Corps thus entered the Vietnam War with a new, small, and largely untested MEF headquarters as its primary corps-level organizational model. That design imposed structural complications when III MAF assumed corps-level responsibilities in I Corps.

Corps-Level Education

The Marine Command and Staff College curriculum reflected the limited emphasis the service placed on corps-level operations. In WWII, the college initiated an abbreviated three-month class to train more field-grade officers in higher staff functions. Reflecting the important role of III and V Amphibious Corps, one-third of the short course featured work on corps-level assaults. After the war, however, the Staff College reestablished its traditional yearlong program with more emphasis on regimental and division operations. The 1948 curriculum of

1,209 classroom hours, for instance, included just four hours spent on corps-level issues. During Korea, the college's treatment of corps-level topics edged up to a still anemic 7 percent of the 1951 syllabus.[17]

Staff College faculty made only minor curriculum modifications between the end of the Korean conflict and America's entry into Vietnam. A rigorous study of amphibious assaults, totaling at least 40 percent of the instruction, remained the school's bedrock. Most student planning problems included an amphibious corps or MEF as the senior Marine headquarters, but these exercises seldom lasted long or incorporated mobile operations beyond the beachhead line.[18] Neither did the wargames test the MEF in prolonged counterinsurgency operations. Student papers from the era underscore the school's limited emphasis on corps operations. Only twelve of 2,932 school essays between 1945 and 1975 assessed topics at that level.[19] Corps-level missions constituted only a small component of the Staff College's overall instruction, and what was included remained in a narrow (amphibious) tactical box. In contrast, the Army Command and General Staff College's interwar curriculum focused on a wide array of operations at division, corps, army, and army group level.[20] The Marine school's limited coverage of corps-level missions and functions did not fully prepare III MAF's planners and commanders for the expanded set of operational challenges they encountered in Vietnam.

Corps-Level Training

Training exercises turn military doctrine and education into combat capabilities. They seek to anticipate and render unnecessary the costly improvements derived from blood-soaked beaches like those of Tarawa. Garrison wargames and field operations tested corps-level staffs. Because the latter become costlier and more difficult to orchestrate with large units, these drills occurred infrequently at the MEF level. Not surprising, all the corps-level Marine exercises between WWII and Vietnam involved amphibious missions. During this period Marine Corps records identify only fourteen (including several US Army) corps-level amphibious exercises. MEFs conducted ten of those large unit drills between 1953 and 1963.[21]

As South Vietnamese troops suffered increasingly serious losses in combat against their communist adversaries, US naval forces conducted two ambitious corps-level amphibious exercises in 1964–1965 to demonstrate their ability to project military power across the sea to assist a beleaguered ally. In the largest amphibious exercise ever, STEEL PIKE (1964) deployed a 150-ship task force, including thirty-five amphibious transports, to land seventeen thousand II MEF Marines in Spain.[22] The following March, West Coast naval forces tested the Marine Expeditionary Corps concept in Exercise SILVER LANCE by landing fifteen thousand troops on California beaches under the command of the Fleet Marine Force, Pacific headquarters.[23] First Marine Expeditionary Brigade (MEB), a Hawaii-based unit scheduled to fight simulated guerrillas in California, proved the value of readiness when it canceled the planned exercise and instead steamed west to serve as a Southeast Asia contingency response force. A month later, the bulk of that amphibious brigade went ashore in South Vietnam as a part of the 9th MEB.[24]

Conclusion

At the beginning of 1965, the Marine Corps mustered 190,000 personnel. All were volunteers. The service's active-duty forces fielded three MEFs, three divisions, and three air wings. Since 1960 a five-year surge in equipment modernization and enhanced training, coupled with recent operational experience in the Caribbean, Middle East, and Southwest Asia, left the Marine Corps in peak condition. Commandant Wallace M. Greene, Jr., who assumed the post in 1964, told Congress his service had achieved "the best condition of readiness that I have seen in my thirty-seven years of naval service."[25]

The Marine Corps of 1965 demonstrated exceptional competence in its amphibious niche. It remained less capable of orchestrating corps-level operations in other settings. Prior to Vietnam, the Marine Corps' only operational experience with corps-level command entailed a series of brutal but brief amphibious assaults and a few months of occupation duty during World War II. After 1945, the Corps developed MAGTF doctrine but no service-specific guidance on corps-level operations, relying instead on US Army manuals. Unlike their Pacific War amphibious corps predecessors, MEFs commanded only a single division and fielded just a few small corps-level troop units, although they gained control of an air wing. The Marine Staff College's treatment of corps command between 1941 and 1965 concentrated almost exclusively on amphibious assaults. The vigorous Fleet Marine Force training program of that era had the same limited focus, with MEFs and MECs commanding the largest exercises.

All these factors—history, doctrine, organization, education, and training—shaped and limited III MAF's preparation for wartime corps-level command in Southeast Asia. Each one influenced how the MAF's leaders waged war, and together they undermined the organization's ability to accomplish its primary tasks. Although not incapable of performing other assignments, corps-level Marine headquarters had developed for twenty-five years the world's largest and most capable amphibious assault force. The amphibious mission formed the primary lens through which Marines viewed emerging threats. The Corps thus entered Vietnam looking for a problem that amphibious assaults could solve. Yet III MAF soon discovered that its principal expertise pertained only to a small subset of its I Corps responsibilities.

1

Corps-Level Marine Command in Vietnam

III Marine Amphibious Force faced a steep learning curve in Vietnam. Its doctrine, organization, training, and experience had not prepared it to exercise corps-level command. In the first section of this chapter, I summarize the ensuing conflict in the Marine sector. The cases I provide in the second section underscore the MAF's struggles to adjust to its new responsibilities as a regional command post. Each instance demonstrates that the way Marine leaders conceptualized and executed corps-level command undermined their ability to win the war in I Corps. The overview of the two-phase campaign, coupled with the operational anecdotes, depict a headquarters that failed to accomplish its primary operational tasks.

The War in I Corps, 1965–1971

III MAF fought in the Republic of Vietnam (South Vietnam) from 1965 to 1971. For most of that period it served as the senior US tactical headquarters in I Corps comprising the country's northern five provinces (see figure 1). During the first three years, US forces in the region were predominantly Marine forces. Their doctrine, organization, and training dictated how the war was waged in the sector that staff officers in Saigon called "Marineland."[1] After 1968 the Marine command received more US Army reinforcements. As they increased in numbers and influence, the "Marine war" turned into a "joint war." This section details that evolution and analyzes the patterns of conflict within I Corps, interpreting the combat narrative through a framework of force, space, and time factors.

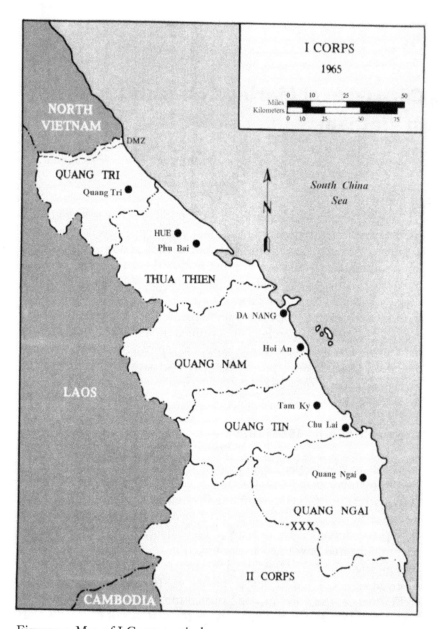

Figure 1.1 Map of I Corps tactical zone

Source: Jack Shulimson and Charles M. Johnson, *U.S. Marines in Vietnam: The Landing and the Buildup, 1965* (Washington, DC: USMC History and Museums Division, 1978), 13.

Phase I: The Marine War, 1965–1967

From 1965 to 1968, General William C. Westmoreland commanded Military Assistance Command, Vietnam, the senior American headquarters in Vietnam. He granted senior Marine commanders broad autonomy to fight the war as they saw fit. They emphasized small unit counterguerrilla actions; conducted battalion and regimental conventional operations; applied their embryonic MAGTF doctrine; learned through trial and error the organizational strengths and weaknesses of the newly designed Marine Expeditionary Force construct; and discovered that corps-level operations in Vietnam entailed far more than prewar Quantico classes and fleet training exercises had anticipated. Senior Marine leaders did not know it at the time, but they were entering a two-and-a-half-year period in which they had the opportunity to prove that the Marine way of war could defeat the hybrid enemy facing them in I Corps.

1965: Arrival and Initial Operations
The dignitaries and giggling schoolgirls who welcomed the 9th Marine Brigade when it splashed ashore at Da Nang on 8 March 1965 offered a poor premonition of the six bloody years that awaited Marines in I Corps.[2] The brigade's 4,608 troops entered a beautiful but harsh region. The size of Maryland, I Corps' five provinces, from thirty to seventy miles wide, stretched 265 miles south from the border with North Vietnam to the boundary with Binh Dinh Province. The Annamite Mountains, up to five thousand feet high, ran down its western border with Laos. Most of its 2.5 million people lived in a narrow strip of cultivated land along the South China Sea coast. Population densities in the rice-growing lowlands exceeded those of the Mekong Delta by a factor of four. Much of the rest of the area was uninhabited, with dense bamboo scrub, canopied jungle, and forested mountains, all deluged with 128 inches of annual rainfall on average, especially heavy during the chilly monsoons from September to February. An alien language and culture made the forbidding locale even more mysterious to the arriving Marines.[3]

The daunting environment also concealed a lethal hybrid enemy: Vietcong insurgents, who posed a dual military and political threat. The latter was represented by a communist shadow government that administered, taxed, and conscripted inhabitants who lived in areas under its control. The military threat started at the hamlet level with local guerrillas protecting the political cadre who ran the shadow government.

Backing the part-time soldiers were district-level companies of VC regional forces as well as main force battalions and regiments that operated across one or more provinces. By 1965 an estimated fifty thousand insurgents operated in the five northern provinces. North Vietnamese Army troops complemented the VC threat. Hanoi started sending its units south the previous year, and several NVA regiments were already inside I Corps. Opposing these communist forces were twenty-five thousand Army of the Republic of Vietnam soldiers organized into two divisions and a regiment. Another thirty-five thousand territorial troops known as Regional and Popular Forces protected provinces, districts, and villages. Nationwide, ARVN was losing a battalion per week to its communist adversaries when US ground forces entered the fray. Despite near parity in regional armed forces, several ARVN battalions within I Corps had been overrun between May and July 1965.[4]

Arriving Marines encountered a complex web of command relationships. On 6 May 1965 III Marine Expeditionary Force uncased its colors in Da Nang, subsuming 9th Brigade as more Marines flowed into I Corps. Fearing negative connotations associated with the legacy of French colonialism, the Marine headquarters immediately changed its moniker from "expeditionary" to "amphibious."[5] For operational matters, the renamed III Marine Amphibious Force reported to MACV in Saigon. Fleet Marine Force, Pacific in Honolulu handled the MAF's administrative and logistic concerns. Lieutenant General Lewis W. Walt, a husky hero of two wars, commanded the MAF from 1965 to 1967.

Westmoreland's initial guidance limited the MAF to defending critical sites such as the airfields whose planes bombed North Vietnam as part of the Operation ROLLING THUNDER. In mid-June, however, given ARVN's declining military fortunes, the MACV commander unleashed III MAF to engage communist forces. Westmoreland's strategy entailed finding and destroying NVA/VC regular units until Hanoi decided to withdraw its support from the insurgency or until it could no longer replace the casualties MACV inflicted. Walt, along with FMFPAC commander Lieutenant General Victor Krulak and the Marine Commandant, General Wallace M. Greene, Jr., believed pacification was a more suitable strategy to win the war. During that first summer, III MAF accordingly established three enclaves—Da Nang, Chu Lai, and Phu Bai—and envisioned gradually expanding them until they merged, covering the majority of the region's populace. Westmoreland thought the Marine method was too slow and vulnerable given the presence of large enemy conventional forces.

Despite MACV's doubts, Walt and his staff initiated a vigorous counterinsurgency program in I Corps. They started an aggressive civic action campaign designed to build support for both the Marines' presence and the legitimacy of Saigon's rule. These programs included distribution of food and clothing, protection of rice harvests, assistance with small self-help projects, and provision of medical aid. The MAF developed the Joint Coordination Council, the first of its kind in South Vietnam, to connect key civil and military leaders, identify and prioritize development projects, and then supervise their completion.[6] Walt quickly identified a major shortcoming in regional security (the poorly equipped and trained territorial forces) and began a program to address their deficiencies. The Combined Action Platoons, one of the best-known and most highly regarded innovations of the war, paired a Marine squad with a South Vietnamese Popular Forces platoon to defend villages.[7] Equally important was the intensive small unit patrolling III MAF employed to clear sectors of guerrillas and thwart their easy access to rural inhabitants.

Walt's troops also pursued enemy conventional units. In Operation STARLITE (18–24 August), the first major battle between American and communist regulars, the 7th Marine Regiment surrounded the 1st Vietcong Regiment a dozen miles south of Chu Lai, killing nearly seven hundred enemy troops. Over the next three months a series of search-and-destroy operations proved less productive. In December, Operation HARVEST MOON, the biggest combined operation of the war thus far, again targeted a revived 1st VC Regiment in the Que Son Valley, forty-five miles southwest of Da Nang. Despite clear superiority in supporting arms, six allied battalions failed to pin down and wipe out four VC battalions. The battle cost more friendly casualties than the reported 407 enemy dead, concluding major combat operations for the year with a whimper rather than a bang.[8]

Overall, 1965 offered mixed results in I Corps. By the end of the year, III MAF comprised the 3rd Marine Division, 1st Marine Aircraft Wing (MAW), Force Logistic Support Group, and Naval Construction Regiment 30. The MAF had expanded to thirty-nine thousand troops, firmly established in three areas that grew a hundredfold from the initial eight-square-mile perimeter around Da Nang's airfield. Coordinated civic action and aggressive small unit operations challenged Vietcong control of the countryside. But no magic talisman appeared to uproot the enemy's political infrastructure. Large unit engagements demonstrated the efficacy of Marine combined arms, yet main force adversaries routinely evaded contact or escaped when located and attacked. Marine leaders claimed 3,476 VC killed, wounded, or captured since March, though their own casualties totaled 2,407. The MAF and its ARVN allies had to improve their military effectiveness if they hoped to decisively defeat their VC/NVA foes.

1966: Seizing the Initiative
Walt needed more forces to simultaneously protect key facilities, pacify the countryside, and attack enemy regulars.[9] In 1966 the 1st Marine Division and Republic of Korea (ROK) 2nd Marine Brigade reinforced III MAF.[10] A few US Army units also arrived, but the fighting remained predominantly an ARVN and Marine affair. III MAF grew to seventy-one thousand troops by year's end.[11] Hanoi matched allied reinforcements, inserting one NVA division in the north and another in the south, with more lurking above the DMZ. As NVA units swelled along I Corps' northern border, Walt shifted 3rd Marine Division to meet the threat. Two allied divisions guarded the region's northern flank while two more, reinforced by two separate brigades, protected the southern three provinces.

The conflict inside I Corps intensified throughout 1966. The North Vietnamese Army tested allied defenses sequentially from south to north. The first five months featured heavy combat in the southern two provinces, smaller conventional and irregular actions in Quang Nam Province, and increasing infiltration followed by sharp clashes in the north. The last half of the year entailed severe conventional combat along the DMZ with less costly but still lethal VC attacks elsewhere. The allies rebuffed both NVA incursions with heavy casualties.

During the spring fighting season, a domestic political crisis flared. On 10 March Premier Nguyen Cao Ky sacked Lieutenant General Nguyen Chanh Thi, the popular ARVN I Corps unit commander. Strikes and protests erupted, led by Buddhists but supported by other dissident groups, local politicians, and army units. For three months troops loyal to Ky opposed those backing Thi. Walt used personal diplomacy and III MAF units to keep the two factions apart. In June Ky's forces subdued the uprising. Brigadier General Hoang Xuan Lam, commanding ARVN's 2nd Division, assumed control of I Corps, a position he retained until 1972. Oddly, the communists never capitalized on the three months of political turmoil.[12]

Pacification progress slowed in 1966 despite the MAF's heavy investment in small war programs. Marine civic action teams visited hamlets twenty-five thousand times during the year, completing 1,100 humanitarian projects such as construction of irrigation canals and schoolhouses. The CAPs expanded while another new initiative, the Kit Carson Scouts, persuaded surrendered Vietcong fighters to hunt their former comrades.[13] Walt also started the Personal Response program to improve relations with the local populace.[14] A new tactic, dubbed "COUNTY FAIR," sought to destroy communist political infrastructure. Troops surrounded and searched hamlets for VC cadre while plying residents with food, medical aid, and entertainment. These promising operations dwindled as the year progressed, derailed by increasing combat.

Westmoreland spurred Walt to get III MAF units "out of their beachheads" and conduct more search-and-destroy missions.[15] Marine units responded by conducting 150 operations of battalion size or larger. They also executed more than two hundred thousand small unit actions.[16] The year 1966 ended in a tactical standoff, with both sides suffering roughly eleven thousand casualties. Communist and allied forces had each improved their abilities to project power, but neither had converted their growing strength into a sustainable military or political victory.

1967: An Expanding War
The new year brought more of the same grinding attrition that had racked South Vietnam for eighteen months.[17] In April, the US Army's Task Force Oregon reinforced the MAF. When Lieutenant General Robert E. Cushman, Jr., replaced Walt in June, III MAF's strength approached one hundred thousand with soldiers representing 21 percent of the total.[18] Including territorial forces, the RVN fielded seventy-seven thousand troops inside I Corps. They focused on pacification, while US forces battled enemy regulars outside the populated areas. Opposing allied forces were forty-seven thousand communists, nearly equally divided between regulars and guerrillas.[19] Since most of the ARVN and almost half the US troops were tied down protecting bases, roads, and cities, the combatants available to both sides for offensive operations approached equity.[20]

This equality led to a tactical stalemate. In clashes along the DMZ, half the friendly casualties resulted from enemy artillery and mortar fire. Attacks on Con Thien, a 525-foot hill located two miles south of the DMZ and overlooking coastal infiltration routes, underscored the indirect fire threat. Fighting around the base cost the allies more than 2,500 casualties in May.[21] At the same time, a series of bloody engagements ensued near the Laotian border to control the hills surrounding the Khe Sanh airfield. Marines forced an NVA division to withdraw but lost 580 dead and wounded in a preview of future bloodletting for that key terrain.[22] Combat intensity in northern I Corps increased in the summer and fall. Con Thien endured a stronger NVA attack in July.[23] Another occurred in September, marked by an even more destructive artillery duel.[24]

A controversial aspect of the border war centered on construction of a barrier, known as the McNamara Line, which US secretary of defense Robert S. McNamara had approved in 1966. The obstacle was meant to hinder NVA infiltration. Constructed of barbed wire, mines, sensors, and fortified outposts, the system stretched from the South China Sea inland to the mountains. From there, strongpoints on high ground monitored sensors and barriers in the valleys to prevent easy access through frontier passes. Beyond the Laotian border, air-delivered ground sensors would pick up enemy movement and trigger allied firepower. Senior Marine leaders scoffed at the barrier's promised effectiveness. The enemy routinely attacked construction crews, guard forces, and outpost garrisons. Despite the III MAF commanders' misgivings, ARVN and Marine forces labored throughout the year to complete the defensive line.

In I Corps' southern three provinces, operations in 1967 proved nearly as costly as the border war. Between June and September, Marines in the south lost 484 dead and 3,788 wounded, with antipersonnel mines inflicting half the casualties.[25] In July rockets destroyed or damaged fifty aircraft, detonated ammunition stores, and caused 184 casualties in Da Nang.[26] Farther south, the army task force, renamed the Americal Division in September, employed air assault tactics and claimed more than 4,500 enemy soldiers killed in the latter half of 1967.

Meanwhile the III MAF pacification campaign focused on population security, destruction of the shadow government, and opening transportation routes. In May President Lyndon B. Johnson placed pacification, formerly split between civil and military agencies, under MACV. The new Civil Operations and Revolutionary Development Support (CORDS) organization, under its brilliant but acerbic civilian head, Robert W. "Blowtorch" Komer, managed most counterinsurgency programs except the CAPs, which grew from fifty-seven to seventy-nine platoons.

The MAF continued its assistance to South Vietnamese security forces. Yet the I Corps Advisory Command was the smallest in Vietnam, less than two-thirds the size of neighboring II Corps' advisory effort and half that of the contingents advising III and IV Corps. More telling, only 12 percent of ARVN's 428 large unit operations in I Corps were conducted alongside US or Korean forces, indicating that the allies were still fighting parallel wars.

In 1967, the region's toll of blood and treasure continued ratcheting up. In May almost twice as many enemy soldiers died in I Corps than in the other three RVN corps zones combined. Twenty-five thousand NVA and VC perished in the III MAF zone during that year, or nearly fifteen thousand more than in 1966. The allies rebuffed repeated NVA incursions while whittling away at Vietcong infrastructure and guerrillas. Despite some progress, however, III MAF had not attained MACV's elusive crossover point, beyond which the enemy could not or would not replace troops lost in the escalating war of attrition.

From 1965 to 1967, III MAF ran the regional war with minimal supervision and limited assistance from the US Army. The MAF's balanced operational style proved effective yet insufficient. The allies demonstrated tactical mobility and proficiency in the use of combined arms but too often allowed enemy formations to escape. More important, III MAF failed to find an operational remedy for the persistent threats posed by the Vietcong infrastructure and NVA infiltration. The MAF's command of large unit conventional operations would soon be tested as Hanoi prepared to unleash the biggest communist offensive the Marines ever faced in Vietnam.

Phase II: The Joint War, 1968–1971

The first half of III MAF's tenure in I Corps featured increasingly bitter fighting that amounted to a grinding struggle of attrition on both regular and irregular fronts. Those trends continued as the conflict transitioned from one highlighting the Marine way of war to a more joint and combined approach. ARVN and US Army units played a progressively more important role as the regional war intensified in 1968 and beyond.

1968: The Tet Offensives
Both sides envisioned 1968 as a year of decision.[27] Saigon and MACV planned to consolidate pacification gains. Hanoi, fearing the South's growing strength, decided to initiate a major military offensive in the hope of sparking a general uprising to bring down President Nguyen Van Thieu's national government. The stage was set for the Tet Offensive, a showdown that dwarfed everything that had come before.

In January a growing concentration of enemy divisions along the northern border prompted MACV to initiate major changes in allied forces and command relationships within I Corps. Westmoreland directed his deputy, General Creighton W. Abrams, Jr., to establish a MACV (Forward) headquarters near Hue to supervise what he anticipated might be the climactic battle of the war. Westmoreland also inserted the 1st Cavalry Division and the 101st Airborne Division, MACV's operational reserve, into III MAF's northern sector to conduct preemptive raids along the Laotian border or to counter expected enemy attacks.[28]

The communists struck first, massing four NVA divisions around Khe Sanh, an airstrip situated in a rural, mountainous area defended by the 26th Marine Regiment. Beginning on 20 January, the enemy cut Route 9, the sole road supplying the base, bombarded the airfield for seventy-seven days, and conducted intermittent attacks against both the main position and its hilltop outposts. The defenders crafted a curtain of fire, Operation NIAGRA, that stymied NVA assaults and delivered ten bombs and shells for each one the enemy fired. Army and Marine units opened Route 9 in mid-April, lifting the siege and ending the Tet Offensive's largest single action.[29]

The brutal battle inside Hue, the densely populated former imperial capital, also captured global attention. Communist troops seized the city on 30 January, triggering a vicious, house-to-house fight to clear the modern district south of the Perfume River and the warren of buildings inside the massive stone walls of the old city. Six hundred allied troops and six thousand civilians died in the one-month urban brawl, and 116,000 residents were left homeless.[30]

The Tet Offensive struck many other I Corps sites, notably Da Nang, South Vietnam's second-largest city and a lucrative target featuring a thousand square miles of ports, airfields, supply depots, and headquarters. Two NVA attacks infiltrated the town but were too weak to reach their objectives. Two more nationwide assaults followed the winter offensive. Neither of these "mini-Tets" proved as powerful as the original. In I Corps, the May offensive centered around Dong Ha and Da Nang.[31] The August attack hit Da Nang again but cost the 2nd NVA Division high casualties with little to show for it. During the last four months of 1968, communist units in I Corps withdrew to sanctuaries to refit, while the allies launched wide-ranging mobile operations in pursuit of the elusive enemy.

The Tet Offensive initially set back pacification as conflict in the cities shifted focus away from the countryside. Of the five hundred villages in I Corps, February assessments recorded a drop in pacification status among forty-nine.[32] Rural conditions nevertheless improved as the year progressed. CAPs, which had absorbed half the communist assaults in the months of 1967 leading up to the first Tet attack, became more mobile, operating from temporary bases in the countryside rather than fortified compounds in the villages. The program expanded again, adding a fourth group headquarters, twenty-eight platoons, seven training teams, and five hundred men during the year. The role of CORDS, headed by a civilian reporting directly to the MAF commander, also increased in 1968. Phoenix, the CORDS initiative to destroy the shadow government, picked up momentum as the year unfolded, killing or capturing four thousand insurgents.

General Abrams, who succeeded Westmoreland as MACV commander in June, launched the Accelerated Pacification Campaign in November. In I Corps, this three-month counterinsurgency surge solidified government control over 140 contested hamlets. By December three thousand communists had rallied to the South Vietnamese cause. More than 225,000 civilians joined the region's People's Self-Defense Force (PSDF) militia. Enemy attacks fell to the lowest level in two years, while nearly 70 percent of I Corps' population resided in secure areas. Despite Tet's hard fighting, the pacification program stood on firmer ground in late 1968 than it had since the Americans entered the war.

Allied command relationships morphed while the war's intensity peaked in 1968. The MACV (Forward) command post transitioned to a provisional corps headquarters in March, which was redesignated as XXIV Corps in August. The new army corps-level headquarters worked for III MAF but commanded US ground forces in I Corps' northern two provinces.[33] In I Corps the MAF's strength crested in August at 159,305 troops.[34] Each year thereafter American power receded, following a gradual path toward withdrawal. Communist forces failed to make lasting gains in I Corps despite the surprise achieved by the Tet Offensive. Vietcong numbers declined even as NVA strength increased by more than 50 percent. Estimated enemy casualties totaled 96,424 for the year; the number of III MAF dead and wounded amounted to 38,033. Despite heavy losses, both South Vietnam and North Vietnam maintained the political will to continue the fight.

1969: Counterattack and Vietnamization

The MAF began its fifth year in Vietnam as the largest combat command in Marine Corps history.[35] It received a new leader in March, when Lieutenant General Herman Nickerson, Jr., replaced Cushman.

Together III MAF and ARVN I Corps faced seventy-four thousand communist troops and sixteen thousand political and logistic cadre. Abrams introduced a MACV "One War" philosophy that mirrored the original Marine prescription for a balanced operational approach: constant combat against enemy regulars, expanded security and development in the countryside, and increased emphasis on building South Vietnamese military capabilities in a program Washington now called "Vietnamization."

The post-Tet allied counteroffensive continued into 1969. In the northern two provinces, the first half of 1969 featured a dozen MAF search-and-destroy operations of one to three months' duration. The 9th Marine Regiment conducted the most heralded, Operation DEWEY CANYON, which raided NVA supply dumps in northwestern Quang Tri Province.[36] The biggest was Operation APACHE SNOW, a 101st Division raid into the A Shau Valley in May. It culminated in the infamous "Hamburger Hill" battle, which inflamed domestic dissatisfaction across the United States with tactics that seized ground at great price only to abandon it.[37]

In I Corps' southern sector, the first half of 1969 also entailed frequent large unit combat. The Marine and army divisions turned back multiple NVA regimental attacks in February. Both units also conducted many sweeps with ARVN. In the largest, 1st Marine Division's Task Force Yankee controlled Marine, army, and ARVN regiments in Operation TAYLOR COMMON. The combined force cleared Base Area 112, one of eight sanctuaries in I Corps, located thirty miles southwest of Da Nang. Task Force Yankee destroyed an NVA regiment and captured more than a thousand weapons.[38] Attacks like DEWEY CANYON and TAYLOR COMMON illustrated the shift to more aggressive air assault tactics targeting the enemy's logistic networks. By the end of the year, III MAF units had conducted sixty-two large unit operations.

Small unit security tasks, though less dramatic than their bigger cousins, nonetheless represented an enormous effort. Marine units defending Da Nang, for instance, conducted 10,600 patrols and ambushes and seventy-eight company-size cordon operations in January alone. In the Marine divisions, nearly two-thirds of the year's 132,490 Marine operations of company size or less occurred at night.[39] The MAF's commitment to the CAP concept remained strong. Working alongside Popular Forces, 1,700 CAP Marines and sailors conducted 145,000 patrols (73 percent at night) and accounted for 425 enemy captured and an estimated 1,938 enemy killed. Between October and

December, III MAF built on the program's concepts by partnering other US squads, platoons, and companies with territorial forces in villages without CAPs.[40] This blanket of allied fire-team, squad, and platoon operations put increasing pressure on enemy forces throughout the region.

Supervising a thousand US military and civilian personnel in I Corps, CORDS orchestrated extensive pacification programs. These included efforts to improve local government, develop the economy, increase agricultural production, expand access to health care, and resettle refugees. Regionally, an astounding 85 percent of the people voted in local elections, unintimidated by Vietcong threats of reprisal. Military engineers constructed two Vietnamese hospitals and restored roads, bridges, and railroads to spur trade. Civil affairs units completed 2,813 aid projects. Medical personnel treated one million I Corps patients, conducted thirty-five thousand dental procedures, and administered one hundred thousand shots. CORDS reduced the region's refugee population from 25 percent to 7 percent in 1969.

Small war security programs also progressed. More than five thousand shadow government cadre were killed or captured, while nearly six thousand (mostly nonmilitary) Vietcong surrendered—more than the total that had changed sides in 1967 and 1968 combined. In both the Phoenix and Chieu Hoi (defection) programs, 80–90 percent of the enemy's losses occurred in the southern three provinces. CORDS recruited more than half a million citizens for the regional militia, training more than half (although arming only 15 percent). In 1969 the number of I Corps citizens rated as secure increased from 69 percent to 94 percent.

South Vietnamese forces, assisted by III MAF's Advisory Command, did much to achieve these gains in security. In 1969 ARVN I Corps units conducted 181 pacification operations resulting in more than seven thousand enemy deaths and 1,604 prisoners. Forty-five ARVN infantry and artillery battalions provided rough combat power parity with their NVA/VC conventional foes. ARVN aspired to field six additional infantry battalions to defend Da Nang's vital port and airfields. MAF planners envisioned sixty-five thousand territorial troops (scheduled to reach eighty thousand) protecting the population, while thirty-four thousand ARVN regulars blunted NVA incursions. Importantly, allied plans also projected a US infantry division remaining in I Corps indefinitely to back up the South Vietnamese security umbrella. MAF advisers reported "steady progress towards self-sufficiency along with impressive improvement in the proficiency of ARVN units in I Corps."[41]

The most significant 1969 development was the US political decision to withdraw its forces. The 3rd Marine Division returned to Okinawa. The year's fighting, although again costly, produced significant
allied gains. Saigon controlled almost all the region's territory. South
Vietnamese forces increased in strength. In I Corps, enemy forces
suffered fifty-eight thousand casualties, with 4,500 more surrender-
ing. The allies once again exercised the tactical initiative. Hanoi had
responded to a similar setback in 1967 with a major attack. This time
its leaders opted for a different strategy.

1970–1971: Downsizing and Redeployment
Diminishing responsibilities and redeployment marked the final year
and a half of III MAF's tour.[42] On 9 March 1970, the MAF ceded to
XXIV Corps its role as the senior US headquarters in I Corps. Lieutenant General Keith B. McCutcheon replaced Nickerson as MAF
commander the same day. Since soldiers outnumbered Marines in the
region, MACV decreed the two corps headquarters exchange positions
in the tactical hierarchy. The MAF sector shrank to Quang Nam Province. Three Marine regiments defended the approaches to Da Nang
while a fourth patrolled farther afield.

Conflict continued at a reduced scale throughout 1970. Sixteen enemy battalions, succored by well-stocked bases inside Laos, posed an
enduring threat inside Quang Nam Province. The 7th Marine Regiment alone recorded 1,100 small engagements in the first six months.
In the year's latter half, ten MAF offensives scoured the rugged Que
Son Mountains and the lowland rice fields and villages south of Da
Nang. During October two cyclones and two tropical storms slowed
the fighting. In November and December, in one of the biggest I Corps
intelligence coups of the war, Marine units seized two enemy regional
command posts.

On the pacification front, daunting challenges persisted. The government functioned and enjoyed support; 83 percent of eligible voters
again turned out for provincial elections in June. Yet only 44 percent of
the province's children attended school, and 20 percent of its 950,000
citizens were impoverished refugees. Marine units, in conjunction
with RVN security forces, focused on improving security.[43] The CAP
program peaked at 2,220 personnel, including a new Combined Action
Force headquarters, but three of its four groups deactivated between
July and September. Only 2nd Combined Action Group, with seven
hundred men in villages surrounding Da Nang, persisted by December
1970.

The VCI remained intractable. The I Corps Phoenix program proved better at amassing information than acting on it. District officials, intimidated and sometimes co-opted by their clandestine foes, remained hesitant to support Phoenix's drive to uproot the shadow government. Some 7,600 VC were active in Quang Nam Province at the beginning of 1970. An estimated 2,500 were captured or killed during the next twelve months. At the end of the year, CORDS rated Quang Nam's security status among the bottom quarter of Saigon's forty-four provinces. The MAF's pacification program was running out of time.

Development of ARVN continued, with emphasis on professionalizing Regional and Popular Forces. MACV ranked Da Nang's 51st Regiment as the third-best ARVN unit in the country. The MAF staff pressed local forces to assume more responsibility for area defense, but most units proved reluctant. South Vietnam's hard-pressed security forces were developing but could not keep up with the precipitous American withdrawal.

The MAF's timeline for departing Vietnam extended. Abrams initially intended to withdraw III MAF by midsummer 1970, but the rapid retrograde outpaced Marine logistic capacity to support it. Instead one brigade departed in March and a second by October.[44] In December III MAF retained just twenty-five thousand Marines. The day before Christmas Lieutenant General Donn J. Robertson took over from an ailing McCutcheon for the final few months of the MAF's tenure. Enemy forces marked time, content to watch allied combat power withdraw faster than they could destroy it. The big-unit war faded in early 1971 even though the guerrilla campaign carried on with its customary lethality.

During its final year and a half in Vietnam III MAF weathered internal frictions undermining Marine camaraderie and discipline. War crimes, drug abuse, racial conflict, and attacks on unit leaders underscored the slipping cohesion. The February 1970 murder of sixteen Vietnamese women and children at Son Thang (4) hamlet was the most egregious crime Marines committed against Vietnamese civilians. Unlike the 1968 My Lai massacre, done by a US Army unit in III MAF's zone but not reported or investigated until long after the event, the four men responsible for the Son Thang atrocity were swiftly identified and court-martialed.[45] Attacks by junior Marines on noncommissioned officers (NCOs) and officers increased as the war wound down. Forty-seven fragging incidents, so named because perpetrators often employed fragmentation grenades against unpopular leaders, occurred within 1st Marine Division as the war ebbed in 1970, leading to one death and forty-one injuries.

Racial unrest and drug abuse also became more prevalent. Commanders estimated that 30–50 percent of their Marines used drugs. Education and punishment lessened the impacts, but senior leaders viewed the epidemic as a social and medical problem deserving rehabilitation rather than dismissal. Black militancy proved equally difficult to curb. African American Marines, objecting to perceived second-class treatment, resisted authority by flaunting nonregulation hairstyles, giving black-power salutes, and forming alternate chains of command in some units. Thirty-two racial incidents occurred in 1st Marine Division in the first ten months of 1970. Several base-camp riots broke out. As the assistant division commander observed, "the aggravation doesn't always come from the black side, it's very often prompted by the white side."[46] Commanders relied on small unit leaders to manage the strife. McCutcheon argued that III MAF never lost the cohesion needed to fight well, but the energy devoted to such issues reflected the fraying of the service and the country that it represented.

III MAF returned to Okinawa on 14 April 1971, leaving 3rd Marine Amphibious Brigade (MAB) with fifteen thousand troops for two more months to complete the final drawdown. By 4 June army units had taken over all Marine installations in Quang Nam Province. The MAB departed on 26 June. Province security had declined during the first six months but recovered during the latter half of 1971 despite the smaller allied footprint. The precarious lull did not last. Less than a year after the MAF's departure, the NVA initiated the 1972 Easter Offensive. Only a few Marine advisers remained in I Corps to help stem the coming onslaught.[47] For III MAF, the war was over.

Patterns of Conflict

Regional actions remain difficult to track and assess in a war that possessed no front lines. Tracing macro-level force, space, and time factors, however, illuminates key operational rhythms of the Marine experience in Vietnam.

American manpower in I Corps waxed from III MAF's introduction in May 1965 through August 1968, when numbers peaked. From that point until the Marine headquarters 1971 departure, troop levels waned as US units gradually redeployed. Table 1 illustrates the quarterly strength of MAF forces between 1965 and 1971.

Estimated enemy strength (table 2), although much less reliable in accuracy, depict an adversary that averaged half the forces deployed by

Table 1.1. III MAF personnel strength

May 1965	17,567	July 1967	102,202	July 1969	144,087
July 1965	23,784	October 1967	102,793	October 1969	130,491
October 1965	42,011	January 1968	117,058	January 1970	115,803
January 1966	44,972	April 1968	151,781	April 1970*	43,521
April 1966	58,815	July 1968	156,223	July 1970*	39,999
July 1966	56,795	August 1968 (peak)	159,305	October 1970*	26,880
October 1966	61,099	October 1968	137,380	January 1971*	25,490
January 1967	76,297	January 1969	139,581	April 1971*	17,947
April 1967	85,991	April 1969	141,137		

* The last five figures do not include American Division and XXIV Corps since they no longer worked under III MAF.

Source: This data derived from USMC III MAF command chronologies.

the United States in I Corps. Communist forces nearly doubled in size and reached their high point in 1969 as US forces began to withdraw. The enemy's swelling ranks reflected larger infusions of NVA manpower rather than increased recruiting of Southerners into the Vietcong. By April 1968 indigenous South Vietnamese represented only 41 percent of the communist fighting forces in the South. Two years later that figure had dropped to just 20 percent. After the Tet Offensive insurgent

Table 1.2. NVA/VC troop strength in I Corps

May 1965	11,041	January 1969	89,300
July 1965	10,106	July 1969	85,400
January 1966	25,913	January 1970	78,600
July 1966	43,015	July 1970*	14,500
January 1967	30,500	January 1971*	15,850
July 1967	42,200	April 1971*	9,500
January 1968	40,943		
July 1968	38,380		

* The last three estimates include enemy forces in Quang Nam Province only (III MAF's Area of Operation during this period).

Source: Data drawn from FMFPAC monthly summaries of III MAF operations in Vietnam. Little was known of enemy strength in I Corps as Marine forces established themselves ashore. These numbers include "confirmed" and "probable" categories for NVA and Main Force VC units as well as guerrilla forces and VC infrastructure when those numbers are available. The numbers also include communist forces stationed just over the RVN border inside Laos, the DMZ, and North Vietnam within proximity of the DMZ. The final estimate is drawn from III MAF's April 1971 command chronology, as the MARFORPAC summary did not include enemy order of battle data for that month.

strength entered a steep decline as NVA regulars increasingly carried a heavier share of the fighting.[48]

The MAF's spatial footprint within I Corps expanded with its growing numbers. Initially, Marines occupied three enclaves around Da Nang, Chu Lai, and Phu Bai totaling just eight of the region's 10,440 square miles.[49] By 1 October 1967, these sectors covered 20 percent of I Corps' land, 40 percent of the area's rural villages, and 50 percent of its total population.[50] Two years later, Hamlet Evaluation System (HES) data indicated that secured areas had expanded to encompass 91 percent of the region's population.[51] When XXIV Corps assumed responsibility for allied operations in I Corps in 1970, III MAF's sector transitioned from all five northern provinces to just Quang Nam Province. By 1971, as its units redeployed, the MAF guarded only a shrinking perimeter around Da Nang.

At the height of its strength III MAF averaged fifteen troops per square mile across the entire region and one American per seventeen South Vietnamese citizens. When combined with eighty-one thousand South Vietnamese soldiers, this troop density achieved a more favorable ratio of one allied soldier to eleven citizens. This fraction exceeded by a factor of four corresponding proportions in Malaya, a case often cited as a useful template for pacification force ratios. Yet numbers alone, using what later practitioners would call "population centric" techniques, did not suffice to squelch the Vietnamese insurgency.[52]

Casualty figures provided a critical measure of the conflict's intensity as well as one of the most contentious aspects of the war. American reports of friendly losses were precise. The notorious enemy "body count," by contrast, proved unreliable. Inflated by commanders eager to earn credit for their military prowess and compromised by the difficulty of assessing casualties recovered by the enemy or lost to explosions that obliterated remains and spread them across a rugged landscape, allied estimates furnish only a rough estimate of the actual damage inflicted on the enemy. Communist counts of their own losses exceeded in aggregate the casualties MACV claimed that it inflicted, but the official US military numbers associated with specific engagements nonetheless require cautious treatment.[53]

The I Corps data for enemy and friendly casualties (tables 3 and 4) reveal several interesting trends. First, Military Region 1 (MR 1) remained an exceedingly dangerous place.[54] US forces lost more troops there than any other region of Vietnam. The year 1968 was an extreme casualty outlier for communist forces, with rates three times the next closest year. Even in 1970, however, the communists lost nearly

Table 1.3 NVA/VC casualties in I Corps

Year	Killed in action	Wounded in action	Prisoners of war	Total
1965	2,627	314	535	3,476
1966	10,627	-	913	11,540
1967	24,452	-	934	25,386
1968	89,202	-	7,222	96,424
1969	30,803	-	916	31,719
1970	5,719	-	475	6,194
1971	520	-	44	564
Total	163,905	314	11,039	175,303

Source: Data for enemy killed in action for 1965–1968, wounded in action for 1965, and prisoners of war for 1965 and 1968 are from USMC official histories for those years. The rest of the data is derived from MARFORPAC's December editions of *Operations of the MAF/Operations of U.S. Marine Forces Vietnam*. Records do not indicate why III MAF stopped reporting enemy WIA figures.

Table 1.4. III MAF casualties

Year	Killed in action	Wounded in action	Missing in action	Total
1965	342	2,047	18	2,407
1966	1,672	10,807	46	12,525
1967	3,602	26,990	61	30,653
1968	6,495	30,902	636	38,033
1969	3,523	24,139	257	27,919
1970	764	5,905	19	6,688
1971	38	482	0	520
Total	16,436	101,272	1,037	118,745

Source: This table also includes the casualties suffered by troops of other services assigned to III MAF. Figures are derived from three sources. The data for 1965 and 1968 were obtained from Marine official histories. The data for 1966–1967 was taken from FMFPAC's monthly historical reports (*Operations of the MAF/Operations of U.S. Marine Forces Vietnam*) for December of each year. Data for 1969–1971 came from III MAF's monthly command chronologies. "Killed in action" includes those who "died of wounds." Of note, many US wounded were not hurt badly enough to be evacuated to a hospital. Just 58 percent of Marines wounded in the war required hospitalization—51,389 hospitalized of 88,633 wounded. The other 42 percent were treated in the field and returned to duty immediately. Merrill L. Bartlett and Jack Sweetman, *The U.S. Marine Corps: An Illustrated History* (Annapolis, MD: Naval Institute Press, 2001), 269.

as many troops as III MAF lost in its bloodiest year. On average, the NVA/VC lost the equivalent of three divisions, or one corps, per year inside the I Corps region.

Second, total casualties (including killed and wounded) for both sides approached a 1:1 ratio in every year except 1968, in which the communists lost 2.5 troops for every American casualty. Although claimed US kill ratios (the number of enemy killed compared to Americans killed) were much higher, including wounded in the calculations leveled the playing field for confirmed American and communist casualties.[55] MACV estimated 1.5 wounded for every enemy combat fatality. That was a conservative factor by historical standards.[56] Even including projections for wounded troops only raised the ratio of enemy casualties to III MAF losses to not quite 4:1. North Vietnam's police state willingly endured this toll, as it did not pay the political price for casualties that Washington did.

Seasonal patterns of combat remained consistent between 1965 and 1971. Each year fighting flared between February and June. July sometimes offered a brief respite, followed by sharper battles in August and September before hostilities lapsed again in the final quarter. This routine corresponded with the drier, non-monsoon periods, when roads and cross-country terrain became easier to traverse.[57]

Annual casualty lists show that 1968, with its three communist offensives, was the bloodiest year of the MAF's tour. Neither 1967 (marked by multiple NVA incursions across the DMZ) nor 1969 (featuring the conclusion of the allies' counterattack in the Accelerated Pacification Campaign and subsequent assaults into communist base areas) generated the toll of friendly casualties suffered in 1968.[58] MAF casualties dropped significantly in 1970 and 1971 for three reasons. First, the tallies no longer included US Army soldiers lost outside of the Marines' reduced sector in Quang Nam Province. Second, redeployment thinned the ranks of the MAF's ground fighting units. Finally, ARVN assumed more responsibility for both conventional and irregular combat duties.

Parables of Proficiency

The cases highlighted below underscore III MAF's struggle to act as a corps-level headquarters, to achieve its three primary tasks, and to develop a campaign that achieved the desired goals for I Corps. Together they reveal an ad hoc, uncertain command post troubled by friction within its own chain of command and with its Vietnamese allies. It conducted many successful tactical operations without establishing the conditions required to ensure the region's long-term security.

Working with ARVN: Operation HARVEST MOON

Throughout its tenure the MAF did not prepare ARVN's I Corps to protect the region independently.[59] Despite the fact American advisers considered it to be South Vietnam's most capable corps, ARVN's I Corps still lacked talented small unit leadership, robust supporting arms, adequate logistic support, sufficient air transport and fires, competent planning skills, and a strong corps staff and commander. And even if it had possessed those capabilities, it was too small to defend the region against the NVA and VC by itself. At the height of the conflict in 1968, ARVN's I Corps, even with the help of six additional allied divisions (measured in regiments and brigades), achieved only a tactical standoff. The MAF could not mandate a larger ARVN I Corps, but it could work to develop the shortfalls in its proficiency. Conducting combined operations was one of the best ways to do so.

Operation HARVEST MOON provided an early example of poor III MAF–I Corps tactical cooperation and one that impeded rather than developed effective combined operations. The chronological narrative above noted the operation's disappointing outcome and high friendly casualties. But HARVEST MOON also illustrated the potential pitfalls of South Vietnamese and American troops working together. Botched combined operations not only constituted missed opportunities to improve ARVN's skills; they also destroyed the mutual trust necessary for effective teamwork. The operation's objective was to trap and destroy the elusive 1st VC Regiment, an iconic unit that I examine in more detail in chapter 3. Two ARVN battalions headed into the Que Son Valley in search of the enemy. They were, said an American planner, "the bait." Their task was to fix the VC regiment while two III MAF battalions helicoptered in behind the enemy to attack the force caught between the US and RVN units. Foreshadowing the fiasco to follow, the ARVN regimental commander received his orders only one day before of the operation, giving him little time to prepare, because MAF leaders feared VC spies inside ARVN would compromise the plan.

The operation veered off track almost immediately. On D-Day, 8 December 1965, a VC battalion ambushed one of the two approaching ARVN battalions. Within fifteen minutes one-third of the RVN unit was killed or wounded; the rest retreated under cover of US air strikes. The next morning two VC battalions struck the other ARVN unit. It, too, was overrun within twenty minutes. MAF advisers, along with US artillery and air support, helped survivors of both ARVN units escape. Helicopters from 1st Marine Aircraft Wing ferried a third ARVN battalion to the scene to support the crippled ARVN battalions. Meanwhile the two Marine battalions were disastrously slow in coming to their allies' aid.

The story of that delay is worth relating in detail. It took twenty-six hours from the initiation of the 8 December VC ambush for the first Marine battalion to link up with ARVN remnants on the ground. On the day of the first ambush, one MAF battalion moved by truck from Chu Lai to its designated helicopter pickup zone in Tam Ky. It did not fly out until 1000 hours the next morning, several hours after the destruction of the second ARVN unit. During that ambush on 9 December, the other Marine battalion trucked from Da Nang to its aviation pickup point near Thang Binh. It arrived at the helicopter zone at 1030 and flew out at 1400 to help the ARVN units. Because the second US battalion flew into a zone much closer to the ARVN remnants, it was the first to reach them midafternoon on the second day. The first Marine battalion never contacted ARVN. Both US units traveled by truck, helicopter, and foot to the battle zone. It was only thirty-six miles by road for the battalion coming from Da Nang and forty-six for the unit coming from Chu Lai. The respective air distances from their initial locations were twenty-four and thirty-five miles. The MAF's ground and air forces dedicated to support the mission were nearby, but they were not close enough or prepared to respond quickly when enemy action disrupted their scheduled deployment timelines. Proper planning would have positioned the Marine units closer and in a posture ready to respond immediately if the ARVN forces encountered trouble, as they did, soon after commencing the operation.

Major General Nguyen Chanh Thi, commanding ARVN's I Corps, was not impressed. In fact, he was justifiably furious at the Marines' tardiness. On 10 December he withdrew all other ARVN forces from HARVEST MOON. He then drew a boundary between ARVN and III MAF forces and commenced an independent ARVN search-and-destroy operation north of that line, leaving Marine forces to fight on their own. South Vietnamese forces had ample reason to be bitter. Their units had advanced to contact, expecting quick and aggressive Marine infantry support once they contacted the enemy. Although no allied commander had anticipated the early destruction of both lead

ARVN battalions, the MAF's response was too slow to assist either RVN unit. Poor command and control procedures (examined in chapter 2), exacerbated by inexperience, led to the muddle.

This episode poisoned the early relationship between Marine and South Vietnamese units. Unsuccessful outcomes like that of HARVEST MOON reinforced mutual judgments of incompetence and undermined trust in integrated operations. While the tactical performance of ARVN and III MAF forces improved over time, early miscues like HARVEST MOON impeded ARVN I Corps' development of the skills required to conduct effective large unit operations.

Corps-Level Leadership at Hue

Marine generalship proved deficient at Hue. The 1968 battle furnished III MAF's most important opportunity to exercise corps-level command of conventional combat operations. The Marine headquarters failed the test. Cushman and his subordinates fumbled the defense of Da Nang; remained strangely inert during the Hue crisis; deferred to a MACV (Forward) command that was not fully established on the ground until two weeks into the offensive; allowed a subordinate Army division headquarters to coordinate efforts inside the old imperial citadel instead of the Marine command responsible for doing so; took a month to block enemy reinforcements into Hue; and then neglected to pursue the defeated enemy. In short, III MAF provided almost none of the command and control necessary to win the vital battle for Hue sooner or more decisively.

A confused defense of Da Nang provided the first indication that Cushman's command post was not on top of its game. As the Tet Offensive commenced, the 2nd NVA Division approached the city. After repulsing an uncoordinated enemy attack on 30 January, the 1st Marine Division commander asked for more troops.[60] Rather than provide them immediately, Cushman waited an entire week to discuss the issue with Westmoreland on February 7. The MACV commander, miffed at Cushman's "absence of initiative," directed US Army forces from Chu Lai to reinforce Da Nang. A small army brigade subsequently fought under 1st Marine Division's control for five days to help repel a second enemy thrust. Cushman later explained that he always sought MACV's approval before shifting US Army units within I Corps. This was a thin excuse. He could have asked sooner. More important, asking was unnecessary because III MAF already exercised operational control of the army forces.[61]

Brigadier General Foster C. LaHue's Task Force X-Ray, under the 1st Marine Division, defended the region around Hue. His headquarters, established fifteen miles south of the city on 13 January, controlled three infantry battalions and two regimental staffs. LaHue was slow to appreciate the strength of the enemy assault. He claimed on 1 February that Marines controlled Hue south of the Perfume River when in fact they did not do so for another ten days. He fed units into the battle piecemeal, never requesting reinforcements even though his need for them far exceeded that of his division commander in Da Nang. LaHue did not enter the citadel to coordinate directly with Brigadier General Ngo Quang Truong, commanding 1st ARVN Division. Other than deploying a dozen artillery pieces and coordinating resupply, LaHue exerted curiously little influence on the battle. Neither III MAF nor 1st Marine Division demanded more drive from the on-scene commander, who barely assisted his embattled ally.[62]

MACV recognized the MAF's command sluggishness and moved to fill the void. On 27 January, Westmoreland ordered his forward command post, not used in Vietnam before or after this episode, to I Corps to direct the allied response to what he believed would be the war's decisive campaign.[63] Abrams, his deputy, assumed command, but the advance headquarters did not become operational alongside LaHue's command post until 12 February.[64] In the interim III MAF, 1st Marine Division, and Task Force X-Ray had done little to reinforce their forces in Hue. On 13 February, Abrams and Cushman met and agreed that Hue represented the region's primary threat. At this point Task Force X-Ray had recaptured the district south of the river and moved one Marine battalion into the citadel to help clear the old city. Meanwhile, two battalions from the 1st Cavalry Division had fought for eleven days to close off the NVA's northern and western approaches to Hue, but the troopers stalled against heavy resistance.[65]

MACV (Forward) moved to assemble the reinforcements Cushman had neither provided from his own forces nor requested of others. On 16 February, Abrams exhorted Cushman to reinforce the army's effort to close the enemy's routes into the city. The next day Westmoreland met with Abrams and Cushman and directed a small brigade from the 101st Airborne Division to reinforce Task Force X-Ray and block enemy egress routes south and southwest of Hue. He also added two more army infantry battalions to 1st Cavalry Division to strengthen the attack toward the city from the northwest. On 20 February, three weeks after the first attack on Hue, Abrams told Cushman that he deemed "the measures so far taken to be inadequate and not in consonance with the urgency of the problem or the resources you command."[66]

That same day Abrams informed Major General John J. Tolson that his Air Cavalry division must clear the approaches to the city within forty-eight hours, establish liaison with General Truong inside the citadel, and come up with a plan to finish the battle. Abrams promised to issue orders to Cushman to support this new guidance. This directive ignored the fact that Tolson worked for Cushman and that Task Force X-Ray, commanding the Marine regiments and army brigade operating south of Hue, did not work for Tolson. The Cavalry Division renewed its attack, inserted its assistant commander into the citadel to help coordinate allied fires, and finally reached the walls of the city on 25 February. South Vietnamese troops and US Marines finished clearing the citadel the day before the cavalrymen arrived to block the enemy's resupply and withdrawal routes. It had taken the army twenty-two days of hard fighting to reach Hue from a starting position twelve miles distant.[67]

Both Abrams and Cushman faltered in directing the recapture of Hue. The operation afforded the opportunity that MACV's strategy had long sought: a conventional fight against the enemy's regular forces, albeit one conducted within a historic cultural center. Yet the battle dragged on for a month because American commanders did not swiftly deploy the troops required to counterattack strongly.

Cushman exercised operational control of all Marine and army forces in I Corps. Following the defeat of the 2nd NVA Division, he could have sent the two-battalion US Army task force from Da Nang, along with several Marine battalions, to block Hue's western perimeter and stanch the flow of supplies and fresh NVA soldiers that poured into the city each evening. Instead he returned the US Army task force to Chu Lai on 11 February. Army reinforcements did not reach Hue until 17 February (two battalions under Task Force X-Ray) and 20 February (two battalions under 1st Cavalry Division). No Marine battalions augmented the three originally at Phu Bai.

Abrams supervised III MAF loosely during the first two weeks of the struggle and then assumed formal command of the region and its US forces on 12 February. His harsh 20 February message registered his dissatisfaction with Cushman's passivity; given his command authority, however, it also underscored his own inexcusable failure to act decisively up to that point. His subsequent direct order to the Cavalry Division, one of III MAF's subordinate commands, made little difference over the final five days of the battle, but it did confirm Task Force X-Ray's previous lack of coordination with and support for ARVN inside the besieged citadel.

Abrams and Cushman crowned their hesitant command by failing to launch a vigorous pursuit of the fleeing communist forces. Instead of following their defeated foes into the mountains to complete their destruction, the two generals directed their army and Marine units to conduct security sweeps of the areas immediately surrounding the city. US Army, US Marine, and ARVN units conducted their own battles in and around Hue. There was no common commander of US forces, much less a combined commander for the operation. The official Marine history concluded: "Both Cushman and Abrams were at too high a level and distracted by Khe Sanh to focus much of their attention, except periodically, to the Hue situation."[68] This verdict gives more credit to the commanders than either deserves.

Hue required the steady hand of a corps headquarters to control elements of four allied divisions and two separate brigades fighting in a small area. Both Cushman and Abrams had authority to command all US forces in the battle. Neither did. Corps exist to orchestrate such battles, yet III MAF failed to do so. Cushman's handling of the Hue operation reinforced the MACV commander's distrust of the Marines' ability to direct large unit operations. It confirmed his decision to replace Abrams's ad hoc command post with an army corps headquarters to control the conventional fight in northern I Corps for the rest of the war.

A Denial Strategy

The MAF did not prevent the NVA from operating inside I Corps. Marine senior leaders, including the MAF's commanders, favored a mobile defense to shield the region. This approach allowed the NVA to enter South Vietnam. The MAF then employed mobility and firepower to strike enemy units before they could reach populated areas. This worked to a degree, but it also ensured that the ground war was waged on friendly territory. The method—search-and-destroy operations—also complied with MACV's theater guidance.

General Westmoreland recommended, and President Johnson approved, a strategy of attrition. Analysts during and after the war debated whether attrition constituted a strategy at all. But the MACV commander used the term to describe his approach, and it accurately conveyed the essence of the method: kill or capture enough enemy troops to convince the communists to give up their aspirations to over-throw the South Vietnamese government.[69] The flaw in this theory of victory was that it allowed the enemy to decide how much pain to endure. The goal was to convince Hanoi and its client insurgency that the potential benefits of aggression were not equal to the costs. Because US policy prohibited ground operations in Cambodia, Laos, and North Vietnam, enemy forces found sanctuary just over the South's long and porous borders. The politically constrained attrition strategy thus ceded the operational initiative to the enemy.

A better phrase for Westmoreland's approach, borrowed from the field of nuclear deterrence theory, was "punishment strategy." The method mimics a slapping contest. Two adversaries square off and deliver sequential blows until one submits or gets knocked out. In such a contest a rational-actor calculus theoretically drives surrender decisions; a foe is expected to yield when the costs or pain of fighting surpass its benefits. The punishment concept also complemented another favored Cold War strategic method: graduated escalation. In this construct, the rheostat of enemy punishment was slowly dialed upward, with pauses to enable a foe to assess his escalating pain. This meter was carefully monitored by politicians, diplomats, and generals, with levels of violence ratcheted up or down to signal degrees of seriousness. The goal was to project the minimum amount of damage, whether conventional or nuclear, necessary to induce an enemy's submission. All this worked well in game theory. In Vietnam, its application to ground combat and aerial bombing did not work at all.[70]

Managing South Vietnam's foremost operational problem—unfettered NVA incursions—required instead a strategy of prevention. This concept, sometimes labeled "denial strategy," also comes from the nuclear deterrence realm. Here the idea was to identify an enemy's war-winning method and ensure that the approach could not work. If, for example, a nuclear state seeks to strike first to disarm its foe, the intended victim would ensure that enough of its own nuclear arsenal remained untouched (e.g., on submarines, on alert or airborne bombers, or in hidden, protected, or mobile ground-based missile batteries) to strike back with sufficient force to dissuade any adversary's thought of a first strike. Conceptually, the key was to render inoperable an enemy's defeat mechanism.

In Vietnam, Hanoi's primary method to achieve its political goal was to send its army south to conquer Saigon. The NVA traveled through Laos or across the DMZ to invade the RVN. An allied strategy of prevention required blocking those routes with ground forces. Denying the enemy's primary invasion paths would have undermined Hanoi's most dangerous military capability, deprived the VC of external aid, and transferred much of the combat to the northern border as opposed to fighting the NVA across the South after it had infiltrated.

American policy precluded building a continuous defensive line from the South China Sea to the Mekong River to block the Ho Chi Minh Trail. The concept generated strong debate during and after the conflict. A complete analysis of the merits and demerits of that strategic alternative exceeds the scope of this study and deserves its own monograph. Three points, however, pertain to III MAF's inability to prevent the NVA from operating inside I Corps.

First, a strategy of prevention offered the only other defensive military option, other than an indefinite continuation of punishment, to defend South Vietnam from conventional attack. The punishment strategy left the decision to an implacable foe of when or whether to quit. A successful prevention strategy, by contrast, promised to obviate the importance of the enemy's will by forestalling his primary operational method. In other words, Hanoi's intent to conquer the South might never flag, but its ability to do so would be blocked. Senior Marine leaders at III MAF, FMFPAC, and HQMC never appreciated this methodological distinction or why a prevention strategy offered advantages that the punishment strategy could not match.

Second, though civilian and military leaders in Saigon, Honolulu, and Washington determined allied theater strategy, III MAF still had a role to play. The senior Marine headquarters in Vietnam had a duty to recommend military strategies that would allow the defense of I Corps. The Marines did not shy from that responsibility in the debate over pacification versus attrition strategies or in the controversy over the US Air Force's management of Marine aviation assets. They had an equally important professional obligation to recognize that their preferred mobile defense construct was not working and to recommend an alternative approach, including the extension across Laos of a fortified line defended by ground units.

Finally, III MAF had an opportunity to assess elements of a prevention strategy, at least on a trial basis, by testing the ability of Secretary of Defense Robert McNamara's barrier to slow or halt NVA incursions across the DMZ. This Generals Walt and Cushman refused to do (see further in chapter 6). Neither did they or their successors initiate any strategic dialogue with MACV on other methods to keep the enemy's army out of I Corps. This lapse contributed to a dearth of strategic reassessment, two failed strategies (attrition and Vietnamization), and a war lost.

A Political Strategy

The MAF did not destroy the insurgency's shadow government. One method of doing so entailed strictly military or, more accurately, police tactics. Allied forces had to develop intelligence on the Vietcong's political and logistic cadre, then apprehend or kill them in discrete raids. Another way to counter the power of the VCI was to defeat its political ideas. This approach required a positive political program advanced from Saigon to the most remote hamlet within I Corps. While III MAF could not influence the political agenda in Saigon, it could work at the regional level to build a "rice roots" political movement that promised and provided better local government than the Vietcong could deliver. The MAF never accepted its supporting role in this realm of political warfare.

Despite the Marines' interest in counterinsurgency and their belief that it represented the key to victory in Vietnam, they refused to help the South Vietnamese implement a political program that would garner more support from the populace. Missing was a political strategy. The concept was not in the American military's doctrinal lexicon in 1965.[71] Neither was it a part of the Marines' small wars tradition. Even the famous *Small War Manual* counseled political neutrality when conducting stability and nation-building operations. This admonition did not serve III MAF, or the South Vietnamese, well in I Corps.

The very idea that an armed intervention on the scale of the US presence in South Vietnam could somehow be politically neutral was disingenuous. American forces were protecting and projecting the political power of South Vietnamese officeholders from Saigon to the hamlets. That reality should have provided all the incentive necessary to forthrightly promote leaders and policies, at every level, that advanced the common interests of Saigon and Washington.

Moreover, American military and political leaders did intervene in South Vietnamese politics, at both national and regional levels. President Diem and his brother learned that truth at great cost in the 1963 coup that brought down his government. Throughout the brothers' tenure MACV and the US embassy sought to influence Saigon's political agenda. While less common at the regional level, such interaction occurred there too. General Walt, for instance, reluctantly engaged local politics in I Corps during the 1966 Buddhist uprising.

In the end, positing US political neutrality in I Corps did not achieve the desired regional end state—a vanquished VC counter-state and effective civil government. The postwar notion that a more aggressive US political program promoting good RVN governance at the local level was somehow underhanded or un-American is risible. Even more absurd is the supposition that the South Vietnamese were somehow incapable or unworthy of effective self-government. War, as Carl von Clausewitz reminds us, is the continuation of politics by other means. In that spirit, if a short definition of counterinsurgency is "armed politics," then III MAF emphasized the first word to the detriment of the second. Marine security, humanitarian assistance, and psychological operations were necessary but not sufficient. Those activities could never substitute for a regional political strategy.

Political warfare entails connecting the people and their leaders. It builds the organizational means to execute policies and programs at every level of government. In I Corps no regional government existed beyond the dictates of the ARVN corps commander. Government officials operated at the province, district, city, and village levels. Beyond the rudiments, Marine leaders possessed limited understanding of either formal or informal government practices in the area. A 1969 MAF G-5 report confirmed the lack of American insight into how local politics worked.[72] This absence of information posed serious constraints on how Americans might have engaged politically had they been inclined. They were not so inclined. The Marines were happy to acknowledge that "winning hearts and minds" was paramount in defeating the insurgency. But III MAF remained relatively unengaged in local politics. Instead American units provided external security while the decisive political contest raged on a playing field they observed from the sidelines.

The 1969 staff study mentioned above, titled *Development's Role in Pacification*, stressed the primacy of politics in III MAF's war. Its authors, two Marine and two US Army junior officers, wrote an insightful, 475-page treatise on political and economic conditions in I Corps. While acknowledging how much more there was to learn about regional political dynamics, they offered several trenchant observations. First, they observed there was little tradition of self-help ventures at the hamlet level, undermining the pacification campaign's effort to spur community cooperation and win political loyalty through local development projects. Building on that insight, they concluded that political work must precede other forms of development. Turning the popular notion of "security first" on its head, they argued that neither ironclad security nor socioeconomic progress alone could achieve pacification. Although projects could not be completed under pervasive security threats, they also recognized that political motivation undergirded the will to fight and build.[73]

In their own methods of expanding the Communist Party's control of the population, the Vietcong employed the "politics first" methodology advocated by the American staff analysts. The communist cadre did not establish blanket security prior to proselytizing in the hamlets. Neither did they initiate elaborate Western-style economic, educational, medical, and construction projects in contested villages. They lacked the resources and recognized that the true contest was one of ideas—a political battle.[74] Saigon competed in the political warfare lane (with its Revolutionary Development cadre, for example) but struggled to match the organizational and ideological work done by communist agents in the villages. Meanwhile III MAF did not engage in this crucial arena beyond its humanitarian aid and propaganda efforts. At the national level, the Nationalist Chinese provided Saigon limited political warfare assistance. But their advice focused more on motivating ARVN's troops than earning the loyalty of the peasants.[75] The Vietcong emphasized both.

The G-5 planners did not lay out a specific agenda for a political strategy in I Corps, but they did recommend focusing on the district level. Like Douglas Pike, whose definitive study on the Vietcong had appeared three years earlier, the III MAF analysts appreciated the need for an "organization in depth of the rural population." Gaps in regional governance were rife. But the district—the linchpin connecting villages and province—promised the largest return on investment. The young civil affairs officers recommended substantially reinforcing that echelon's political and development capacity, using both US personnel and Vietnamese Revolutionary Development cadre.[76] While experts from the US State Department and US Agency for International Development should have provided this assistance, by 1969 these agencies had already proven they lacked the means and determination to meet the requirement. Indeed, the US embassy's failure to marshal a stronger socioeconomic and political response had triggered CORDS's standup in 1967.[77] Unfortunately, MACV's new pacification command also neglected substantive political development opportunities. In I Corps, CORDS's small district advisory teams never attained the expanded capacity the G-5 study called for.

A "rice roots" political strategy required policies that motivated I Corps' citizens to support the government. Such policies had to offer improvements in wealth, status, and power to those on the lower end of Vietnam's socioeconomic stratum. As such, they entailed revolutionary social changes that the RVN's central government was slow to authorize. These included land reform, progressive tax policies, enhanced authority for village leaders, opportunities for peasants to advance within the RVN's civil and military hierarchies, and more effective administration of local economic development projects. MAF political advisers needed to help village, district, and province politicians develop and implement such policies within their means. For regional policies driven by national decisions, MAF advisers needed to work with their American counterparts in Saigon to promote policy implementation. Some of these initiatives, especially land reform and programs to strengthen village-level civil-military authority, came online by 1970. But these changes were slow to develop, and III MAF invested little effort promoting them with regional political parties or through American civil and military officials working at the national level.[78]

Whatever the policies and mechanisms that might have been developed, the 1969 study stressed that the crux of the problem was to tie together the society and its political system. "These tasks are not peripheral to the pacification campaign," said its authors. "Quite the opposite. They are the guts of it."[79] The report's analysis anticipated that of Jeffrey Race's influential 1972 book, *War Comes to Long An*. In Race's words, III MAF and ARVN I Corps lacked a social strategy to match their military strategy.[80] Sadly, the young officers' prescient insights and sound recommendations fell on deaf ears. This enlightened G-5 report exerted little influence on III MAF's approach to pacification.[81] Local politics proved too foreign to Marines who had no experience or education that prepared them to assess or apply the seemingly radical proposals advanced. Forging a regional political strategy remained a promising operational concept left untried.

Conclusion

The parables highlighted above reflect paths not taken. Opportunities existed for III MAF to work more closely with ARVN from the beginning, to directly control multiple divisions in combat, to pursue other methods to deny NVA access to I Corps, and to compete politically with the Vietcong. Strong leadership was required to keep the MAF focused on the primary tasks: improving the RVN security forces at every level; keeping the NVA away from I Corps and its people; and uprooting the insurgency through a combination of patient soldering, police work, and effective political countermobilization. Battles won, even many such tactical victories, could not make up for a campaign that did not accomplish these three key operational objectives. The result was stalemate—and eventually defeat.

Operational patterns of the six-year American war in I Corps reveal that the war in 1965 was chiefly an insurgency. North Vietnamese troops were already present, but in small numbers. That ratio reversed steadily and then completely by the aftermath of the Tet battles in 1968. For the rest of the war Vietcong conventional troops and guerrillas posed a diminishing threat, though the shadow government still proved difficult to eradicate. Control of territory, for both sides, reflected troops available and time to expand their purview. Security conditions in the countryside shifted with swings in tactical initiative, but the enduring trend favored the expansion of Saigon's writ over broader portions of I Corps. Time, however, favored Hanoi for two reasons. First, its territory, though intermittently bombed as the war ground on, suffered far less devastation compared to the South, especially in III MAF's sector. The Northern homeland was never threatened by US ground forces because Washington was unwilling to invade North Vietnam. Thus, Hanoi's army remained on the offensive. More important, the communist government did not face the same domestic political opposition that challenged leaders in South Vietnam and America. The politburo in North Vietnam generated and enforced superior political will, enabling its people to persevere despite terrible losses.

The war in I Corps exhibited two overarching phases, initially Marine-centric and then joint in character. During the first three years of fighting, III MAF stressed an approach balanced between conventional tactics executed by battalion to brigade units and small war techniques designed to protect the people from communist guerrillas and political cadre. Unlike MACV, which espoused an equitable employment of conventional and irregular methods but in practice emphasized offensive search-and-destroy missions as the primary way to defeat the enemy, the MAF invested heavily in counterinsurgency operations. As the conflict escalated, Walt and Cushman discovered they needed more forces to simultaneously pursue conventional, counterinsurgency, and advisory missions.

Between 1968 and 1971 III MAF fought a joint and combined war that far exceeded previous levels of combat intensity. It also enhanced operational cooperation among US Army, Korean, US Marine, and ARVN formations. Despite significant US Army reinforcements, however, the MAF managed only to maintain the costly regional impasse. During the Tet Offensive, the MAF lost the interservice battles to operate in accordance with Marine doctrine as a corps-level headquarters controlling both ground and aviation forces in its assigned sector. In chapter 2 I will examine how and why those command-and-control consequences emerged.

2

III MAF Command and Control

Responsibilities associated with command and control (commonly referred to as "C2") represent the most important of the warfighting functions because they determine how the other functions—intelligence, operations, logistics, and plans—work together to accomplish assigned missions.[1] Larger unit size, a broader range of capabilities, and more expansive threat conditions make C2 especially challenging at the corps level. In Vietnam, the commanders of III Marine Amphibious Force directed between 30,000 and 160,000 troops. The scale of their tasks resembled the daily management of a midsize city. The array of concerns in I Corps broadened considerably because of the hybrid nature of the war. Each of the MAF headquarters' three primary missions—conventional combat, pacification, and training and advising ARVN—incorporated a unique set of C2 challenges. Together they represented a joint and combined operational environment far more complex than anything Marines had encountered previously. Ironically, just four months before III MAF deployed to Vietnam, Victor Krulak, the FMFPAC commander, recommended against expanding the headquarters, still at cadre strength, to a full-time and fully manned corps-level staff.[2] The MAF and its mission would suffer for its lack of preparation.

Contemporary Marine Corps doctrine identifies three constituent parts in a command-and-control system that must work in harmony: *leaders*, *processes*, and *organization*. Personnel include commanders—the leaders who wield formal and informal authority to direct action—and the headquarters staff that supports them. Processes address ways that commanders and staffs handle information and generate, supervise, and assess tasks. Structural considerations encompass the size and layout of the staff, the number of subordinate units and the command relationships among them, and the corps' own place within the theater's web of adjacent and senior headquarters.[3] In this chapter I examine each component of III MAF's C2 system. I then look at two instances of special interest: the service friction that led to the establishment of a second US Army corps headquarters under the MAF, and the commencement of the single-management system that placed control of Marine fixed-wing aircraft under the US Air Force.

Command and control determined how III MAF conducted operations in I Corps. Problems associated with all three C2 functions—leaders, processes, and organization—undermined the headquarters' performance. These difficulties also contributed to the MAF's struggles with its joint partners and, even more important, its inability to accomplish its missions and win the war in I Corps.

Commanding the Corps

Six different general officers commanded III MAF during its six years in Vietnam. The first and last served only a few months and did not have a substantial impact. Major General William R. Collins opened the headquarters in Da Nang in May 1965 but completed his command tour just a month later. Lieutenant General Donn J. Robertson assumed command from the ailing Lieutenant General Keith B. McCutcheon in December 1970 and redeployed the command back to Okinawa less than four months later. Between Collins and Robertson, four general officers guided III MAF through its formative and defining challenges in I Corps. Lewis W. Walt (June 1965–June 1967), Robert E. Cushman, Jr. (June 1967–March 1969), Herman Nickerson, Jr. (March 1969–March 1970), and Keith B. McCutcheon (March–December 1970) determined III MAF's operational style, with the first two exerting the greatest influence.

The corps occupies a unique niche within the overall architecture of combat command. In 1965, and based on the experience garnered over the previous fifty years, a corps headquarters was expected to control several divisions and report to a field army. Corps were designed to direct a shifting pattern of subordinate divisions and independent brigades in the accomplishment of larger tactical tasks. They typically lacked robust administrative and logistic elements, with such support coming from the parent field army when required. Vietnam shattered the previous doctrinal norm. In that theater they became regional headquarters, their duties being joint and combined in character. No longer mobile, the stationary staffs ballooned in size to cover their burgeoning responsibilities. These included advising South Vietnamese security forces, combating conventional and irregular opponents, and implementing nation-building tasks outside the traditional purview of military headquarters.

Major General Walt, the MAF's new commander, set out to master this complex C2 environment. He boasted one of the strongest Marine combat pedigrees of the era. The burly officer had captained the football and wrestling teams at Colorado State University before commissioning in 1936. Winner of two Navy Crosses and a Silver Star in WWII, Walt added a Bronze Star in Korea. His peacetime career was a mixture of command and professional education up to the National War College, albeit with no significant staff assignments at either Marine Corps headquarters or the Department of Defense. Although still the most junior major general in the Marine Corps, he assumed command of III MAF on 5 June 1965.[4]

"Soon after I arrived in Vietnam," Walt later recalled, "it became obvious to me that I had neither a real understanding of the nature of the war nor any clear idea as to how to win it."[5] That initial confusion included his direction of III MAF's command-and-control system. Walt initiated the continuing effort to comprehend and adapt to the conflict's hybrid character. He also began the process of building and refining the staff processes and organizational constructs necessary to win the war. Nonetheless, either through lack of experience or lack of interest, he did not fashion a reliable C2 instrument to implement his will. A charismatic leader more comfortable inspiring people directly than working through staff procedures, Walt never built a strong, cohesive corps-level team to translate his intent into effective operations.

Another of Walt's challenges was his relationships with his operational and administrative bosses. The stiff, starched Westmoreland, in Saigon, challenged Walt's emphasis on pacification. The diminutive Victor "Brute" Krulak, in Honolulu, challenged nearly everything else. Walt treated both superiors with deference but resented the latter's overbearing attempts to drive operations in Vietnam. Krulak's long shadow hovered over the MAF throughout his 1964–1968 tenure as FMFPAC commander.

A frequent visitor to Vietnam, Krulak conveyed copious tactical advice to MACV and III MAF. A personal letter penned by Walt's G-3 Operations officer in 1966 underscored the vexing nature of the FMFPAC commander's constant interference. "Krulak is still bouncing around causing misery. I've stayed completely away from him this time. He really gags me. I am positive he is out here just to heckle."[6] Krulak defined his role with respect to III MAF as "command minus operational control."[7] While technically correct, this verbiage

underplayed the fact that III MAF in I Corps worked for MACV.
FMFPAC rendered essential administrative and logistical support, but
it did not upstage MACV's preeminence in directing III MAF's operations. Krulak understood this but, convinced that he knew best, often
strayed into operational matters in Vietnam.[8]

Walt forged friendly relations with his Vietnamese I Corps counterparts, another precedent subsequent MAF commanders strove to
emulate. The political intrigues of spring 1966, in which protesters in
Hue and Da Nang supported Lieutenant General Nguyen Chanh Thi
against the Saigon regime of Premier Nguyen Cao Ky, tested Walt's
political acumen. As the senior American on scene, he capably managed the transition from General Thi, with whom he had established
strong personal bonds, via a succession of temporary commanders to
Brigadier General Hoang Xuan Lam, whose subsequent command of
ARVN forces in I Corps endured beyond the Marines' departure in
1971. Throughout this unanticipated and perilous transition of I Corps
command, Walt displayed admirable courage, at one point even facing
down a belligerent ARVN warrant officer who threatened to detonate
a key bridge in Da Nang while both men stood on it. That the 1966
political crisis ended without greater damage to the larger South Vietnamese cause attested to Walt's steady and engaged leadership.[9]

Walt's affable nature (he was admired as "Uncle Lew") and reputation for fearlessness earned his men's admiration. He personified the
"muddy boots" commander. Walt visited units in the field, sometimes
arriving just after a contact to discuss the engagement with the Marines involved.[10] He later wrote: "Since Guadalcanal . . . I had chafed
at my progressive isolation from the places where the battles were being fought. . . . The helicopter ended this dismal restriction. . . . This
new Pegasus allowed me not only to see what was going on, but also to
know, first hand, what the men of my command were enduring, and to
learn, assess, and pass on to others each unit's response to the circumstances of Vietnam."[11]

Walt's personal style of command had worked well at the battalion
and regimental levels, but he lacked division and corps command experience. Before the war he served as an assistant division commander,
but III MAF was his first experience commanding a division and a
corps, leading both simultaneously until March 1966. Not surprising, he and his staff suffered growing pains as they wrestled with a
host of challenges for which neither experience nor education had
prepared them. Walt's early stewardship of a relatively small corps-
level command element, though not without flaws, committed the new

headquarters to a balanced approach between pacification and conventional operations. Subsequent MAF commanders continued his policy. Unfortunately, balance alone was not enough when clear ideas on how to win the conflict remained elusive.

Lieutenant General Robert E. Cushman, Jr., Walt's replacement, arrived in 1967 with a slightly less formidable combat résumé but broader experience in politico-military assignments. As a battalion commander, he was decorated for valor at Bougainville, Guam, and Iwo Jima. After WWII, Cushman instructed at both Marine and joint staff colleges, did a tour with the naval staff in London, and commanded a regiment and three divisions. He also served at the Central Intelligence Agency (CIA), worked for four years on Vice President Richard M. Nixon's national security staff, and directed the intelligence and operations staffs at Headquarters Marine Corps.[12]

One might expect, given Cushman's extensive command, staff, and teaching experience, the general to have imposed firm structure and processes on III MAF's C2 system. Instead he appeared to have accepted the organization he inherited and did little to improve it. His aloof style, lack of energy, and poor tactical judgment led one prominent Marine historian to label Cushman's command "lackluster."[13]

Cushman's direction, or lack thereof, prompted Westmoreland to initiate major C2 modifications in I Corps. Unlike Walt, who maintained cordial relations with his higher headquarters in Saigon despite some tactical differences, Cushman's relations with the MACV commander were frosty from the start. Partly this disparity reflected different command styles, including approaches to managing higher headquarters. Westmoreland was the prototypical "Organization Man," a Harvard Business School graduate and notorious micromanager who placed great emphasis on professional staff work. Cushman ran a much looser ship. As corps commander, he identified missions for his subordinates but did not interfere with their tactical implementation. He relied heavily on his chief of staff, Brigadier General Earl Anderson, to orchestrate III MAF's staff and coordinate with outside agencies. Cushman may have been badly served in this choice. Anderson, a technophile with a bent for "authoritarian decision-making," did little to balance the MAF commander's own detached leadership.[14]

Within six months of his arrival, Cushman had lost the confidence of his boss. In 1967, Westmoreland faulted the III MAF commander for poor supervision of the DMZ barrier construction project. During the runup to and the crisis of the 1968 Tet Offensive, the army theater commander concluded Cushman was too passive in the face of increasing NVA threats to Khe Sanh, slow to respond to the crises at Da Nang and Hue, and unwilling to use Marine aircraft to support US Army divisions in I Corps.[15] Merited or not, those judgments cost III MAF direct command of both the ground war in the northern two provinces and of the 1st Marine Aircraft Wing's reconnaissance and strike aircraft.

The My Lai massacre also occurred on Cushman's watch. In March 1968, an army platoon murdered 107 Vietnamese noncombatants in Quang Ngai Province. The extensive investigations of the war crime reflected no blame on the III MAF staff or its commander. Both were unaware of the incident and its coverup. The American Division, parent command of army First Lieutenant William L. Calley, who led the unit that committed the atrocity, did not submit reports of its internal inquiry to the MAF (its superior command for operations), US Army, Vietnam (its higher administrative headquarters), or MACV.[16] In records of that month's actions, the American Division reported seventy-seven civilian deaths, a low total for the division that normally led the MAF in that grisly category. In the nine months between January and October 1968, the American Division acknowledged killing nearly five times as many civilians as its Marine counterparts and accounted for 38 percent of the civilian deaths reported by the five US divisions under III MAF.[17] Cushman did not investigate this anomaly or the methods that may have explained it.

Cushman's successor, Lieutenant General Herman Nickerson, had a distinguished combat record in Korea. He commanded 1st Marine Division around Da Nang in 1967 and served as Cushman's deputy in 1968 before assuming MAF command in 1969.[18] Nickerson instituted few changes in the way the corps command post operated beyond putting a force-level headquarters over the CAPs, previously supervised by a MAF staff officer. During his one-year in command, Nickerson presided over the start of the Marine drawdown in I Corps, including the 3rd Marine Division that withdrew to Okinawa by October 1969. He also dealt with the poisonous fruits of social upheaval addressed in chapter 1, including racial tension, drug use, and fragging (attacks by enlisted personnel on their own leaders).[19]

Like Walt and Cushman before him, Nickerson learned that corps command entailed new C2 challenges. As a division commander, Nickerson had personally welcomed incoming officers and SNCOs and shared his views on their complex mission. Because the larger span of control prevented such briefings at the MAF level, he initiated instead a column in the III MAF weekly newspaper to convey his perspectives on the enemy, civil-military aspects of the conflict, and the South Vietnamese people and their armed forces.[20] These missives revealed no significant changes from his predecessors' command philosophy or operational approach. In dealing with the US Army, he maintained mostly friendly relations. With the air force, Nickerson continued the MAF's consistent efforts to regain full control of its fixed-wing aircraft, with limited success.[21] He competently and quietly managed declining resources.

In many ways Lieutenant General Keith B. McCutcheon represented the most intriguing of the MAF's four primary commanders. An aeronautical engineer, he won a Silver Star and Distinguished Flying Cross in the Pacific during WWII and pioneered Marine close air support tactics for army forces in the Philippines. McCutcheon also led a helicopter squadron in the Korean conflict, an aviation group in North Carolina in 1958, an amphibious brigade in Hawaii in 1962, and the 1st Marine Aircraft Wing in Vietnam in 1965. He served four years at Headquarters Marine Corps before returning to command III MAF in 1970.[22] In Vietnam, he became the first aviator to lead a corps-level Marine headquarters since General Roy Geiger in WWII.

McCutcheon lacked prior experience commanding ground forces. He initiated no new C2 arrangements during his nine-month tour, which focused on drawing down the Marines' stake in the war. Like Nickerson, he inherited a command facing increasingly serious internal strife. He continued drug-abuse education and treatment programs, promoted efforts to resolve racial unrest, and expanded procedures to crack down on fraggings. Unlike the previous MAF commanders, McCutcheon's corps headquarters no longer served as the senior US command element in I Corps. Instead it served as a subordinate of the army's XXIV Corps, responsible for only one of I Corps' five provinces. As the service's ablest advocate for Marine aviation, McCutcheon won a partial victory over the US Air Force in the bureaucratic struggle over who directed strike/reconnaissance aircraft missions. Picked to replace General Walt as the assistant commandant in 1971, McCutcheon seemed destined to become the first Marine aviator to serve as Commandant. Only the invidious return of a previous cancer, which took his life just six months after he returned home for treatment, prevented this brilliant and widely respected officer from further shaping the Corps in the years following the Vietnam conflict.[23]

In this hybrid war, corps-level Marine generalship proved competent over the long term but fell short when it mattered most. The MAF commanders employed different leadership styles. Walt exemplified the heroic leader, inspiring subordinates and relying on superior human qualities to win battles. Cushman and Nickerson were managers, dependent on the MAF's shaky staff processes, unevenly resourced and administered, to produce results. McCutcheon combined leadership and management prowess. All four generals ardently defended the integrity of the MAGTF, conducted a balanced conventional and irregular campaign, and avoided micromanagement of division and wing commanders. Yet the corps they created and wielded failed in its mission. Cushman was the least effective. His lethargic response to the 1968 Tet Offensive—the greatest tactical test faced by any of the MAF commanders—inspired General Westmoreland to sideline the senior Marine headquarters by initiating the new I Corps command structure examined in the next section.

Staff Structure and Processes

The corps staff enabled III MAF commanders to control the organization's sprawling enterprises. Walt established the MAF headquarters at Da Nang, the site of ARVN's I Corps command post in addition to being the region's largest city, principal airfield, and major port. Three hundred meters west of the air base and adjacent to 1st MAW's command post, this site facilitated coordination with the South Vietnamese corps commander and his staff, the air force's 366th Tactical Fighter Wing, and the US Naval Support Activity.[24] In June 1966 Walt moved the III MAF command element into a new facility in eastern Da Nang.[25] When XXIV Corps assumed command of US forces in I Corps in March 1970, it moved from Phu Bai into the III MAF command post, while the Marines shifted their senior headquarters into a compound evacuated by the Seabees at Camp Haskins, just a few miles away on Red Beach in northwestern Da Nang.[26]

Walt organized the MAF headquarters staff by the standard functional specialties: G-1 (Administration), G-2 (Intelligence), G-3 (Operations), G-4 (Logistics), and G-5 (Plans). In October 1965, the G-5 converted from Plans to Civil Affairs. CORDS, added in 1967, partly absorbed existing G-5 military personnel but operated as a separate branch nominally under the MAF headquarters' supervision. Serving as the "pacification staff," CORDS had no precedent in military command systems. More typical were the many smaller staff specialties augmenting the primary directorates and reflecting the theater's varied demands. By August 1969 these special staff sections included

Psychological Operations, Supply, Legal, Engineer, Adjutant, Comptroller, Food Service, Chaplain, Surgeon, Dental, Combat Information Bureau, Motor Transport, Staff Secretary, Protocol, Special Services, Ordnance, Inspector General, and a team of liaison officers.[27] While the G-3 Operations staff played the most visible part in orchestrating corps-level actions, each of the other principal departments and special staffs performed important roles in the MAF's day-to-day operations.

Perhaps because they believed the MAF's primary function was to support amphibious campaigns, Marine Corps schools had envisioned a "suitcase" MAF staff that was collocated with the division or wing staff and used the same personnel to fill billets at both levels simultaneously. The prewar III MEF staff existed only in cadre form, and there was no comparable but established Marine headquarters that could provide either trained personnel or proven practices.[28] The larger III MAF staff that emerged over time was not planned but improvised and ad hoc. It grew by fits and starts, cobbled together by contingency and hard-earned experience. Successive commanders inherited but did not alter Walt's initial staff construct, one that was not organized, trained, or equipped to handle competently its expansive duties.

Officers working for the MAF soon realized their responsibilities within a corps differed from those within the division or the wing they were more comfortable with.[29] They found that the corps dealt with manpower policy issues like managing force structure and strength caps, whereas divisions focused on casualty replacement concerns. The corps held a regional view of the enemy threat and integrated operations across all five I Corps provinces, whereas a division was responsible only for its sector. The corps coordinated force-wide supply, maintenance, and medical concerns, including integration with theater and sister service logistics capabilities, whereas the division concentrated on pushing supplies out to troops in the field. The corps incorporated a broad array of civil-military considerations into plans developed with adjacent and higher joint and combined headquarters, whereas divisions directed local humanitarian assistance projects. The corps communicated with an array of external commands and agencies with which divisions did not have to bother. Neither Walt nor his staff at first recognized the vast differences between corps and division responsibilities. Help from higher headquarters remained absent. Thus both Walt and his staff fell back on what they were comfortable with: running the corps like a division or even a regiment.

It was naïve to assume that the same staff officers could fill both corps and division/wing billets simultaneously or that a cadre MAF

staff could swiftly expand and operate efficiently upon war's out-
break.[30] That this perception prevailed across the Marine Corps is astounding in retrospect. Cruel experience soon taught the lessons that
the schools had missed. In 1970 and 1971, when the MAF began to
shrink its size and responsibilities in preparation for departing Vietnam, Marine leaders realized that the service's senior headquarters in
I Corps could not parasite again off a division or wing staff. Instead
they maintained a smaller, but still separate, MAF staff until it transitioned to a Marine Amphibious Brigade staff two months before the
last Marine units departed for Okinawa.[31] In 1965, however, Walt, who
liked to lead his subordinates face-to-face, seemed quite happy with
the flattened C2 architecture. The ad hoc staff, whatever its flaws,
reflected the commander's personality and command style.

Walt's multi-hatted role provided another indication that no one
considered corps-level command more than a part-time job. Senior
Marine leaders did not appreciate what the corps echelon of command
really did. Walt served simultaneously as commander of 3rd Marine
Division, commander of US Navy forces ashore in Vietnam, and commander of III MAF until March 1966.[32] In addition to confusing three
separate staffs that served the same boss, this arrangement split Walt's
time and attention between very different spheres.

No precedent for a dual division/corps command existed in either
US Army or Marine experience in WWI, WWII, or Korea. Neither
was it duplicated for the duration of the Vietnam conflict. Less im-
pactful, but similarly ill-advised from both practical and organizational
standpoints, Marine division and wing commanders served concur-
rently as deputy MAF commanders between June 1965 and April 1967
and again from March 1970 to April 1971. In the intervening three
years, officers held the deputy MAF commander billet as a full-time
position. In 1968, an army general served as an additional MAF deputy
"for Army matters." An army brigadier also filled the MAF deputy
chief of staff (Plans) position in 1969. Both billets reflected the growing importance of US Army forces in I Corps.[33]

When Walt discovered he could not make up for his headquarters
staff's deficiencies by double-tapping division/wing assets, he sought
structural remedies. These chiefly entailed adding more personnel. In
December 1965 (the first month for which data is available), the MAF
staff numbered 249 men.[34] By 1967 the staff, not including support
personnel such as cooks, mechanics, security guards, and radio op-
erators, totaled 574.[35] Staff numbers, including officers and enlisted

personnel, crested at 997 in August 1968.[36] By comparison, the army's I Field Force (corps-level) staff in the Central Highlands numbered five hundred personnel, while its II Field Force staff, supervising US forces stationed around Saigon, grew to a thousand.[37] Large staffs added capacity for analysis and increased ability to respond to high levels of information, but they also tended to slow down operational tempo as more people became involved in the decision-making process.

As the MAF's responsibilities grew, Walt and Cushman requested more personnel. But records of message traffic do not indicate that they were asking for more talented staff officers. Neither did service commandants or FMFPAC commanders push their best officers to the III MAF staff. Unlike in the army, Marine officers viewed staff duty as a career-killer. Almost to a man, they strove to get posted to divisions, regiments, and battalions, with command being the ultimate prize. These cultural norms channeled motivated Marines away from the corps-level headquarters, and Walt's staff functioned poorly as a result. Its slow start and haphazard performance reflected a newly formed team with no peacetime training to prepare for its duties.

An early example of shoddy command and staff work surfaced in December 1965 during Operation HARVEST MOON. Early in the operation, Walt fired Marine Brigadier General Melvin D. Henderson for unsteady command of a brigade-level task force. Sometimes represented as the work of a no-nonsense MAF commander with a low tolerance for subordinates who lacked his own confidence in combat, this incident represented the only Marine sacking of a general officer in the war.[38] Long after the conflict, details of this event remained murky. Records released in 2011 revealed actions less flattering to Walt. Henderson, commanding his first engagement in Vietnam, moved his command post five times in the first twenty-nine hours, disrupting control of the nascent operation, which lasted another ten days.

But Walt and his own staff bore equal responsibility for the initial confusion. The complex operation was hastily planned by an ad hoc task force staff, with inadequate communication resources and confused command relationships between Marine forces ashore and afloat. Walt's staffs and his own direction accounted for some of the mixups, as the subsequent inquiry revealed. A full investigation conducted by III MAF's superior army or Marine headquarters likely would have found the III MAF commander equally or even more culpable for the chaos than the officer Walt relieved. The casualties and confusion that occurred during the brief period in question could not be attributed to a single factor or commander.[39] The relief was not Walt's finest hour. More important, it illustrated that his C2 system, a victim of both institutional and individual deficiencies, lacked proficiency.

The developing III MAF staff also suffered from a lack of education, since not everyone had attended the Amphibious Warfare and Staff College courses that taught higher-level staff duties. Few Marine officers and SNCOs had served on a corps-level staff, much less one engaged in a complex hybrid war. Another factor contributing to second-tier staff work was the dizzying pace of turnover. In the Civil Affairs section, nineteen men served as the principal staff officer in the six years the MAF operated in Vietnam, averaging less than four months each. Other primary staff section heads served similarly brief tours, often staying less than six months in the same billet before rotating to a new post or redeploying back to the United States.[40]

Lack of continuity among senior staff officers hindered development of the proficiency required. In March 1966 the MAF Operations officer, Colonel (later general) John R. Chaisson, wrote: "We don't have as strong a group in the III MAF staff as we did in the 2d Marine Division. It is sort of a jerry-rig organization." A month later he lamented that "the staff is zilch. It is a crime that we are fighting 50,000 Marines with a 3d string outfit." In May he observed: "Our basic problem is lack of talent and numbers."[41] Chaisson's criticism reveals that III MAF's staff problems emerged early—and should have been corrected early.

The MAF commanders and their struggling staffs employed several techniques to synchronize subordinate operations. Regular meetings allowed primary and special staff officers to coordinate regional actions, but MAF commanders called subordinate commanders to conferences on an infrequent basis. Instead they toured the region, visiting divisions, regiments, and even battalions at their camps and in the field. Walt was by far the most active in this role. His tendency to appear in the field without notice earned him a reputation as the "three star grunt."[42]

Neither he nor his successors, however, employed the "directed telescope," a type of control used by commanders such as George Patton and Bernard Montgomery in WWII. Then, designated agents (such as trained junior staff officers) or senior representatives (such as deputy commanding generals) moved about using the commander's authority to check on subordinates' status or performance.[43] Improved communications and the widespread availability of helicopter transport made the directed-telescope technique less prevalent than in previous conflicts.

The traditional method of coordinating corps-level action entailed commanders and their staffs dispatching written orders to subordinate divisions. Some of those orders addressed standard operating procedures designed to develop common techniques. The III MAF 1968 CAP Standard Operating Procedure exemplified that genre of administrative order.[44] The most common type of order, however, addressed operations. These could be time-sensitive directives concerning a brief operation or instructions that remained in effect for months or even years. For the entire six-year span of its service in I Corps, the MAF operated off just four standing MACV orders.[45] In turn, III MAF generated few written orders to its subordinate division, wing, and logistics commands. In the first year of its time in I Corps, Walt's dual command of the corps and division allowed him to issue MAF orders directly to regiment-size combat units. This occurred, for example, in January 1966 when 3rd Marine Division's Task Force Delta executed Operation DOUBLE EAGLE.[46]

All the III MAF commanders and their staffs crafted operational orders featuring directive, not detailed, language. They assigned tasks to subordinate units in the broadest possible terms rather than trying to anticipate and account for every potential factor that might influence the outcome. The 1968 Letter of Instruction directing 1st Marine Division to conduct its part of the Accelerated Pacification Campaign around Da Nang, for example, tasked it to "find and destroy NVA/VC units and installations," "expand combined spoiling and preemptive attacks," and "conduct mobile operations . . . to eliminate the VCI."[47] Guidance to army formations was couched even more diplomatically. Major General Samuel B. Koster, commanding the Americal Division in 1968, remarked: "I got the distinct feeling that I was to work my TAOR [Tactical Area of Responsibility] as I saw fit." Cushman averred that he treated the army division like a Marine division.[48] Orders to regional CORDS directors were equally generic. Roger "Blowtorch" Komer, Westmoreland's first deputy for CORDS, claimed "the corps commanders left us alone. The pacification business was run autonomously."[49] In their hands-off approach, the III MAF staff and commanders anticipated modern Marine doctrine and best practices, which condemn detailed orders in favor of directives that provide only essential information.[50]

The crux of these MAF orders concerned assigned objectives.

Information detailing "who," "what," "where," and "when" determined the ways and means; "why" established the desired ends. Then, as now, setting this goal such that it matched available resources and feasible methods constituted the essence of operational art. Orders generated by III MAF often identified valid, if sometimes vague, objectives. The MAF order launching DOUBLE EAGLE in 1966, for example, aimed to "locate and destroy enemy forces."[51] The challenge, like the problems identified with corps-level plans of longer duration (covered in chapter 8), always entailed attaining the goals with the forces and methods at hand.

In short, it was easier to describe an outcome than to achieve it. DOUBLE EAGLE amassed three ARVN, army, and Marine divisions—working across corps boundaries, covering two thousand square miles, and serving under four ARVN and US corps-level headquarters—to trap and destroy seven thousand NVA/VC. The combined operation lasted a month and accounted for approximately two thousand enemy killed and captured. Although successful in the aggregate, the Marine portion of this operation was less productive, claiming 331 of the adversary's casualties. Adding insult to injury, a follow-up III MAF sweep failed to locate the ever-elusive 1st VC Regiment.[52] This operation, like many others, underscored the difference between staff work, however sound, and actual results on the ground.

Organizational Framework

The complex web of organizations operating in I Corps and the tangled command relationships that flowed from that network represented the most convoluted C2 architecture that the American military had yet experienced. Since the Vietnam War, such multifaceted command systems have become more common, but I Corps' mix of forces and authorities was unprecedented. Under Westmoreland's oversight three US corps-level headquarters (two army and one Marine) directed America's ground war in Vietnam. An ARVN corps directed civil and military actions for Saigon in each of the country's four numbered regions. In each sector except the one covering the Mekong Delta, a US corps worked with its ARVN counterpart to defend the area's people and resources. III MAF, teamed with ARVN's I Corps, furnished the US corps-level command post in the northern five provinces of South Vietnam.[53] MACV exercised operational control of III MAF, while the latter reported administratively to Fleet Marine Force, Pacific in Pearl

Harbor and directly to Headquarters Marine Corps in Washington for specific service-related issues.

Walt and his successors also coordinated with adjacent US Army and Air Force commands. The former included I and II Field Forces, also corps-level headquarters, stationed in South Vietnam's II and III Corps sectors, respectively. Inside I Corps the MAF exercised operational control over US Army Special Forces units, which conducted cross-border reconnaissance and trained or led South Vietnamese unconventional forces such as the Civilian Irregular Defense Groups.[54] The primary air force headquarters that III MAF worked with was Seventh Air Force in Saigon. This command and III MAF engaged in a contentious spat over control of aircraft, detailed in this chapter's final section.

Marine interface with regional navy forces morphed as the war continued. In his first year in Da Nang, Walt commanded all US Navy forces within I Corps and reported to Pacific Fleet in that capacity. In April 1966 the navy lifted that burden by establishing a new service headquarters in Saigon to command its forces in Vietnam. By 1968 in I Corps alone twenty-two thousand sailors served in supply, maintenance, engineering, and hospital units. To employ Marine amphibious forces, which belonged operationally to the navy, III MAF communicated with United States Seventh Fleet through MACV and Fleet Marine Force, Pacific.[55]

Control of amphibious units remained controversial throughout the conflict, especially the blurred lines of command when landing forces came ashore into sectors already managed by other allied headquarters. Naval forces afloat desired more autonomy to control units and fires ashore, as established in amphibious doctrine. MACV wanted these naval forces to come under its command as soon as they landed. Two conferences in Okinawa in 1966 smoothed the friction, but complaints continued from both sides throughout the war. Several landings led to bureaucratic riffs between MACV and the navy rather than to fights with the enemy. Westmoreland believed that the tenets of amphibious doctrine, in which the navy controlled the beachhead and its airspace, were irrelevant in Vietnam, where friendly forces already managed the coastal landing sites and were engaged in conventional land operations for a prolonged period. Given the administrative nature of many of the landings, Westmoreland chose to leave the C2 issue unresolved rather than spark another dispute with the navy over a type of operation that delivered little tactical value in South Vietnam.[56]

In addition to joint force collaboration, III MAF commanders also coordinated with ARVN's I Corps command, collocated in Da Nang. This headquarters directed the 1st and 2nd ARVN Divisions plus the Quang Da Special Zone, a division-level command in Da Nang that by 1970 managed twelve infantry battalions, including those of the 51st ARVN Regiment.[57] The Republic of Korea's Marine Brigade, which deployed to I Corps in August 1966, cooperated with III MAF. Like ARVN's I Corps, the Korean brigade reported to neither III MAF nor MACV. The brigade's national reporting chain ran back to Seoul via the senior Korean army general in Vietnam. The ROK–US Marine relationship, with the Korean brigade accepting III MAF's "operational guidance" in the official (nondoctrinal) terminology, remained one of coordination, not command, throughout the conflict. Frustrated by his lack of authority, Cushman observed the Korean Marines "didn't do a thing unless they felt like it." Annoyed by the brigade's national mandate to keep their casualties low, he also groused privately after his tour that the Korean force was "totally useless" because it avoided aggressive large unit sweeps.[58]

Beyond the wide array of external players, the MAF's organizational structure grew increasingly complex with its own organic and assigned forces. Although serving under just two reinforced Marine divisions, leatherneck ground forces in III MAF numbered eight infantry regiments at their 1969 peak. This total was just one regiment shy of the number at Iwo Jima in 1945 and represented two more than landed on Okinawa. Overall, however, the Vietnam MAF employed a much bigger corps than its WWII antecedents because of its subordinate army elements. In August 1968, under Cushman's watch, III MAF topped out at just over 159,000 personnel, compared to V Amphibious Corps' 71,000-man force at Iwo Jima or the similarly sized III Amphibious Corps at Okinawa.[59] Measured in regiments, allied regular units in I Corps included by 1968 the equivalent of nine divisions: the Korean Marine Brigade; two reinforced Marine divisions; three army divisions; two ARVN divisions; and the division-size ARVN forces protecting Da Nang and serving as regional reserves.

The MAF's expanding force list incorporated several structural novelties. The first of these was the aviation command. A Marine air wing had never deployed for sustained operations ashore to fight under a MAF headquarters. A standard MAW in 1965 comprised two fixed-wing and two rotary-wing air groups. By 1969 1st Marine Aircraft Wing in I Corps had added an additional jet and helicopter air group for a total of six groups flying from five separate airfields and supporting allied ground forces of field army size. In addition to the large ground and air components, the MAF developed a much larger version of its organic logistics regiment, the Force Logistics Command, which attained a top strength of 9,766 Marines.[60] Walt also created a new formation, the two thousand–strong Combined Action Force. This unit deployed as individual squads operating with RVN Popular Forces platoons in the villages, but it was organized administratively into four battalion-size groups reporting directly to the MAF.[61] In 1967 the MAF added the novel CORDS organization, whose civilian and military personnel conducted development work with their South Vietnamese village, district, province, and regional counterparts.[62] Finally, the MAF commanders controlled the unique I Corps advisory command, led by a US Army colonel and staffed mostly with soldiers, which assisted and trained I Corps' ARVN forces.[63]

Two factors compounded the challenges inherent in the MAF's large size and the diversity of its command relationships. First, though all the allied forces in the region fought against a common foe and sought the same operational goals, no single command directed the disparate elements in a synergistic fashion. The South Vietnamese, Koreans, and Americans in I Corps coordinated their efforts but never established a combined headquarters. This decision mirrored the relationships in place at the national level, since allied political leaders elected not to establish a unified military or civil-military command.[64] Instead their forces waged war in a cooperative manner, settling for "unity of effort" rather than the more effective and efficient "unity of command." Even among I Corps' US forces, unified command did not exist. III MAF functioned as the senior US military headquarters in Saigon's northern region, but army logisticians, the air force fighter wing, and the Naval Support Activity's supply, construction, and some medical personnel did not serve under III MAF's command or operational control.

The second problem concerned "span of control." Both military doctrine and business organizational theory suggest three to seven major subordinate elements as an optimal span of control for a single headquarters.[65] Thus corps traditionally control two or three divisions plus the battalion- or brigade-size units serving as corps troops. In December 1967 III MAF directed eight major subordinate commands: three divisions (two Marine and one army), an air wing, a logistics command, the CORDS program, an advisory group, and the Combined Action Force while also coordinating with external ARVN, Korean, and sister service forces.[66] Two more army divisions and a US Army corps headquarters joined the III MAF force mix in 1968. At least three company or battalion size units also served as "corps troops" under III MAF. This array of subordinate formations far exceeded a doctrinal Marine Expeditionary Force headquarters' intended command capacity—a single division and air wing plus a logistics regiment—and equaled the designed control capabilities of a field army command post.[67] If a multi-division corps exceeded the MAF's capacity to command comfortably, subordinate forces of field army size certainly dwarfed its envisioned span of control.

III MAF's commanding generals had little control over their corps' unity-of-command and span-of-control challenges, but they bore direct responsibility for another organizational flaw. At every level of command from rifle company to amphibious force, Marine commanders exhibited a marked tendency to mix units in ad hoc task forces fitted to emergent missions. At one level this flexible task organization enhanced responsiveness and demonstrated the interchangeability of platoons, companies, battalions, and regiments.[68] Both the 1st and 3rd Marine Divisions frequently established temporary task forces commanded by the assistant division commander, staffed by one or more (often mixed) regimental staffs and populated by battalions and regiments from subordinate units representing two to four separate commands. Two examples among many illustrate the trend. In Operation DOUBLE EAGLE (1966), the five thousand–man Task Force Delta, led by 3rd Marine Division's assistant commander, formed its staff with personnel from the staffs of the division and two regiments and directed four battalions from four separate regiments.[69] In Operation ALLEN BROOK (1968), a battalion from 7th Marines commanded three companies from three other battalions but none of its own.[70]

Unit interchangeability proved a minor blessing but a major curse. On the plus side, it allowed commanders to swiftly employ available units regardless of their organizational origin. Unit leaders and their staffs also learned new ways of operating, including unfamiliar tactical techniques and new command processes. Perhaps most important, the ad hoc task forces prevented division commanders and their staffs from being consumed by major named operations like ALLEN BROOK, allowing them to keep a watchful eye on other important activities ongoing across their sectors at the same time.

These marginal advantages paled in comparison to the drawbacks of routinely mixing units. While the constantly fluxing organizational permutations did not lead to battlefield failure, they exacted penalties on unit cohesion, staff efficiency, and combat effectiveness as commands that had not previously worked together formed and jelled under fire. Marines at the time noted the deficiencies inherent in this approach.[71] Major General Raymond G. Davis, 3rd Marine Division commander in 1968, abhorred the organizational patchwork in the division he inherited. Colonel Robert H. Barrow, commanding 9th Marines at the time, likened the division's regimental commanders to warlords and its battalions to "roving bands of mercenaries." Davis set about restoring battalions to their parent regiment's control and later attributed his units' subsequent success to these changes.[72] Unfortunately, the 1st Marine Division never instituted similar measures to stabilize companies and battalions under their respective parent commands, though Cushman did direct the two Marine divisions to restore "organizational integrity" by returning battalions belonging to the other division.[73]

The Marine penchant for constantly changing task forces carried organizational flexibility to the point of dysfunctionality. Although III MAF did not mandate the kaleidoscopic rotation of forces at the company to division level, it could and should have recognized and done more to prevent its deleterious effects. Spenser Wilkinson, in his classic study of the German General Staff, noted "the corps must have had so much practice in working together as a whole that it has none of the weaknesses of a 'scratch team.'"[74] The MAF fought as a scratch team.

III MAF fielded additional units in addition to its major subordinate wing, division, and logistic commands. These formations included infantry, artillery, engineering, communication, transport, and aviation units. (See table 2.1 for reinforcing ground units.) None of them resided in III MAF's organic structure. Instead they came to I Corps from external Marine, navy, and army commands to supplement the capabilities of the MAF. Together these augmenting units mustered four regimental headquarters, thirty-two battalions, and two independent companies. Doctrinally a corps headquarters may employ augmenting units directly, working under its own control (where they are called "corps-level troops"), or by assigning them to subordinate commands to reinforce their capabilities. In I Corps, III MAF allocated most of these externally sourced units to the two Marine divisions, underscoring their need for additional forces simultaneously to protect key cities and installations, attack enemy regular units, and conduct pacification operations throughout an extended battlespace. Although the employment of these reinforcing units varied over time (as table 2.1 shows), III MAF consistently retained for its direct use only the radio (signals intelligence) battalion, psychological operations battalion, and civil affairs company.

Table 2.1. Units reinforcing III MAF

Unit	Type	Assigned to	Source
26th Marine Regiment (three battalions)	Infantry	1st Marine Division	5th Marine Division
27th Marine Regiment (three battalions)	Infantry	1st Marine Division	5th Marine Division
5th Tank Battalion (two companies)	Armor	1st Marine Division	5th Marine Division
Naval Construction Regiment 30	Engineer	Force Logistics Command; Naval Support Activity*	U.S. Navy
7th Engineer Battalion	Engineer	III MAF, 3rd Marine Division, 1st Marine Division	I MEF
9th Engineer Battalion	Engineer	III MAF, 3rd Marine Division, 1st Marine Division	III MAF
11th Engineer Battalion	Engineer	III MAF, 3rd Marine Division	5th Marine Division
1st Field Artillery Group HQ	Artillery	11th Marine Regiment, 1st Marine Division	Force Troops, FMFPAC
1st Battalion, 13th Marine Regiment	Artillery	11th Marine Regiment, 1st Marine Division	5th Marine Division
2nd Battalion, 13th Marine Regiment	Artillery	11th Marine Regiment, 1st Mar Division	5th Marine Division
7th Motor Transport Battalion	Truck	Force Logistics Command	1st Marine Division
9th Motor Transport Battalion	Truck	III MAF, 3rd Marine Division	3rd Marine Division
11th Motor Transport Battalion	Truck	1st Marine Division	FMF Pacific
5th Communications Battalion	Communications	III MAF, 3rd Marine Division, Force Logistics Command	5th Marine Division
7th Communications Battalion	Communications	1st Marine Division; III MAF	1st Marine Division
1st Radio Battalion	Signals Intelligence	III MAF	FMF Pacific
1st Force Reconnaissance Company	Intelligence	III MAF, 3rd Marine Division, III MAF	FMF Pacific
U.S. Army 29th Civil Affairs Company	Civil Affairs	III MAF	U.S. Army
U.S. Army 7th Psychological Operations Battalion	Psychological Operations	III MAF	U.S. Army
1st MP Battalion	Military Police	Force Logistics Command, III MAF	1st Marine Division
3rd MP Battalion	Military Police	Force Logistics Command, III MAF	3rd Marine Division

* On 1 April 1966, the US Navy Seabees in Vietnam were transferred to the command of US Naval Forces, Vietnam in Saigon. After that date, in I Corps they reported to the Navy Support Activity in Da Nang, although they cooperated with and essentially continued to work for III MAF.

Source: The information in this table was derived from the III MAF tables of organization contained in the six USMC official histories, supplemented by data from III MAF command chronologies. This table shows only ground force augmentations. In addition, two Marine air groups and twenty-two more flying squadrons reinforced 1st Marine Aircraft Wing between 1965 and 1968.

In previous wars, corps headquarters often kept more units at the corps level than III MAF did in Vietnam. These troops, normally at brigade strength, fought or managed operational functions under centralized corps control. Corps artillery groups, for example, operated independently to reinforce division guns or orchestrate the corps counterfire battle. Engineer brigades frequently supervised critical corps-level construction or repair tasks. Reconnaissance regiments screened advances or covered defensive sectors. By 1968 the doctrinal US Army corps included all these formations, as well as air defense, logistics, medical, aviation, signal, psychological operations, civil affairs, and smoke-generation units of battalion to brigade size.[75] In I Corps, however, III MAF never established such brigade-level corps troops commands. No independent artillery or signal brigades (or battalions) worked directly for III MAF.

Partly this organizational choice reflected the distributed nature of the I Corps fight with discrete combat actions seldom exceeding a single regiment's scope. In this environment the decentralization of most tactical assets made sense. The Marines' preference—pushing resources down to major subordinate commands rather than centralizing their control and employment at the MAF—flowed also from their limited experience with corps-level operations, a C2 doctrine that did not emphasize the MAF's role as a fighting rather than an administrative headquarters, and the size and type of the forces available. In two specific instances, however, III MAF missed opportunities to employ its operational resources in a more centralized fashion to achieve better outcomes. First, a corps artillery headquarters could have controlled the counterfire fight along the DMZ.[76] And second, a corps-level engineer brigade could have coordinated regionwide base construction, road and railroad maintenance, and DMZ barrier construction tasks.[77] In both cases such corps-level units' senior leaders, staff capability, and focus would likely have enhanced performance of those critical tasks.

Doctrine dictates that C2 resources, like combat forces, must be tailored to match the assigned task.[78] In I Corps, III MAF encountered a complex civil-military operational environment that tested the capability of its preferred MAGTF command construct. The Marines enjoyed neither unity of command nor a reasonable corps-level span of control. They did, however, for the first time field an air-ground-logistics team fighting under a common service headquarters.[79] Despite this doctrinal achievement, the initial MAF structure proved too small in practice to manage the complexity of its regional responsibilities. Additional resources flowed to meet the emerging requirements, including significant augmentation by external Marine and joint units and even, in CORDS and the Force Logistics Command, by influxes of civilian personnel.[80]

Given the challenges the MAF faced in I Corps, it is surprising that Fleet Marine Force, Pacific did not employ the Marine Expeditionary Corps concept, creating a larger and more capable command element designed to control multiple divisions. No evidence suggests that this option was ever seriously considered.[81] Nonetheless by 1968 III MAF was a corps headquarters in fact if not in name. The MAF's early staff miscues, ad hoc nature, incremental growth, and uneven talent undermined its performance, but the command deficiencies outlined in the final two sections below stemmed from senior leadership failures rather than organizational shortfalls.

Friction with the Army

Throughout its existence, III MAF experienced various forms of friction with US Army headquarters and commanders in Vietnam. These conflicts included senior, adjacent, and subordinate army commands. With MACV, the disagreements centered on strategy. Westmoreland viewed III MAF's reluctance to leave its coastal enclaves and hunt the enemy as undermining MACV's attrition strategy. The Marines' lack of enthusiasm for Secretary McNamara's DMZ barrier concept, manifested by slow progress in the project's construction, proved equally irritating. Occasional complaints from I Corps' South Vietnamese officials about unilateral Marine civil-military operations buttressed Saigon's concern about III MAF's performance. Adding to these difficulties, Walt and his I Field Force colleague to the south, Lieutenant General Stanley R. Larsen, disliked one another. Their personal animosity soured relations between their staffs trying to coordinate operations along the two commands' shared boundary. Despite these challenges, Westmoreland kept his official and personal relations with Walt amiable lest interservice contretemps damage the war effort. Upon Walt's departure in 1967, the MACV commander presented him an award. Later he also recommended him for the post of Marine Commandant.[82]

The shaky Marine–army partnership deteriorated further under the new III MAF commander. Generals Westmoreland and Cushman represented a study in contrasting styles. The former, a formal, somewhat rigid officer who thrived on detailed staff work, never hit it off with Cushman, a fatherly figure who operated with more relaxed staff protocols. Continuing debates on the priorities of pacification versus engaging conventional units, as well as more controversy over McNamara's DMZ line, further strained relations. Cushman, like Walt, deemed the barrier a waste of resources. Westmoreland, though he, too, held reservations about the obstacle's potential to prevent North Vietnamese infiltration across the DMZ, nevertheless expected III MAF's full compliance once the secretary of defense mandated the project. At Khe Sanh, doubts about III MAF's indifference to the growing threat and the isolated base's poor defensive posture further undermined MACV's confidence in Cushman's leadership. Army leaders viewed Marine generalship as substandard, featuring poor supervision of key tasks, reluctance to ask for outside help when needed, and deficient tactical performance.[83] By the end of 1967, Westmoreland's confidence in the MAF's capability to command effectively had faded. In the words of MACV's official history, he "increasingly doubted its competence to direct the expanding and increasingly violent battle for I Corps."[84]

As the threat posed to I Corps by the North Vietnamese Army grew in late 1967 and early 1968, General Westmoreland decided to make a substantive change in the region's C2 construct. He elected to deploy a MACV (Forward) headquarters, under his deputy General Creighton Abrams, to manage the conventional fight anticipated in northern I Corps. The advance echelon of the army's new command post arrived at Phu Bai, ten miles south of Hue, just a few days before the commencement of the communist Tet Offensive. Slow to deploy, the new MACV headquarters did not become operational until two weeks into the enemy's nationwide attack. One reason Abrams's command post took so long to establish was because it did not exist previously; it had been created out of other existing staffs on the spur of the moment. Westmoreland chose to put a portion of his own headquarters into the field to avoid the interservice uproar that would ensue should he put an army corps commander, an officer with the same rank as Cushman, directly in charge of the expected battle inside the Marine sector.[85]

MACV quickly confirmed the continued requirement for this unique command arrangement on 17 February 1968, when Westmoreland announced that his own forward headquarters would be replaced by a provisional corps commanded by an army officer. Lieutenant General William B. Rosson, the former commander of Task Force Oregon and the American Division serving under III MAF at Chu Lai, established the new army corps command post at Phu Bai on 10 March. It directed the 3rd Marine Division, 1st Cavalry Division, and 101st

Airborne Division in the northern two provinces of I Corps. Rosson was also responsible for coordinating his divisions' tactical actions with ARVN's 1st Division. The army's provisional corps served under III MAF's operational control.[86]

Underscoring the tenuous nature of Cushman's actual authority over the new army corps, Westmoreland authorized General Rosson to report directly to MACV, providing only an informational copy of message traffic to his nominal Marine headquarters in Da Nang.[87] This communication arrangement mirrored the direct access the Joint Chiefs of Staff granted MACV rather than going through (and possibly being filtered by) the navy's theater headquarters in Pearl Harbor. In both cases, the protocol sped up communication at the cost of the naval headquarters' ability to control the ostensibly subordinate army commands' actions. On 16 July 1968, the provisional corps was renamed XXIV Corps, a command element that remained in I Corps beyond III MAF's tenure in Vietnam.[88]

The Marine and army corps headquarters each had a turn commanding the war in I Corps. In 1969 Lieutenant General Herman Nickerson, Jr., inherited the army corps still operating under III MAF's nominal control. During his tenure, this arrangement continued with XXIV Corps directing the war throughout Quang Tri Province and most of Thua Thien Province. By 1970 there were more soldiers than Marines in Military Region 1. On 9 March 1970, the day Lieutenant General Keith McCutcheon took command of III MAF, the two services' corps-level command posts reversed positions in MACV's hierarchy of headquarters.[89] The MAF served under XXIV Corps for the remainder of its time in Vietnam. The army corps spent its first twenty months under Marine command, while III MAF spent its final thirteen months in Vietnam under the operational control of XXIV Corps.

During the period of Marine ascendency, III MAF staff officers and commanders sometimes had to remind their army counterparts of their position within the chain of command.[90] Soon after the change of relative positions, XXIV Corps' commander, General Melvin Zais, underscored the army's reluctance to view the MAF as a true corps-level headquarters when he publicly argued that XXIV Corps should be able to communicate directly with the Marine division and air wing without going through III MAF. General Abrams vetoed that demand, a command encroachment that Zais himself did not suffer and would have rejected when III MAF served as his own superior headquarters.[91] Despite such squabbles, the Marine and army corps headquarters' exchange of seniority proceeded relatively smoothly. The MAF's final year in Vietnam produced minimal command drama, as the Marines essentially guarded a single province and protected Da Nang under still dangerous yet greatly reduced enemy threat conditions.

The command arrangement Westmoreland invented in I Corps was unprecedented in twentieth-century US military history. No previous case featured an American corps serving under another corps in a shared battlespace.[92] One Army historian noted: "It seems clear that Westmoreland expected a much bigger Communist offensive in the north than actually developed. He did not trust III MAF to handle it and wanted Abrams on the scene with a headquarters to control the battle if necessary. Westmoreland authorized Abrams at MACV (Forward) to give tactical direction to III MAF's subordinate units if the situation required."[93] In short, deploying Abrams and the MACV (Forward) command post registered a vote of no-confidence in Cushman's tactical direction. That interpretation was confirmed by a 28 January 1968 cable from Westmoreland to US Army General Earl Wheeler, chairman of the Joint Chiefs of Staff. The MACV commander noted that Marine professionalism in Vietnam had sunk "far short of the standards that should be demanded of our armed forces" and that the service's performance, top to bottom, "required improvement in the national interest."[94]

Replacing the ad hoc MACV (Forward) command post with a provisional corps (which also had not previously existed) underscored Westmoreland's verdict that Cushman required a safety net even after Tet. This judgment, further validated by Abrams's subsequent decision to keep a numbered army corps in I Corps until June 1972, reflected both commanders' distrust of III MAF's tactical competence. Westmoreland claimed the new arrangement eased Cushman's stretched span of control. Moreover, he argued that the move, rather than diminishing his status, elevated the MAF's senior general to the equivalent of a field army commander.[95] Doubters concluded that Cushman had been kicked upstairs. In effect the new army headquarters took the crux of the conventional fighting in I Corps out of the hands of the MAF's commanders.

Naturally, many senior Marines took a dim view of this turn of events, though Cushman responded graciously to the tacit rebuke at the time and said little more about it in his postwar assessments. Other senior Marines reacted less charitably. Most determined that the new army headquarters represented an unnecessary echelon of command that added little value to the prosecution of the regional war. Although the episode never achieved the notoriety or emotional impact generated by the 1944 "Smith versus Smith" controversy on Saipan,[96] partly because Westmoreland's public commentary downplayed the "soft relief" nature of the action, it nonetheless struck Marine observers at the time as a professional insult of the highest order. Major General Raymond L. Murray, III MAF deputy commander, correctly concluded that MACV did not trust III MAF. General Rathvon McC. Tompkins, 3rd Marine Division commander, called the move "unpardonable" and noted that it would never have happened unless MACV was "very, very worried about the local commander, afraid he can't hack it."[97]

General Westmoreland's decision followed an earlier judgment in which he refused to set up a US field army in Vietnam to control subordinate corps. Instead MACV established US Army, Vietnam as an administrative and logistic headquarters controlling all nontactical army matters. Westmoreland did not want to subcontract operational control of ground operations to a subordinate commander. General Bruce Palmer, who commanded the new US Army, Vietnam headquarters in 1967, argued MACV needed a fully functional field army to enable Westmoreland to concentrate on politico-military responsibilities.[98] A field army headquarters would have facilitated the splitting of I Corps into two US corps sectors rather than subordinating one American corps under another. In this arrangement XXIV Corps would have covered the two northern provinces while III MAF controlled US forces in the southern three provinces. This construct might also have entailed the switch of the Americal and 3rd Marine Divisions to give each corps sector an army and Marine pure force, but that decision would have left the southern zone short of forces once the 3rd Marine Division departed in 1969.

With no field army in place, creating two separate US corps zones in I Corps would have burdened MACV with yet another major subordinate command in its already large span of control. Of course, as noted above, XXIV Corps already had direct access to MACV. A more cynical reason for Westmoreland rejecting two separate corps sectors instead of maintaining one embedded inside the other, as well as ensuring that both corps sectors retained Marine forces within them, was that he did not want to undermine MACV's rationale for greater sharing of Marine fixed-wing aircraft sorties in support of army units in I Corps. It is also true that splitting the region into two US corps sectors would have forced ARVN's I Corps commander to coordinate with two American corps rather than one, though this concern could have been mitigated by placing the field army's headquarters near

ARVN's I Corps command post and using it to advise the South Vietnamese. On balance, however, setting up two separate US corps rather than embedding one inside the other, with or without an intermediate army headquarters between the two corps and MACV, would have enabled more efficient control of US forces across the northern five provinces and avoided the strange "corps within a corps" command construct.

The Battle Over Centralized Aviation

Marine friction with the US Army over the war in I Corps hinged on competence and span-of-control issues. In the US Air Force the struggle concerned operational control of fixed-wing aircraft. The distress generated by the insertion of MACV (Forward) and then XXIV Corps paled in comparison to that of the single management controversy—the only dispute that Westmoreland claimed caused him to consider resignation. US Air Force doctrine called for centralized control of aviation resources. Marine doctrine posited the primacy of the air-ground team fighting under the direction of the MAGTF commander. Air force leaders argued that the senior airman in a theater should control all airplanes to maximize efficiency. Senior Marines claimed that stripping aircraft from the service's fighting units robbed them of their combined arms punch. Marine ground and air forces had operated separately throughout most of WWII and the Korean conflict. To prevent that from happening again, the Marine Corps had developed modular task forces with embedded aviation components ranging in size from squadron to group to wing. Marine leaders justified their need for a large aviation branch because the amphibious assault mission required heavy aviation fires to complement naval gunfire in the vulnerable period before artillery could move ashore.[99]

The situation in I Corps, however, the first long-term combat operation ashore by a MAF, did not match the standard amphibious template. While some leatherneck squadrons supporting actions in Vietnam flew from navy carriers, most Marine jets operated from airfields ashore. Marine ground forces received fire support from many sources: Marine and army artillery, naval gunfire ships, and aircraft from all four US services. As army units flowed into I Corps in response to increased North Vietnamese incursions in 1967–1968, the buildup stretched 1st MAW's capacity to support the growing allied forces. By 1968 the Marine air wing was backing the equivalent of

nine allied divisions in I Corps. Seventh Air Force shared responsibility for supporting this large ground contingent, but both services
struggled to meet the demands posed on their combined air forces.
A regional shortage of jet-capable runways exacerbated the challenge
and prevented the deployment of more air force attack aircraft. During the Tet Offensive Westmoreland worried that the 1st Cavalry and
101st Airborne Divisions would not receive adequate close air support.
Worsening threat conditions strengthened Seventh Air Force's claim
that a single manager of all fixed-wing aircraft would improve the equitable distribution of available air support to army formations.[100]

On 10 March 1968 General Westmoreland appointed Seventh
Air Force as the single manager of all aircraft in South Vietnam. At
a stroke, the US Air Force gained operational control of all Marine
fixed-wing strike and reconnaissance aircraft. The new arrangement
did not address rotary-wing aircraft, since neither MACV nor Seventh Air Force wanted the army to lose control of its vast fleet of helicopters. Previously MACV Air Directive 95-4 established a system
in which the air force coordinated but did not control employment of
all fixed-wing aircraft in South Vietnam. The pre-1968 system allowed
III MAF to retain operational control of its own strike and reconnaissance aircraft, providing only sorties not needed by Marine, joint, and
combined forces in I Corps to Seventh Air Force for use elsewhere
in South Vietnam or beyond. In the first few months of 1968, the air
force and Marines had worked out a hybrid system to manage the pro-
liferation of aircraft flying in the limited airspace around Khe Sanh.
The MAW controlled planes in the airspace closest to the base, while
the air force managed the air umbrella covering most of the surrounding area. The new single-manager system fundamentally altered those
protocols. It transferred control of Marine strike and recon aircraft to
MACV's air commander, who allocated only some of those assets back
to III MAF based on his own headquarters' assessment of the needs in
I Corps compared to competing demands elsewhere.[101]

The MAF, not surprising, cried foul. Cushman protested the loss
of relative combat power that resulted when Marine ground forces experienced diminished air support. Westmoreland held firm, citing the
theater commander's inherent right to apportion available resources,
including aircraft, to best prosecute the war. Krulak contested the decision with Admiral U.S. Grant Sharp, Jr., heading Pacific Command
in Hawaii, while General Leonard F. Chapman, Jr., the new Commandant, asked the Joint Chiefs to overturn the policy. Within the Pentagon, the army and navy supported the Marine position. Ultimately

Paul Nitze, the deputy secretary of defense, affirmed the MACV commander's authority to run the war, including management of its airpower, as he saw fit. On the ground, Marine divisions experienced a slight decrease in close air support. Army divisions in I Corps received increased jet attack sorties under the new system. The procedures imposed by the air force to request preplanned strikes changed the process from three to seven steps and doubled the standard eighteen-hour timeline from request to delivery of ordnance for preplanned missions. In Vietnam, both the army and the air force were delighted: The former saw increased aviation support with access to more Marine bombers, and the latter validated its long-cherished tradition of air force management of all ground-based theater aircraft.[102]

Between 1968 and 1970, the single-management system evolved. In May 1968 Seventh Air Force accepted a change that returned 70 percent of III MAF's sorties back to 1st MAW for tasking, although these aircraft were still obliged to appear on the air force's weekly frag order, carry preplanned ordnance loads, and predict estimated strike times several days in advance rather than tailoring the missions from the start to a specific target. From the Marine Corps' perspective, centralized air force direction took too much time and decreased the MAW's efficiency, but at least the modification allowed III MAF to determine where most of its attack sorties were applied. Meanwhile the wing met many of the ground forces' urgent unplanned requests by exceeding authorized airframe usage rates, which generated additional sorties amounting to 17 percent of the total flown. Highlighting the decline in efficiency, the new system decreased preplanned Marine sorties from 88 percent to 40 percent of all flights, while immediate air support missions jumped from 10 percent to 25 percent of the total flown. Throughout 1969 Lieutenant General Nickerson advocated a return to the original rules, but Abrams elected to continue Westmoreland's single-manager policy.[103]

Lieutenant General McCutcheon, the most talented and influential Marine aviator of the period, continued the battle to regain MAF control of its bombers in 1970. The wing received permission to set aside 18 percent of its attack sorties for special missions such as helicopter escort and landing zone preparation. In August 1970 McCutcheon convinced MACV and Seventh Air Force to modify the theater's aviation instruction to restore much of III MAF's control over its own aircraft. The new language limited Seventh Air Force to tasking authority but prevented it from reorganizing Marine aviation forces, designating objectives, and exercising mission command. Technically, this agreement ensured III MAF retained "operational control" of its planes. In practice, the new directive still allowed air force centralized control while placating Marine sensitivities over command. As American involvement in the war drew down, such written agreements mattered less than decreasing demand for aviation support based on diminished combat intensity and good-faith efforts by aviators of both services to cooperate and provide the best available support to allied ground forces.[104]

All the armed services exhibited double standards in their positions on single-management principles. The air force kept its B-52 strategic bomber fleet operating under a separate chain of command, external to Seventh Air Force, even though the large bombers performed close air support missions inside South Vietnam. Moreover, MACV rather than Seventh Air Force retained targeting authority for the strategic bombers, so the latter lacked the same level of tasking authority for some air force bombers that it claimed was vital to exercise over Marine Corps planes. The army approved single management of aviation for jets, which it did not own, but not helicopters, which it possessed in abundance. The admiral commanding Pacific Command allowed air force management of Marine aviation but refused to allow Seventh Air Force to control navy aircraft flying from carriers at sea. Meanwhile Marines declined to employ their own doctrinal concept of fighting two wings simultaneously under the same MAF headquarters. Why? Because Marine aviators insisted on single management of all the wing's aircraft within the MAF's airspace. The 1st Marine Aircraft Wing employed nearly twice the aircraft normally commanded by a single wing. Nonetheless, III MAF declined to establish a second wing-level aviation C2 system, just as Seventh Air Force refused to accept a subordinate Marine air force operating independently in I Corps.[105]

Although rejecting air force calls for single management of its aircraft and airspace, all of III MAF's commanders championed the same tenets when integrating Marine helicopters afloat into the 1st MAW's airspace. Amphibious doctrine called for establishment of an Amphibious Objective Area, in which the amphibious force controlled all naval ground and air forces until command transitioned to the landing force ashore. South Vietnam did not meet the classic circumstances of an assault against a defended enemy beach. Instead naval landing forces entered an ally's sovereign territory in conditions that, by 1966, represented a mature theater with established C2 architecture and friendly forces operating ashore. Within I Corps, it made sense to III MAF for Marine helicopters flying from ships to work under the air wing's existing command system, yet the Headquarters Marine Corps stance on this issue supported existing amphibious doctrine and argued against the intraservice application of single management principles ashore.[106]

Cushman and Nickerson also encountered a separate single-management conundrum in their employment of the MAF's organic helicopters. Army commanders thought the Marine Corps was too centralized in its management of Marine rotary-wing aircraft. By late 1968 senior Marine leaders such as Major General Ray Davis, seeing what the army's airmobile divisions could do with more than four hundred assigned helicopters each (especially the powerful, nimble, and ubiquitous Hueys), developed a case of helicopter envy. By comparison, Marine helicopters seemed too few, too slow, too big, and too unresponsive. The Marine wing, not unlike Seventh Air Force, insisted on centralized control of its own aircraft. Davis complained enough to briefly obtain for 3rd Division its own aviation liaison officer, a brigadier general heading an auxiliary (forward) wing command post, and a provisional air group to improve helicopter availability and responsiveness.[107] The MAF and Headquarters Marine Corps deemed the issues raised by this intramural fracas serious enough to commission in 1969 separate studies that reached similar conclusions. Both analyses recommended training, education, and equipment modifications to improve combat performance of III MAF's aviation element but validated the wing's single-management protocols for its helicopter fleet.[108]

The Marine Corps lost its doctrinal fight with the air force over centralized control of its organic aviation resources. Its argument—that stripping Marine task forces of their organic aircraft put Marines on the ground at risk by depriving them of needed firepower—fell before the logic of a joint commander's prerogative to use assigned forces in the way best calculated to increase his total combat power. The underlying Marine justifications for the service's heavy reliance on and investment in attack airplanes—that they were necessary to complement naval gunfire during the assault phase of amphibious operations and, once ashore, to make up for limited organic artillery support—went unquestioned in Vietnam. Both explanations proved irrelevant in an environment featuring sustained land operations supported by sufficient artillery. Neither did Marine commanders or their staffs explore whether fielding more artillery and naval gunfire might provide a cheaper solution to insufficient firepower in continental and littoral environments. Instead the service's expensive commitment to attack jets continued as an article of faith. The bitter rivalry for control of those aircraft generated dissention but not consensus.

Both the air force and the Marine Corps departed Vietnam convinced of the correctness of their respective doctrinal positions and prepared to continue the same dispute in future conflicts.[109]

Conclusion

Vietnam provided the stage for the first combat test of the Marine Corps' new corps-level headquarters. There the Marine Expeditionary Force, designed to control air, ground, and logistic elements, received its trial by fire. The general officers who led the new formation brought distinguished pedigrees, but the first two struggled to integrate their command smoothly with their joint counterparts. Westmoreland doubted the MAF's command and staff proficiency, objected to its emphasis on pacification, and resented its reluctance to share Marine attack planes with army units. These issues came to a head during the 1968 Tet Offensive, when Cushman lost control of his air force as well as direct command of the US divisions fighting along the DMZ. More aggressive supervision of the MAF's divisions and wing could have prevented both of those outcomes.

The Marine Expeditionary Force, designed to supervise a single division-wing team, was overwhelmed by the expanded span of control that III MAF encountered in Vietnam. New in the early 1960s, the MEF construct lacked the organization, manpower, and training to hit the ground running in I Corps. The doctrinal Marine Expeditionary Corps, intended to command multiple divisions and wings, was more concept than reality in 1965. The Marine Corps would have had to cobble one together, using the III MAF and Fleet Marine Force staffs as its nucleus. The easier choice, and the one taken, entailed employing the small but available III MEF staff on Okinawa and building it up to suit the conditions encountered in Vietnam.

Once on the ground in I Corps, the MAF demonstrated great organizational flexibility, supervising naval component responsibilities, an Advisory Command, the Combined Action Force, the civil-military CORDS command, and extensive liaison elements linking the command with ARVN, Korean, and US Army units. Yet the lack of emphasis on corps-level operations in the prewar Marine Corps' training and education regimes, coupled with high staff turnover and the frequent reshuffling of constituent units, undermined the MAF's cohesion and proficiency.

A corps-level command-and-control system, to be effective, must view itself and act as a warfighting entity, not simply as an administrative headquarters pushing resources down to subordinate commands that control all tactical operations. The latter mindset left Cushman and the MAF headquarters unprepared to maneuver multiple divisions and exploit tactical opportunities such as occurred during the Hue battle. Despite the growing intensity of conventional operations between 1965 and 1968, the tendency of both Walt and Cushman was to allocate to their subordinate divisions almost all reinforcements and corps-level troops. No force-level commands existed to focus on and conduct critical tasks such as the DMZ counterfire fight or McNamara's barrier construction project.

In this chapter I have identified some of the C2 challenges III MAF experienced in Vietnam and the strengths and deficiencies it displayed in meeting those tests. Arguably, the senior Marine headquarters adapted and performed as well as its US Army counterparts in II and III Corps. The MAF had, or soon developed, adequate if not consistently excellent leaders, processes, and organization to prosecute the war in I Corps. Notwithstanding the available C2 means, however, it still struggled to find the recipe required to pacify, protect, and develop the region. The following chapters show how command and control orchestrated the other warfighting functions and fashioned an unsuccessful corps-level campaign against a hybrid enemy. In chapter 3 I examine how III MAF's intelligence team assessed those conventional and irregular threats.

3

III MAF Intelligence

The Marine Amphibious Force G-2 (Intelligence) section was not prepared for the challenges it encountered in I Corps in 1965. Initially it lacked the size and expertise required to assess the complex enemy and environment it faced in Vietnam. By 1968 it had added additional intelligence capabilities and capacity required to furnish more useful assessments, but the improvements exerted little influence operationally. Throughout the conflict, the MAF's intelligence specialists analyzed enemy conventional units more effectively than they did irregular civil-military threats. Yet it was the G-2's desensitization to the presence and capability of enemy conventional forces inside I Corps, along with its lack of recognition of the long-term threat they posed, that represented its primary failure.

The G-2 directorate exhibited many of the problems that plagued III MAF throughout the war. In common with other branches of the MAF staff, there was little continuity in leadership and personnel. The intelligence section rarely produced informed analysis that was crucial in operations leading to decisive victories against the MAF's regular or irregular foes. Over time, the G-2 became desensitized to the presence of large NVA forces inside I Corps and contributed to the MAF headquarters' lack of interest in finding other ways to prevent this permanent intrusion. Although III MAF's intelligence specialists gradually developed a better feel for the nature and extent of the shadow government, they never tracked its size, membership, and activities with the same passion and commitment they devoted to conventional units. Reflecting the MAF headquarters' general disinterest, G-2 devoted little attention to the most critical intelligence estimate affecting ARVN—how much capacity was needed for RVN armed forces (RVNAF) to protect the region themselves. Finally, the G-2 branch's underestimation of the enduring NVA threat undermined the operational impact of III MAF campaign plans.

In this chapter I examine the Marines' intelligence organization and activities. I will survey three cases that illustrate how III MAF employed its G-2 section and how corps-level intelligence enabled or undermined regional operations. The first case investigates the 1965–1967 intelligence appreciations of two major communist conventional units in I Corps, one main force VC and one NVA. The second case evaluates the MAF's predictive acumen in anticipating the 1968 Tet Offensive. The third considers intelligence support for pacification in the eighteen months following that offensive. Together these examples highlight the evolving role intelligence played in the MAF's war in I Corps. They also reveal a headquarters either unable or unwilling to draw from its intelligence analysis the insights needed to refine corps-level operations. In the final section I explore III MAF's most important intelligence assessment: whether the conventional or insurgent threat posed the greatest long-term danger to South Vietnam.

Intelligence in I Corps

Marine G-2 analysts provided information about the adversary's capabilities and intentions as well as the environment. The knowledge the intelligence system developed supported III MAF's decision-making. Intelligence information was developed and refined through a six-step process: planning, collection, processing, production, dissemination, and employment. At the end of that cycle intelligence specialists delivered two types of analysis: descriptive and estimative. The first included basic geographic, political, economic, social, and military data of encyclopedic nature like maps or insights on enemy doctrine as well as reports on more fluid factors such as recent enemy troop movements or activity patterns. Estimative analysis, which is more demanding, predicted the enemy's future actions. Both types of intelligence aided MAF commanders and staffs better understand threats, warned of pending enemy action, refined targeting, and improved assessment of friendly operations.[1]

These intelligence appreciations mattered because an understanding of the foe influenced the appropriate operational response. In South Vietnam, allied intelligence faced two related but dissimilar threats. The North Vietnamese Army posed the first danger. The second peril—indigenous Southerners fighting for the Vietcong—consisted of guerrillas and conventional military units plus the most advanced subversive political organization ever fielded by a Maoist-style insurgency. The NVA and VC represented separate branches of the same tree; Hanoi's politburo directed both the insurgency and its own army.[2] Regardless of their common master, the internal and external adversaries represented discrete challenges that required different intelligence capabilities.

As in the rest of South Vietnam, in I Corps Vietnamese communists employed a form of hybrid war. Vietnamese communists called this approach a "war of interlocking," total war combining conventional and guerrilla forces and conducted, in General Vo Nguyen Giap's words, such that "[p]olitical activities [are] more important than military activities."[3] The insurgency conducted regular and irregular military operations, but it also advanced its political interests via acts of terror, propaganda, spies, clandestine party agents, antigovernment protests, networks of seemingly innocuous organizations covertly controlled by the Communist Party, land reform policies that promised ownership for the indigent, and social transformations that weakened traditional family and religious values to champion class and party interests.[4] These civil and military means undermined Saigon's authority and together posed a formidable risk to the RVN's independence. Unchecked, either the VC or the NVA could topple the South Vietnamese government. Intelligence agencies had to address the symbiotic threats simultaneously. This dual challenge constituted a tall order for military intelligence specialists whose training had emphasized assessing Soviet-style conventional rather than irregular opponents.

Further complicating the intelligence picture, the nature of the threat was different in each of I Corps' five provinces. Quang Tri and Thua Thien endured constant conventional war. Quang Ngai, in the far south of III MAF's sector, featured a deeply embedded insurgency. The two middle provinces, Quang Tin and Quang Nam, suffered from hybrid warfare combining the worst aspects of both regular and irregular combat.[5] Lessons learned from experience in one province did not always transfer directly to another.

From the time of its arrival, the III MAF intelligence section had to make sense of these assorted threats. Like other MAF staff elements, G-2 specialists were not well prepared to operate in the forbidding new environment. Their education and experience focused on conventional enemies, not Maoist-style insurgents. They lacked proficient linguists necessary to translate captured documents and interrogate prisoners and defectors. Moreover, Marine intelligence officers received little training and seldom stayed in the job long enough to develop proficiency.[6] Between March 1965 and April 1971, III MAF fielded seventeen G-2 officers for an average of just eighteen weeks each in the job.[7] The 1967 split between the CORDS intelligence staff and the MAF's G-2 directorate—the former concentrating on insurgents while the latter specialized on assessing conventional forces—produced an organizational divergence that threatened unity of effort.[8]

Vietnam-era doctrine situated most intelligence capability at the army level under a Military Intelligence battalion. Independent corps operating remotely, like III MAF, received army Military Intelligence detachments with personnel trained in order of battle, photo interpretation, technical systems, document translation, interpreter translation, prisoner interrogation, and counterintelligence duties.[9] In 1965, however, III MAF received no such detachment of intelligence specialists from MACV, the equivalent theater-army headquarters in Vietnam. In its first year in Vietnam only two Marine intelligence units augmented the MAF: a detachment of counterintelligence specialists, and a radio battalion (signals intelligence) detachment. The initial G-2 staff's resident expertise remained relatively sparse. Its contribution to the monthly 1965 command chronologies, for example, focused on weather reports and enemy orders of battle, operations summaries, and casualty tallies.[10]

Despite its limited resources, bifurcated systems of analysis, and high G-2 turnover, III MAF's intelligence capacity expanded over time as it responded to the complexity of the conflict. In January 1967 (the first available roster), III MAF's G-2 section included thirty-two officers, almost half of whom were of field-grade rank. Their duties encompassed plans, collections, order of battle records, signals intelligence, counterintelligence, ground reconnaissance, target information, electronic warfare, aerial reconnaissance, and operations center watch responsibilities.[11] In late 1967 MACV decentralized direction of its collection and analysis capabilities, allowing III MAF to control the regional intelligence process more efficiently. By 1968 the MAF fielded a separate intelligence battalion, a counterintelligence element to ferret out enemy moles and spies, a signals intelligence collection unit, a combined corps-level interrogation center, a US officer in each province headquarters to coordinate sharing of intelligence information, a US officer stationed with the ARVN I Corps G-2 shop, Vietnamese intelligence analysts working with their American peers, and Vietnamese G-2 personnel supporting US field units to quickly translate captured documents and interrogate captured personnel.[12] Nevertheless the MAF's expanded intelligence apparatus struggled to keep up with the tracking, analytical, and predictive duties associated with the intelligence staff function in I Corps.

Between 1965 and 1971 III MAF G-2 compiled hundreds of intelligence summaries. These products followed a standard format, divided into five sections: (1) enemy situation in each I Corps province; (2) enemy operations organized by type (reconnaissance, antiaircraft fire, indirect fire, ground attacks, etc.); (3) other intelligence factors (unit organization, equipment, personalities, casualties, etc.); (4) counterintelligence—usually covered in detail in a separate annex; and (5) enemy capabilities and vulnerabilities. Annexes addressed the enemy orders of battle; information derived from interrogation of prisoners and deserters, agent reports, and captured documents; and counterintelligence. Later in the war separate annexes appeared covering reconnaissance/ sensor activity and sometimes weather. These weekly intelligence reports, often forty pages long, featured more data than analysis. They focused much more on VC/NVA conventional actions and threats than the irregular activities of guerrillas and clandestine infrastructure.[13]

Assessing Conventional Forces, 1965–1967

The MAF G-2's strong suit was evaluating the enemy's conventional orders of battle, incorporating both NVA and VC regular units. Intelligence analysts excelled at tracking these forces' movements and strengths. Their assessments did not, however, make the connection between the order of battle data emphasized and the success or failure of the MAF's operations. This section highlights two frequent antagonists within I Corps to illustrate the strengths and weaknesses of the G-2's analysis.

Tracking the 1st VC Regiment

A brief explanation of the VC's military wing, encompassing three levels, situates the role of the first unit examined. The Guerrilla Popular Army (paramilitary militia forces) furnished local security for communist hamlets and villages. These ubiquitous, black pajama–clad guerrillas, farmers by day and fighters by night, remain an iconic image of the Vietnam conflict. One step up the military chain, Regional or Territorial forces provided full-time but still geographically restricted security. These local troops normally served within their own district and seldom ventured farther afield. Main force units, by contrast, roamed across their home province and sometimes moved across province lines in support of regional offensives. They encompassed the best-trained and -equipped insurgent formations and were designed to engage ARVN on equal terms in conventional battle. Fighters at the bottom of this VC hierarchy could be promoted, or conscripted, into higher-level units. Proven hamlet militia often augmented local district forces, who in turn furnished troops to casualty depleted main force units.[14] III MAF's experience tracking the 1st Vietcong Regiment illustrates the military challenges posed by these insurgent regulars.

MAF intelligence reports indicated that the 1st Vietcong Regiment formed in 1962 and subsequently carved a bloody swath across I Corps.[15] It had conducted seven battalion-size attacks on ARVN units during the year prior to III MAF's arrival. Subsequent assaults expanded in size and tempo. Three regiment-size attacks occurred between April and July 1965. The last battles represented epic triumphs, for which the victors assumed the honorary title "Ba Gia Regiment" for the site of its victories.[16] By the time III MAF began searching for VC formations outside its enclaves, this famous unit had established its reputation and became a high-priority target for Marine intelligence officers.

The Marines' first contact with the Ba Gia Regiment took place in August 1965. III MAF's intelligence shop received multiple reports that the VC regiment was staging a few miles south of the Chu Lai airstrip and planning an attack on the base.[17] The MAF intelligence officer, Colonel Leo J. Dulacki, and his team mapped the locations emerging from a stream of incoming information. The plots indicated the enemy regiment was moving toward the Marine base. A deserter and fresh signals intelligence soon confirmed the regiment's location in a village just twelve miles south of the airfield.[18] Lieutenant General Lewis W. Walt launched a regiment-size spoiling attack on the 1st VC. The resulting operation, code-named STARLITE, claimed 614 dead insurgents, captured nine prisoners, and detained forty-two suspects.[19] By doctrinal standards the VC regiment was destroyed.[20] But it rose to fight again. This battle only foreshadowed how difficult it would be in I Corps to trap and destroy main force insurgents who chose when and where to fight.[21]

Like Ahab pursuing the white whale, III MAF intelligence personnel hunted the elusive 1st VC Regiment over the next two years. During that period allied forces found and fought the unit a dozen times, administering catastrophic losses. In 1965 MAF intelligence reports claimed 1,340 1st VC dead in four battles. In 1966 the G-2 noted 753 more soldiers from the unit killed in action (KIA) in three operations.

In 1967 the regiment's toll of dead climbed to 1,515. Given its consistent two-thousand-man organizational strength, these figures indicate losses of 67 percent in 1965, 38 percent in 1966, and 75 percent in 1967. The numbers do not include wounded, or those killed by supporting arms, or those who died of wounds whose bodies were not recovered. Using the MACV estimate of 1.5 wounded for each combat death, the projected wounded would have added another 5,412 casualties to the regiment's total losses over the thirty-month period. By doctrinal standards, counting only "confirmed" dead and prisoners and excluding "estimated" dead, the Ba Gia Regiment was destroyed twice in 1965, once in 1966, and two more times in 1967. If estimated wounded are included in the total losses, then the unit was destroyed thirteen times during that short period.[22] A veritable phoenix, the 1st VC Regiment nevertheless continued to reconstitute, strike, and evade allied forces for the rest of the war.

The III MAF intelligence directorate, exploiting ARVN, MACV, and national resources as well as its own ground, aviation, and signals collection capabilities, tracked the 1st VC Regiment closely. Almost every Marine intelligence summary listed this main force formation's location and strength, sometimes adding information on its soldiers' health, morale, training, tactics, leaders, and even unit alias titles used for deception purposes.[23] Over time, more NVA regulars filled out the depleted ranks of the nominally Southern insurgent formation. By July 1967 MAF intelligence reports indicated one of its infantry battalions contained mostly North Vietnamese regulars who infiltrated into the RVN via the Ho Chi Minh Trail.[24] In MAF intelligence summaries, Vietcong who deserted the 1st VC Regiment consistently cited low morale, poor health care, and little food—although never a shortage of ammunition.[25] Such insights gave analysts a good sense of the personnel composing the regiment, but the continuous scrutiny did not enable allied forces to fix and finish their weary and wary foe.

The MAF's intelligence directorate followed the insurgency's conventional forces closely. But surviving III MAF intelligence records do not indicate how its G-2 section assessed the order of battle numbers it so assiduously gathered. How they explained, for example, the 1st VC Regiment's amazing recuperative ability is the most important, but missing, element of the G-2's reports on that unit. The data collected suggests two explanations for the resiliency of the enemy's main force units. The first was communist access to a rural population that could be persuaded or coerced to send its sons and husbands to fight under the VC banner. The second was a steady resupply of fresh regular troops infiltrated from the North. Together these manpower reservoirs enabled savaged VC main force battalions and regiments in I Corps to reform and continue to fight.

III MAF's experience with the 1st VC Regiment may provide an explanation for the continued regeneration of VC forces throughout South Vietnam despite regular mauling by superior allied firepower. If so, it indicates that Westmoreland's attrition program, coupled with the interdiction effort, had not attained the elusive "crossover" point beyond which the enemy could no longer make good his losses. Nor had the ROLLING THUNDER bombing campaign convinced Hanoi to stop sending its forces south to rebuild shattered VC units. The resilience of the various VC formations prior to the 1968 Tet Offensive also highlighted the failure to pacify South Vietnam's countryside and convince its people to support the Saigon government. The lengthy MAF intelligence reports provided the data to reach those conclusions, but they never did. G-2 analysts tabulated enemy strengths and activities without acknowledging that the strategy employed by MACV and III MAF was not working. While it was or should have been obvious that allied military operations in I Corps were not keeping out NVA replacements or preventing local VC recruitment to replenish units like the 1st VC Regiment, III MAF G-2 products never said so directly. Instead they reported the facts and figures without highlighting the "so what." This was a critical failure of both the MAF's intelligence and operations staff.

Tracking the 324B NVA Division

In addition to hunting Vietcong units such as the Ba Gia Regiment, the MAF G-2 also focused on the North Vietnamese Army, which began sending its formations into the South early in 1964.[26] Intelligence specialists at III MAF did not see the looming NVA border threat as early as did their MACV counterparts. In January 1966 Westmoreland's G-2 identified twenty-two enemy battalions in Quang Tri and Thua Tin Provinces, whereas Marine analysts acknowledged only nine.[27] These diverse assessments fueled the discrepancy between the Marines' preference for a strategy focused on pacification operations versus MACV's desire for more aggressive search-and-destroy operations. The MACV assessment suggested more focus on tracking down NVA and main force VC units. The Marine interpretation, although still identifying a division's worth of conventional combat power, indicated a less serious problem on the border, one that allowed allied forces to concentrate on protecting coastal population belts.

Between May and July 1966 further Marine reconnaissance confirmed the presence of the 324B NVA Division in Quang Tri Province.[28] Thereafter that NVA division became a frequent foe of allied forces along the DMZ, one that III MAF's intelligence analysts came to know well. Their order of battle reports on 324B grew quite detailed, listing aliases for the unit's subordinate elements and even personnel rosters, down to company-level executive and political officers, based on captured documents and interrogation reports.[29]

The 324B Division waged a bitter border war against the allies in the summer and fall of 1966 and throughout 1967. MAF G-2 reports traced those conventional clashes, including many battles along the DMZ and a series of failed attempts to capture the Marine bastion at Con Thien, a prominent hill overlooking direct invasion routes into the South. The intelligence summaries cited the NVA's constant activity inside I Corps: raiding bases, ambushing convoys, shelling airfields, establishing supply depots, fortifying villages and caves, and constructing hundreds of bunkers.[30] Some of those defensive positions, reinforced with concrete and steel, were stout enough to stand direct hits by 500-pound bombs.[31]

Fighting near the DMZ intensified in 1967. In February, the MAF G-2 termed NVA infiltration and attacks along the border "active screening and reconnaissance" despite more than seven thousand NVA soldiers operating inside I Corps.[32] By September, as many NVA as ARVN troops occupied Quang Tri Province. MAF intelligence confirmed the presence of two regiments of the 324B NVA Division along with four other regiments. Together these units totaled ten thousand troops, the equivalent of a full-strength NVA division.[33] That month the MAF G-2 highlighted the enemy's failure to prevent widespread turnout in the national election, but it also noted the heaviest monthly bombardment of allied installations thus far in the war (7,800 rounds of mortar, artillery, and rocket fire along the DMZ). Intelligence analysts characterized the recent series of fights around Con Thien as both "probing actions" and a "large scale offensive" to capture the Marine strongpoint.[34]

Despite allied attempts to prevent the enemy intrusions into I Corps, NVA troops operated in the zone just south of the Demilitarized Zone for weeks and months at a time. Some of the soldiers' provisions came from local villages. But MAF intelligence sources indicated porters carried much of the required food, ammunition, and medicine across the border to units like the 324B Division. This was a major undertaking. Feeding the sixteen thousand NVA soldiers that the MAF estimated to be in Quang Tri Province in May 1967 required eight tons of provisions per day ferried by porters. Each NVA regiment had a transport company with three bearer platoons of thirty men each. These troops hauled supplies into South Vietnam and departed with the sick and wounded. Soldiers initially crossed the border with ten days of rations. A battalion transport detachment then delivered another food ration for each company every ten days.[35]

At short distances this simple logistics system proved resilient throughout the conflict.[36] Its limitations, however, supported III MAF commanders' belief that the NVA could not operate deep inside I Corps without VC logistic support. Since allied forces did not supply themselves with porters, and MAF G-2 analysts knew Hanoi was developing the Ho Chi Minh Trail to enable transport and support of conventional forces far inside South Vietnam, it was a mistake for the Marines to conclude that the NVA could and would never develop a more conventional long-range logistic capability. ARVN learned otherwise in the 1972 and 1975 NVA invasions. Equally important, this G-2 information on NVA logistics was reported but not analyzed or exploited to devise operations that curtailed the enemy's cross-border sustainment capability. The MAF's intelligence cell had identified an enemy limitation, but that information did not turn into an effective allied attack on the vulnerability.

Intelligence reports indicated that NVA casualties climbed precipitously as the conventional fighting along the border intensified. In 1966 approximately two thousand North Vietnamese regulars died in action in Quang Tri Province. The following year that figure quadrupled as allied forces swept the area in two dozen named operations.[37] If casualties for the 324B Division matched the overall rate of NVA killed and wounded in the province, then the division lost nearly half its strength in 1967.[38] Yet III MAF order of battle analysts maintained the division at full strength (9,600 men) at the beginning of both 1967 and 1968.[39] Their assessments indicated that Hanoi's manpower pipeline effectively replaced the 324B Division's combat losses.

The growing border war against the 324B Division and its sister NVA units, like the struggle farther south against the 1st VC Regiment, revealed important insights about the efficacy of the allied strategy in I Corps. The boundary with North Vietnam, neither demilitarized nor impermeable, permitted an influx of combatants at the time and place of the enemy's choosing. Meanwhile President Lyndon B. Johnson forbade US conventional units from attacking into Laos and North Vietnam to disrupt and destroy the NVA bases supporting the incursions. By the end of 1967, it was apparent that US efforts to coerce or prevent Hanoi from continuing its policy of invading the South had failed. Analysis by the III MAF G-2 section did not elucidate that reality.

The DMZ war against the NVA also desensitized III MAF's staff and commanders to the mounting threat, akin to the proverbial frog in a pot of slowly boiling water. By the end of Marine intelligence analysts' third year in I Corps, the gradually escalating violence along the border had conditioned them to be comfortable with repeated clashes of increasing intensity. They assessed frequent conventional engagements against elements of division-size enemy forces on South Vietnam's sovereign territory as routine counter-reconnaissance activities. The MAF and its ARVN I Corps counterpart could not stop this infiltration, allowing NVA battalions and regiments to come across the border and stay for months at a time in bases inside South Vietnam and located just a few kilometers from allied outposts. Walt and Lieutenant General Robert E. Cushman, the MAF commanders during this period, seemed satisfied so long as the increasingly sharp fighting resulted eventually in the 324B NVA Division and its peers withdrawing back across the Laotian and North Vietnamese boundaries. The combat's cumulative costs sparked concerns about casualties among Marine generals in Washington, Honolulu, and Da Nang, but all remained optimistic that tactical trends favored the allies. The looming events of 1968 would soon challenge the MAF's prevailing view of a situation well in hand.

Anticipating the 1968 Tet Offensive

The communist 1968 Tet Offensive struck the biggest blow III MAF endured during its six years of combat in I Corps. The enemy attack stirred controversy over the degree of the surprise associated with the countrywide assault.[40] The extent of the enemy's effort stunned American citizens and caused them to doubt the previous optimistic assessments emanating from MACV and their political leaders. Despite the domestic shock, US military commanders had recognized a building threat for several months before the attack. In a 20 December 1967 message to Washington, General Westmoreland concluded: "I believe the enemy has already made a crucial decision to make a maximum effort."[41]

American military intelligence officers had noted indications of a pending attack since October 1967. These warnings came from seized documents that mentioned forthcoming assaults on cities, agent and prisoner-of-war reports, captured battle plans and propaganda tapes, increased traffic on the Ho Chi Minh Trail, troop buildups along the DMZ and near major cities, and shaping attacks in the Central Highlands.[42] In November and December 1967, CIA analysts in Saigon sounded three warnings about a strike around the time of the Tet holiday (late January).[43] It was not the general timing of the 1968 attacks around Tet that surprised MACV but their breadth and unprecedented focus on urban areas. Westmoreland's intelligence specialists accurately identified most enemy units and their locations prior to the offensive.[44] But his J-2, Major General Phillip B. Davidson, confessed that the number of sites struck simultaneously and the fact the enemy chose to attack the cities (locations of allied strength) constituted the real tactical surprise.[45]

The postwar NVA official history claimed its attacks targeted the South's cities because they represented its weakest points.[46] Saigon was the principal objective, but Da Nang and Hue also represented valuable prizes. Communist planners reinforced each city with hundreds of political agents to establish control following the anticipated victories. Hanoi's Communist Party leaders believed that ARVN would collapse, Southern citizens in both urban and rural areas would revolt, and that communist forces could destroy enough American troops and equipment to favorably alter the military balance. Four NVA divisions massed on the northern border, threatening Quang Tri City and Khe Sanh. Ten regiments (five artillery, three antiaircraft, one infantry, and one engineer), all separate from the NVA divisions, augmented communist strength in the northern sector of I Corps.[47]

The intent, according to the North's official history, was to draw allied mobile forces away from the cities, leaving them less protected.[48] If so, Westmoreland's focus on the Khe Sanh and DMZ buildups played into Hanoi's deception. Whether the NVA border threat was designed as a main effort or a diversion, it reflected astute planning. Sound campaign design incorporates multiple ways to win. Communist commanders certainly recognized the dilemma imposed on MACV by simultaneous attacks against remote outposts and cities; by threatening each locale at the same time, they gave their units an opportunity to succeed against either or both sets of objectives. Allied leaders, identifying signs of forthcoming enemy attacks on both rural and urban targets, had to protect them all.

Marine assessments of the looming threats aligned with those of the MACV analysts in Saigon. Despite the sense that the enemy might soon make a major assault, allied commanders remained confident they would defeat such initiatives, just as they had deflected previous communist thrusts. Krulak's monthly report to Washington in November 1967 presented a general tone of inexorable progress on all fronts in I Corps.[49] Cushman's end-of-year assessment for 1967, dated 12 January 1968, cited "substantial progress" and anticipated that "accelerated progress in all areas will continue in 1968."[50] By early January 1968, some American intelligence officers anticipated attacks on cities, including Hue. Unfortunately, the 1st ARVN Division, the South Vietnamese unit responsible for protecting the northern two provinces of I Corps, doubted the communists' intent and capability to assault urban centers.[51] This misconception left the unit poorly positioned for the subsequent attack on Hue.

The MAF G-2 report published on 14 January 1968 noted the continuing threat to Khe Sanh, listed Con Thien–Geo Linh–Quang Tri City as likely targets for regiment-size attacks, anticipated interdiction of roads to isolate the northern two provinces, highlighted the vulnerability of Combined Action Platoons, predicted more attacks by fire, and projected further acts of terror throughout the region. In order of likelihood, analysts forecast minor unconventional and psychological operations, indirect fire attacks, and regiment-size ground assaults on objectives along the DMZ, near Quang Tri, or against isolated units farther south.[52] In other words, at midmonth III MAF expected more of the same, not a country and regionwide assault.

With the benefit of hindsight, the 1968 MACV *Command History* characterized enemy actions at Khe Sanh as a diversion and not a main effort.[53] But at the time, Westmoreland and his subordinates in I Corps saw the matter differently. They judged the purported threats against the cities as the distraction, designed to cover an attempt to gain a Dien Bien Phu–like triumph over the Marines at Khe Sanh. MACV war games concluded that such border threats posed the enemy's most likely and most dangerous course of action.[54] On 13 January 1968 Cushman warned Major General Rathvon McC. Tompkins, 3rd Marine Division commander, that an attack on Khe Sanh was expected on 18 January.[55] Messages on 12–13 January 1968 between Chairman of the Joint Chiefs Earle G. Wheeler and Westmoreland, with commentary by Krulak to Cushman and Admiral U.S. Grant Sharp, Jr., reflected the senior leaders' emphasis on Khe Sanh rather than on other developing threats.[56] The American intelligence assessment of border attacks as the enemy's main effort hinged on recognition that its supplies, based just across the borders in North Vietnam and in Laos, best supported the multi-division force required to seize the base and perhaps even conquer the two northern provinces. However logical, this allied evaluation supported the communists' bid to distract attention from their planned urban assaults.

This misdirection, however, proved inadequate to allow sustained communist success in the cities during the 1968 offensive. Intelligence allowed MACV forces to reposition and be on high alert going into the Tet holiday. In December 1967 and January 1968 General Westmoreland postponed planned allied operations in the Central Highlands, drew American units closer to Saigon, cancelled Operation YORK along the Laotian border in I Corps, and transferred the 1st Cavalry Division to Thua Thien Province in anticipation of the enemy's pending attacks. On 22 January the MACV commander cabled Wheeler predicting regiment-size attacks on Hue and Quang Tri City.[57] US forces went on maximum alert for the Tet holiday. ARVN also issued a final warning to its four corps on 29 January 1968.[58]

While Major General Frederick Weyand, commanding III Field Force, indicated that he received no "useful" intelligence prior to the Tet Offensive, Cushman acknowledged "ample forewarning" of the impending offensive (although no identification of specific targets).[59] Indeed, III MAF headquarters had been certain of communist intentions to launch major attacks even before Christmas 1967. On 20 December, the Marines executed Operation CLAXTON, an innovative but unsuccessful deception that detonated explosives around the Da Nang airfields and supply dumps to simulate enemy rockets and trigger a premature ground assault. Cushman opposed observance of the normal Tet truce and canceled it in I Corps six hours prior to its planned start. III MAF units stood on 100 percent alert when the attacks commenced.[60]

After the offensive, President Johnson's Foreign Intelligence Advisory Board conducted a study for the National Security Council to determine how much surprise the Tet attacks achieved. Its report noted major differences in readiness among the four corps tactical zones. The most prepared was I Corps. The investigation reported that Cushman had expected attacks during the Tet holiday. His staff anticipated assaults on Khe Sanh and Quang Tri City, though G-2 analysts had identified no specific date. Despite the failure at Hue, most ARVN units in I Corps remained on high alert and near full strength. The extent and coordination of the attacks caught the allies by surprise, as did the focus on the region's cities. But overall, the board gave III MAF the highest marks of any US corps headquarters for its readiness.[61]

An internal study, conducted by the MAF G-2 section, arrived at similar conclusions. It reported that III MAF's intelligence resources predicted the nature, scope, and timing of the Tet Offensive and disseminated that information to subordinate commanders in a timely fashion. It acknowledged a "flood of information" between 15 and 30 January 1968 warning that a large attack was imminent. Marine G-2 analysts disputed the national board's view that attacks on I Corps' cities were unexpected, since most of the NVA/VC units they were tracking had moved within twelve hours' march of the region's cities by late January. Almost all the communist units engaged during the offensive matched the ones identified, located, and predicted to participate in the anticipated major attack. The high correlation between projected and encountered formations, they suggested, indicated that the MAF's intelligence section had a strong grasp of NVA and VC conventional forces' location, strength, and intent.[62]

The biggest intelligence failure in I Corps during the runup to the Tet Offensive was the lack of information on the communist attack on Hue. Eight enemy infantry battalions, one rocket battalion, three engineer battalions, several local force companies, and six commando teams participated in the initial assault.[63] In the days before the 31 January strike this division-size force infiltrated the area as supplies and munitions were covertly carried into the city and stored. Given the cultural sensitivities of the site, III MAF had made a conscious decision not to garrison or defend Hue. South Vietnamese troops, including the 1st ARVN Division, its headquarters positioned in the town's citadel, were charged with its protection. Unlike Da Nang, no web of bases, barriers, and constant ground and air patrols secured Hue's perimeter.

The fact that such a large NVA/VC force approached undetected over a period of days indicated that the local population either actively supported the communist cause, feared to report the impending attack, or adopted a fence-sitting posture toward both pro- and antigovernment forces. That even South Vietnamese police, paramilitary units, and regular soldiers stationed in the area had no inkling of the impending blow underscored the failure of the allied hearts-and-minds campaign to convince citizens to report signs of enemy activity.

Allied intelligence in the months leading up to the 1968 Tet Offensive delivered mixed results. A mid-1967 study by Westmoreland's

Plans directorate sought to predict new enemy tactical or strategic initiatives between September 1967 and September 1968, but it did not anticipate a Tet-style, countrywide attack on the cities in an effort to trigger a general uprising, collapse ARVN, and destroy the South Vietnamese government.[64] The US G-2 system nevertheless gathered many indications of a pending enemy offensive. Evidence of conventional forces massing along or infiltrating across the northern border proved sufficient to allow MACV to shift US forces and III MAF to reinforce Khe Sanh.

Despite a mature intelligence organization and three years' experience, however, allied analysts did not foresee the full extent of the enemy's Tet effort or the ambitious goals the offensive pursued. Despite a profusion of low-level agent reports predicting imminent offensive action, human intelligence still proved inadequate to detect the communist troops approaching their targets, especially at Hue.[65] An overreliance on technical intelligence capabilities characterized the US approach.[66] Although high-resolution photographic, seismic/acoustic, and signals intelligence information provided much useful data, this could not make up for the dearth of reliable agent and man-on-the-street reports necessary to consistently preempt attacks by elusive insurgent and conventional forces.[67] Because they didn't anticipate the strength and extent of the communist attacks, US intelligence officers and commanders also failed to anticipate or forestall the psychological effect on the home front.[68] This strategic impact far outweighed the temporary loss of local tactical initiative that accompanied the offensive's unexpected extent.

Measuring Pacification's Progress, 1968–1970

Walt's emphasis on counterinsurgency spurred the MAF staff to develop a monthly assessment system to measure pacification levels. Starting in February 1966, he required subordinate commanders to rate conditions in villages within their sectors. Marine leaders analyzed five categories to arrive at a total numerical score on a 100-point scale. Criteria included destruction of enemy conventional units and shadow government, establishment of RVN security forces and local government, and degree of economic development. Each category included several supporting factors, each of which was also assigned a numerical grade. A score of 80 points overall earned a village a "pacified" status. Building on this early work, the CIA later developed III MAF's assessment tool into the better-known Hamlet Evaluation System administered by CORDS.[69]

Gauging allied progress in the pacification campaign proved more challenging than tracking enemy conventional units. Some aspects of the problem, such as the number of people driven from their homes or the number of villages with functioning chiefs, lent themselves to counting. Others, like the extent of the communist infrastructure or the level of prevailing security, entailed more difficult assessments. A split in civil and military intelligence capabilities complicated matters. Robert Komer, head of CORDS, insisted the organization's intelligence apparatus separate from the military G-2 directorates.[70] At the regional level, III MAF's limited reporting on CORDS initiatives, despite CORDS's status as a major subordinate command under Marine control, reflected this dichotomy.

The introduction of CORDS in 1967 with its attendant reorganization of allied pacification duties, coupled with the enemy's Tet and mini-Tet Offensives of 1968, delayed and disrupted, but did not completely derail, ongoing pacification programs. These hearts-and-minds initiatives sought to forge an enduring compact between the South Vietnamese people and their government. Goals included the elimination of communist shadow government infrastructure; the expansion of village, province, and national authority; development of government services; resettlement of citizens displaced by fighting; and the protection of both urban and rural populations from Vietcong intimidation and terror. A variety of actors contributed to these programs. In the Marine zone, ARVN's I Corps headquarters along with the province chiefs directed the RVN pacification program set out in the late-1968 Accelerated Pacification Campaign and the 1969 Pacification and Development Plan. For III MAF, CORDS supervised most of the US civil and military programs supporting the RVN effort.[71]

Unraveling the VC's complex civil-military command structure proved the most difficult aspect of the counterinsurgency campaign. The intelligence required differed in kind from that needed to track conventional units and anticipate their actions. The Vietcong movement's political dimension was more dangerous than its more visible military component. Communist infrastructure was the key to the irregular intelligence puzzle because it represented the revolution's principal source of organizational strength. In military terms the infrastructure was the insurgency's operational center of gravity because political cadre motivated and controlled the personnel who recruited, supplied, and supported the guerrillas, local force troops, and main force units. VC military units, by contrast, served only as a tactical center of gravity because they protected and helped expand the shadow government.[72] Communist ideology, political promises, and social organizations inspired the masses who supported the VC cause. Douglas Pike, in a seminal study of the Vietcong published in 1966 (and thus available to Marine analysts early in the war), observed that the infrastructure's purpose was to "restructure the social order of the village" and achieve "victory by means of the organizational weapon."[73] To destroy the insurgency, the allies had to eradicate its core: the shadow government.

Supplementing unclassified studies by outside experts such as Pike, allied military intelligence officers built up extensive dossiers of information on the Vietcong. After three years of analyzing the insurgency's regional infrastructure, III MAF's G-2 section had developed a solid understanding of its purpose, organization, and strength. The twofold purpose of the VCI was to provide food, money, intelligence, refuge, recruits, and guides to military units and to set the stage for the assumption of power in the South by a communist government. Perhaps reflecting CORDS's growing influence on pacification and its need for intelligence support, a III MAF G-2 study released in August and September 1968 detailed the shadow government's history, structure, and personnel across the five provinces of I Corps. This 150-page document named many of the infrastructure's key leaders, identified the sectors controlled by subordinate echelons, and charted extensive wire diagrams of the shadow government's varied party, front, and military components.[74] This assessment, however, was an exception to the MAF G-2 shop's more consistent emphasis on reporting conventional enemy unit intelligence.

Both the military and the political wings of the Vietcong movement suffered significant losses during the 1968 Tet and mini-Tet Offensives. When clandestine political agents surfaced to support the military assaults, the leaders, stripped of their cloak of anonymity, became vulnerable. Allied forces killed or arrested more than two thousand VCI cadre in I Corps during the offensives, while another 2,800 VC troops and agents surrendered.[75] As the 1968 Tet offensives faltered, the RVN and MACV counterattacked with the Accelerated Pacification Campaign, a comprehensive push to wrest control of the countryside from depleted communist forces. Within three months, this campaign reclaimed 155 contested hamlets in I Corps and moved 1.7 million more peasants nationwide into secure sectors.[76]

Attacking the shadow government, especially when its members remained concealed, was a more difficult task than engaging guerrillas. CORDS and G-2 intelligence analysts supported the MAF's counter-VCI programs, but even the dossiers they had developed on specific cadre prior to the start of the Accelerated Pacification Campaign did not lead to swift elimination of the regional infrastructure. Allied line units performed numerous cordon-and-search operations of I Corps hamlets, with RVN police interrogating suspicious detainees. CAP Marines, working with their South Vietnamese Popular Forces partners, sought to identify and capture or kill civilian VC agents in the villages. Allied psychological operations encouraged communist civilians and troops to surrender. Finally, the controversial Phoenix program, run by the RVN police and supported by both the CIA and US military advisers, targeted infrastructure personnel via intelligence-driven raids. Only Phoenix routinely employed G-2 data to apprehend specific VC cadre. From an intelligence and operations perspective, the rest of the anti-VCI programs resembled a blunderbuss firing over open sights rather than a scoped sniper rifle removing a critical specified target. During 1969 these programs collectively reported 5,363 killed, captured, or surrendered members of the VCI within I Corps. While this figure exceeded the region's annual goal by more than 10 percent, it still left a projected nineteen thousand cadre in the field.[77]

The insurgency was strongly established in I Corps, especially in the southern three provinces. Quang Nam, home of Da Nang, contained more VC political cadre than any of the RVN's other forty-three provinces.[78] The estimate of VCI in Quang Nam alone equaled 81 percent of the projected number in the eleven III Corps provinces surrounding Saigon. A September 1969 assessment of cadre in I Corps' provinces indicated 1,658 in Quang Tri; 2,501 in Thua Thien; 6,973 in Quang Nam; 4,897 in Quang Tin; and 4,584 in Quang Ngai. Some 57 percent of the total had been identified with confidence through intelligence sources; the remainder was projected based on unconfirmed reports.[79] The VCI numbers killed, captured, or surrendered in I Corps in the year following the Tet Offensives accounted for only 20 percent of the communist shadow government cadre operating in the region. The insurgency's political infrastructure thus remained a problem even though the number of guerrillas protecting and projecting it continued to decline after Tet. Given this level of cadre strength after years of combat, the III MAF G-2 concluded: "The military war will not be won until this infrastructure is eliminated or neutralized."[80]

Although the MAF G-2 knew that attacks on the VCI were important, in practice it was still quite difficult to eradicate the shadow

government. On the final day of 1969, Alexander Firfer, the I Corps
CORDS director, wrote a letter to Ambassador William E. Colby, director of CORDS for MACV, lamenting that attempts to destroy the
infrastructure were not working. He attributed part of the failure to
a lack of means to put double agents inside the shadow government.[81]
Several other problems also contributed to the limited counter-VCI
progress. The district intelligence and operations centers were better
at collecting information than acting on it. Much of the work required
policing and detective expertise, but the programs were manned by
army personnel without investigative training. The RVN government, at all levels, had a mixed record of supporting the attacks on the
shadow government.[82] Even though 1969 represented the best year yet
in attacking the shadow government's cadre, Firfer recognized that
the all-important effort to destroy communist infrastructure still had
many aspects to improve.

For the broader allied pacification campaign, the Hamlet Evaluation
System, initiated by MACV in December 1966 and administered by
CORDS, provided the best (although not faultless) indication of overall progress. The MAF's intelligence system contributed data to HES,
but the evaluation incorporated inputs from CORDS, staff G-2 and
G-3 analysts, and the Advisory Command. The monthly HES reports
tracked eighteen factors ranging across six areas: VC military action;
subversion and political activities; friendly force security capabilities; government administrative and political progress; health, education, and welfare programs; and economic development. Letter grades
ranged from A (most secure) to D (most contested), with a V rating
for hamlets deemed under communist control. Over time CORDS ad-
ministrators lengthened and improved the instrument to better reflect
realities on the ground. While not flawless (and less reliable once the
South Vietnamese assumed full responsibility for the system's administration during the Vietnamization process), HES data nonetheless
provided a useful metric for gauging the social, political, economic, and
security trends of the pacification program.[83]

The MAF's assessments of pacification going into 1970 reflected
several positive trends. Communist infrastructure losses spiked in
1969. Humanitarian assistance projects continued to grow in number
and sophistication. In December 1969 alone, 545 civic action missions
were conducted and nearly sixty-five thousand Vietnamese civilian
patients received medical treatment.[84] The RVN government was re-
settling the large number of refugees, a tragic byproduct of fighting a
defensive war on South Vietnamese territory, with increasing dispatch

and improved, if still imperfect, competence. Of the region's 509 villages, 91 percent (and 99 percent of its hamlets) had leaders selected in free and fair local elections. Security improved markedly with the post-Tet withdrawal of North Vietnamese regular formations and Hanoi's relapse to lower-intensity guerrilla warfare concentrated mainly in I Corps' southern three provinces. The flood of newly armed rural militia made it harder for small VC units to intimidate and control Southern villagers. CORDS's HES statistics mirrored the improving conditions. The percentage of population under government control in the III MAF zone jumped from 74 percent to 94 percent. Quang Tri and Thua Thien Provinces boasted 100 percent HES pacification rates by June and September 1969.[85] The most unsettling aspect of the pacification problem lay in the persistent, although diminished, presence of VC cadre and guerrillas.[86] They proved difficult to defeat and disband despite the array of allied tools, programs, and units deployed against them.

In January 1970, shortly before III MAF transferred regional command to XXIV Corps, the interagency Vietnam Special Studies Group in Washington published a study of conditions in the countryside in twelve RVN provinces, including two within I Corps. It observed that the VC was more proficient at establishing "control" of the hamlets through VCI, while the allies were more capable of establishing "security" because of their superior conventional military power. The studies group concluded that the shadow government in Thua Thien was broken, even though two thousand cadre remained. In Quang Nam, the VCI was eroded but in better shape. The conventional fighting there had destroyed 45 percent of the province's hamlets in just one year. In both provinces, RVN political control was poor, while the social fabric was rent by too much fighting and resettlement.[87] The MAF deputy CORDS director, Carl R. Fritz, called the Washington report's analysis "outstanding" and its conclusions "valid," although he felt the authors underemphasized recent improvements in People's Self-Defense Force militias, village governments, and urban conditions overall.[88]

By the summer of 1970, XXIV Corps reported that Quang Nam and Quang Tin Provinces were running the best counter-VCI programs in the country despite uneven American support at the province and district levels, too few precision raids based on strong intelligence leading to neutralization of upper-level VC cadre, and an RVN judicial system too slow to prosecute and confine shadow government suspects.[89] It was not enough. American efforts to eradicate the VCI ran out of time as US forces began to withdraw. When the MAF departed in 1971, followed by XXIV Corps a year later, I Corps had not developed the South Vietnamese leaders or taken full ownership of the civil-military processes needed to continue an aggressive campaign against the shadow government.

Prioritizing Hybrid Threats

The way the Marines Corps conceptualized its problems, prioritized its enemies, and evaluated progress determined how it operated in Vietnam's most challenging region. Assessment was not just the intelligence section's purview. It was commanders' business, and the entire staff contributed to the process by drafting appraisals, conducting war games, and preparing studies focused on specific issues. The MAF used a variety of staff experts and processes, including a new Systems Analysis section, to improve the command's grasp of its tactical environment and thereby improve its operational response.[90] These tools and processes were essential to do what doctrine posited each level of command must do: periodically reexamine its assumptions and actions to determine if those things needed adjustment based on a changing enemy situation or other new circumstances.[91] Fundamental to this process—and thus the MAF's most important intelligence assessment—was deciding whether the insurgency or the conventional war posed the greatest operational challenge. Evidence indicates that neither combat experience nor intelligence studies ever altered the MAF commanders' answer to this question.

Among their three primary missions—pacifying the countryside, fighting enemy regulars, and developing ARVN—III MAF's leaders made pacification first among equals. This viewpoint was shared among Marines from Commandants down to division commanders and represented a consensus that the key to victory—the "defeat mechanism" in planner language—rested on winning the hearts and minds of the South Vietnamese people. The consensus maintained that the insurgency represented the biggest threat because leaders believed that the NVA was unable to sustain itself in the South without the assistance of the Vietcong. Thus, once the populace supported Saigon, the contest would be over in both the big war and small war arenas. That view was more justified in 1965 compared to 1970, but senior Marine leaders never altered their convictions to match changing circumstances.

G-2 and other III MAF analysts' assessment of the war against

Vietcong and NVA conventional forces downplayed the severity of their persistent carnage and perhaps confirmed the MAF's focus on the insurgency. Marine intelligence specialists became accustomed, almost numbed, to high intensities of enemy activity across I Corps. A G-2 report covering action in July 1969, for instance, described nearly 1,200 incidents of ground combat and 2,500 rounds of enemy artillery fire as "light" activity. Compared to earlier levels of violence, it was minimal. The July tally represented the fewest number of attacks in six months, half the monthly average of indirect fire incidents over the last year, and the lowest monthly sum of enemy casualties in I Corps since December 1967. When the MAF G-2 staff summarized more than seven attacks per day in each province and a regional count of 3,364 enemy dead for the month as "minor" contact, it highlighted the sustained high-intensity character of the conflict.[92]

More consequential than their desensitization to the conventional war's growing costs, the Marines were wrong on pacification's war-winning potential. As Westmoreland argued, the enduring NVA conventional threat represented the larger and more lethal problem for the South. By 1970 the Vietcong presence in I Corps was small enough for RVN regional security forces to handle. By contrast, the NVA generated military power that ARVN alone could not match. Combat outcomes from 1965 to 1971 indicated that, even with up to five reinforced US divisions in support, the best the allies could manage in I Corps was a tactical stalemate. For the foreseeable future ARVN, without US ground forces and firepower, was doomed.[93] The Marine assessment to the contrary—that is, emphasizing pacification as the key to victory— was a fundamental misread of the threat environment and one that the war's literature has largely ignored.

The flawed Marine appraisal started at the top. The Commandant in 1965, General Wallace Greene, Jr., supported enclaves, an application of the spreading-ink-spot theory of pacification. He opposed MACV's plan to win by locating and destroying large Vietcong units. Instead he advocated slowly clearing an expanding territorial bubble—pushing the guerrillas away and then keeping them from returning. For Commandant Greene, search-and-destroy tactics, though necessary to blunt the enemy's conventional attacks, served only as an auxiliary to the main task of pacification. The Commandant saw MACV's focus on the large unit war as a mistake. "From the very beginning," he claimed, "the prime error had been the failure to make the population secure." Greene was convinced that "pure military action will not win," but his judgment did not convince his fellow Joint Chiefs or carry weight with

Westmoreland in Saigon. It did, however, influence his subordinate Marine commanders in Honolulu and Da Nang.[94]

General Krulak, at FMFPAC, shared Greene's views, arguing even more ardently for the prominence pacification deserved. He conceptualized the war based on his previous experience as the Joint Chiefs' special assistant for counterinsurgency during President John F. Kennedy's administration. In that capacity he studied Vietnam and visited eight times between 1962 and 1964. Influenced by Sir Robert Thompson's ideas on how to defeat communist insurgencies, and by the British pacification experience in Malaya, Krulak believed strongly in the ink-blot strategy. Westmoreland and Secretary of Defense Robert McNamara listened politely to the FMFPAC commander's advice but concluded that clear-and-hold techniques were "a good idea but too slow." Krulak countered that the allies "didn't have time to do it any other way" and that to "attrit the enemy to a degree which makes him incapable of prosecuting the war, or unwilling to pay the cost of so doing . . . has to be regarded as inadequate." He argued that search-and-destroy tactics were a waste of time, since "the real war is among the people."[95]

Krulak became the strongest and most vocal Marine advocate for pacification. Although others minimized the distinctions inherent in the argument as matters of minor tactical emphasis, he characterized his professional disagreements with Westmoreland's methods as profound. As FMFPAC commander he held only an advisory capacity with respect to Vietnam's operational matters. Nevertheless he outlined his reservations about MACV's approach and his own countervailing proposals in copious message traffic, forty-six additional visits to Saigon and I Corps, a detailed monthly summary of III MAF actions, and a series of personal meetings in Hawaii and Washington with senior military commanders, influential politicians, and media moguls. Krulak also provided constant operational advice concerning the war to Admiral Sharp, Westmoreland's boss. In the war's first year he forwarded to the secretary of defense a seventeen-page appraisal outlining an alternate strategy. The consistent theme of these communications was the importance of protecting the people and earning their support for the South Vietnamese government. Nothing that transpired in I Corps between 1965 and 1971 changed his assessment.[96]

General Walt, commanding III MAF from 1965 to 1967, shared his Marine superiors' views on how to fight the war in I Corps. In his 1970 book on Vietnam, Walt stressed the formative influence of career mentors who had learned their small wars craft in Nicaragua or

Haiti. His memoir acknowledged the North Vietnamese threat but highlighted the importance of defeating the Vietcong and winning over the population.[97] Walt's 29 December 1966 letter to the HQMC's chief of staff, penned after nineteen months in command of III MAF, captured his view on the nature of the principal peril facing I Corps:

> I believe far too much emphasis is being placed on the importance of the infiltration threat. I base this on my conviction that our primary enemy here remains the guerrilla. . . . [T]he mass of infiltrators must be considered as NVA or main force VC types. As the record shows, we beat these units handily each time we encounter them. In my mind, therefore, we should not fall into the trap of expending troops unduly seeking to prevent the entry of individuals and units who pose the lesser threat to our ultimate objective, which remains the people of South Vietnam.[98]

General Cushman, who followed Walt in command of III MAF, proved less of a pacification zealot compared to Greene, Krulak, or Walt.[99] And yet he still believed in the importance of the small war mission. In a message to the Commandant and the FMFPAC commander in December 1967, Cushman noted that "population control would eventually be decisive." His theory of victory reflected the Marines' balanced approach and anticipated success in both the political and military dimensions. When a visiting congressional delegation asked how the allies would ever win, he replied: "Keep the pressure on militarily and fight and destroy enemy units; behind this shield go full force on RD [Revolutionary Development] and Pacification to include rooting out the VC infrastructure. When Hanoi finds out it has no political machine to control the population, since it already knows it cannot conquer the country militarily, in my opinion they will simply pull out their main force units."[100] Cushman was at best a partial prophet. Hanoi's 1969 withdrawal of main force strength served only as an operational pause, giving the NVA space and time to rebuild its shattered legions while waiting for the allies to depart.

One of Cushman's most aggressive subordinates, Major General Ray Davis, commanding 3rd Marine Division, also misjudged the NVA's post-Tet tactical respite. He crowed in April 1969 that his unit and the ARVN troops operating in his sector "totally control Quang Tri Province."[101] Enemy conventional forces in that province had diminished over the previous four months, but III MAF intelligence reports for April still listed elements of five NVA regiments, an estimated 3,480 troops, operating in the province.[102] Whether the other NVA units were forced or ordered out of northern I Corps, the comparative lull in conventional combat allowed both American and South Vietnamese troops to refocus on pacification, a mission that had taken a back seat during the Tet and mini-Tet Offensives of 1968. Like Cushman, Davis underestimated Hanoi's political will as well as the staying power of its regular and irregular military components. Moreover, President Richard M. Nixon's withdrawal policy quickly rendered moot the big and small war tactical accomplishments of Davis and his division, which had returned to Okinawa by the end of 1969.

Davis's pride in his division's work and his overconfidence in how much it mattered underscored a larger point: Not only was Cushman wrong to believe that the North would give up its conventional attacks because the Vietcong failed to control the population; he and Davis and other senior Marine leaders were also wrong to think that the NVA, with or without insurgent assistance, posed the lesser—and certainly not a vanquished—threat. The Vietcong's power had dwindled by 1970 to manageable proportions. The remaining guerrillas, animated by a Vietnamese strain of Marxist political ideology, did not conquer Saigon in 1975. North Vietnamese regulars, employing multiple corps-level combined arms attacks, earned that laurel. The people of the South remained the ultimate prize as the counterinsurgency enthusiasts had theorized, but the Marines consistently turned a blind eye to the notion that those citizens were more vulnerable to a conventional assault than to an insurgent-sponsored revolution. Even a successful pacification campaign would not defeat the NVA.

The Marines were nonetheless right to find fault with Westmoreland's reliance on an attrition strategy to defeat the NVA. Krulak observed in 1965 that the casualty math associated with MACV's preferred tactics looked grim. At the then-prevailing rate of 2.5 enemy dead for each American, it would "cost something like 175,000 lives to reduce the enemy manpower pool by a modest 20 percent." Krulak's projection proved uncannily accurate: seven years later the United States and South Vietnam had lost 220,000 dead and cut Hanoi's manpower pool by just 25 percent.[103] He foresaw that attrition cut both ways. The communist regime's willingness to suffer its costs exceeded that of a democracy engaged in a limited war.

But Krulak's prescience vanished in his estimation of the conventional war's ultimate impact: "The conflict between the North Vietnamese/hard core Vietcong, on the one hand, and the [United States] on the other, could move to another planet today and we would not have won the war. On the other hand, if the subversion and guerrilla efforts were to disappear, the war would soon collapse, as the enemy would be denied food, sanctuary and intelligence."[104] On this point Krulak could not have been more wrong, as subsequent conventional campaigns in 1972 and 1975 proved.

Up and down the chain of command, Marine assessments on this fundamental issue proved equally faulty. The conventional war was not irrelevant or a distraction to the main show of eradicating the Vietcong. Neither had the allied mobile defense afforded I Corps an effective defensive shield against the NVA. Although pacification was important, it was not the crux of the problem or the sole key to victory. The war could not be won without an effective counterinsurgency campaign, but it could be lost despite defeating the guerrillas and the shadow government. Pacification was necessary but not sufficient. Vietnam's hybrid war demanded decisive action on all fronts. In theory, both MACV and III MAF commanders recognized this fact. Their plans called for simultaneous action against both conventional and irregular threats. But in practice the United States Army relied on the big war and the Marines on the small war to bend the enemy to their will. In chapter 4 I examine why both approaches fell short.

Conclusion

The III MAF G-2 and its supporting CORDS intelligence analysts registered both successes and failures in their assessments of the enemy. During the first three years of the Marine intervention, the G-2 directorate tracked the locations, movements, and composition of the VC main force and NVA units in all parts of I Corps with impressive fidelity. In the months leading up to the 1968 Tet Offensive, allied intelligence noted the buildup of forces along the corps' northern border as well as the shifting of some units toward attack points near their objectives. In all the targets except Hue, allied forces either repulsed or swiftly ejected enemy assault forces. After the last of the three communist offensives faded later in that year, allied commanders launched a counterattack on the pacification front with the Accelerated Pacification Campaign, followed by the annual campaign plan for 1969 that focused on seizing additional territory from enemy forces. Intelligence assessments supported these successful counterinsurgency initiatives, even if MACV and III MAF intelligence agencies never assigned the same analytical emphasis to understanding and locating the insurgency's operational center of gravity—the shadow government—as they did its tactical center of gravity—fielded military forces.

On a higher level, however, failure marked each of these intelligence case studies. The 1st VC Regiment rebuilt itself many times after disastrous encounters with allied forces because it recruited more South Vietnamese troops and imported more North Vietnamese manpower. Units like the 324B NVA Division suffered similar recurrent losses in Quang Tri Province in the 1966–1967 period yet returned repeatedly because they refitted across the borders in North Vietnamese and Laotian sanctuaries and then reemerged on Southern battlefields where and when they chose. The 1968 infiltration of more than a division's worth of VC and NVA troops into and around Hue without raising an alarm indicated that a social environment sympathetic to the communists still existed within I Corps.

All three examples pointed to unsuccessful allied interdiction, attrition, and pacification campaigns. Even the more aggressive pacification operations of 1968–1970 did not unearth and eradicate the deeply rooted communist infrastructure in I Corps. Marine intelligence evaluations recognized those facts, but MAF commanders never used them to alter operational approaches or to recommend new strategies to better address recurrent problems. The biggest intelligence shortcoming in I Corps, however, was the MAF's conviction that the insurgency was the most dangerous element of the hybrid war. This assessment led the MAF to discount the long-term danger posed by continued NVA incursions—a vulnerability that proved fatal once ARVN stood alone.

4

III MAF Operations

In Vietnam the Marine Corps encountered a conflict fundamentally different than any it had experienced before. The war encompassed, in equal measures, a Maoist insurgency and a conventional campaign between two rival states. The former featured a dynamic political component in conjunction with vicious violence targeting civilians. The latter showcased fierce combat between two Vietnamese light infantry armies, each aided by superpower sponsors eager to supply advice, weapons, and manpower.[1]

Marines had encountered guerrilla and conventional fighting before, but never so seamlessly knitted together as they were in Southeast Asia. Both enemy threats posed an existential peril to Saigon's sovereignty. The Vietcong, unchecked, threatened to supplant the Republic of Vietnam's control of the countryside, instigate rebellion among the urban masses, and undermine the legitimacy of the national government. The North Vietnamese Army aimed to crush its rivals on the battlefield and impose communist rule. The Marine Amphibious Force sought a way to deny both ambitions.

The operations that followed unfolded under the rubric of the service's new doctrine: the Marine Air-Ground Task Force. Vietnam provided the initial operational trial for that organizational concept. In this chapter I examine the outcome of the clash between a novel threat and a new doctrine. I explore III MAF's response to the hybrid war conditions it faced, assess the effectiveness of its campaigns and programs, and end with a reflection on the command's operational style. The evidence demonstrates how the MAF's choices undermined aspects of its effectiveness, how it failed to accomplish its primary tasks, and how it succeeded tactically but failed to fashion a campaign that won the war in I Corps.

III MAF's Operational Response

Throughout its six years of combat in I Corps, III MAF implemented a balanced operational approach to address the communists' lethal dual-track strategy. Advisory efforts strengthened ARVN and its territorial forces. Conventional actions held at bay VC main force units and the rising tide of NVA invasions. Pacification programs protected the people and strengthened their ties with the RVN's local, regional, and national governments. During the MAF's tenure, these three complementary tracks forestalled a communist victory in the RVN's most embattled region. The Marine response to I Corps' unique blend of challenges featured applications of tried-and-true techniques, including amphibious assaults, airpower, combined arms, local militias, and aggressive ground combat tactics. This menu of means reflected an organization employing its traditional operational methods, for better or worse, against a new problem set.

Advising and Assisting ARVN

Enabling RVN security forces to stand on their own against their VC and NVA enemies represented an essential MACV mission, but this did not receive priority until the decision to commence withdrawal of American forces in 1969.[2] In August 1965 General William C. Westmoreland designated US corps commanders as senior advisers to their regional ARVN counterparts, responsible for improving the effectiveness of Saigon's conventional and irregular forces. Yet III MAF commanders devoted scant attention to this task. Lieutenant Generals Lewis W. Walt and Robert E. Cushman, Jr., did conduct weekly staff meetings with their deputy senior advisers, followed by a coordination conference with ARVN's I Corps commander.[3] Developing ARVN, however, remained last among the three primary missions under the first two MAF commanders.

Walt hardly mentioned ARVN in his memoir of his command tour. His greatest personal accomplishment with I Corps' leaders entailed defusing the political tensions of the 1966 Struggle Movement, which threatened the RVN government.[4] Most ARVN generals spent more time on domestic politics than fighting, but that behavior became less of a problem in I Corps after Lieutenant General Nguyen Chanh Thi's 1966 ouster and Lieutenant General Hoang Xuan Lam's ascension.[5] The MAF commanders maintained professional relationships with

their I Corps counterparts, but too many of their professional inter-
actions resembled staged diplomatic visits, with accompanying pomp
and circumstance, rather than senior commanders and their staffs engaged in serious, collaborative soldiering.

Marine leaders viewed ARVN's development as a back-burner task,
well behind pacification and conventional combat duties. In August
1966 III MAF listed its three primary objectives as destruction of VC
forces, pacification, and base defense.[6] Advising did not consistently
appear as a category of operations in the MAF's monthly command
chronology, which detailed the unit's activities across the range of its
command and staff functions. Neither did Fleet Marine Force, Pacific,
the MAF's service superior in Honolulu, acknowledge the advising
mission in its monthly and semiannual reports of Marine actions in
Vietnam. All the MAF commanders were content allowing the primarily US Army–staffed Advisory Command to handle the critical
advising/training task. Few Marines participated in this effort. The
deputy senior ARVN advisers, always soldiers, carried the load for the
South Vietnamese army's development in I Corps.[7] Approximately
forty-five Marines worked for the MAF's eight hundred–strong Advisory Command. Marines trained and supported Vietnamese Marine
units that operated nationwide as a strategic reserve, supported ARVN
units with Air-Naval Gunfire Liaison Company (ANGLICO) detachments, and worked extensively with territorial forces in the Combined
Action Program, but US Army advisers provided most of the assistance to South Vietnamese regulars in I Corps.[8]

The US Army assigned advisers to ARVN's fielded forces, schools,
and staffs. By the end of 1965 the number of US military advisers in
Vietnam had increased to more than eight thousand. Five years later
this sum had grown by another six thousand troops. Just 11 percent of
that total worked in I Corps, split between combat units (that advisory
contingent was reduced to 560 men by 1970) and pacification duties
with CORDS (1,011 men). For the former, detachment strengths varied
by echelon: In 1965, 143 advisers served at the ARVN corps, fifty-two
soldiers supported each of the two ARVN divisions, just three personnel worked with each regiment, and five advisers assisted each battalion. CORDS detachments received twenty advisers at the province
level and five military personnel at each of the subordinate districts.[9]

Initially the III MAF Advisory Group controlled both tactical and
administrative teams, but district and province advisers reported to
CORDS after its establishment in 1967. Army advisers did not support ARVN's territorial forces until 1968, when MACV established

353 Mobile Advisor Teams to assist Regional and Popular Forces. These six-man teams typically trained territorial units for about a month before moving on to the next designated command. Territorial force advisers concentrated on fundamentals such as marksmanship, patrolling, and ambush drills.[10] Their conventional unit counterparts devoted less attention to basic soldiering skills, serving primarily as liaisons with nearby US forces, operations planners, and coordinators of ARVN's logistic and fire support.

Combined operations offered another effective way to develop ARVN's fighting capabilities. With no unified command structure, I Corps and III MAF units operated together based on coordination and cooperation rather than within a single chain of command. American units proved reluctant to work closely with ARVN until 1968.[11] Prior to that point MACV relegated South Vietnamese security forces mostly to area security duties while US commands concentrated on finding and destroying communist conventional forces. The MAF's fusion with I Corps ranged from no coordination at all (Operation STARLITE, 1965), to completely ineffective integration (Operation HARVEST MOON, 1965), to simultaneous but separate operations in contiguous zones (Operations HASTINGS, 1966, and HICKORY, 1967), to model cooperation resulting in a decisive outcome (Operation VINH LOC, 1968).[12]

Coordination improved as ARVN units shouldered more of the conventional fight after the Tet Offensive and the Vietnamization program began to emphasize South Vietnamese self-sufficiency in 1969. Brigadier General Ngo Quang Truong, commander of ARVN's 1st Division, later cited Operations DELAWARE (April 1968) and NEVADA EAGLE (September 1968), for example, as exemplary combined operations that strengthened Saigon's conventional and irregular security forces in I Corps. He credited US Army Lieutenant General Richard G. Stilwell, commander of XXIV Corps, with instituting a close and effective partnership between the ARVN's 1st Division and the US Army corps.[13] It is instructive to note that Truong did not credit 3rd Marine Division or III MAF, which had worked alongside ARVN's 1st division for three years prior to XXIV Corps' arrival.

Throughout the conflict ARVN's forces in I Corps earned strong endorsements from the MAF's Advisory Group. Most American analysts, both in Da Nang and Saigon, counted I Corps as the most capable of South Vietnam's regional commands. The 1st ARVN Division, despite its brief dalliance with the protest movement in 1966, consistently ranked as the most effective of Saigon's ten infantry divisions.

Later in the war, the 2nd ARVN division, operating in Quang Tin and Quang Ngai Provinces alongside the US Army's Americal Division, also developed an admirable reputation.[14]

Adviser assessments, reported via SEER (System for Evaluating the Effectiveness of RVNAF), were not always reliable because evaluators felt pressure to report their unit's progress and cast their own performance in a positive light.[15] Like Hamlet Evaluation System reports in the pacification realm, however, the adviser reports furnished the best available data and tracked trends that provide useful insights into ARVN's growth and proficiency. In 1968 the Advisory Group's deputy commander reported that I Corps was proficient in pacification support duties, its primary emphasis from 1965 to 1967, but was not yet proficient in offensive operations.[16] Two years later his successor reported that I Corps was "combat proficient not just as compared to other ARVN units in Vietnam but by absolute military standards: there are no 'problem units' at this time."[17] A host of SEER report data over time backed up his verdict.

Tactical outcomes buttressed the advisers' positive reviews of I Corps' infantry formations. They fought well, winning most of the engagements with their communist foes. I Corps boasted some of the most effective ARVN troops in South Vietnam. In 1969 they killed more than twenty-four thousand enemy and captured 3,454. They accounted for nine thousand more enemy casualties than the US Marine forces had, despite fielding only 26 percent of the conventional troop strength. South Vietnamese conventional and irregular troops delivered 44 percent of the enemy's losses in I Corps.[18] They grew in confidence and proficiency with experience, especially from the combined operations with US forces. I Corps units led the RVN's conventional forces in time spent on active combat operations as well as kill ratios. They also led the other corps sectors in amounts of artillery and air support employed; ARVN units provided 82 percent of the former but only 14 percent of the latter. American advisers also rated General Lam's corps as the most proficient in staff work. Countrywide, only ARVN airborne and RVN Marine units exceeded I Corp's ratings for operational effectiveness.[19]

The MAF's experience with advising and supporting I Corps security forces did not square with standard postwar accounts of ARVN ineptitude or unwillingness to fight.[20] The US Army's official histories of the advisory experience conclude that the South Vietnamese army's overall poor performance reflected the weak political and social base upon which it was built.[21] Yet I Corps offered an intriguing paradox: Its units experienced the same socioeconomic and political disadvantages facing their countrymen in other regions, and yet these challenges did not prevent them from fighting effectively. The troops of ARVN's 1st and 2nd Divisions as well as the 51st Regiment at Da Nang consistently matched and, with US support, exceeded the combat prowess of their NVA and VC adversaries. They lacked neither the will nor the skill to defend their country in the conflict's harshest cauldron of combat.

South Vietnamese generals saw their army's weakest link at the corps level, especially in staff planning for mobile combined arms battles and in grooming competent senior leaders to direct multi-division operations.[22] Too often US staffs and advisers planned combined operations, leaving their ARVN contemporaries, dubbed "blindfolded executors" by the final I Corps commander, without practice, expertise, or confidence.[23] General Lam's corps-level command and staff deficiencies were manifest during the conventional combat of Tet 1968, the Laos incursion in 1971, and the initial NVA onslaught in the 1972 Easter Offensive.

The MAF, itself unpracticed as a headquarters directing corps-level maneuvers, proved an unreliable mentor for Lam and his staff between 1966 and 1970. The US Army's XXIV Corps proved more effective in its tutelage of 1st ARVN Division from 1968 to 1970, but its efforts to develop the I Corps commander and his staff after it assumed the senior regional advisory role in 1970 also fell short when put to the test of battle in 1971, 1972, and 1975. Corps command mattered in the campaigns in Military Region 1 that decided the South's fate. ARVN's American tutors did not develop the senior I Corps staff officers and commanders required to fight competently when it counted the most.[24]

Conventional Combat Operations

All of III MAF's commanders viewed conventional combat in I Corps as a mission of secondary importance, as an enabler of successful pacification. Senior Marine leaders considered combat by large units to be a shield behind which the war-winning work of counterinsurgency could proceed unhindered. They reasoned that, if the allies could separate NVA and VC main force units from the people, then the enemy's conventional forces could not sustain themselves or attack the government. Walt explained that Marines had nothing against fighting enemy regulars, but they did not want to waste time beating the bush in fruitless pursuit of elusive enemies. They preferred swift strike operations based on reliable intelligence like the initial STARLITE attack in August 1965.[25] Successful search-and-destroy operations were easier conceived than carried out, as Vietnamese communist forces usually fought only when they chose to while evading allied troops when conditions remained unfavorable. Regardless, Westmoreland pressured III MAF to spend more time conducting large unit attacks, and strong enemy incursions into I Corps provided more opportunity to do so between 1966 and 1969. The conventional ground operations that ensued incorporated a variety of techniques, all of which the MAF employed under the rubric of its MAGTF doctrine.

In the pantheon of preferred Marine tactics, amphibious operations occupied a lofty perch. The Fleet Marine Force, Pacific commander, Lieutenant General Victor H. Krulak, noted that he clung to the amphibious role "like a drunk hangs onto a lamp post."[26] Several advantages commended the practice. The sea presented an undefended flank for enemy units operating on or near the coast. The Navy–Marine Corps team had the organization, training, and equipment to exploit this potential vulnerability. Marine forces afloat represented a reserve for the entire Pacific theater as well as for III MAF when threats and opportunities in I Corps beckoned. Finally, landing exercises, with or without enemy opposition, also enabled the Marine Corps to sustain its congressionally mandated proficiency in the art and science of amphibious warfare. American naval forces conducted seventy-four landings in Vietnam. All but nine occurred in I Corps. Only two exceeded battalion size. Most landings were unopposed, and few generated the tactical surprise and success achieved in the initial foray during Operation STARLITE.[27]

Search-and-destroy operations commenced within months of III MAF's arrival in country and continued throughout its six-year stay in I Corps. Large unit actions often employed either "hammer and anvil" tactics or cordon tactics designed to trap enemy concentrations. When possible, MAF forces sought to engage their foes far from the populated coastal plains to minimize the fighting's impact on the people. Marines and soldiers spent far more time searching than destroying, patrolling the backcountry for days and weeks to locate their wary communist prey. When they did encounter the enemy, it was usually because the opponents chose to fight, normally from tactically advantageous, well-defended positions.

American units tended to attack field fortifications with copious quantities of artillery fire and air-delivered bombs and rockets. This softening-up process preceded the ground assaults necessary to winkle the enemy infantry from their spider holes and bunkers. When allied bombardments continued through the night to prepare for a dawn assault, the attacking force often discovered a vacated position, the enemy having slipped away under cover of darkness. Few large unit search-and-destroy operations entailed allied movement after dark. Instead most American battalions harbored in defensive laagers overnight.

The MAF's offensive operations, a total of 411 of battalion size or larger, lasted anywhere from a few hours to a few months in duration.[28] The longest, Operation PRAIRIE I–IV, a four-phase series of fights along the DMZ, lasted from August 1966 to May 1967.[29] Such sweeps blunted and rebuffed NVA incursions, but they seldom resulted in the complete destruction of entire enemy units. Instead the battered antagonists limped back into their cross-border sanctuaries to recuperate.

Despite the organizational preference for offensive operations, the MAF could not escape defensive missions. Marines deployed to Vietnam initially to defend the airfield at Da Nang. That responsibility never went away. As the MAF footprint grew, other bases, airfields, ports, ammunition depots, and headquarters also required protection. Effective point defense of fixed sites around the clock for months and years on end absorbed enormous tolls of manpower, resources, and command attention.[30] Communist attackers had the luxury of conducting selectively timed and carefully planned assaults, whereas allied defenders had to maintain constant vigilance. Repetitive sapper and rocket attacks tested the various bases' guard forces. These assaults took a small but steady toll on allied installations throughout the war despite increasingly sophisticated anti-access patrols, counterbattery schemes, and aerial surveillance. Nonetheless enemy attacks exerted little sustained impact on the MAF's overall operational posture. This outcome reflected immense efforts by Marines over a prolonged period and remains one of the underappreciated aspects of the war.

At the height of its strength, the MAF devoted an entire infantry division as well as organic security units from subordinate tenant commands to guard Da Nang's thirty-seven-mile perimeter.[31] Even after III MAF's sector shrunk to just one province in 1970, protecting the region's biggest and most important city, port, airfield, and logistics node remained a key duty for what eventually devolved to a single Marine infantry regiment. Those defenders, working in conjunction with ARVN's 51st Regiment, enabled the mostly uninterrupted operation of Da Nang's many critical facilities throughout the conflict, including the vulnerable period of the US military drawdown. The troops engaged in securing the city's approaches remained unavailable to conduct offensive operations farther afield. This drawback motivated

Westmoreland's frustration with the MAF's focus on protecting the people and key nodes rather than getting "out of their beachheads" to find and destroy the enemy's regular forces.[32]

Facility protection demanded constant vigilance, but guarding the border under the bombardment of North Vietnamese artillery remained the most dangerous task. The 3rd Marine Division, arrayed along the northern frontier, suffered 47 percent of its casualties from indirect fire between January 1968 and June 1969. Marine units along the DMZ defended key frontier positions such as Khe Sanh and Con Thien. These fortified outposts featured trenches, bunkers, artillery revetments, minefields, acoustic sensors, and other refinements required to protect their garrisons. Marines proved reluctant (some observers claimed incompetent) defenders of such fixed sites. Westmoreland criticized Marine field fortifications on the DMZ. He instructed III MAF to send representatives to the US Army's 1st Infantry Division to learn how to build more effective defenses. The MACV J-2, Lieutenant General (US Army) Philip B. Davidson, noted Khe Sanh's limited defensive works during a liaison visit on 20 January 1968.[33]

Even senior Marines echoed these critiques of inadequate fortifications. Colonel Richard B. Smith of the Marines, commander of 9th Marine Regiment in 1967, criticized his troops' lack of expertise in constructing bunkers and trenches at the Con Thien outpost two miles south of the DMZ. He blamed the shortcoming on insufficient training. Cushman, like Davidson, found 26th Marine Regiment's fortifications at Khe Sanh in a poor state of readiness during an inspection visit on 17 January 1968 just prior to the base's seventy-seven-day siege. Cushman's deputy, Major General Raymond L. Murray, explained that Marines were offensive-minded and thus "don't do well in organizing defenses." Other Marines blamed any deficient defensive positions on the lack of equipment and materials rather than on lack of training or an ingrained offensive ethos that eschewed proper defensive preparations.[34]

Most Marine commanders favored mobile defenses over static or positional defenses. The latter relied primarily on fixed fortifications to stop enemy infiltration. The former employed reconnaissance and screening forces to locate the enemy, followed by ground units to destroy opponent forces.[35] III MAF lacked enough troops to garrison a static defense along I Corps' borders with North Vietnam and Laos, so the mobile defense served as an economy-of-force measure to block and repulse enemy incursions. Initially III MAF employed 3rd Marine Division, using search-and-destroy tactics, to repulse NVA invasions via a series of bloody operations such as HASTINGS in the summer of 1966.[36]

The planned 1967 McNamara Line, covered in more detail in chapter 6, was intended to counter infiltration of small groups across the border rather than invasions by large conventional forces. Combining elements of both static and mobile schemes, the McNamara Line concept envisioned fortified outposts, mines and wire strung between them, and reaction forces arrayed behind the frontier trace to reinforce threatened sectors, counterattack breaches, and seal penetrations. But MACV abandoned this approach toward border defense in 1968. Thereafter, the MAF and its subordinate XXIV Corps—responsible for protecting the northern third of I Corps—returned to more aggressive offensive tactics, enabled by the influx of new army divisions and hundreds of new army helicopters to increase their agility.

The mobile defense reached its culmination with the air assaults that the 1st Cavalry and 101st Airmobile Divisions conducted in MR 1 after the Tet Offensive. Marines dubbed these heliborne attacks "high mobility operations."[37] Major General Ray Davis's 3rd Marine Division became an ardent practitioner of the new techniques in 1968 and 1969, often using borrowed army helicopters to conduct his unit's maneuvers. Both Marine and army battalions used these air assaults, supported by a web of fire bases, to block NVA advances and to scour the jungles and mountains that hid the enemy's bases.[38]

Heliborne operations prevented communist conventional forces from overrunning I Corps' populated coastal plain, but they were not a tactical panacea. While rotary-wing aircraft enabled quick deployment of infantry units, rapid emplacement of supporting artillery, timely supply replenishment, and swift extraction of casualties, in the end these helicopter-supported search-and-destroy operations boiled down to soldiers on the ground slogging across inhospitable terrain for days and weeks at a time. Intermittently, they located and engaged the enemy's tenacious light infantry in sudden, violent clashes often triggered at close quarters. Despite the many contributions of aviation technology, the actual infantry engagements still resembled the brutal, close-in combat that the US Army and Marine Corps had experienced in the Pacific twenty-five years earlier during World War II.

Pacification Operations

MACV defined "pacification" as "the military, political, economic, and social process of establishing or reestablishing local government responsive to and involving the participation of the people." The campaign aimed to secure territory, destroy the enemy's shadow government, and establish self-sustaining social and economic development. These goals remained easier to describe than to achieve. The South Vietnamese had tried many pacification programs in the decade before III MAF arrived on the scene. All approaches focused on winning the rural population's support for local, regional, and national governments. By 1966 the RVN's effort to forge those links, so-called Revolutionary Development (and managed by a national ministry of the same name), featured fifty-nine-person teams to improve hamlet security and local living conditions.[39] American civilian and military advisers assisted, sometimes working at cross purposes with both the Vietnamese and each other. But the effort to defeat the Vietcong remained an important common objective for the allies.

In *The Army and Vietnam*, Andrew Krepinevich argued that the US Army focused too much on conventional warfare in Vietnam and not enough on pacification.[40] No historian has levied that critique against the Marines. Generals Walt and Krulak, as well as Commandant Wallace M. Greene, Jr., considered pacification to be the key to winning the war. They saw search-and-destroy operations as a shield behind which the more important work of nurturing a South Vietnamese social contract might blossom. Walt emphasized small unit patrolling to eliminate village guerrillas rather than battalion and larger operations targeting larger NVA or main force Vietcong units. Krulak maintained that "there was no virtue at all in seeking out the NVA in the mountains and jungle . . . [and thus] our efforts should be addressed to the rich, populous lowlands." Greene chided MACV's failure to "stamp out the VC hidden in town and hamlet."[41] Circumstances conspired to constrain the MAF's initial operational preference to focus on guerrillas, but pacification remained the favored method in the Marines' bid to vanquish the hybrid threats found in I Corps.

The techniques the MAF employed to support its small war emphasis reflected the recommendations found in counterinsurgency manuals of that period. Tribal wisdom, derived from the Banana Wars and the *Small Wars Manual*'s sage advice to emphasize "tolerance, sympathy, and kindness" while reestablishing community "peace, order, and security," influenced the MAF's approach in Vietnam, but counterguerrilla tenets prescribed in contemporary schools and doctrine swayed Marine planners and commanders even more.[42] The pacification methods of the Vietnam era, despite the Kennedy administration's newfound enthusiasm for nation-building, rested on tried-and-true small war tactics. These proven methods included separating the people from the guerrillas, preventing external support of the rebellion, and relentlessly pursuing insurgents. Military manuals acknowledged the primacy of politics in this new/old form of warfare but saw political warfare as someone else's job.[43] Accordingly, both army and Marine practitioners concentrated on security tasks, though augmented by supporting efforts such as civic action and psychological operations.

In I Corps the security emphasis translated into a protective screen surrounding enclaves that gradually widened to encompass more territory. Within two years of its arrival in country, the MAF had expanded its protective ink blots from just a few square miles to nearly 1,700, approximately one-third of the coastal plain.[44] The US Army Field Forces in II and III Corps did not dedicate as many troops or as much energy as III MAF did to protecting the Vietnamese population with area security measures. MAF units from company to fire-team size conducted a constant array of offensive patrols, ambushes, raids, and search-and-destroy missions. They also guarded roads, bridges, base perimeters, and likely approaches to villages and towns. The scale of this intensive 24–7 blanket of security operations beggars the imagination. In the year prior to the Tet Offensive, for example, III MAF units conducted 421,496 small unit operations, accounting for approximately eight thousand enemy killed (33 percent of the total during that time frame).[45] During the same period, psychological operations convinced 2,539 enemy to surrender to allied forces; 5 percent of those defectors joined American units as scouts to fight against their former communist comrades.[46]

The diversity of III MAF's civic action programs complemented the scale of its security actions. In December 1967 alone civil affairs teams issued 227 tons of food, sixty-six tons of cement, seven tons of soap, four tons of clothing, and 2,768 school supply kits, completing distribution of these educational materials to every eligible child in I Corps. Medical and dental specialists treated 142,171 Vietnamese patients that month, and engineers completed forty-seven construction projects, including wells, clinics, schools, farm improvements, and a police station.[47] Civil affairs detachments also helped Vietnamese authorities resettle refugees driven from their homes by the fighting. These acts of benevolence were intended to convince the Vietnamese, especially rural peasants, that the United States was an ally, not an occupier, and that the Republic of Vietnam's government deserved backing.[48] Despite the extensive security, psychological, and civil affairs activities by the end of 1967, however, less than a month later the enemy managed to clandestinely infiltrate a division into Hue and launch widespread attacks across I Corps. Humanitarian assistance and development had not fostered improved security conditions.

As the war intensified in 1968 and 1969, the MAF expanded its pacification campaign along parallel tracks. Territorial security and civil affairs operations grew larger and more sophisticated. The main effort, however, shifted to the CORDS program established in May 1967. Civilians ran the program in I Corps and reported directly to the MAF commander, thereby putting most pacification programs under the military's control for the first time. Perhaps Westmoreland acceded to the new arrangement because it allowed him to subcontract a mission that he did not prioritize. Phillip B. Davidson, the MACV G-2, observed that Westmoreland treated pacification as a "stepchild." The official Marine history hints at a similar dynamic in III MAF, since Cushman did not exhibit the same zeal for pacification that Walt had, but such interpretations overstate the case.[49] Both Westmoreland and Cushman profited from having a single touchpoint to coordinate local governance, economic development, territorial security forces, psychological operations, police programs, refugee resettlement, attacks on VCI, and assessment of these varied operations.

CORDS, though organizationally unwieldy, proved effective in focusing command attention and resources on "the other war." At the end of 1969, I Corps reported more than half a million People's Self-Defense Force militia (half of whom were trained and 15 percent of whom were armed); 144 new Popular Forces platoons formed and trained; a Phoenix program meeting its goals of communist infrastructure reduction (more than five thousand VC cadre for the year); 336 Revolutionary Development cadre active; 91 percent of hamlet and village official jobs filled; more than three thousand village-level construction projects completed; and a refugee count of 169,000 (still high but reduced by 75 percent since the beginning of the year).[50] These statistics reflect the impact of the programs CORDS managed in I Corps, yet oddly neither III MAF nor FMFPAC referenced the organization responsible for overseeing pacification in their monthly command synopses. With or without command recognition, CORDS gradually undercut the Vietcong's position in I Corps. By 1970 III MAF's HES reports reflected 94 percent of the population in I Corps living under areas controlled by the South Vietnamese government.[51]

The Combined Action Program, working with Popular Forces to protect the region's villages, logically fit into the CORDS portfolio. Yet III MAF refused to allow its premier small wars force—the only one of its kind in South Vietnam—to fall under CORDS's direction despite Ambassador Robert W. Komer's initial desire to control the program.[52] Regardless which headquarters it reported to, CAP stands as one of the conflict's most innovative counterinsurgency creations. It developed territorial security forces that became the most efficient and least expensive fighters in Saigon's armed forces. By the end of the MAF's tour in I Corps, Regional and Popular Forces units represented 51 percent of the RVN's security forces, suffered 60 percent of the South's combat deaths, accounted for 33 percent of the enemy's battle casualties, and cost only 4 percent of Saigon's total security budget.[53]

The MAF's program to hone this untapped capacity developed from the bottom up, the brainchild of infantry officers securing Phu Bai in the first summer of the Marines' tenure.[54] Walt quickly recognized the concept's potential and spread CAP throughout I Corps. This innovation grew from seven combined platoons in December 1965 to 114 platoons four years later. The force—barely over twenty-one hundred Marines and sailors by the end of 1969—conducted that year around their assigned villages 145,000 mini operations, three-quarters of which transpired at night. This web of local security actions claimed 1,938 enemy killed and 425 prisoners, representing 6 percent of III MAF's claimed KIA tally for the year.[55] Operational records and assessments indicated that CAP platoons patrolled more, and to more lethal effect, than Popular Forces units without integrated Marines. Popular Forces in CAPs also proved less likely to desert.[56]

Despite its achievements, the CAP during this period drew mixed reviews from commanders and senior staff officers. Opponents asserted that putting Americans in every village unsustainably taxed manpower. They also disliked having to coordinate operations around the combined platoons' village-size sectors. Finally, they resented having to come to the rescue of units big enough to start fights but too small to finish them.[57] All these complaints underscored a calculus of operational risk versus gain. Small units were more vulnerable, and thus coordination with nearby joint and combined conventional forces remained a requirement.

Putting a detachment of Marines into each of I Corps' villages would have required about five hundred squads—an infantry division's worth of manpower and seven times more than III MAF invested in the program at its 1970 peak. Yet the goal was not simultaneous coverage of all villages but rather a sequential tutelage that left Popular Forces platoons able to protect their villages without Marine assistance. Once a Popular Forces platoon became self-sufficient, the CAP would move on to a new village. Whatever the naysayers' criticisms, the enemy saw CAPs as a problem worth eradicating. In the three months leading up to the Tet Offensive, CAPs absorbed 49 percent of the attacks in I Corps. In 1967 these small units, representing just 2 percent of the MAF's manpower, received 17 percent of communist attacks. In 1968 they endured 20 percent of NVA/VC assaults.[58]

Perhaps noting the enemy's attacks on an effective counterinsurgency initiative, each of the MAF commanders supported the CAP program despite its detractors. In 1969 General Nickerson created the Combined Action Force, controlling three subordinate groups, as a separate command that reported directly to his deputy commander.[59] With the corps headquarters' support, the CAPs persevered until the Marines departed Vietnam. They gradually deactivated as the MAF's area of operations declined in 1970, but some remained in the field in the spring of 1971, among the last of the diminishing Marine forces.

No war-winning silver bullet emerged among the various III MAF pacification programs and techniques. Food denial operations, raids, ambushes, cordon-and-search tactics, intensive patrolling, reconnaissance and surveillance efforts, defensive screens, site security, psychological operations, intelligence networks, informants, and police work combined to whittle away at the strength of the armed guerrillas and their shadow government structure. These counterinsurgency "sticks" wielded by regular and irregular allied forces complemented "carrots" such as medical care, refugee resettlement, local self-government, agricultural assistance, land reform, and education initiatives. Together they gradually undermined the Vietcong's power and persuasion. In the 1968 Tet Offensive the South Vietnamese people did not abandon their government and rally to the NVA/VC aggressors. ARVN and its territorial forces did not give up or change sides. Local, regional, and national governments did not collapse. Communist revolutionary warfare, though persistent, failed utterly in spurring a mass uprising in the 1968 campaigns, the 1972 Easter Offensive, or even in the final, and militarily effective, 1975 conventional invasion. In each case the vast majority of South Vietnamese civilians fled their Northern assailants rather than greeting them as liberators. These outcomes, throughout and even after the MAF's service in I Corps, revealed a resilient but still unsuccessful Southern insurgency.

Progress in the pacification campaign nonetheless proved slow and inconsistent. In 1965 III MAF initiated most of the tactics mentioned above, but it took time to orient to the new environment, learn the ways of its ally, and understand the nature of the communists' threats.

In 1966 the Buddhist Struggle Movement and the social, political, and security chaos it unleashed disrupted pacification's momentum. In 1967 the North Vietnamese Army stepped up its conventional attacks throughout I Corps, crowned the following year by the Tet Offensives. The year 1969, marked by allied counterattacks on both conventional and counterinsurgent fronts, proved nearly as bitterly contested as 1968 but still entailed significant progress in the pacification realm. As the MAF's role receded geographically to focus only on Quang Nam Province during 1970–1971, the regional insurgency remained potent. The Vietcong political presence and security threat endured. In December 1970 Saigon's control over I Corps' population ranged from 93 percent in Quang Tri Province to 66 percent in Quang Ngai. CORDS rated Quang Nam Province, the Marine sector, just 68 percent secure three months before III MAF departed in 1971. Analysts estimated that four thousand members of the VC shadow government still operated there.[60] In March 1971 I Corps endured 399 terror attacks, the most recorded in a single month since the American intervention.[61] Six years of grinding attrition, exerted and complemented by a variety of pacification techniques and programs, had decimated but not destroyed the persistent insurgent menace.

Assessing III MAF's Operational Response

To solve, manage, or mitigate its operational problems, III MAF shouldered the three main missions detailed above: build ARVN up, keep the NVA out, and keep the VC down. The allies had to attain any two of those objectives to win the war in I Corps. Strong South Vietnamese security forces and a diminished insurgency promised a sustainable stalemate despite a continued NVA cross-border threat. Similarly, with competent South Vietnamese security forces and enemy regulars that could not penetrate the border, even a robust local insurgency remained manageable. Finally, if the allies decisively defeated both regular and irregular communist forces, then ARVN's short-term performance would not prove vital. None of these three conditions, after six years of effort, pertained when III MAF departed Vietnam in 1971.

This outcome prevailed despite I Corps serving as the stage for the US Army's and Marine Corps' best units, strongest forces, and most promising operations. Sophisticated intelligence programs, heliborne mobility, search-and-destroy tactics, saturation patrolling, cordon-and-search maneuvers, raids on communist base camps, amphibious assaults, combined operations, mentoring village security forces, extensive use of combined arms, clever psychological warfare, and the most ambitious civil affairs program ever employed failed to win the war in I Corps. Three reasons, each associated with an essential task, explain why.

Building ARVN Up

The South Vietnamese army's I Corps was not ready by 1971 to defeat the NVA without American assistance. The MAF's mostly army-led Advisory Group helped I Corps become the finest of Saigon's four corps. Its subordinate commands consistently ranked at the top of ARVN's ten divisions and featured some of its best tactical leaders. Yet I Corps remained a weak corps-level headquarters with a poor tactical commander, as General Lam demonstrated in Laos in 1971 and again during the 1972 Easter Offensive. The Vietnamization process initiated important improvements in ARVN's I Corps' size and capability, but the new equipment and forces proved too little and too late for the South Vietnamese to assimilate and employ effectively without continued US advisory, fires, and logistic support.

III MAF was culpable in three ways for ARVN's subsequent tactical collapse in I Corps: It did not develop its counterpart Vietnamese corps headquarters' ability to command and control the campaign in MR 1; it did not practice combined operations enough at the division, task force, regiment, and even battalion levels; and it did not press MACV with recommendations on how and how much I Corps should grow. The first oversight was not surprising given III MAF's reluctance to manage its own corps-level campaign more directly. Admittedly, I Corps' greatest tests as a corps command post occurred after III MAF was no longer responsible for its performance. But the Marines had five years to develop staff proficiency in the I Corps headquarters as well as General Lam's individual command skills before the 1971 raid into Laos revealed their deficiencies.[62]

The second error—insufficient combined operations—was a trend that extended across multiple commanders and unit levels. Allied units did fight alongside one another on the battlefield, but too few US Marine and army leaders saw those operations as a primary way to develop their ARVN counterparts' proficiency. Combined operations were seldom conducted as training missions that deserved as much emphasis as the tactical outcome of the current engagement. In 1968 and 1969 the 101st Airborne Division did some excellent combined-operations work within I Corps. The best of these efforts, especially in the post-Tet period, entailed close cooperation at the battalion level and integrated territorial security forces in cordon operations that destroyed entire communist units. Such decisive tactical outcomes were a rarity in Vietnam, and in I Corps, throughout most of the conflict.[63] The 1st and 3rd Marine Divisions missed many opportunities, especially during their first three years in country, to conduct similar closely integrated tactical operations.

The third mistake—concerning ARVN's capability—entailed campaign-level shortsightedness. In 1968 ARVN deployed just one-third of the total allied ground combat power in III MAF's sector. By that point it was apparent that ARVN's I Corps had to grow in strength, as well as in firepower and logistic support, if it ever hoped to stand alone. Even with continued American advisory, logistic, and air support, I Corps needed more troops to defend the region, as the 1972 Easter Offensive demonstrated. While these decisions ultimately resided in Saigon, the MAF had a responsibility to make recommendations on how much ground combat force I Corps required to protect the northern five provinces. Consumed by its own tactical challenges, III MAF's staff and commanders ignored this crucial dialogue and lost the chance to positively influence the decision. The Marines' failure to shape ARVN's I Corps' development at the national, regional, and local levels, combined with the precipitous American withdrawal from Vietnam, left I Corps unready to face independently its internal and external foes.

Keeping the NVA Out

The second reason III MAF attained only a tactical stalemate rather than a clear-cut victory was its inability to keep the NVA out of I Corps. Here, too, the challenge rested partly on policy decisions made above the corps level, especially the prohibition of raids on NVA sanctuaries just across the Laos and North Vietnam borders. But the problem was bigger than that. With respect to the conflict's conventional operations, III MAF concurred with MACV's reliance on search-and-destroy tactics. Most of these operations entailed heliborne sweeps and raids. Their purpose was to defeat enemy incursions and inflict more casualties than Hanoi could bear. The fights that ensued bloodied but seldom destroyed enemy formations, left the initiative in the communists' hands (because they could retreat to and later return from those cross-border sanctuaries), and devastated I Corps' land while turning nine hundred thousand of its people into refugees.[64] In short, the allies' mobile defense did not protect the region. This conclusion was apparent even before the 1968 Tet Offensive.

Traditional tactics offered two ways to stymie NVA invasions: area or mobile defenses.[65] The first featured static fortified positions linked together in a continuous chain of strongpoints, obstacles, and sensors, backed by local counterattack forces and supporting fires. The alternative way to keep North Vietnamese troops at bay was the mobile defense favored by MACV and III MAF. This approach allowed enemy units to cross the border before attacking them and forcing them to retreat. Two problems undermined the MAF's preferred mobile method of defense: It did not protect the Republic of Vietnam's territorial integrity, and it generated high allied casualties.

Examples of the mobile defense's deficiencies occurred early and often. In the spring of 1966, the NVA's seizure of the A Shau Valley and the MAF's battle with the 21st NVA Regiment outside Quang Ngai City underscored the danger of waiting for enemy formations to come into I Corps to fight them. In the A Shau battleground, superior forces overran small, allied border outposts. No MAF counterattack ejected the enemy from the valley—an important approach route and base area supporting attacks on Hue and Da Nang. In the Quang Ngai City events, a four-day battle claimed six hundred enemy dead but cost 526 allied casualties. These engagements, and many others like them, demonstrated how difficult and costly it was to prevent NVA infiltration. These frustrating affairs also established III MAF's inability to capture or wipe out enemy light infantry formations operating well inside I Corps.[66]

Such costly, incomplete victories became the pattern, as the operational records reveal. Two additional cases illustrate the point. In July 1966 elements of the NVA 324B Division infiltrated across the DMZ and established supply dumps and fighting positions in the foothills surrounding the Ngan River Valley two miles south of the border. Five Marine battalions choppered into the area to drive the enemy back. In Operation HASTINGS, the largest of the war to that point, eight thousand Marines and three thousand ARVN troops fought an equal number of NVA regulars. The allies lifted six hundred troops daily with a total of ten thousand helicopter flights, employed 1,677 bombing sorties, and fired 34,500 artillery shells. Each side lost six to seven hundred casualties. The battered enemy division withdrew into North Vietnam to replenish its ranks.[67]

In the first five months of 1967 a series of operations code-named PRAIRIE scoured the same area. They featured intensive use of combined arms and tough infantry combat at close quarters. Despite the battlefields' location inside South Vietnam, most of the engagements required Marines to assault NVA ensconced in quickly prepared field fortifications. The North Vietnamese, by American estimates, lost three thousand killed, but III MAF also suffered 552 dead and 3,467 wounded.[68] Again, the Marines "won," but the butcher's bill was extravagant. The vaunted mobile defense proved both porous and costly.

III MAF does not seem to have recognized that its emphasis on the assault, whatever its short-term battlefield success, had long-term political consequences. Tactical aggression was a key feature of the Marines' institutional culture, inculcated by training and a mythology of glorious attacks from Belleau Wood to Suribachi. They disliked defending fixed positions and, by their own admission, performed that sometimes necessary function poorly. The MAF's objection to MACV's DMZ barrier scheme highlights the ample evidence. But the alternative mobile defense ensured that allied infantry would repeatedly cross the deadly last fifty yards against entrenched enemies. Hundreds of mini-Tarawas resulted.[69] The number of III MAF casualties averaged more than one thousand per month in the first thirty-four months of the war.[70] High mobility operations, dependent on helicopters and attack airplanes, also took a heavy toll in aircraft. In 1966 alone III MAF lost 22 percent of its 234 Marine helicopters and 25 percent of its 201 fixed-wing aircraft.[71]

Mobile defenses blunted and turned back NVA incursions, but employing a tactical offense in support of a strategic defense guaranteed a steep cost while ceding the operational initiative to the enemy. And while Marine mobile operations promised local tactical initiative, they never prevented the enemy from determining where and when NVA formations would enter South Vietnam. Although it seems counterintuitive, a positional defense offered better prospects because it aims to prevent the enemy from crossing the border to begin with. In that scenario, Hanoi would retain the initiative to attack where and when it chose along the defended line, but its troops would no longer be infiltrating through unobserved and uncontested avenues. Instead they would crash up against prepared defenses the way they did at Khe Sanh in 1968. In that kind of battle, tactical advantage shifts to the defenders. The enemy must concentrate to penetrate, making his formations vulnerable to massed fires and counterattack. For a denial strategy to work, of course, the defensive line had to extend from the South China Sea across the DMZ and through Laos to the Mekong River border with Thailand.

In I Corps, however, III MAF championed the mobile defense based on a strategy of punishment rather than an area defense based on a strategy of denial. Allied losses mounted. By September 1967 the Marine Commandant and Fleet Marine Force, Pacific commander recognized that the Corps was suffering too many casualties along the DMZ.[72] Throughout I Corps, it was clear by the end of that year that Marine operational art was working to win the battles but not the war. The years 1968 and 1969—bloodier yet—only reinforced the verdict.[73]

In the conventional realm of its trifold mission, III MAF exhibited several deficiencies. It provided scant tactical direction to its divisions; held close its aviation assets rather than sharing them generously with allied forces; employed no corps-level engineer or counterfire command; remained reluctant to move US Army assets it controlled; scrambled the unit integrity of its own regiments and divisions; and grew desensitized to multiple NVA units of battalion, regimental, and even division size homesteading in I Corps. All these issues contributed to a composite failure to protect the region's territory and population from NVA attacks. The primary culprit, however, was a mobile defense that could not, even when conducted by nine allied divisions, prevent continuous enemy incursions or clear all the communist conventional forces that operated in I Corps.

Keeping the VC Down

Of the three primary tasks, III MAF did its best work against the Vietcong. The Marines emphasized the task from the beginning. They initiated a variety of operations, including small unit patrols and ambushes, civic action, humanitarian assistance, psychological warfare, and of course the Combined Action Program. Estimated Vietcong combatant strength in I Corps decreased by two-thirds, from forty-five to fifteen thousand, between December 1966 and December 1970.[74] Yet Vietcong political cadre, as well as conventional and guerrilla troops, proved difficult to eliminate completely. Despite III MAF's focus on counterinsurgency and its belief that the small war campaign represented the key to victory in Vietnam, the Marines struggled with two critical aspects of an effective operational response: They did not develop a precise way to target the VC shadow government, and they did not advocate a larger militia to improve territorial security. Oddly, both shortcomings flowed in part from the MAF's most effective small war innovation: the Combined Action Program.

The MAF deserves credit for recognizing and acting immediately upon an insight that MACV did not: hamlet security represented an essential element of the small war campaign. More important, III MAF's commanders dedicated force structure taken from other Marine units, up to a regiment in strength, to stand up and expand the new regional program. Marine leaders warranted, but did not receive, equal credit for their conventional units' extensive saturation patrolling to clear villages of guerrillas. This was a level of effort US Army commands in other regions seldom duplicated, especially during the war's first three years. For the Marines, small unit patrolling became a major effort that they captured and touted in their monthly operations summaries.[75] And yet Westmoreland and his staff largely ignored and downplayed III MAF's significant, early, and persistent counterguerrilla achievements.

CAP, III MAF's most celebrated innovation, earned mixed reviews during and after the war. Observers disagreed on its potential to improve rural security nationwide. Proponents saw it as a model worthy of emulation and more resources. Opponents deemed it too manpower-intensive for any but limited implementation. Yet Vietnamese village and district leaders strongly supported the CAPs and valued the increased protection their presence provided. That security, however, also relied on ready access to the fire support, medevac, and reinforcement capabilities of nearby conventional units.

Three flaws tainted the CAP's otherwise impressive operational record. First, Vietnamese officials did not fill their Popular Forces manpower quotients, so the ratio of Marines to local troops never exceeded 1:2 rather than the 1:3 proportion the MAF considered essential.[76] This shortfall in locally assigned manpower reduced the combined platoons' operational impact. Second, the process suffered from the slows, another way of saying that producing self-sufficient village security forces took too long. Over the six-year course of the program ninety-three CAPs moved on to new villages because they had developed Popular Forces platoons that could operate independently.[77] Yet too many South Vietnamese Popular Forces units never developed the technical and tactical proficiency required to stand alone without the aid of Marine communications, firepower, and fighting skills. Even when they did attain the necessary skills, the slow process prevented more than half of I Corps villages from ever receiving CAP security assistance. In the end the program, like American assistance writ large, ran out of time before it achieved its desired goals.

Both CAP advocates and skeptics have overlooked the program's third and most significant shortfall: it failed to destroy the Vietcong political infrastructure. This task—listed first among six in the 1968 CAP Standard Operational Procedure—mirrored the primary mission of the Popular Forces that the CAPs supported.[78] The CAP's own operational reports paid almost no attention to this priority task. Its monthly summaries did not consistently track progress on this crucial metric.[79]

The communist shadow government functioned as the insurgency's operational center of gravity.[80] As the local manifestation of the Vietnamese Communist Party, it controlled political and military activities across the South. The Vietcong infrastructure motivated, recruited, supplied, disciplined, and directed the guerrillas who protected and projected its local party leaders' dominion. Marine planners and commanders knew full well, from both classified and unclassified studies, the critical role the VCI played.[81] Yet CAP—III MAF's primary instrument to identify and uproot the shadow government—made little discernable headway on that most important task.[82] A more tailored counter-infrastructure system, the Phoenix program initiated in 1967, used police and military intelligence methods to locate VC cadre. Phoenix also fielded the most efficient special action units targeting the shadow government between 1968 and 1971, but Marine commanders knew little about Phoenix and supported it less.[83] Eventually MACV distanced itself from Phoenix because of bad publicity, a case where communist propaganda helped neutralize the effectiveness of a program that was endangering the VCI's control of the rural population.

The historian Mark Moyar argues that the aggregate impact of widespread small unit conventional actions, the improved security created by Regional and Popular Forces (including those assisted by CAPs), intelligence-driven raids by Phoenix strike teams, and the steady toll of the Chieu Hoi defection program eventually eroded VCI numbers. Together these allied security measures gradually diminished the Vietcong's ability to access and control villages. Those shadow government cadre who survived became more vulnerable and began moving out of the villages to remote bases where communist regular troops could protect them. The wartime RVN and US statistics tracking VCI agents are not reliable. While the exact numbers are elusive, the trends are clear: the 1970 VCI was less formidable than its 1965 counterpart.[84]

Ironically, it was not the NVA but the VC's guerrillas and shadow government who suffered most from attrition. Despite its degradation over time, the VCI remained surprisingly resilient in I Corps beyond III MAF's tenure. Increased Marine support for the Phoenix program offered the best way to do even more damage to the regional shadow government.

The second missing link in III MAF's initial counterinsurgency construct was a local militia. The Marines' pacification campaign rightly emphasized protection of I Corps' citizens but lacked one of the most effective ways to achieve it. No amount of external security, whether provided by American or South Vietnamese forces, could safeguard all of I Corps civilians from insurgent threats and violence. The people, when armed and motivated, provided the best protection of their own interests. Comprehensive territorial security required more than regular troops, full-time Regional Forces, and part-time Popular Forces soldiers assisted by CAPs. It required a volunteer militia. Unfortunately, Saigon did not trust its rural peasants enough to take this step until it formed the People's Self-Defense Force in the aftermath of the 1968 Tet Offensive. Within eighteen months seventy-three thousand PSDF militia helped guard I Corps. But five years had been lost.[85] The MAF could not mandate the national decision to form a militia, but it should have recognized that only an armed citizenry could provide the blanket of security that conventionally trained soldiers and police forces could never hope to match. Marine leaders should have pushed earlier, through MACV, for an I Corps militia program.

During the Marine phase of the war (1965–1967), III MAF primarily employed CAP and County Fairs (large unit cordon-and-search operations) to find and destroy the VCI. Neither program efficiently targeted the shadow government. Meanwhile CAP exerted an enormous tax on the MAF's organizational energy. It consumed senior leaders' attention and left little prospect for alternate counter-VCI programs. The MAF missed the opportunity to develop sooner a program like Phoenix, which the CIA initiated, and CORDS later managed for MACV and its regional commands. Similarly, CAP's focus on Popular Forces, while productive, also tended to preclude III MAF's equally strong support for a broad-based militia like the PSDF. Both Phoenix and the PSDF were essential components of a comprehensive small war campaign. They came to I Corps eventually thanks to sponsors outside III MAF, but three years were lost before the allies reaped the operational advantages of an intelligence-driven counter-VCI program and a self-defense militia.

Operational Style

III MAF's operational repertoire reflected its institutional comfort zone. As a naval corps–level headquarters, it applied tactics and techniques that Marine Corps experience, doctrine, training, and culture had prepared its forces to execute. Among its three primary missions, the MAF emphasized pacification. It engaged in conventional combat, including preemptive strikes, when and to the extent necessary to block NVA incursions, protect the counterinsurgency campaign, and satisfy MACV. To run the ARVN advisory command, III MAF relied on American soldiers to train and assist their South Vietnamese counterparts. This marriage produced the most combat-effective ARVN corps and regular army divisions in Saigon's fighting force. MACV, however, largely ignored territorial security forces until CORDS began to stress them as a key ingredient of the pacification campaign. In the interim III MAF filled the void in I Corps by developing the Popular Forces with its CAP program, which continued to grow even after MACV and Saigon began to invest more resources in Regional, Popular, and People's Self-Defense Forces.

The MAF's tactics relied on several proven methods. Marines exercised their amphibious capability, though with gradually diminishing results, throughout the conflict. The MAF stressed combined arms, especially the integration of artillery, naval gunfire, and aviation fires, at all levels. US Army and Marine units used fires to suppress and destroy enemy infantry when they fought from field fortifications. In this style of fighting III MAF mirrored US combat norms in other regions of Vietnam as well as longer-term trends in the American way of war. Finally, as the conflict continued, the Marines in I Corps developed an increasing reliance on helicopters. Marines pioneered vertical assault techniques in the Korean conflict, but it was in Vietnam that the US Army and Marine Corps honed air assault methods and came to rely on them extensively for much of their maneuver, fires, and logistic support.

III MAF conducted no corps-level ground combat operations in Vietnam. This reflected the fact that the war was chiefly a smaller unit fight. Infantry battalions served as the primary ground maneuver force; their rifle companies and platoons did most of the fighting and dying. But the lack of corps-level operations in Military Region 1 also comported with Marines' perspective on warfighting. Organizationally, the Marine Corps stressed and valued actions at the regimental level and below. Seldom did prewar planning and field exercises include division or corps operations. In I Corps the Marines conducted no operations under direct division command, much less MAF command. Instead Marines employed ad hoc task force headquarters, under brigadier generals and built around regimental staffs, that were not initially organized, trained, or equipped to control large unit maneuvers. Equivalent army corps–level headquarters did control some field operations. In 1967 these included II Field Force's CEDAR FALLS and JUNCTION CITY operations, followed in 1968 by that headquarters' QUYET THANG and TOAN THANG. The US Army's XXIV Corps also conducted Operation DELAWARE in the A Shau Valley in 1968.[86] While none of the army's corps-level operations proved decisive in the sense of permanently destroying enemy formations, several seriously damaged their foes.

Massing overwhelming combat power at a regional level was one of the responsibilities of corps commanders, but the idea that they should aggressively shift regiments and brigades, even temporarily, within I Corps to concentrate combat power on discrete targets did not occur or appeal to III MAF's commanders in Vietnam. The Hue example detailed in chapter 3, when III MAF missed an opportunity to end the Hue battle sooner and more decisively, illustrates the cost of failing to mass larger forces. MAF commanders did not think of the MAF as a warfighting headquarters and appeared more comfortable playing small ball, that is to say, providing subordinate divisions with a set of resources but not orchestrating their maneuver and fires at a larger tactical level.

The war on the ground constituted a strategic defensive, protecting South Vietnam from NVA incursions and VC depredations while limiting US attacks outside Saigon's territory (apart from the brief 1970 Cambodian raid) to air forces and small-scale special force missions. Within this overarching operational framework, III MAF employed defensive techniques along the DMZ and around cities, bases, logistic sites, and transportation nodes. But the Marines preferred more aggressive offensive tactics inside I Corps, opting for mobile rather than static or positional defenses when possible. Still, Westmoreland believed the Marine enclaves tied down too many US troops guarding the people, protecting key locales, and chasing guerrillas rather than finding and attacking communist conventional forces. This difference in operational emphasis contributed to Westmoreland's low opinion of the MAF's ability, and willingness, to capably conduct effective larger unit operations as the test of Tet loomed. This assessment in turn led the MACV commander to insert his deputy into the operational chain

of command and then transition control of the war in the northern
I Corps sector to a provisional army corps that became XXIV Corps.

Ironically, the balanced Marine small war/big war approach that
frustrated Westmoreland provided the template, often lauded by subsequent analysts, for MACV operations under General Creighton
Abrams. His One War concept reflected the operational style III MAF
had employed since 1965. These methods still included conventional
combat to push back the enemy's regulars but placed greater emphasis
on pacification to expand the territory under Saigon's control and increased the focus on training and equipping South Vietnamese security
forces. Scholarship in the twenty-first century has highlighted more
continuity than change in the mix of operations conducted by Westmoreland and Abrams.[87] Conditions between 1969 and 1971—especially
Hanoi's decision to curtail larger attacks in favor of more political agi-
tation, guerrilla warfare, and acts of terror while the allies gradually
withdrew—enabled and required MACV to place more prominence on
counterinsurgency tactics. In I Corps, the shift in emphasis, however
slight in practice, proved less stark than in other regions because of
the strong small war foundation laid by III MAF in the early years of
the American intervention. The Marines' relentless small unit security operations during the first half of their Vietnam service, coupled
with the grievous losses the VC suffered during the 1968 Tet Offensives, enabled Abrams's later efforts to build atop a firmer foundation
in I Corps than would have existed without the MAF's earlier focus
on pacification.

Conclusion

The Vietnam War provided the Marine Corps its first combat test
of MAGTF doctrine. The emphasis on air-ground integrity triggered
parochial service conflicts with Seventh Air Force and MACV that
led to the MAF's loss of operational control over its fixed-wing strike
and reconnaissance aircraft. Simultaneously, the doctrine's lack of focus on traditional corps-level operations left III MAF unprepared to
command five US divisions, a large but manageable corps-level span of
control, when the Tet Offensive drew two additional US Army divisions into the region.[88]

Beyond the MAF's miscues with aviation support and large ground
unit maneuvers, its operational record featured both accomplishments
and failures. III MAF and its ARVN allies kept NVA units mostly

out of the populated zones, aside from the 1968 Tet Offensive's urban assaults. In the countryside, the Marines' never-ending small unit battles against guerrillas eventually eroded the armed strength of the Vietcong to a level ARVN could manage. Despite these achievements, however, MAF operations ultimately did not accomplish the three most critical security tasks: keeping NVA units out of I Corps' territory altogether; destroying the insurgency's shadow government; and developing South Vietnamese security forces that could independently withstand both the NVA and VC. This mixed scorecard underscores that MAGTF operations, emphasizing combat at the regimental level and below, succeeded tactically but failed operationally.

Marine Major General William R. Collins (*right*) arrives in Da Nang on 17 May 1965. As the first of III MAF's commanders in Vietnam, he served only a few weeks before passing the colors to Major General Lewis W. Walt. Archive Branch, Marine Corps History Division, Quantico, VA.

Major General Lew Walt talks with Marines of Regimental Landing Team 4 shortly after taking command of III MAF in June 1965. Walt was the most junior two-star general in the Corps when he assumed simultaneous command of 3rd Marine Division and III MAF in Vietnam. Archive Branch, Marine Corps History Division, Quantico, VA.

10 December 1965. General Walt confers with the commanding officer of Echo Company, 2nd Battalion, 7th Marines during the ill-fated Operation HARVEST MOON. Walt, a "muddy boots" general, frequently visited his units in the immediate aftermath of a major action. In this operation he sacked a subordinate Marine general for cause, the only such instance in III MAF's six-year tenure in Vietnam. Archive Branch, Marine Corps History Division, Quantico, VA.

The commander of ARVN's I Corps, Major General Hoang Xuan Lam, with Lieutenant General Walt in 1966. Walt, and all subsequent MAF commanders, enjoyed good relations with Lam. Despite five years of Marine and army mentorship, however, Lam failed to perform effectively as a corps commander during ARVN's 1971 invasion of Laos and the NVA's 1972 Easter Offensive. Archive Branch, Marine Corps History Division, Quantico, VA.

Marine Lieutenant General Victor H. Krulak receives a brief in the field from the commander of the Special Landing Force on operations ashore, 7 May 1967. Krulak held administrative command over Marine forces in Vietnam, but he shared his operational advice more than MACV and III MAF commanders preferred. Archive Branch, Marine Corps History Division, Quantico, VA.

16 July 1967. Marine Brigadier General John R. Chaisson confers with General Abrams (Deputy MACV), Major General Hochmuth (CG, 3rd Marine Division), and Lieutenant General Cushman. Chaisson served as the III MAF G-3 and then as a trusted aide to General Westmoreland at MACV. His candid insights into both headquarters, revealed in a constant stream of letters to his wife, provide some of the most valuable information on army–Marine command relationships in the first half of the Vietnam War. Archive Branch, Marine Corps History Division, Quantico, VA.

10 August 1967. General Wallace M. Greene, Jr. (*left*), Commandant of the Marine Corps, talks with General Westmoreland (*right*), MACV commander, while Lieutenant General Cushman listens. Cushman commanded the MAF from 1967 to 1969. His rocky relationship with Westmoreland led in 1968 to the MAF ceding control of the ground war along the DMZ to a subordinate US Army corps headquarters while the US Air Force gained control of Marine fixed-wing strike and reconnaissance aircraft in I Corps. Archive Branch, Marine Corps History Division, Quantico, VA.

11 September 1967. Lieutenant General Cushman with III MAF's primary staff officers. Shown here are two major generals, one brigadier general, thirteen colonels, three US Navy captains, three lieutenant colonels, seven majors, one sergeant major, and one civilian political adviser. At its height the entire III MAF staff numbered approximately one thousand. Archive Branch, Marine Corps History Division, Quantico, VA.

Lieutenant General Herman Nickerson, Jr., assumed command of III MAF in March 1969 and held the reins for one year. Like his predecessors, Nickerson possessed a distinguished combat record from previous wars. He presided over the start of the Marine drawdown in I Corps. Archive Branch, Marine Corps History Division, Quantico, VA.

Lieutenant General Hoang Xuan Lam (*left*), Commanding General, I Corps. General Cao Van Vien (*center left*), Chairman of the Joint General Staff, ARVN Forces. Lieutenant General Richard G. Stillwell (*center right*), commanding US Army XXIV Corps. Major General Ngo Quang Truong (*right*), Commanding General, 1st ARVN Div. They are at the Phu Bai airport during General Cao Van Vien's visit on 4 April 1969. Vien was one of South Vietnam's best military leaders, while Truong was its finest combat commander, recapturing Hue during the Tet Offensive and driving the NVA back in I Corps during the Easter Offensive. Archive Branch, Marine Corps History Division, Quantico, VA.

Marine Lieutenant General Keith B. McCutcheon commanded III MAF from March to December 1970, when cancer cut short his tour and shortly thereafter claimed his life. This renowned aviator, in some ways the most intriguing of the MAF's commanders in Vietnam, developed World War II close air support techniques for US Army units in the Philippines and introduced innovative helicopter tactics in Korea. McCutcheon was a strong candidate to become Commandant of the Marine Corps had sickness not forced his early retirement. Archive Branch, Marine Corps History Division, Quantico, VA.

Marine Lieutenant General Donn J. Robertson in front of the III MAF logo in Da Nang. He served as the final III MAF commander in Vietnam from December 1970 to April 1971. Robertson's brief tour, like that of his predecessor, focused on redeployment to Okinawa. Archive Branch, Marine Corps History Division, Quantico, VA.

5

III MAF Personnel and Logistics

No "L" for logistics graced the MAGTF acronym. Yet expeditionary operations, the Marines' forte, demanded special expertise in supply, transport, maintenance, engineering, and medical support. Unlike campaigns occurring in theaters with modern ports and airfields, developed roads and rail lines, and strong agricultural and manufacturing sectors, military operations conducted by early entry forces in less developed areas put a high premium on come-as-you-are capabilities. The US Navy and the Marine Corps, designed to project power into austere and contested regions, thus provided in 1965 an attractive option for MACV's mandate to move American military forces quickly into Vietnam. The Marines brought a relatively light logistical structure, optimized for short-duration, high-intensity combat. The navy furnished the logistical tether that enabled the landing forces to sustain operations ashore. Together they seemed tailor-made to protect Da Nang's air base, assist ARVN, and fight Vietcong guerrillas and main force units as required. As the missions in I Corps expanded over time, logistic support requirements grew apace. Within four years of their initial arrival, the navy and Marine logistics elements supporting III Marine Amphibious Force had increased twentyfold in size.

In this chapter I examine that growth, focusing on how III MAF adapted its organizational model and logistic processes to sustain its morphing missions. Difficulties emerged that challenged the Marines' existing and preferred practices for combat service support. Some of the problems were self-inflicted, underscoring my claim that Marine organizational and leadership choices diminished the MAF's effectiveness. Some reflected challenges associated with Vietnam's operational environment and enemy initiatives. Others derived from Washington policy decisions. The MAF managed most of the logistic obstacles it encountered in ways that either prevented or minimized their impact on operations. The army and navy provided essential aspects of the burgeoning supply, medical, construction, and port/base operations capability. Perhaps surprising is that personnel, the most fundamental commodity of warfare, presented the most intractable dilemma. Equally unexpected, the US Navy's improvised land-based logistics organization provided superb support. In a similar cobbled-together manner, the Marines created a capable new corps-level construct for logistics by reconfiguring existing units. The resulting ad hoc naval logistics system sufficed for a static regional war but revealed that the MAF lacked sufficient organic capability to support multiple divisions.

Manpower

Lieutenant General Lewis Walt knew soon after arriving in 1965 that the MAF needed more troops to defend and pacify I Corps. Walt's initial force totaled approximately sixteen thousand Marines. Within three years that number had grown by a factor of more than five.[1] During the first four years of the American intervention, Marine Corps strength overall grew from 190,000 to 315,000 to feed the insatiable demand for more troops.[2] In 1966 Headquarters Marine Corps reestablished the 5th Division in California as a pool of trained reinforcements for III MAF. It subsequently deployed two of the new division's three infantry regiments to Vietnam. The number of Marines serving in I Corps peaked in 1968 at eighty-eight thousand, which included eight of twelve infantry regiments and one-fourth of the service's total manpower.[3] Filling the increasing demand for more men, while ensuring that those sent remained fully capable of fulfilling their combat duties, represented the most vexing of the MAF's logistic challenges.

The first Marine units that deployed to Vietnam had formed and trained together. This approach enhanced unit cohesion and simplified the planning and execution of combat deployments. American political leaders, however, sought to limit Vietnam's impact on the home front and thus preferred policies that kept total military manpower at the lowest possible levels. This decision mandated individual rotations because that approach more efficiently filled the ranks with a smaller aggregate service strength. In a unit rotation policy, to keep a single battalion or squadron in I Corps required a second unit of equal size training to replace the deployed command. Meanwhile, a third unit would be recovering from its recent turn in combat. In short, unit deployments required a total force at least three times the size of the one deployed in country. Thus, a MAF that fielded eighty-eight thousand Marines in I Corps and employed unit rotations required a total service strength of at least half a million men.[4] This manpower requirement necessitated a shift in personnel policy, initiated in September 1965, from unit to individual rotations. The new rule remained in place for the duration of the conflict.[5]

Mobilizing reserves offered another way to deal with the emerging manpower crisis. President Johnson decided not to call up the reserves in 1966, even though the Joint Chiefs, including General Wallace Greene, the Commandant, favored it.[6] President Johnson rejected reserve mobilization, like he rejected raising taxes to finance the conflict, because both underscored the war's growing costs, threatened his ambitious Great Society domestic agenda, and spurred increased domestic dissent.[7] Many historians have identified the failure to mobilize reserve forces as a primary cause of the personnel problems the US Army experienced in Vietnam.[8] In contrast, Marine personnel officers viewed employment of reserve forces as a mixed blessing. Although composed of better-educated and more experienced men than the newly enlisted active-duty force, the entire Organized Marine Reserve promised only forty-eight thousand men for a single, one-year deployment. By law, once activated, these troops owed no additional service obligation and could not be used again. Existing war plans envisioned mobilization of the entire reserve Marine component. When the Joint Staff suggested a partial reserve mobilization in 1968, Marine planners scrambled to devise ways to activate and deploy smaller portions of the reserve division/wing team. Because the reserve component was designed to provide a one-time-only augmentation, the new Commandant, General Leonard F. Chapman, Jr., agreed reluctantly to its use. Afterward the service would need a generation to rebuild its reserve. In a war with no end in sight, Chapman judged the playing of this personnel chip chancy. In the end the Defense Department elected to call no Marine reservists in 1968, so the Corps searched for other ways to supply III MAF with the men its responsibilities demanded.[9]

Although the Marines had resorted to conscription before, the service prided itself on attracting volunteers motivated to join an elite force. The threat of the draft itself, of course, inspired many of those who wished to control their own destiny to join the Marines, but it was not enough to meet the growing demand. Headquarters Marine Corps thus accepted 19,537 draftees as the service expanded from 231,000 to its new authorized strength of 286,000 in 1966. Two years later the Corps again accepted three allotments of draftees, totaling 7,702 men. In 1969 the Marines added 12,872 more men via nine small monthly draft calls. The Corps ended its dependence on conscription in February 1970, seven months after III MAF's Vietnam drawdown commenced. Not all those drafted served in Southeast Asia, and the entire complement of conscripted Marines represented less than 10 percent of the nearly half-million Marines who did deploy to Vietnam.[10] Without the draft, however, III MAF would not have been able to replace its losses.

Adjusting lengths of enlistment provided an even more important technique for ensuring a steady flow of manpower to the MAF. Paradoxically, shortening terms of service enabled more men to deploy overseas. Before the war Marines enlisted for a minimum of three years, with 80 percent of recruits signing on for four or more years. Two-year enlistments began in 1965 and grew to half of all enlistments by 1968. Because Defense Department policy required two years outside a war zone between combat deployments, even a four-year contract allowed only one thirteen-month Vietnam tour. Within two years of the MAF's entry into the war, most Marines had already deployed to Vietnam once. Since service end strengths were capped, the only way to get more men into theater was to shorten individual enlistments. Given five months required to train recruits followed by thirteen months in theater, the last six months of even a two-year contract represented wasted time from a manpower perspective. To free up those spaces for new Marines who could train and deploy sooner, the Marine Corps discharged seventy thousand men up to six months early in 1969. Three years into the war more than one-third of enlisted Marines had less than one year of service. Vietnam thus changed the composition of the Corps from a force characterized by long service and stable units to one of high turnover, unit instability, and limited individual experience.[11]

The Marines who served in III MAF also took on a different cast as the war progressed. The Defense Department launched Project 100,000 in October 1966. This program, designed to complement President Johnson's Great Society initiatives by providing jobs and training for less-qualified Americans, increased all the services' ratio of recruits from Mental Group IV, the lowest category allowed to serve in the armed forces. The Marines' assigned quota from this group totaled 20–25 percent of those who joined. The Corps had already lowered its admission standards in 1965, accepting candidates with otherwise disqualifying test scores if they possessed a high-school diploma. The percentage of high-school graduates dropped as the war continued, standing at 65 percent in 1965, 57 percent in 1968 (though still 2 percent above the national average for civilians), and 49 percent in 1973. Some analysts have blamed the lowering of mental standards for the surge in disciplinary cases that arose in the second half of the conflict, but this verdict confuses correlation with causation. Between 25 percent and 30 percent of Marines who fought in WWII were in Mental Group IV. During the Korean War that category accounted for 40 percent of Marines. By 1969 one in four Marines in Vietnam possessed scores in Group IV.[12] Accomplishments of these men in all three wars suggest that strong leadership, and the support shown back home for their sacrifices on the front, did more to determine troops' performance and morale than a score on an intelligence test.

Regardless of their mental acuity, recruits headed for III MAF received less entry-level training as the war continued. This reduction, like shortened enlistments, reflected the need to get troops into units and into action sooner. Prior to the conflict, Marine boot camp lasted for eighty days. Four weeks of Individual Combat Training followed. A new Marine obtained initial eligibility for overseas service only after another three months of on-the-job training. This prewar seven-month training cycle shrank to seventeen weeks by January 1968. Boot camp shaved off twenty-four days. Individual training lasted two weeks rather than the previous four. Basic Specialist Training (one month) replaced three months of on-the-job training. A three-week Vietnam orientation course completed the preparation phase. The curtailed training pipeline reduced recruits' wait for the war while introducing some efficiencies that provided adequate, in some respects perhaps even improved, preparation for their duties. Nonetheless, in April 1968 the Commandant claimed that another month of entry-level training (two more weeks on the drill field and two additional weeks of individual training) would improve the basic trainee product.[13] Arguably, the several months of wasted (nondeployable) time remaining at the end of a two-year enlistment did allow more initial preparation, but the relentless demand for manpower drove the initial training cycles toward shorter rather than longer durations.

The war also adversely impacted III MAF's enlisted training and experience levels. Many new leadership positions opened as the Corps expanded. Junior Marines received swift promotions to NCO ranks, while former NCOs quickly advanced to SNCO status. The newly promoted SNCOs furnished a seasoned cadre of leaders quickly, but the new generation of NCOs lacked the experience and training that had been the prewar norm. Before 1965 60 percent of Marine sergeants had served more than ten years. By 1968 more than half of the sergeants had less than four years of service. Small unit leadership, so critical at the rifle squad and infantry platoon levels, suffered accordingly.

Of course, young Marines quickly gained some combat experience in I Corps, which served as a partial antidote for their reduced training levels and lack of previous operational service.[14]

Retaining qualified enlisted personnel remained a problem. In the first year of the war Headquarters Marine Corps lacked enough troops to sustain the Vietnam rotation in 42 percent of the 270 occupational specialties IIII MAF required. Aggressive training and manpower management policies reduced this deficiency to 20 percent by 1967, but the challenge continued.[15] Rising casualty tolls exacerbated the numbers problem and compounded retention difficulties. Reenlistments plummeted. First-term enlisted reenlistment rates plunged from 16.3 percent in 1965 to 4.7 percent in 1970. During the same period enlisted reenlistment rates among combat arms Marines of all grades fell from 88.3 percent to 72.5 percent. Given the service's traditional peacetime manpower model, in which most Marines served only a single tour before returning to civilian life, these retention numbers made it hard to build and sustain an experienced NCO force. Unlike previous Marines in World War I, World War II, and the Korean conflict, few combat veterans returned for a second tour in Vietnam.[16]

The MAF faced similar challenges with numbers but not with experience among its junior commissioned leaders. Officer accession programs struggled to fill their quotas as the conflict continued. College students increasingly steered away from Officer Candidate School, Platoon Leaders Class, and Naval Reserve Officer Training Corps programs. Meanwhile more enlisted Marines filled the company-grade officer gap via the Enlisted Commissioning Program.[17] This remedy further diminished the already inexperienced enlisted leadership ranks. More than four thousand warrant and staff noncommissioned officers received commissions as lieutenants in the first two years of the MAF's tenure in Vietnam. The influx of new lieutenants from prior enlisted and warrant officer ranks led to a paradoxical inversion of experience among company-grade officers. By 1968 60 percent of Marine first lieutenants had over ten years' service compared to only 20 percent of the captains. Meanwhile officer retention rates, like those of their enlisted counterparts, dropped 12 percent between 1964 and 1967. From 1966 to 1969 augmentation spaces for regular Marine commissions went unfilled because too few reserve officers applied. Finding and keeping "a few good men" grew increasingly difficult.[18]

Manning shortfalls in the air wing proved even harder to manage than those experienced in the ground combat and combat service support elements. Long training pipelines in the aviation community demanded extended service commitments from officers and enlisted Marines. Pilot shortages emerged in Vietnam within six months of the MAF's arrival. HQMC mitigated the deficiency by involuntarily retaining key aviation personnel who wished to depart the service and prohibiting pilots from attending professional education courses; the MAF did its part by using nonaviators to fill the wing's ground-based jobs. Despite these measures, Marines in aviation fields remained in short supply in Vietnam until elements of the air wing began to redeploy in 1969.

Helicopter pilot billets proved the most difficult to manage. The Marine Corps sent fixed-wing pilots to train with the air force in 1967 to open more seats for helicopter pilots in Pensacola's naval flight training course. Marines began training at the army's helicopter course in 1968. Some propeller and jet aircraft pilots transitioned to the helicopter community. Still as late as 1969 1st Marine Aircraft Wing fielded less than 80 percent of its 703 required helicopter pilots. Aviation mechanics, with mandatory four-year enlistments due to their long entry-level training syllabus, also hovered just below their 80 percent manning quota.[19] Shortages of both air and ground aviation specialists, coupled with flying rates that commonly exceeded authorized Navy Department airframe limits, contributed to maintenance woes and high noncombat operational losses.[20]

Manpower turbulence continued once Marines reached their III MAF unit destinations. Troops faced a potential gauntlet of transfers from one unit to another throughout their thirteen months in Vietnam. The policy switch from unit to individual deployments required shuffling men to new units to ensure that all Marines in the same command would not have identical rotation dates. The decision to adopt individual redeployments meant that every unit, once initially set, would thereafter endure an 8–9 percent rotation of personnel each month not counting casualty replacements. As units began to withdraw from Vietnam in 1969, another round of mass transfers ensued. Those with less than seven months in country shifted to commands scheduled to remain, while men who had completed more time in combat returned home. Per the MAF, the initial deployment and later redeployment manpower adjustments became Operation MIXMASTER. Personnel specialists engaged in constant, detailed planning across multiple deployment cycles to maintain mandated ranks, required skills, and time in country, all of it complicated by adjustments due to casualties, varying troop ceilings imposed by the Pentagon, and last-minute changes to units slated to stay or go. Staff frustration, decreased unit efficiency, and lowered troop morale accompanied MIXMASTER's constant churn. Sometimes an individual Marine served in six different units in as many months. Given the endless whirl of manpower movement, the wonder is that the system, and the units that soldiered on under the confusion that reigned, worked as well as they did.[21]

The case of Regimental Landing Team 27 (RLT-27) illustrates the practical consequences of the manpower mess. MACV summoned the Marine regiment, activated in 1966, to reinforce III MAF during the early days of the 1968 Tet Offensive. The regiment's first battalion, redirected to Vietnam from a Pacific training cruise, arrived with so few men eligible for a combat tour that its rifle companies averaged 40 percent of their authorized strength. Fleet Marine Force, Pacific sent two hundred Marines taken from security guard duty on naval stations, various headquarters billets, and the 9th Marine Brigade plus two hundred recruits fresh from entry-level training to flesh out that battalion. Back in California, only 693 men out of 2,160 assigned to the RLT met the deployment criteria. Prior to its departure for Da Nang the unit's nondeployable personnel transferred out. More Marines arrived to fill the ranks. The regiment still lacked nine hundred infantrymen. General Krulak removed three hundred of those billets by accepting a "marginal" rather than a "full" combat readiness rating for the command. Then he assigned four hundred noninfantry Marines to the infantry regiment. One hundred men already on hand waived their statutory disqualification to deploy; the final one hundred replacements joined from the Camp Pendleton Staging Battalion. Within a week the regiment had transferred fifteen hundred Marines out and another nineteen hundred men in as it rushed to deploy.[22]

The first planeload of RLT-27 Marines left for Vietnam within forty-eight hours of notification. The last group departed on 22 February, just ten days after the unexpected deployment order. Nearly a thousand of these men were involuntarily ordered to return to Vietnam despite not having the two-year break that Defense Department policy previously required. Nevertheless, all three battalions of the regiment were engaged in combat by 1 March. This deployment, though muddled in implementation, matched a similar emergency deployment by 1st Marine Brigade to Korea during the Pusan Perimeter crisis in the summer of 1950. On its way back to the United States in the fall of 1968, only eight hundred of the 27th Regiment's 3,500 Marines met the redeployment criteria, so 2,700 men transferred to units staying in South Vietnam while an equal number of troops from other units who were ready to return home departed with RLT-27.[23] The constant administrative anarchy that Marines of all commands suffered in Vietnam exacerbated the inherently dangerous and volatile environment.

One way the MAF sought to curtail the manpower chaos affecting infantry battalions was through intra-theater unit rotations. Periodically the MAF sent a battalion from Vietnam to Okinawa for rest and refit. Simultaneously an infantry battalion on Okinawa shifted to the Special Landing Force role on amphibious ships, while the formation that had been afloat replaced the one that departed for Okinawa. This program allowed a one- or two-month respite for units to rejuvenate personnel and equipment in Japan while keeping all hands proficient in amphibious operations. The rotation ended in March 1966 and then restarted five months later. Battalions participating in the intra-theater movements enjoyed somewhat more stability while outside Vietnam, but they still experienced the roil of monthly personnel rotations.[24]

Unit strengths fluctuated over time, but the smaller commands closest to the action faced the largest manpower deficiencies. In June 1968 III MAF's Marine rifle companies averaged 73 percent of their assigned manning level. Sometimes the companies dropped to half-strength and fielded a single officer. Headquarters fared better. Higher-level headquarters fared best of all. Infantry battalion command posts stood at 92 percent strength. Regimental commands filled 95 percent of their billets. Division headquarters reported 150 percent of their authorized manning; the MAF command post also exceeded its official manpower limits. Meanwhile the two Marine divisions remained 4,130 men below authorized strength, with most of the shortfalls coming at the sharp end. The CAP program, which lacked an authorized table of organization yet syphoned off infantry to assist South Vietnamese Popular Forces, accounted for nearly half the divisions' personnel shortfall. Other elements of the MAGTF fell just shy of their assigned manpower levels. Overall III MAF, despite the losses resulting from the Tet Offensive and the disruptions associated with constant individual rotations, fielded 98 percent of its authorized troop strength on 31 July 1968.[25] This tally reflected a manpower system that struggled mightily but managed, by a system of expedients, to keep the MAF's units supplied with the men required to keep fighting. The measures that enabled this outcome came at a price: unit integrity, small group cohesion, and continuity of command. In the manpower realm, Marines grudgingly traded aspects of military effectiveness for the efficiencies required to keep III MAF operational.

Navy Logistic Support

The Marines could not have operated in Vietnam without the navy's assistance. Tactical tasks that sailors performed included resupply of vessels operating offshore, guarding coastal and inshore waterways against communist infiltration, salvage of damaged vessels, shore bombardment, special operations, and bombing missions. In this section I highlight the navy's critical role in supporting III MAF logistically. The navy stepped into that role, reluctantly, in 1965 when the army could not provide theater-level support for the Marines.[26] Sailors provided supply and public works services, a full suite of medical capabilities, and half the US engineering capacity in I Corps. The navy furnished major aspects of the support that a field army or a US Army theater support command would normally provide to an army corps.[27] The organizational structure and terminology varied somewhat in their naval applications, but these key logistic functions enabled the MAF's tactical operations across a ten-thousand-square-mile sector.

Supply

The Naval Support Activity (NSA) supervised the US supply management chain in I Corps. The command activated in October 1965 and reported directly to III MAF until General Walt relinquished his responsibility as Vietnam's Naval Component Commander to Rear Admiral Norvell G. Ward on 1 April 1966.[28] Administratively, NSA fell under Service Force, US Pacific Fleet, whose WWII predecessor established forward supply bases and provided the mobile fleet logistic trains that supported the Third and Fifth Fleets in their Central Pacific campaigns.[29] Its Vietnam-era offspring, also implemented and refined in the midst of war, provided common supply items to all services in I Corps, developed ports, and oversaw base development. At its peak in 1969 NSA employed ten thousand sailors and eleven thousand civilians (mostly South Vietnamese).[30] Together, under harsh environmental and tactical conditions, they fashioned a superb logistics command that lived up to its motto: "They Shall Not Want."

Of all the challenges inherent in an undeveloped theater, ports—the entry points for the massive flood of supplies pouring into I Corps— proved most problematic. Da Nang offered the only major harbor, but it lacked protected anchorages, deep-draft piers, and adequate warehouse space. Its waters, vulnerable to northeastly monsoon winds that produced swells of fourteen feet in the winter, made unloading ships at anchor or pier side a perilous proposition. Improving the region's primary port thus became an immediate priority. The navy dredged channels and anchorages, built piers to accommodate larger vessels, and constructed vast storage facilities.[31] Initially the poor conditions kept transports idly anchored for weeks before stevedores could unload them. This shipping backup unclogged by February 1966.[32] Thereafter Da Nang's freight throughput became increasingly efficient. In July 1965 NSA processed thirty-five thousand tons of cargo through the port. Two years later it moved that much in a day and matched the monthly tonnage delivered in WWII's Okinawa Campaign.[33] By 1969 Da Nang received 550,000 tons per month, making it a busier harbor than Baltimore.[34] This improvement represented a triumph of naval engineering and supply management.

As the MAF expanded from its initial lodgment, it sought new ways to support its forces advancing up and down the coast. The single rail line through I Corps, vulnerable to interdiction, never proved a reliable means of transporting military supplies.[35] Roads were essential to project forces inland, but a single Landing Craft Utility carried the cargo of thirty trucks.[36] Not until 1970 did tonnage moved by vehicles equal that carried by landing craft.[37] The Marine enclaves at Chu Lai and Phu Bai depended on lighterage to sustain their forces, since neither site offered an established deepwater port. The former relied on amphibious vessels delivering material across the beach. The latter required landing craft to move twelve miles up the Perfume River to Hue, where trucks then hauled the cargo an equal distance south to the base at Phu Bai. Later, as the war in the region's northern and southern fringes heated up, small, shallow-water ports at the mouth of the Cua Viet River and tiny Sa Huynh Island (dubbed "Gilligan's Isle" by the sailors) fed supplies to bases eight miles upriver in Dong Ha and to American Division units operating in Quang Ngai Province.[38] Sailors in Task Force Clear Water manned gunboats to help protect vessels plying the shallow rivers to Hue and Dong Ha. By 1969 more than 350 amphibious ships, specialized harbor vessels, and landing craft provided a reliable littoral lifeline to ground and air forces throughout I Corps.[39] The largely unsung achievements of this colorful coastal fleet empowered III MAF's actions ashore.

Fuel became one of the most challenging commodities coursing through the naval supply line due to its hazardous nature, a lack of port facilities to handle it, and the sheer volume imported for the thousands of ships, aircraft, and trucks employed in MR 1. Da Nang lacked tanker piers that would have simplified and speeded the offload of petroleum products. Instead floating and underwater pipes, ten and twelve inches in diameter, connected fuel buoys to storage tanks ashore. Tankers anchored near the buoys, connected to the input valves, and pumped their gas to waiting fuel farms. During poor weather the physical connection between ship and pipeline often parted, and storms frequently cut or tangled the underwater and floating hoses.[40] Smaller fuel systems, designed to support amphibious assaults in austere conditions, supplemented the larger storage tanks with bladders holding three hundred thousand gallons at Da Nang and Chu Lai.[41] Medium landing craft hauled fuel upriver to Dong Ha in ten-thousand-gallon bladders from the landing ship ramp at Cua Viet.[42] Capacities of this nascent petroleum distribution system grew over time. In 1965 eight million barrels came ashore. That amount tripled within the first year and increased by another 50 percent in 1967.[43] NSA proved that an army-size campaign could be fueled without deep-draft tanker piers.[44]

The NSA also facilitated the flow of ammunition, even more hazardous to handle than gas and oil products. Weight and bulk further complicated its handling, while enemy activity influenced how much ammunition was required, making it the most unpredictable supply item to manage effectively. The amount of aviation munitions used in I Corps jumped by a factor of almost eight from the four thousand tons employed in June 1965 to the amount delivered in May 1968. Illustrating the increasing appetite for explosives, planes from the USS *Enterprise* dropped twice the bombs by weight in Vietnam in a single month than its namesake had in all of WWII. Monthly expenditures of naval gunfire shells ramped up more than sixteen times between July 1965 and March 1968.[45] The navy imported nearly all the ammunition used by the allies in MR 1, and it did so across beaches, via landing craft up shallow rivers, and over storm-exposed anchorages and piers. The war could not have been waged without the stream of munitions NSA managed.

Over time the navy's supply focus in I Corps shifted from cargo handling to common item management and distribution ashore. Refrigerated storage space increased from nothing to half a million cubic feet.[46] Warehouse space mushroomed to nine hundred thousand square feet. Open storage lots around Da Nang grew to 113 acres by 1967.[47] One year later the NSA offered 105,000 individual items to support allied forces, received 186,000 supply requests, and met 165,000 requisitions for an 89 percent fill rate. Approximately 80 percent of the navy's supply business serviced other US services or assisted Korean Marines. Furnishing common supply items via a single service conduit improved the allies' military efficiency and allowed other branches to focus only on parts, equipment, and consumables unique to their own needs. Overall, the Naval Support Activity distributed 98 percent of the food, fuel, ammunition, and other supply commodities used by allied forces in the region.[48]

In the process of taking care of this expanding supply empire, NSA developed the largest US Navy public works department in the world. It managed twenty-two separate installations in Da Nang alone, along with other real-estate holdings sprinkled across I Corps. NSA's Public Works maintained barracks, mess halls, repair shops, communications centers, motor pools, and recreation facilities.[49] It ran a rock crusher that processed five hundred tons of gravel per day, an ice plant that produced fifteen tons of block ice daily, 986 generators producing 122 megawatts of electricity, and thirty water treatment plants producing seven million gallons of water daily. This key player in the war effort also employed four hundred pieces of construction equipment, built and repaired navy and Marine permanent structures, maintained seven hundred miles of road, operated 2,300 vehicles, and transported four hundred thousand passengers monthly via buses and taxis.[50] All these base-support services allowed III MAF personnel to concentrate on their own primary duties.

US Army logistic elements also provided support to III MAF in I Corps. Initially this assistance focused on soldiers deployed to the region. US Army Support Command, Da Nang furnished tactical logistics for army units akin to what Force Logistics Command supplied to Marine organizations. The army's regional logistics element grew as its fielded forces increased in 1968. By 1969 it totaled 7,500 logistics troops in a depot hub and two general support groups sustaining army forces in northern and southern I Corps. In 1970, as the navy redeployed along with the Marines, most of the NSA's logistics functions transferred to Army Support Command. Marines watched this shift with bated breath, expecting a major dropoff in support as the long-established navy–Marine working relationship shifted to a less familiar army–Marine support contract.[51] The MAF G-4, Colonel Wilbur F. Simlik, noted: "All of a sudden with the NSA leaving we had a sinking feeling—almost one of despair." The switch entailed minor dramas driven by institutional and cultural frictions, but in the end even Simlik admitted that "our fears were groundless. The Army was perfectly capable of giving us the support that we needed."[52] Army logisticians provided excellent operational-level assistance—including port operations, hospital care, and engineering services—for the last year of the MAF's presence in Vietnam.

Medical Care

The navy's supply services made operations in I Corps possible, but its medical system earned the deepest appreciation from those who bore the war's physical costs. Every Marine platoon had an assigned navy hospital corpsman. Each company had a senior corpsman, often a chief petty officer. Battalions and regiments fielded aid stations manned by a physician and a small team of corpsmen. From World War I to the present, an almost mystical bond has existed between Marines and the navy docs who accompanied them in the field. Although coming from different service cultures, the two groups forged a brotherhood based on shared risk and suffering. A letter home from a young corpsman in training captured the connection. "Someday I will see before me a wounded Marine," wrote Petty Officer 2nd Class Chris Pyle in 1968. "My training has prepared me for this moment. I really doubt if I will be a hero, but to that Marine I will be God." To prepare them for their lifesaving mission and the rigors of combat medicine, Vietnam-era corpsmen like Pyle attended a sixteen-week medical course, followed by a three- to five-week field skills course.[53] Their duties, often conducted under fire and in the worst of environmental conditions, focused on dressing wounds, splinting bones, treating for shock and pain, and preparing casualties for evacuation.[54]

In Vietnam evacuation most frequently occurred by helicopter.[55] Unlike the army, the Marine Corps did not design aircraft or designate crews tailored for the medevac mission. Regular transport helicopters and aircrew instead filled the role. Nonetheless, their ability to whisk patients from the battlefield to hospital services, often in less than an hour, drastically diminished evacuation timelines attained in previous conflicts.[56] On the receiving end of this process, surgical care resided at several echelons. Marine divisions included medical battalions, commanded by a doctor who was a navy captain, with four collection and clearance companies capable of handling up to fifty patients per hour and providing short-term care for sixty nonambulatory patients. One company supported each infantry regiment while the fourth remained with the division headquarters. Designed to be mobile, these small field hospitals remained static in Vietnam, although occasionally they deployed detachments to a landing zone or fire base to provide emergency room services closer to the action. In Operation HARVEST MOON (1965), for example, a team of six doctors and twenty-five corpsmen accompanied Task Force X-Ray and treated ninety-four patients in one twenty-four-hour period.[57] Similarly, a small surgical team was located at Fire Support Base Cunningham during Operation

DEWEY CANYON (1969) to care for casualties who could not be immediately evacuated during unflyable weather conditions.[58]

The division-level medical battalions provided first-echelon surgical care, supplemented in 1966 by an independent navy hospital company emplaced in Da Nang with beds for one hundred patients and
reinforced three years later by another separate medical company that
established a 240-bed hospital.[59] In 1966 the navy also established a
six-hundred-bed fleet hospital at Da Nang to provide longer-term and
more elaborate medical services. This facility, staffed by forty-eight
physicians, twenty medical service officers, twelve dentists, thirty-
four nurses, and 485 corpsmen, offered the most comprehensive
medical support in Vietnam. It featured a preventive medicine unit,
an optical shop, eleven operating rooms, an intensive care unit, five
surgical wards of fifty to sixty beds, and an equal number of beds dedicated to rehabilitation from tropical diseases. The naval hospital also
incorporated a research group, which investigated ailments specific to
Vietnam, developed new diagnostic techniques, and improved shock
trauma treatments.[60] Doctors at Da Nang pioneered the use of frozen blood for the massive transfusions required by combat casualties,
identified the optimal mix of blood and IV fluids to manage shock,
employed new dialysis procedures, and created improved clamps for
vascular injuries. These advances sparked subsequent improvements in
civilian trauma care.[61] The hospital provided these lifesaving services
until May 1970, when it closed in conjunction with the rest of the
Naval Support Activity.[62]

In addition to the hospitals ashore, the navy deployed two more
afloat. The first, USS *Repose*, arrived in February 1966. The second,
USS *Sanctuary*, deployed to Vietnam fourteen months later. Both had
served as hospital ships in WWII and undergone renovations before
returning to the fleet. These ships cruised offshore from active combat
zones. Their mobility and proximity cut the time required to move casualties to lifesaving care. Each vessel furnished 560 beds managed by
three hundred medical personnel, including twenty-five doctors, seven
medical service doctors, three dentists, twenty-nine nurses, eight dental technicians, and more than two hundred corpsmen of various specialties. Both ships stayed on station eighty days per quarter. *Repose*
averaged 850 patients per month during its first twenty months in
Vietnam; *Sanctuary* still handled 567 casualties per month during 1968
despite both ships splitting the patient load. Despite their capacious
recovery wards, new surgical suites featuring the latest equipment, and
a well-staffed mix of medical specialists, the hospital ships suffered

from several key drawbacks. They lacked sufficient helicopter pads and triage spaces. These constraints slowed initial casualty delivery and impeded patient flow once aboard. More important, the ships provided only three operating rooms, which limited their ability to handle casualty-intensive surge periods.[63]

The network of medical services—from individual corpsmen providing immediate battlefield treatment to skilled surgeons operating at Marine field hospitals, the naval fleet hospital, and aboard ship—achieved a new standard of combat casualty care. Some 3,200 sailors, 14 percent of all those navy service members deployed to Vietnam, supported III MAF's medical system. This total included two hundred doctors, seventy dentists, fifty medical service doctors, 150 dental techs, and 2,700 corpsmen.[64] The field hospitals alone provided six hundred beds. Adding the fleet hospital and two hospital ships raised the Navy's total to 2,300 beds in I Corps at peak capacity. At times, occupancy levels rose as high as 80 percent, but normally the treatment facilities averaged roughly 50 percent fill rates, which indicated that the health care system met both sustained and surge treatment requirements.[65] During III MAF's tenure in Vietnam, 78,756 Marines suffered wounds in combat. Indirect fire caused nearly a third of those casualties, followed by booby traps and mines (28 percent) and bullets (27 percent).[66] For those wounded in action, 44 percent received treatment in the field and returned to duty.[67] Of those Marines admitted to a hospital for combat wounds, 87 percent returned to duty, 7 percent separated from the service as a result of their disability, and 5 percent remained in long-term medical treatment facilities.[68] In I Corps the percentage of Marines who died after receiving medical treatment totaled just 1.4 percent. This ratio was less than half that of WWII and a full percentage point less than that of the Korean conflict and US Army rates in Vietnam.[69] In short, the navy's medical system provided III MAF the best combat casualty care in military history up to that point.

Construction

Sailors in the Construction Battalions (CBs, from whence "Seabees") also won the Marines' lasting gratitude for their work in I Corps. Seabees were formed in WWII to build advance bases in support of naval campaigns. During that conflict they fielded 150 battalions, grew to a strength of a quarter-million men, and earned an enviable reputation in both the Atlantic and Pacific theaters for building while fighting.

After WWII the new force shrank to two battalions, then expanded to eleven for the Korean conflict. Early in 1965 the Seabees maintained ten battalions totaling just 8,500 sailors worldwide. The few peacetime battalions tallied only half the strength of their thousand-man WWII predecessors. Vietnam War Seabees were a more junior force as well, averaging twenty-three years of age compared to the thirty-five years of their 1940s forefathers. The younger sailors also paid a steeper price in blood for their service. Just three years into the war in I Corps the navy's construction units had already suffered more wounded than the much larger Seabee force did in WWII. The ratio of Seabees killed in action compared to the number deployed eventually reached four times the mortality rates of World War II.[70]

Whatever their differences with their elders, the Seabees in Vietnam sustained the organization's legendary can-do spirit. In the years before the 1965 buildup, the Seabees supported Army Special Force camps across the country and assisted MACV's expansion around Saigon. In a program dubbed the "military peace corps," Seabees also sent thirteen-man detachments into South Vietnamese hamlets to provide medical and engineering support to peasants. Those civic action teams worked initially for the US Agency for International Development and later CORDS, using their engineering skills to win villagers' hearts and minds. This little-known effort started with four detachments in the 1963–1966 period, doubled in 1967, and reached seventeen teams countrywide for the last few years of the war.[71] After American ground forces arrived, Seabees began to build and maintain facilities for US Navy riverine, commando, and coastal interdiction forces across the country. But their main effort centered on I Corps, where their unique skills quickly became indispensable to III MAF. General Wallace M. Green, Jr., the USMC Commandant, underscored the point, claiming: "Without the Seabees we could not do it! This is more evident on each of my trips to Vietnam."[72]

Within the northern five provinces, Seabees formed the uniformed nucleus of the expansive NSA Public Works (described in the "Supply" section above). Public Works Seabees designed and constructed buildings, acquired and managed real estate, ran utilities and transportation systems, and maintained facilities within the region's many allied enclaves.[73] Both inside and outside established bases, naval construction units developed ports, built airfields, constructed missile sites, paved roads, dug fortifications, and furnished every conceivable form of general engineering service. As the war intensified, Seabee support became less garrison-oriented. The Seabees expanded the units' initial charter to support ARVN's allied advisers and the new US Army formations arriving in I Corps.[74] Eventually 25 percent of the effort was devoted to army units. By June 1968 half of all Seabee units worked north of Hai Van Pass, in the area controlled by XXIV Corps, and devoted half their time to tactical support tasks. Six US Navy construction battalions, for example, toiled to repair and reopen Routes 1 and 9 from Hue to Khe Sanh following the Tet Offensive, refurbishing 133 bridges along the 138-mile stretch. The emphasis on field engineering increased again to 75 percent of all Seabee workdays in 1969.[75]

A 1965 construction battalion project, just one example among many throughout the conflict, illustrates the formidable skills and feverish energy that won the Commandant's praise and his Marines' admiration. Early in the conflict the MAF needed a second air base. The US Air Force pledged to complete a new field at Chu Lai in eleven months. General Krulak promised the secretary of defense that a strip would be operational in twenty-five days. Naval Mobile Construction Battalion (NMCB) 10 got the job. Working around the clock in 100-degree temperatures, the Seabees struggled to emplace an eight-thousand-foot runway composed of aluminum plates atop shifting sands. Eight Marine A-4 Skyhawk attack jets landed on the half-completed strip twenty-five days later and flew the first combat missions from the new facility on the same day using catapults and arresting gear simulating a carrier deck ashore. Thanks to the Seabees' science and sweat, Krulak kept his promise to the defense secretary. It took thirty-three more days to finish the second half of the runway and six major repair projects over the next six months to stabilize the soil and prevent dangerous buckling of the landing surface. Early in 1966, however, the Seabees finally cracked the technical challenges and produced a "tinfoil strip," as it became known, that lasted under heavy use for the remaining five years of III MAF's tenure. General Walt, citing the ceaseless obstacles such construction skills overcame at Chu Lai, extolled: "These Seabees, they just wouldn't quit."[76]

Achievements like the Chu Lai airfield ensured the flexible organization's charter kept expanding, and Seabee force structure in I Corps grew along with its evolving tasks. Four battalions deployed to I Corps in 1965. Three more arrived in the spring of 1966, with a fourth joining in August. Three additional battalions reinforced the engineering effort in 1967, the final NMCB deploying in 1968.[77] The navy created a force of twenty-one battalions worldwide during the war, including two mobilized reserve units, to sustain the twelve NMCBs active in I Corps. Five battalions served at Da Nang, two at Chu Lai, two at

Phu Bai, one at Camp Evans, one at Quang Tri, and one at Dong Ha. During the conflict the size of each battalion increased, from 589 men to 762, in conjunction with the growing mission set. Seabee command arrangements also expanded to control the growing force. In May 1965 the navy formed the 30th Construction Regiment to command the first three battalions. The 32nd Regiment stood up in August 1967 to control the new battalions in northern I Corps. The 3rd Construction Brigade activated in Saigon in June 1966 but moved to Da Nang to direct the two Seabee regiments soon after the second one formed in 1967.[78]

Initially the 30th Regiment and its Seabee battalions reported directly to General Walt in his capacity as Naval Component Commander. Later they reported to the navy admiral in Saigon who had assumed that role in 1966. But III MAF always exercised de facto operational control of the Seabees in I Corps. The navy offered its Construction Brigade to serve as the MAF's Force Engineer Group headquarters, controlling all general support engineering battalions in I Corps. General Walt refused. By 1968 there were three Marine and four army force/corps-level engineer battalions in the region along with the twelve Seabee battalions.[79] This nineteen-battalion force, the equivalent of two divisions of general support engineering capacity, never responded to a single higher engineer command. It is no surprise that the 1st Marine Division G-4 complained in 1969 of blurred lines of responsibility among the many competing engineer units. "I never saw so many engineers in all my life working in a given area," Colonel Nicholas A. Candoza wrote, "and I must admit that I don't think I've ever seen so much attendant confusion as to who is supposed to do what and why and who is in charge of this and that."[80]

Marine Logistic Support

Marine logisticians complemented the navy's supply, medical, and construction services and enabled III MAF to project combat power from its enclaves throughout I Corps. The Marine Corps' tactical logistic system connected allied forces ashore with the navy's operational-level support. Neither the army nor the navy was ready to provide port development and base management functions in 1965, so the Marines struggled to perform those tasks as well as their own organic logistic missions until the Naval Support Activity assumed its new responsibilities during the year's last quarter.[81] The army dominated allied logistic support in the rest of South Vietnam but played little role in I Corps until the 1st Cavalry and 101st Airmobile Divisions arrived in 1968. At that point, the army established its own tactical logistics network that eventually subordinated III MAF's system in 1970 and then replaced much of the navy's port, medical, and engineering capacities in 1971 as naval forces withdrew. But III MAF orchestrated the region's tactical logistics effort for all but the final year of its six-year campaign.

On the MAF staff, the G-4 officer and his section supervised the corps-level logistics effort. Unlike its counterpart intelligence section, which infantry officers led, the G-4 employed senior logistician colonels and subordinate staff officers trained and experienced in their respective subdisciplines. By July 1968 the MAF logistics staff included ten field-grade officers tracking supply stockpiles, embarkation, naval cargo imports, ground and air transport, engineer operations, food services, ordnance maintenance, and medical care.[82] Like other elements of the MAF staff, the logisticians experienced rapid turnover. The average tour for G-4 section heads averaged just twenty-three weeks between 1965 and 1971.[83] Such a short period hardly allowed managers time to master the complicated logistic difficulties associated with the support of a force of field army size.

The range and magnitude of those problems were unmatched in Marine Corps experience. The amphibious corps of World War II developed minimal organic supply, maintenance, and transport capabilities because their mission was to conduct brief island campaigns that did not require sustained or distant operations ashore.[84] The organizational design of 1965 MAGTFs reflected that precedent. Marine divisions and wings, supported by their organic logistic units, were designed to operate largely independently. Marine Expeditionary Forces fielded one service regiment to support a division, an air wing, and force-level troops. That regiment was small for its intended task and not designed to support a corps of multiple divisions. Despite the MAF's lack of robust supply and maintenance capability, a reputation for US Navy–Marine logistic self-sufficiency in an expeditionary environment influenced the initial decision by the Pentagon and MACV to commit Marines to I Corps. The combat that ensued bared the deficiencies of the MAF's minimalist approach to corps-level logistics.[85]

III MAF did not employ its designed logistics construct in Vietnam. Rather than deploy its organic service regiment to support the division and wing, the MAF left most of its force-level logistic unit, 3rd Service Regiment, on Okinawa. The MAF's replacement logistic command, dubbed the Force Service Logistics Group, quickly grew from battalion to brigade strength by the end of 1965. Its personnel and equipment came primarily from the 3rd Division's Service Battalion, reinforced by elements of the 1st Marine Division's Service Battalion and pieces of the 3rd Service Regiment on Okinawa.[86] General Krulak, recognizing the need for more logistic capacity as the MAF's forces expanded, had his staff devise a larger and more capable Force Logistics Command (FLC), which he activated on 15 March 1966.[87] The new logistics headquarters morphed again in February 1967, when it assumed the colors and organizational construct of I MEF's California-based service regiment.[88] Thus, III MAF's senior logistic command required augmentation from two subordinate divisions and a sister corps-level headquarters to perform its assigned functions. This makeshift arrangement underscored the inherent logistic deficiencies in III MAF's organizational design.

The corps-level headquarters lacked enough organic logistics capacity and scrambled to create it. The MAF removed the two Marine divisions' organic Services Battalions and assigned them to the FLC. The Logistics Command used these units to form two subordinate elements: Force Logistics Support Groups Alpha and Bravo (FLSG-A/B) at the Phu Bai and Chu Lai enclaves.[89] In 1968 the southern FLSG shifted north as the war along the DMZ intensified and army logisticians began to support the American Division operating around Chu Lai. FLSG-A, based on the 3rd Service Battalion, remained at Phu Bai to support elements of the 1st Marine Division operating near Hue. FLSG-B, built from the 1st Service Battalion, moved to Dong Ha to support the 3rd Marine Division near the border.[90] In other words, the logistics battalion organic to 1st Marine Division supported 3rd Marine Division and vice versa. Aside from reversing established command relationships, this arrangement complicated matters in 1969 when 3rd Marine Division redeployed, forcing the FLC to shift FLSG-B back to Phu Bai so 3rd Service Battalion could redeploy with its parent division.[91] No explanation survives to justify this organizational chaos.[92] But an anemic force-level logistics capacity triggered the MAF's decision to centralize control, shuffle units and responsibilities, augment FLC capacity by robbing divisions of their organic service battalions, and replace them with similar organizations that reported directly to the FLC.

The wonder was not that the resulting improvised logistics system experienced glitches but that it performed as well as it did. In the early going III MAF experienced serious supply deficiencies. The Marines

adopted a form of just-in-time delivery employing computerized requisition and inventory management practices. They switched from
the so-called push logistics system used in World War II and Korea
(sending supplies forward at regular intervals in predetermined quantities) to a pull system in which units ordered only what they needed
when they needed it. The new requisition processes, tropical weather
that caused increased spoilage of poorly packaged supplies, and un-
expectedly high demands for almost all commodities led to periodic
extreme material shortages. "Charlie Med," one of 3rd Division's field
hospitals outside Da Nang, at one point in 1965 held only thirty-six
bottles of IV fluid.[93] General Walt admitted that the MAF operated
on a supply shoestring.[94] Two FMFPAC initiatives alleviated but did
not rectify the shortfalls. The first, REDBALL, prioritized designated
critical items to speed their global transit and expedite their arrival in
I Corps. The second, CRITIPAC, reinstituted a mini version of the
old push system, sending regular shipments of four-hundred-pound
boxes packed with high-demand supplies identified by Marine battalions in Vietnam.[95]

   As facilities, organizations, and processes improved, supply gradually caught up with the ever-growing demand. Intermittent shortages, even of basic items like uniform items, repair parts, and radio
batteries, still occurred in the war's middle years, but they became
the exception rather than the rule.[96] The FLC established a series of
static supply hubs—satellite installations under the FLSGs—for surrounding units to access more easily. Shore-party companies, designed
to facilitate movement of supplies across beaches during an amphibious assault, supported infantry regiments while smaller detachments
supported battalions and companies. Units in the field submitted resupply requests to the nearest logistics command by 3 p.m. each day.
Trucks or helicopters delivered requested items to the field the next
day. Shore-party Marines, cross-trained as helicopter support teams,
guided in aircraft, unloaded supplies, and loaded damaged equipment
and wounded or redeploying personnel.[97]

   The FLC's absorption of division logistics commands prompted a
switch from the doctrinal unit delivery system to a point distribution
method.[98] Under the former approach, designed for a war of movement, a subordinate command received support from the logistic element of its parent headquarters. This proved unnecessary in I Corps,
in a campaign confined to the same sector, once the FLC established
enough stationary supply nodes to support the major troop concentrations spread across the region.

Enemy action proved a much greater hazard to Marine sustainment than the learning curve associated with the newfangled MAF logistics system. Vehicle staging areas, supply warehouses, fuel depots, and ammunition dumps constituted high-value targets for communist sappers and gunners. Between January and June 1968, for instance, Marine supply points along the DMZ lost 551,850 gallons of fuel and 11,380 tons of munitions to communist artillery fire.[99] Despite such setbacks, the MAF supply system met combat demands and even gained a capacity to supply the troops some luxuries as well as necessities. In August 1968, at the height of its support responsibilities, FLC received half a million short tons of cargo via 730 ships and landing craft, purchased 1.1 million pounds of bread, issued 574,000 gallons of milk, and produced 8,698 gallons of ice cream.[100] In Operation DEWEY CANYON (1969), Marines operating along the Laotian border received soft drinks via helicopter.[101] In 1970 Marines patrolling in the deadly Arizona Territory of Quang Nam Province enjoyed weekly company-level cookouts with steaks, milk, bread, and all the fixings.[102] Such largesse indicated a fully functioning supply system.

Maintenance—the upkeep and repair of weapons and equipment—constituted the second major function of Marine logistics. The FLC's centralized management system also changed the flow of the maintenance cycle. Units that operated the equipment performed organizational maintenance, the first two echelons of care that included minor repairs and scheduled preventative upkeep such as vehicle oil changes. At the intermediate level, echelons three and four, mechanics performed more extensive repairs and replaced major components. Echelon five maintenance, done by depots in the United States, entailed major overhauls or complete rebuilds. By doctrine, logistic units in direct support of units using the equipment provided intermediate-level maintenance. In Marine divisions, the service battalions provided level-three support, while the force-level service regiment handled most fourth-echelon repairs. Once the divisions' service battalions became part of the FLC, third-echelon repair responsibilities no longer resided in the divisions but were handled by the Force Logistic Support Groups. Initially 3rd Force Service Regiment on Okinawa performed most fourth-echelon repairs for the MAF, but this became too costly in both time and money, so in the summer of 1966 the FLC began conducting fourth-echelon work in I Corps and some fifth-echelon maintenance on Okinawa.[103]

Broken equipment in I Corps often reflected a lack of parts to effect repairs. As the supply situation gradually improved, maintenance levels upgraded as well. The overall rate of inoperable equipment throughout III MAF dropped from 12 percent to 8 percent in 1966 and stood at 6 percent in January 1967.[104] Providing sufficient aircraft parts remained a problem even during 1968 and 1969. Aviation investigative boards determined that the primary culprit was not just the availability of helicopter parts, which hovered around 70 percent, but excessive flying. Marine helicopters routinely surpassed their authorized Navy Department flying rates, which led to increased demands for repair parts. As a result, helicopter deadline rates remained high, between 25 percent and 50 percent in 1968.[105] The 1st Marine Aircraft Wing completed an extensive repair program for its CH-46 medium-lift helicopter fleet in February 1968. The wing had grounded these aircraft four months prior when their rear pylons began failing in flight. Maintenance personnel shuttled 105 helicopters to Japan for major structural modifications. A second phase of structural modifications, including installation of new tail sections and transmission mounts, continued until the end of the year. These emergency repairs restored the CH-46s to full reliability but decreased the MAF's rotary-wing lift capacity in the interim.[106]

The most controversial maintenance problem III MAF faced stemmed from the M-16 rifle. The new weapon, which replaced the trusted and reliable M-14 in 1967, received strong criticism from infantry Marines due to its tendency to jam in action. Participants in the spring 1967 fighting in the hills around Khe Sanh blamed the weapon's malfunctions for many Marine deaths. Congress opened an inquiry. Marine official records assert the investigation's evidence did not substantiate claims that the rifles' failures had caused friendly battle casualties, but other sources disagree. Regardless, the hearings exposed serious deficiencies. Investigators discovered use of the wrong cleaning lubricant, quality control problems with the new 5.56mm ammunition, an excessive cyclic rate of fire, not enough cleaning kits, and inadequate training in how to care for the new rifle. Most important, technical inspections revealed defects with the rifles' chamber that caused a failure to extract spent cartridges. Marine headquarters and the MAF initiated corrective measures to fix identified supply and training deficiencies. At the same time, the Force Logistics Command upgraded all the issued M-16s' chambers with new chrome linings and modified their buffer groups, converting 61,100 weapons in 1967 and 1968. The improved rifle, dubbed the M-16A1, soon earned allied troops' appreciation for matching the increased firepower of communist infantry wielding variants of the deadly AK-47 assault rifle.[107]

Transportation represented the final major category of Marine logistic support. Landing craft and trucks carried most of the supplies required to keep combat forces in action.[108] Each Marine division had a truck battalion to haul cargo, and the FLC operated a large truck company. Three force-level truck battalions reinforced this organic capacity. Rather than operating those units under centralized control, the MAF attached one to each division and the third to the FLC. Roads required major engineering work to upgrade their condition and to keep them passable during the monsoon season. Gradually the prolonged construction effort paid off in improved travel conditions. By 1969 the transit time by road from Da Nang to Hue (sixty miles) had decreased from six hours to two. That year III MAF trucks logged 6.8 million miles, carried 2.4 million passengers, and hauled 770,000 tons of cargo. Those figures become even more impressive considering that each trip represented not just a convoy but also a security operation. Roads required constant sweeping for mines, and Marine Rough Rider convoys included security detachments, heavily armed gun trucks, and aerial escort to deter harassing fire or fight their way through ambushes en route to their objectives.[109]

Air delivery complemented the extensive ground transportation network. Both fixed- and rotary-wing aircraft contributed to the FLC's logistic distribution system. Marine C-130 cargo planes delivered critical supplies such as ammunition, medical stores, and engineering equipment to four expeditionary airfields around I Corps.[110] More common were the light, medium, and heavy helicopters that flew in all conditions of visibility, weather, and enemy opposition to deliver vital loads and extract casualties and broken equipment. Helicopters, for instance, supplied the embattled hill posts during Khe Sanh's siege in 1968; during February Marine helicopters flew 2,335 sorties, carried 4,607 passengers, and lifted 1,545 tons of cargo in support of that besieged base.[111] When airplanes and helicopters could not land, the Logistic Command's air delivery specialists parachuted supplies to Marines on the ground. While Route 9 was closed for repairs in 1967 for two months, the FLC air delivery platoon delivered fifty-one tons per day to Khe Sanh's garrison. The following year during the siege, US Air Force C-130s parachuted in two-thirds of the twelve thousand tons of material transported to the base by aircraft.[112]

Redeployment posed the most challenging logistic problem facing the MAF during its last two years in I Corps, one that required careful integration of supply, maintenance, and transport functions. The FLC opened a retrograde facility in January 1970 to manage the process. Designated units had to withdraw from combat operations, transfer their tactical responsibilities to other allied commands, prepare their equipment for departure, and move men and gear back to Da Nang for redeployment. MAF logicians established a small detachment to help units prepare their equipment to pass the rigorous agricultural inspections required before gear was allowed back into the United States.[113] At its peak, this group prepared for embarkation one thousand weapons, eight hundred radios, and five hundred vehicles per month. The first redeploying Marine units transferred some of their best equipment to sister commands remaining behind. Later, as part of the Vietnamization process, MACV ordered American forces to turn over serviceable equipment to ARVN units if they wanted it. The FLC initiated a redistribution center to manage that procedure and ensure the transferred gear was shipshape. The South Vietnamese accepted 94 percent of the 11,480 items the MAF offered.[114]

In January 1971 the Commandant, General Leonard F. Chapman, directed III MAF to retrograde from Vietnam every usable piece of Marine equipment and all material worth more than five dollars. Redeploying units thus carried back excess stocks of supplies, weapons, and vehicles. Depots in Japan and the United States repaired and rebuilt unserviceable items. In preparation for the next post-Vietnam contingency, logisticians used the salvaged resources to replenish the service's thirty-day unit mountout and augmentation supply blocks.[115] The MAF transitioned real estate as well as equipment and material. It transferred twenty-six US bases to ARVN units during 1970–1971. American units demilitarized the camps the South Vietnamese declined, stripping them of all buildings, bunkers, mines, wire, and the like, leaving just barren lots. Marines cleaned and renovated the bases that ARVN accepted to ensure serviceable buildings, utilities, and fortifications for the transition. The MAF also identified 144 hulks scattered around the region—destroyed trucks, amphibious tractors, tanks, and aircraft—and removed 125 deemed safe to recover. Roughly 90 percent of the Marines' departing material left on ships, most of it in amphibious vessels, thereby saving $18 million in commercial transportation costs. True to the Commandant's guidance, the FLC stowed away among the last of the departing ships fifty-five dissembled steel warehouses, bound for Okinawa, where III MAF needed additional postwar storage facilities.[116]

The Marine logistics system in Vietnam, though unorthodox and makeshift in structure, supported force troops, two reinforced divisions, and a reinforced air wing conducting sustained operations ashore for six years. MAF logisticians also provided some support for the Korean brigade, elements of the other US services fighting in I Corps, ARVN troops, and South Vietnamese civilians displaced from their homes by the fighting. Initially Marine support, even for its own forces, proved tenuous. But it grew more robust over time and met the increasing demands by the peak of the Tet Offensive. Eventually the naval logistics system proved almost profligate in its bounty. Colonel Simlik, the III MAF G-4 in 1970, observed that "never have troops been supported in such abundance as in the Vietnamese war. The chow, the ammunition, the supplies, the transportation, were there when we needed it, in abundance; as a matter of fact, probably too much."[117] The FLC and its subordinate logistic commands earned this backhanded accolade with a force of just ten thousand military personnel. This FLC footprint, reinforced by nearly thirty thousand soldier, sailor, and civilian support personnel, reflected a joint tooth-to-tail ratio of four supported troops for each logistician at III MAF's peak strength in August 1968.[118] As the Marine contingent incrementally withdrew from I Corps between 1969 and 1971, each component of its support force downsized in concert. The 3rd MAB's final logistics element looked very much like the one that landed with 9th MEB six years previously—a battalion-size logistics command configured to provide support to a brigade-size MAGTF.[119]

Conclusion

Marine supply, maintenance, and transport operations represented only the tip of the logistics iceberg in I Corps. The MAF could not have survived, as this chapter makes clear, without the supply, medical, and construction support of the US Navy. Indeed, navy support was one reason why the ratio of support personnel the FLC required was so low. The navy, and the army after it replaced the NSA in June 1970, furnished the operational logistic framework that III MAF plugged in to with its own tactical support capabilities. By 1968, the influx of US Army divisions into the region exceeded the FLC's capacity to support. The army's version of the FLC, US Army Support Command, Da Nang, deployed to I Corps in February 1968 to take care of the second American corps in the sector. For the rest of the conflict, army and Marine logistic commands cooperated to sustain ground forces of both services in an increasingly symbiotic support relationship. Manpower, the Marines greatest logistic challenge, became an increasingly difficult problem as the war went on. The Corps managed, with difficulty, to keep the ranks filled, but the personnel strain was one reason why senior Marine leaders welcomed 3rd Division's early redeployment in 1969 and the MAF's subsequent withdrawal in 1971.

The primary logistics lesson derived from III MAF's campaign in I Corps was the need for more organic logistics capacity to support sustained corps-level operations ashore. One small MAF services regiment proved completely insufficient to support multiple divisions' logistic needs. The Marines created an ad hoc substitute by turning division service battalions and the I MEF services regiment into a larger Force Logistic Command with two subordinate Force Logistic Support Groups. This centralized, top-down arrangement sufficed in a static defensive conflict, but divisions need their own logistic support element in a war of movement. Even under the conditions pertaining in I Corps, many observers at the time felt the Marine divisions would have been better served with their own organic support elements.[120] Regardless which headquarters directly controlled division logistics, however, a MAF commanding multiple divisions in an undeveloped theater required an organic corps-level logistic command of division size.

A longer view reveals that logistic operations in Vietnam marked a watershed in the development of corps-level support capabilities. American corps in previous twentieth-century wars contained few organic logistic units. Corps were tactical headquarters that directed multiple divisions in combat. Divisions contained organic logistic units to service their assigned equipment. When they required higher-echelon supply, maintenance, and transport resources, the corps' parent field army supplied them to the divisions. This construct worked well in World Wars I and II as well as Korea. In Vietnam, the absence of an army headquarters over the three American corps, the long-term and static nature of the conflict, and the distinct environmental and tactical requirements of each military region led the two US Army field forces and the Marine Amphibious Force to develop more robust logistic capabilities than had previously been the norm. Postwar US Army corps continued this trend, adding additional organic logistic capabilities.[121] (In the epilogue I will explore how the Marine Corps responded to this development, along with other corps-level organizational initiatives, in the two decades after Vietnam.)

In Vietnam, as in all wars, logistics dictated the art of the possible. Manpower, supply, maintenance, and distribution factors determined the feasibility of potential military operations and the strategic options they supported. For instance, MACV's preference in 1968 for large operations along the western boundary of III Corps and major forays into Laos were influenced and partially constrained by estimates of logistic supportability.[122] Nonetheless, the adaptive allied logistic innovation demonstrated in I Corps suggests that these limitations, while important, were not prohibitive. Overcoming supply challenges in distant expeditionary operations required proper planning, the subject of chapter 6.

6

III MAF Plans

Historians of the Vietnam conflict have devoted scant attention to ground combat plans other than the invasions of Cambodia in 1970 and Laos in 1971.[1] This contrasts with the extensive literature devoted to air plans and to the larger debates over military strategy. But varying circumstances across South Vietnam called for distinctive plans to address the unique challenges associated with each of the four southern sectors. Thus corps-level planning provides a valuable way to study the regional war in I Corps and III Marine Amphibious Force's response to the hybrid threats it faced.

General Dwight Eisenhower concluded after WWII that military "plans are useless, but planning is everything." He noted that off-the-shelf plans rarely address the actual challenges of emerging threats, but the process of preparing them informs and improves future responses to new circumstances.[2] In I Corps, however, neither plans nor the planning process led to improved operational outcomes. Once again, aspects of Marine organization, training, education, and leadership undercut the headquarters' performance. In this chapter I examine three representative cases: the 1966 manpower plan, the 1967 barrier plan, and the 1969 I Corps combined campaign plan. Together they illustrate the obstacles that prevented III MAF plans from contributing more to victory in I Corps.

Marine Planning in I Corps

In simplest terms, plans chart a path from an organization's current position to a designated end state. Plans are orders prepared in advance, allowing commanders to trigger them at a designated time or based on a set of anticipated conditions. The process of developing plans includes assessing the environment and problem, establishing goals, laying out a vision of how to achieve the desired objective(s), and establishing ways to measure progress. Plans meld resource (troops, fires, supplies, etc.), space (start points, avenues of approach, terrain objectives, etc.), and time (initiation, frequency, duration, etc.) considerations into a cohesive framework of actions that mitigate risk and maximize the potential for success. Military plans exist in two broad categories: *Force plans* address organization, personnel, training, equipment, or facility factors that prepare a service or unit for employment; *operational plans* focus on military action that may cover a single major battle or sequence several operations into a larger campaign. The MAF engaged in both types of planning.[3] The first case in this chapter is a force plan. The second combines elements of both force and operational planning. The last case represents an operational plan.

At the corps level, operational plans direct subordinate divisions' tactical actions. In I Corps these subordinate units included both Marine and US Army divisions. After XXIV Corps arrived in 1968, the MAF's planning documents also guided the subordinate army corps. This odd arrangement—a corps directing a corps of another service— continued until the Marines' departure in 1971. As a naval corps with an organic fixed- and rotary-wing air force, III MAF's plans likewise incorporated guidance for its division-size aviation component. Corps-level Marine plans also covered Force Logistics Command, the Combined Action Force, and force-level units such as a civil affairs company and a psychological operations battalion. Because it cooperated with but did not command the Korean Marine brigade and I Corps' ARVN divisions, MAF plans sometimes included but did not always task those allies unless the plan was jointly issued by all three nations' commanders. Annual I Corps campaign plans, which I address in the final section, provide rare examples of this more formal combined approach.

The Marine staff organization for planning evolved over the course of III MAF's service in Vietnam. Initially the Plans section served as the G-5 directorate on the primary staff, responsible for developing all force-level plans.[4] In October 1965 General Walt converted the G-5's responsibility from Plans to Civil Affairs, transitioning the former section into a new G-6 staff code.[5] This organizational switch enhanced the status of Civil Affairs, making it a primary rather than a special staff section, while downgrading the relative importance of the planning function. In February 1966 the MAF Plans section consisted of a single officer. He represented the only major and the only reservist serving on the MAF's primary staff. By contrast, the staff's Special Services (Morale, Welfare, and Recreation) officer was a colonel with five subordinate officers, underscoring the relative lack of emphasis placed on planning.[6]

The MAF Plans section acquired more resources but no more influence as the war intensified. Despite Walt's 1965 designation of the Plans section as the G-6, III MAF planners apparently continued to work under the supervision of the G-3 in 1966–1967.[7] By the end of 1966 force-level planners, now under a lieutenant colonel, worked within the G-3 (Operations) section, where they represented just two of the thirty-six officers.[8] Six months later the chief of plans position elevated again to a colonel's billet.[9] In May 1968 that colonel remained under the cognizance of the G-3, but his Plans section had grown to fifteen officers, including three from the army.[10] At the end of the summer Plans moved out from under the G-3. The senior planner, now an army brigadier general, and his staff reported directly to the III MAF chief of staff.[11] This arrangement continued until 1970 when the Plans section, reduced again to four or five personnel led by field-grade officers, folded back under the G-3, where it remained until the MAF departed Vietnam the following year.[12] In six years the Plans section served in four different portions of the MAF staff. This continuous migration bespoke planners' low status and weak influence.

The MAF planning section's limited role and diminished prominence matched its suspect professional reputation outside I Corps. General Westmoreland was not impressed with Marine plans early in the war. His dissatisfaction stemmed partly from General Walt's reluctance to emphasize search-and-destroy operations at the expense of pacification efforts, but the MACV commander also judged the quality of Marine plans to be poor. To address the former discrepancy, Westmoreland required III MAF to plan operations against enemy concentrations and base areas. To improve the planners' proficiency, he assigned numerous staff studies and war games, personally reviewing and critiquing their products. Westmoreland frequently used planning drills to make subordinate units prepare for potential contingencies, but among the three US corps-level headquarters, the MACV official history singled out only the Marine command for its poor planning.[13]

Several factors contributed to the MAF's planning deficiencies. As noted in the prologue, prewar Marine schools emphasized amphibious planning, not conventional or pacification operations conducted during a prolonged campaign ashore. Another reason was the notion, common among the initial wave of senior Marine commanders and staff officers (see chapter 2), that the MAF was more of an administrative than a tactical headquarters. This concept encouraged planners and commanders to view operations plans as the primary purview of divisions and regiments. In keeping with this mindset, III MAF rarely developed corps-level operations plans. Even when attacks crossed division boundaries and involved elements of several divisions, as they did at Hue in February 1968, the MAF did not generate corps-level plans.

Limited staff experience, time on station, and numbers undermined the Marines' planning proficiency. The officers who served as chief of plans, like other members of the MAF staff, suffered from short tours and frequent rotations. Fifteen officers filled the chief of plans billet in six years, averaging less than five months each in the job.[14] Four officers served in the role during the pivotal year of the Tet Offensives. Marine culture simply did not value staff expertise; neither did officers aspire to serve in that capacity, especially on high-level staffs. Recognizing the Marines' need for assistance, the army in 1968 and 1969 augmented III MAF's staff as part of that service's reinforcement of I Corps. Several of the new officers served in the Plans section, including two brigadier generals who led the planning effort.[15] The staff at Fleet Marine Force, Pacific in Honolulu also mitigated III MAF's limited planning capacity by furnishing supporting plans and studies, similar to the planning assistance US Army, Vietnam provided MACV.[16]

One indication of the MAF's deemphasis of corps-level planning is the paucity of plans preserved. Few of III MAF's Vietnam plans survive for military historians to assess. Archival records of division- and regiment-level planning products dwarf those of the senior Marine headquarters in Da Nang. The MAF dedicated no separate space in its monthly command chronologies to plans considered, developed, war-gamed, or approved. Neither did the compilers of the MAF's monthly command chronologies deem many plans suitable for inclusion as important historical documents. Fleet Marine Force, Pacific headquarters in Honolulu produced monthly summaries of III MAF actions in Vietnam, but these analytical overviews seldom mentioned plans and they did not dedicate a separate section to them as the annual MACV command histories did. MACV's records, unfortunately, focused only on plans at its level rather than those prepared by subordinate corps. Thus the voluminous MACV records also contain little information on III MAF's planning efforts. Brief references to various plans in message traffic remain difficult to interpret without the relevant context or the documents themselves to evaluate. Absence of evidence, of course, does not imply evidence of absence. The III MAF staff did generate plans, however infrequently or ineffectually. The sections below examine three of the most important examples.

The 1966 Force Structure Plan

One of the most revealing Marine plans for I Corps is also among the least known.[17] Released in October 1966, it tackled a tricky personnel question: How much is enough? In other words, how much force, measured in battalions and squadrons, was necessary to win the war in I Corps? Planners from III MAF and FMFPAC furnished supporting data and analysis, but the Headquarters Marine Corps staff wrote the 107-page plan.[18] It sketched a service-level view of how the MAF's regional campaign should be waged and how long the process would take. Despite its pedestrian title ("Force Requirements and Long Range Estimates for I Corps Republic of Vietnam"; hereafter I will refer to it as the "Force Plan"), it proved in many respects to be a model plan. In clear prose this document defined what "winning" meant in I Corps, laid out underlying assumptions, applied insights from III MAF's first eighteen months of operations in theater, boldly established and justified force requirements, projected timelines, and made clear the trade-offs between troop levels and conflict duration.[19] This staff estimate deserves recognition for its logic and foresight, including the caveat that ultimately rendered its most important projection erroneous.

The Force Plan analyzed the manpower resources of a growing Marine Corps against the service's expanding role in Southeast Asia. In 1965 the Pentagon authorized the Marine Corps to reactivate the 5th Marine Division of Iwo Jima fame.[20] The 1966 Headquarters Marine Corps personnel study sought to determine if the addition of this division would suffice to win the war in I Corps. The resulting estimate confirmed that the scheduled expansion of service strength would provide enough ground forces to successfully conclude III MAF's ongoing campaign. The Commandant thought highly enough of his team's work to share it with National Security Advisor Walt Rostow, serving under President Lyndon Johnson, in December 1966.[21]

Realistic plans rest on accurate assessments of current conditions, and the HQMC estimate did not shy from describing I Corps in stark terms. Enemy forces inside the northern five provinces remained formidable. They included seventeen thousand NVA regulars, eight thousand main and local force Vietcong, and twenty-seven thousand guerrillas. Data derived from eighteen months of war indicated 4,600 new troops augmented the region's enemy formations each month. These reinforcements included 2,600 soldiers infiltrating from North Vietnam plus two thousand South Vietnamese joining the ranks of the Vietcong either voluntarily or under coercion.[22] To defeat the fifty-two thousand armed communists, I Corps fielded thirty-four thousand ARVN troops and fifty-one thousand Regional and Popular Forces in 1966, augmented by eighteen US and three Korean battalions. Only 36 percent of the region's 2.6 million civilian population resided in areas controlled by allied forces. The plan's authors dubbed South Vietnam's state, regional, and local governments "not impressive," noting lack of leadership, citizen apathy, and no historical precedent for a strong, democratic state. Changing those norms required a nationwide social revolution whose "starting point is close to zero."[23]

To overcome these political and military challenges, the HQMC estimate identified four primary objectives. First: defeat the North Vietnamese Army via destruction, erosion, or negotiation, resulting in its withdrawal from the region. Second: render main force Vietcong formations ineffective as organized military units. Third: reduce the threat posed by communist guerrillas to a level manageable by South Vietnamese security forces. Based on I Corps' eighty-five thousand RVN security forces, this goal was set at 7,500 armed rebels to maintain an 11:1 ratio of friendly-to-enemy troops. The final goal—to protect the government from armed subversion and encourage its evolutionary, progressive reform—entailed both civil and military programs.[24] The attainment of these four conditions constituted "winning the war." While the criteria were not original, the planners deserve credit for proposing the type and number of opponents that regional security forces could manage independently. They also firmly espoused the need to eject all NVA units from I Corps territory while acknowledging the necessity for significant South Vietnamese political change.

The 1966 plan's concept of operations designed to achieve these outcomes mirrored the balanced approach General Walt had employed from the beginning. HQMC planners called for strikes on identified enemy bases and conventional units, extensive small unit operations targeting guerrillas and their supporting political infrastructure, and civic action coupled with psychological operations to buttress Saigon's authority in the hinterlands. The plan viewed communist military forces as a continuum. Once defeated, NVA troops would withdraw or reinforce VC main/local force elements. Similarly, remnants of defeated VC units would bolster local guerrilla cells. This connection implied that NVA and organized full-time VC forces must be defeated and driven away before the guerrilla threat could finally be reduced and held to manageable proportions. Since conventional and irregular enemies boasted nearly equal numbers, the best way to shorten the war (reaching the goal of just 7,500 guerrillas remaining) was to attack the entire force spectrum simultaneously, working both ends against the middle. The plan also recognized that South Vietnamese revolutionary development was essential to prevent the reappearance of Vietcong forces capable of overthrowing the government even without NVA assistance. Only a balanced approach promised concurrent gains in both conventional combat and pacification realms.[25]

Planning factors drove the key calculations, and the estimate explained the rationale behind each of those considerations. Planners projected future enemy strength based on anticipated augmentation (NVA infiltration and VC recruitment) minus estimated communist losses over time. Communist combat casualties, based on historical data, correlated to varying allied force levels.[26] The staff estimated total enemy casualties at the conservative MACV standard of 1.2 enemy wounded for each combat death. Enemy losses from other causes such as sickness and desertion were written off to compensate for friendly forces' potential overestimation of adversaries killed in action. A mathematical formula employed the various factors to determine how many months it would take, with the number of allied battalions serving as the equation's dependent variable, to reduce the existing enemy force to the desired 7,500 threshold. The most important assumptions were, first, that RVN civil and military forces would expand enough to control cleared territory, and second that communist reinforcement rates would be cut in half every twenty months based on expanding allied territorial control (resulting in fewer VC recruits) and increasingly effective operations interdicting NVA infiltration.[27]

Friendly ground forces represented the key variable in the study's calculations. Marine planners assessed the impact of adding between zero and seventeen allied infantry battalions (approximately twenty thousand troops) to the existing I Corps force mix. The plan also addressed how much air support the additional battalions would require based on a planning factor of two hundred jet attack sorties per month per battalion. Required aviation reinforcements varied based on how many fixed-wing sorties III MAF provided the air force and navy. When providing only "excess" sorties to joint air forces, Marine aviators anticipated needing forty-two total squadrons commanded by two air wings. This figure exceeded by eleven squadrons the number flying in I Corps in 1966.[28] The extra units also demanded a new air base, with additional ground defense obligations, to service the added aircraft. Supply support for the maximum proposed allied force list totaled 250,000 more tons per month, carried in thirty-two additional ships, and required the construction of a new port featuring two piers, nine landing ramps, and two fuel lines. South Vietnamese security forces also required expansion to consolidate and secure territory cleared by ARVN and allied combat units. The territorial security force shortfall included one thousand Regional Forces, eighteen thousand Popular Forces, five thousand National Police, and nine thousand Revolutionary Development cadre—a total of thirty-three thousand military and paramilitary personnel.[29]

Planners projected campaign timelines that varied inversely with force levels—the larger the allied ground force, the faster the expected victory. The estimate's attrition formula predicted the 1966 contingent of eighteen US Marine and three Korean Marine battalions would take fifty-one months to reduce the enemy's numbers by forty-five thousand. Conversely, thirty-five allied battalions would need only twenty-eight months to arrive at the same point. The estimate predicted ten months, without additional forces, to expand existing Marine enclaves to encompass the entire coastal plain of I Corps (another one thousand square miles). But planners were less sanguine in their forecast of the time it would take (at least twenty but more likely thirty-one months) for South Vietnam to muster, equip, and train the additional thirty-three thousand security personnel needed to control the newly cleared territory. Most important, the HQMC estimate anticipated that it would take a generation—twenty years—to complete the political, economic, and social reforms required to stabilize the South Vietnamese government.[30]

Based on the tradeoffs identified by its analysts, the HQMC team recommended that III MAF receive seven additional allied battalions, two more fighter attack squadrons and eleven more helicopter squadrons, along with the thirty-three thousand Vietnamese civil-military territorial security forces, as the optimum mix to win the war in I Corps. This reinforcement, based on planning factors reflecting progress made during the first year and a half of combat, promised to extend RVN control over the rest of the populous coastal plain, including 90 percent of the region's people and rice, within thirty-five months. Marine planners deemed it wasteful to send more than seven additional battalions to I Corps because nearly half the South Vietnamese forces needed to secure the region did not exist and would not be prepared to operate before a twenty-eight battalion allied force had cleared the rest of the designated littoral zone.[31] HQMC's manpower plan to win the war in I Corps, like all blueprints that don't pan out during their execution, would be easy to dismiss as a wasted or misguided effort. But both its process and its conclusions warrant further consideration.

The 1966 Force Plan accurately assessed the problems facing I Corps, both in terms of enemy threat and the region's need for political, economic, and social development. The plan leveraged eighteen months of operational experience to project anticipated achievements over the next few years. Its authors did not fall victim to the planner's trap—settling for vague and innocuous objectives rather than establishing measurable goals. One can debate their definition of military victory or question the number of guerrillas they deemed manageable by regional RVN security forces, but the HQMC team clearly and logically explained the rationale for both criteria. Most important, the estimate offered an exit strategy for allies seeking to limit their long-term role while acknowledging that the struggle to maintain a free, independent, noncommunist South Vietnam would likely endure for decades.

Many of the plan's assessments and predictions proved accurate. It underscored the criticality of Revolutionary Development, the need for active US assistance in the pacification realm, and the necessity for simultaneous action on both the civil and military fronts, with equal attention in the latter paid to counterinsurgent as well as conventional operations. The estimate foresaw that the NVA/VC could prevail in occasional small engagements but lacked the strength to pull off another Dien Bien Phu in I Corps. The plan anticipated the shortage of helicopters that plagued III MAF's Marine divisions in 1968–1969. It forecast that civilian agencies would not be capable of orchestrating the pacification campaign, a fact borne out the following year when CORDs assumed the mantle for that program under MACV's direction. The Force Plan also projected the gradual expansion of allied territorial control.[32] By the end of 1969, three years after the plan's initial release, allied forces did control the region's populated littoral plain and CORDS's metrics counted 94 percent of I Corps' citizens secure. Vietcong guerrilla strength had shrunk to twelve thousand, still above the indicated goal. But RVN security forces had expanded beyond what HQMC planners had envisioned to a force of two hundred thousand full- and part-time personnel, including ARVN regulars, Regional and Popular Forces, National Police, and armed civilians in the Civilian Irregular Defense Groups and People's Self-Defense Force. The resulting ratio of government security to guerrilla forces exceeded the plan's 11:1 goal. South Vietnamese security forces could manage the residual guerrilla threat by 1970. The problem was that guerrillas that year comprised only 16 percent of the 76,115 enemy within I Corps.[33]

Despite some impressive analysis, the authors of the 1966 Force Plan relied on one faulty assumption that scuttled their work. The planners anticipated that allied military operations could decrease NVA infiltration by 50 percent every twenty months. They also acknowledged that failure to reduce the flow of enemy combatants across the border would delay or imperil the goal of shrinking the composite enemy threat in I Corps to 7,500 troops.[34] Table 6 tells the story. The MAF's failure to achieve the plan's estimated reduction in NVA infiltration meant that the allies continued to face an enemy force several times the size HQMC had envisioned.

The Force Plan projected that thirty-two US and Korean battalions would whittle down the enemy's composite strength from 52,500 to 7,500 in thirty-one months. Even though the tally of US and Korean battalions in I Corps climbed as high as fifty-four, the number of enemy combatants never fell to the desired goal. Communist conventional strength never fell below twenty-one thousand troops over the next thirty-nine months. That nadir came in the wake of the 1968 Tet Offensive, following extensive enemy casualties during the costliest phase of the fighting. Adding Vietcong guerrilla forces to the sums shown in the rightmost column of table 6 makes it unlikely that the total enemy in I Corps ever dipped below thirty thousand. The Marine planners had not anticipated the war's sharp escalation over the next three years. They did not expect multiple NVA divisions to invade I Corps or foresee that MACV would meet these incursions by reinforcing III MAF with three US Army divisions and two more Marine regiments. Those force ratios, based on the analytical work done for the study, should have achieved the desired victory conditions sooner,[35] but only if III MAF found a way to systematically reduce or forestall completely the NVA's steady infiltration. It did not.

The 1966 Force Plan provides a classic example of a good scheme undone by a faulty assumption. The planners knew that attrition worked in their favor only if allied forces could reduce enemy recruitment and infiltration. Decreasing the former proved easier than the latter. As pacification operations continued and RVN control of I Corps' territory expanded, communist guerrillas and their recruits gradually diminished in number. Meanwhile Vietcong main and local forces filled

Table 6.1. 1966 Force Plan estimates of enemy strength versus actual numbers given thirty-two allied (non-ARVN) battalions operating in I Corps

Date	Actual # of US battalions in I Corps	Plan's projected enemy force level*	Actual enemy force level***
October 1966	21	52,500 (start point)**	25,000
June 1967	33	No estimate	26,660
December 1967	33	35,000	27,110
February 1968	51	30,000	21,925
May 1968	54	25,000	28,255
August 1968	54	20,000	35,055
January 1969	45	15,000	25,485
July 1969	45	10,000	27,140
January 1970****	36	7,500 (goal)	30,815

* Conventional and irregular forces included. This column shows the total numbers the plan projected for NVA, VC Main and Local Forces, and guerrillas in I Corps. Once thirty-two allied battalions were operating in the region, composite enemy strength was projected to diminish at the rates and levels indicated. Enemy force levels reflect a monthly influx of 2,600 NVA and 2,000 VC recruits. Projections shown anticipate decreasing those reinforcement numbers by 50 percent every twenty months.

** This number includes 25,000 NVA and 27,500 guerrillas.

*** Conventional forces only. This column indicates actual NVA as well as VC Main and Local Forces in I Corps. No guerrilla strength figures are incorporated, as these numbers were not consistently included in III MAF's monthly command chronologies.

**** This was the date at which thirty-two allied battalions had been operating within the I Corps AO for thirty-one months—the force level and duration that the plan called for to reduce communist presence in the region down to 7,500 combatants.

Source: HQMC Force Estimate, 2, Table B-III, Annex B; III MAF CCs in VDA: June 1967, 35; December 1967, 26; February 1968, 23–24; May 1968, 28; August 1968, 28–29; January 1969, 23–24; July 1969, 25; January 1970, 24.

their unit losses with replacement troops from the North. Over time NVA infiltration played an increasingly important role in determining the size of the enemy's total combat forces. The Force Plan counted on improved interdiction results without identifying the mechanisms, beyond more or better bombing, that would achieve the desired outcome.[36] In the next section I explore another Marine planning effort, initiated shortly after the release of the Force Plan, designed to address the infiltration problem.

The 1967 DMZ Barrier Plan

Between 1966 and 1969 MACV planned but only partially constructed a barrier system, known colloquially as the McNamara Line, to impede North Vietnamese incursions into South Vietnam.[37] The American effort was modeled on the Morice Line the French constructed in 1957–1958 to prevent Front de la Liberation Nationale insurgents from infiltrating into Algeria from Tunisia. That two-hundred-mile barrier, extending from the Mediterranean Sea to the Sahara Desert, featured electric fencing, antipersonnel mines, searchlights, sensors, and mobile reaction forces. Within the first seven months of its installation the Front de la Liberation Nationale lost six thousand men in unsuccessful attempts to breech the line. The lethal combination of obstacles, fires, and response forces effectively denied vital external support for the Algerian revolution.[38] McNamara's namesake barrier project never matched the effectiveness of its North African antecedent. In this section I examine why and how III MAF—the headquarters responsible for the project's detailed plans and construction—undermined the concept's operational potential.

The possibility of an effective barrier across the Demilitarized Zone and into Laos has drawn skepticism in the war's historiography.[39] Naysayers cite the region's challenging terrain, doubting that the allies could sustain a blocking force to cut the Ho Chi Minh Trail that Hanoi's army constructed through the same wild territory. Some critics also challenge the efficacy of such an obstacle, asserting that walls never work. But well-constructed and guarded defensive lines have proven their value throughout history.[40] Vietnam's own past underscores the point. In the seventeenth century the southern Vietnamese Nguyen kingdom constructed and defended for seventy years two walls stretching from the mountains to the sea (near modern Dong Hoi, thirty miles above the DMZ) to protect its realm from the depredations of the Trinh regime centered on the Red River Plain.[41] Three hundred years later Hanoi's leaders appreciated the peril that a barrier posed to their infiltration strategy. Senior NVA leaders feared the prospect of any system physically blocking their troops' access to the South and wondered why the allies never adopted this obvious course of action.[42]

The barrier's purpose was to reduce the influx of North Vietnamese troops. MACV estimated sixty-seven thousand NVA entered the South in the ten months prior to the barrier plan's release in 1966.[43] At the time construction began six months later, NVA soldiers represented

48 percent of the communist combat and combat support troops in South Vietnam. By the following year this had grown to 69 percent of all communist fighting troops in the South.[44] In 1967 eighty thousand men infiltrated, the equivalent of an army corps in strength and 10 percent more enemy soldiers than there were Marines in I Corps. Of that total 17 percent came across the DMZ. In the first half of 1968 the DMZ infiltration tally doubled to 38 percent of the NVA in South Vietnam.[45] From October 1965 to May 1968, MACV estimated, Hanoi had dispatched nearly 214,000 troops into the South.[46] Anything a barrier could do to disrupt or slow this onslaught would save allied lives in the battles fought in I Corps.

In early 1966 Roger Fisher, a Harvard Law School professor, submitted a plan to the Defense Department for a physical barrier system arrayed along the DMZ from the South China Sea to Tchepone, Laos.[47] In the summer of 1966 a group of US scientists, the JASON group working for the Institute for Defense Analysis, evaluated the barrier concept and recommended an air-delivered anti-infiltration system. The sixty-six-page proposal envisioned thick minefields coupled with arrays of sensors that could identify human and vehicle intrusions across the barrier. An antipersonnel sector (twenty by one hundred kilometers) covered the DMZ, while an antivehicle sector (forty by one hundred kilometers) blocked the Ho Chi Minh Trail in Laos. Orbiting aircraft would continuously monitor the system, relaying intelligence on incursions to a sophisticated command center in Thailand that coordinated immediate counterattacks by allied ground maneuver forces, artillery, and aircraft. The study group estimated the barrier could be deployed within a year and operated for an annual cost of $800 million. In September 1966 Secretary of Defense Robert S. McNamara directed the Joint Chiefs to develop and implement the concept.[48]

General Westmoreland thought the scientists' plan impractical, but he appreciated the need to curtail NVA infiltration and saw the potential of the sensors to help identify incursions. He had the MACV staff develop a modified barrier proposal, code-named PRACTICE NINE, featuring three geographic sections. A physical barrier, employing barbed wire and mines overwatched by fortified posts, stretched thirty kilometers from the South China Sea to the highlands rising near Dong Ha Mountain. From there to the Laotian border, obstacles laced the valleys, overlooked by strongpoints on the high ground. In Laos, air-delivered sensors and mines, covered by aviation fires, blanketed the Ho Chi Minh Trail. Seventh Air Force supervised the barrier's

Laotian segment. Allied mobile reaction forces operating from fortified bases backed the portions of the barrier located in South Vietnam.
This section fell under III MAF's control. The MACV barrier plan
combined aspects of both positional and mobile defensive schemes.
It envisioned an ARVN regiment and a Korean division manning the
DMZ border fortifications while US troops provided reserve counterattack capability. PRACTICE NINE required additional units, more
bases to house them, new airfields, enhanced logistics facilities to support construction and supply demands, and a combined command
structure to supervise its constituent parts. Westmoreland's planners
concluded that the proposed system would substantially decrease truck
movement through Laos but "not significantly reduce enemy personnel infiltration."[49]

The Marines turned the MACV concept into a detailed operations
plan for execution in 1967. Initially General Walt subcontracted the
planning effort to 3rd Marine Division, which had no authority to task
MAF units outside the division to support the construction effort.[50] It
made sense for the unit responsible for much of the implementation
to participate in the planning, but the barrier was a corps-level project,
one that impacted at least one US and one ARVN division, and thus
deserved to be planned and supervised by the MAF. The first barrier plan written by III MAF appeared on 26 December 1966. Its mission statement listed three tasks (build, man, and operate the barrier
system) but failed to identify MACV's stated purpose: impede NVA
infiltration through the DMZ and Laos and detect invasion through
the former. The MAF plan called for eight company-size strongpoints
and five battalion base areas behind the barrier. That layout incorporated seven fewer company forts and three less battalion camps than
MACV's initial guidance. The MAF intended to commence construction by 1 April 1967 and complete the project by 1 August.[51] Figure 6.1
depicts the obstacles that would block the eastern segment of the line.

Marines up and down the chain of command resisted the barrier
concept. McNamara told President Johnson in September 1967 that
the Commandant had opposed the idea "from the beginning."[52] General Krulak saw it as a diversion.[53] General Walt's endorsement on the
initial 3rd Marine Division barrier plan forwarded to MACV noted
that the project would not "be worth the time and the effort that
would be put into it."[54] Major General Wood B. Kyle, commanding the
3rd Division, told the undersecretary of the navy that the barrier was
feasible, but unnecessary, since mobile forces could do a better job of
sealing the border without tying down troops in fixed fortifications.[55]

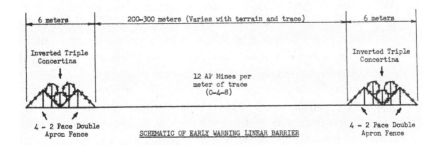

Figure 6.1. MAF obstacle plan for DMZ barrier. III MAF Operation Plan 121-66 (PRACTICE NINE), Annex E, Appendix 1, Tab A, Enclosure 1, Box 156 (III MAF), Entry "Records of Units and Other Commands, 1953–1993," RG 127, NARA II.

General John R. Chaisson, at MACV's operations center, described the line as "fantastic, absolutely impractical."[56] General Cushman initially saw the barrier as a potential economy-of-force measure but soon soured on the effort, calling it "stupid" after the war.[57] The primary Marine complaint reflected service culture. Marines preferred attack over defense and thus favored the more aggressive assault tactics inherent in a mobile defense rather than guarding fixed positions. Moreover, Marine commanders stressed that more than 90 percent of the NVA infiltration was coming into South Vietnam via Laos rather than across the DMZ, a fact that MACV's PRACTICE NINE plan acknowledged.[58]

The operational prospects of the DMZ barrier rose and then receded in 1967. In late January MACV released an updated plan that changed the project's name from "barrier" to "anti-infiltration system" to dampen expectations that it would provide an impermeable border barricade. Semantics aside, the new guidance delayed the completion date for the line's eastern segment from 1 August to 1 November 1967 and pushed the western portion's finish until after the 1968 winter monsoon season.[59] The MAF published a new plan in June, reflecting the delayed schedule, dropping several fortified posts, and adjusting garrison sizes. In June and July security concerns prompted a change to the system's code name from PRACTICE NINE to ILLINOIS CITY and eventually DYE MARKER.[60] Meanwhile increased enemy action along the DMZ in the spring and summer slowed the barrier's construction and inflicted casualties on its builders. A III MAF/3rd Marine Division staff study dated 10 August identified the challenges: an increasing enemy threat (three NVA divisions backed by more than

a hundred artillery pieces), delayed and deficient construction and fortification materials, and insufficient space (bases and bunkers) dedicated to house supporting units. Most important, the effort to build
and protect the anti-infiltration system was taking up nearly all of 3rd
Division's operational focus.[61]

September 1967 proved the decisive month for the barrier's future. General Cushman sent Westmoreland a message on 5 September relaying his concerns and pressing for a determination on how
or whether to proceed.[62] The MACV commander met with Cushman
in Da Nang on 7 and 13 September. Influenced by a Marine casualty
projection of 780 dead and 4,400 wounded if work continued under
the enemy's guns, Westmoreland directed that installation of obstacles
be postponed until the threat receded. Meanwhile, efforts to silence
NVA artillery and complete supporting port, airfield, base, road, and
strongpoint construction continued.[63] Updated MAF plans in September and November reflected MACV's changes and made additional
modifications to strongpoint and base locations and fortifications.[64] By
the end of the year all but two of the fixed sites were complete.[65] But
the barrier, bereft of obstacles connecting them, remained "fenceposts
without the fence" for the rest of the war.[66]

The mines and sensors received their test in Laos beginning in early
1968. The US Air Force employed the air-delivered portion of the barrier against the Ho Chi Minh Trail with disappointing results during
the first four months.[67] Aircraft attacked only 6 percent of the targets
reported, investigated, and confirmed. While aviation attack sorties
triggered by sensors proved four times more effective than those without cueing, truck kills attributed to the DYE MARKER system still
accounted for only 13 percent of the total vehicles estimated destroyed
on the Ho Chi Minh Trail.[68] Vehicle kills in Laos increased as the war
continued, averaging six thousand in 1968–1969 and twelve thousand
in 1970–1971. Despite the sophisticated sensors, mines, and one million
tons of bombs dropped on the trail, however, fifty thousand tons of
enemy ammunition, one hundred thousand tons of food, four hundred
thousand weapons, and 630,000 NVA troops entered South Vietnam
via the trail between 1965 and 1971.[69]

The MAF redirected the antipersonnel mines and sensors intended
for the barrier's eastern DMZ segment to the area surrounding Khe
Sanh in January 1968. There the sensor network, emplaced in valleys
around the base, warned Marine commanders of NVA infantry massing to attack the airfield and its supporting hilltop defensive positions.
Sensor warnings triggered B-52 strikes, tactical aviation bombing,

and artillery concentrations that prevented the three besieging NVA divisions from overpowering the base.[70] Based on this experience, a III MAF staff study in March 1968 recommended using sensors to warn mobile defense forces of an enemy's approach but not to use them in conjunction with a physical obstacle belt as Westmoreland had proposed.[71] General Creighton Abrams assumed command of MACV in June and approved the MAF's sensor recommendation, which resulted in a new MAF border barrier plan (DUAL BLADE II) published in November 1968.[72] For the rest of the war, in the DUCK BLIND program (later DUFFLE BAG), Allied forces protected critical sites with sensor arrays derived from the barrier concept.[73] The employment of these barrier-based sensor-strike systems in Vietnam spurred further postwar development of precision-guided munitions and recon-strike technology.[74]

Senior army and Marine leaders took very different views of the barrier. In addition to seeing a positional defense as less effective than a mobile variant, Marines resented being forced into static positions when MACV initially promised that non-US forces would garrison the trace. The reversal constituted a tactical bait-and-switch. In a prescient message to Walt on 22 October 1966 Krulak noted "it is important that we begin to look for ways to avoid being tagged for the DMZ barrier defense task. The problem is real and approaching fast."[75] He was right. Three months later the III MAF plan acknowledged that the "delay in arrival of additive forces" would require the Marines to initially garrison part of the barrier, to be relieved by other troops later.[76] That never happened. In April 1967 III MAF protested the lack of additional units to support the project.[77] In July Krulak wrote Cushman that "Westy will continue to nibble at III MAF assets in order to permit his use of the add-on forces elsewhere."[78] Cushman complained again to Westmoreland in August about the need for more forces along the border, while Krulak admonished the MAF commander that if he didn't get relief from army or allied forces the manning requirement for the barrier would "come out of your hide."[79]

Army leaders, conversely, blamed III MAF for poor planning, coordination, and execution of the barrier system. As the 1 November 1967 completion deadline approached, Westmoreland and his army staff officers unleashed a torrent of criticism. On 2 October the MACV commander noted in his command diary that materials Cushman had requested were "out of the question or possibly of marginal need." Ten days later he complained of inadequate quality control and a lack of Marine discipline in the barrier strongpoints.[80] On 19 October he cited reports from his staff's recent inspection, reporting III MAF's low priority for and attention to the task as well as a lack of command follow-up on his supervision concerns. The Marines, Westmoreland noted, "were dragging their heels."[81]

Three days later Westmoreland penned a blistering message to Cushman citing inadequate management as an unacceptable cause for delays and demanding immediate corrective steps for construction deficiencies of the whole DYE MARKER system. "I would like to see," he wrote, "the same high degree of motivation concerning DYE MARKER installation as is apparent at Quang Tri airfield construction."[82] The MACV commander's assessment had not improved by Christmas, when he lamented in his journal: "I'm still concerned as to the lay-out of the defenses south of the DMZ, which are not conforming in all cases to the best military practice. . . . I've had no end of problems with the strong-point obstacle system. The reason seems to be that the Marines have had little experience in construction of fortifications and therefore lack the know-how to establish them in the way I had visualized."[83] One week afterward another MACV inspection team toured the barrier system and identified major unresolved issues.[84]

Neither service acquitted itself well in the barrier project. Westmoreland and his staff demonstrated varying levels of interest; continually changed garrison strength, site location, and fortification parameters; and assigned Marines to a static defense while blaming them for a supposed lack of mobility.[85] Because their heart was not in the mission, the Marines failed to finalize a workable plan, dawdled in its execution, and then exaggerated their level of effort. III MAF did not coordinate well with either MACV or ARVN's I Corps, a fact underscored by the changes of post size, location, layout, defensive requirements, and command responsibilities that continued up to the 1968 Tet Offensive. Portions of the 3rd Marine Division participated in the barrier's on-again, off-again construction, but III MAF committed only a fraction of its total engineering units and consistently failed to meet the estimated construction timelines identified in its own orders.[86]

Marine commanders at the time, as well as postwar service histories, cited man-days of effort, equipment lost, and financial costs to paint a picture of a massive investment in a fruitless cause. But only two of III MAF's thirty assigned infantry battalions and two of nineteen engineering battalions helped construct the barrier in 1967.[87] Marine commanders still decried the loss of men, money, equipment, and time expended on the project. In the first four months of construction this cost totaled fifteen killed, 147 wounded, nearly eight hundred thousand man-hours, and almost $104,000 of equipment destroyed. These casualties represented a fraction of those suffered in large search-and-destroy operations, and the labor amounted to two battalions working eight-hour days for just seven weeks. The equipment lost (seventeen vehicles by the end of July) equaled just 14 percent of the cost of a single A-4E attack jet, yet no senior Marine leader called for the cessation of close air support when four 1st MAW Skyhawks were downed in action in August 1967 alone.[88]

Westmoreland recognized but did not resolve the crux of the problem: III MAF was persistently resisting his command guidance. The MAF's level of effort in constructing the barrier paled in comparison to its enthusiasm for opening ports, carving Chu Lai's short-takeoff airfield out of a barren beach and creating a host of bases, supply points, and headquarters around the region. Ironically, in 1968 III MAF unilaterally initiated a similar thirty-mile barrier around Da Nang to prevent communist rocket fire on the vital base. That linear obstacle also required clearing land, installing barbed wire and mines, building bunkers and observation towers, and patrolling the system with five Marine and ARVN battalions. Twenty-four miles of the Da Nang project (a distance longer than that planned for the eastern segment of the DMZ barrier) were completed in less than four months.[89] Apparently III MAF did not oppose barriers in principle—just the one protecting South Vietnam's northern border.

Both III MAF commanders involved in the project, Walt and Cushman, allowed if not encouraged their subordinates to delay the barrier's planning and development. They did lodge legitimate concerns about physically blocking the ground least traversed by NVA infiltration columns when only air-delivered mines and sensors interdicted the Laotian portion of the Ho Chi Minh Trail. Army Chief of Staff Harold K. Johnson, reinforcing that objection, likened the MACV scheme to closing the DMZ window while leaving the Laotian door wide open.[90] The Marines building the DMZ barrier also faced significant attacks from NVA artillery and infantry as well as serious weather woes.[91] But they failed to install the assigned barrier primarily because they did not support the concept and did not want their own troops stuck in defensive positions.

III MAF's main argument against completing the barrier was that the increasing artillery threat made the project too costly.[92] Enemy indirect fire on the DMZ had been a problem since the start of the barrier's construction in April 1967. It more than doubled in intensity from July to September before diminishing again to previous levels in November and December.[93] The obstacles could have been emplaced in the three months before the artillery intensified, at night, under improved counterbattery coverage, or during inclement weather to lessen friendly casualties. The MAF never pursued those options.

Communist ground forces also posed a growing threat. Too many enemy troops, the Marines asserted, made the obstacle belt both costly to emplace and vulnerable to NVA units able to smash their way through an inadequate barrier. By May 1968 Westmoreland was parroting the Marine claim that the barrier had been designed to disrupt limited covert infiltration yet now the allies faced overt large unit intrusions across the DMZ.[94] This excuse for not completing the barrier was disingenuous. The obstacle system was never intended to stand alone but to identify, slow, and attrite incursions so allied fires and maneuver forces could counterattack to block invaders. The absence of a barrier ensured that allied forces encountered the same large enemy units but without the benefit of sensor warnings and without the enemy suffering delay or casualties while crossing the border. Large enemy forces crossing the DMZ were not a new phenomenon. Prior to commencing the system's construction, allied intelligence already listed five NVA infantry regiments (18,750 men) operating inside Quang Tri Province.[95] In the first four months of 1967 MACV estimated more than eight thousand NVA had crossed the DMZ.[96] The influx increased in early 1968 as the enemy prepared for the Tet Offensive, but a significant border-crossing problem was apparent much earlier. With no physical barrier to impede the enemy's approach, the continuing incursions underscored the failure of the MAF's preferred alternative: a mobile defense.

Walt and Cushman may have even intentionally delayed construction of the barrier. In response to Westmoreland's October 1967 rebuke, Cushman told the 3rd Marine Division commander: "The screws are tightening. This was not unpredictable."[97] He then assigned his deputy, Major General Raymond L. Murray, to get the obstacle system back on track, but Murray admitted after the war that he and the MAF staff "never had a handle" on the project. Cushman later crowed that he "just quit" installing the barrier after the Tet Offensive opened because his higher headquarters finally had something else to focus on.[98] Ultimately the efficacy of a fully installed and defended barrier went untested because it was never completed. There is little doubt that a mobile defense fronted by a continuous barrier would have been more effective than one without. But III MAF's dilatory planning and

execution—a form of operational shirking and subversion—undermined and eventually scuttled the theater commander's strategy to
defend the DMZ.

The Marines' judgment on the barrier project was suspect. They
missed an opportunity to test the efficacy of a static defense by completing as directed the DMZ obstacle. Had it worked, it would have
constituted a strong argument for continuing the line into Laos and
garrisoning it properly. The key insight is that the MAF, as a corps-
level headquarters responsible (along with ARVN's I Corps) for defending the border between North and South Vietnam, failed to do
so using its preferred tactics *and* failed to institute and test the only
realistic alternative. In evaluating III MAF's performance, this case
represents a crucial test.

The 1969 Campaign Plan for I Corps

The allies' 1969 campaign plan for the I Corps sector reflected
III MAF's perspective on how to achieve military victory, sans a border barrier, in its regional war. This blueprint, based on MACV's guidance and incorporating the views of the Army's XXIV Corps and the
American Division working under the Marines, represented a joint US
service approach. The plan was also combined in nature, done in cooperation with ARVN's I Corps and the Korean Marine brigade.[99] Its
contents addressed both conventional and irregular aspects of the hybrid conflict. Written in the autumn of 1968, the campaign plan ben-
efited from three years of hard-earned operational experience. Coming
on the heels of the enemy's Tet Offensive, it integrated the lessons
and insights derived from that costly struggle. This document, penned
at the peak of the MAF's numerical strength, was the last regional
campaign plan produced before the decision was made to commence
withdrawal of US forces in the coming year. The one-year campaign
it prescribed proved the final one that III MAF executed as a corps-
level headquarters, since XXIV Corps would assume responsibility for
regional operations early in 1970. For all these reasons, this plan merits
study as a window into III MAF's views on how best to fight the war
in I Corps.

The 1969 plan for I Corps stressed the Marines' balanced operational style, with equal emphasis on pacification and fighting conventional communist formations. The mission, the plan's most concise
statement of essential tasks, described this dual approach as "defeat

NVA/VC forces" and "assist the [Government of South Vietnam] to extend its control." The operational concept characterized both aspects of the mission as exploitation of a beaten foe, a foe reeling from losses suffered in the Tet Offensives. ARVN and allied forces planned to share command, as had been the case since 1965, with regional activities coordinated rather than directed by a single controlling hand. The base plan describing the campaign totaled thirty pages, with another 278 devoted to twenty annexes addressing in more detail functions such as intelligence, specific types of operations ranging from combat actions to refugee support, and logistics. While comprehensive and organized in a standard military plans format, the document was still difficult to follow. The base plan alone listed four overarching military roles, nineteen subsidiary tasks supporting the two primary ones highlighted in the mission statement, six South Vietnamese responsibilities spread across eight types of units, and 118 additional assignments divided among twenty-two different kinds of allied commands. The score of annexes added many more considerations and tasks.[100]

The document's welter of categories, functions, and tasks reflected the construct of MACV's annual campaign plan.[101] The III MAF plan mirrored the combined theater plan in both form and substance. The regional plan added nothing original beyond a short section on CAP's role in the pacification process. Almost all its many tasks copied verbatim those found in the higher headquarters' national plan issued on 30 September 1968. The I Corps version also emulated the MACV annexes that contained most of the detailed guidance for specific functions and operations. Annex B, for example, detailing military support for pacification, incorporated only minor variations from the senior plan's organization and language. Annex J, addressing the allied attack on Vietcong infrastructure, duplicated its national counterpart nearly verbatim. At one level this parallel construct was both necessary and helpful, as nesting concepts and rhetoric contributed to clarity and consistency. At another it suggests I Corps' planners were just going through the motions. At a minimum they missed an opportunity to customize the national document's ideas to their own area's unique circumstances.[102]

The MAF's 1969 combined plan featured both continuity and change compared to its predecessors. The 1966 I Corps plan anticipated linking the three Marine enclaves via a spreading-ink-blot methodology that would enable allied control of the coastal plain from the DMZ to the southern boundary with II Corps.[103] The Buddhist crisis and more aggressive NVA incursions foiled this goal. The 1967 plan shifted ARVN's focus to pacification duties while freeing US units to more aggressively pursue communist conventional forces.[104] That year enemy troop strength inside I Corps matched allied buildups, leaving III MAF unable to simultaneously meet base defense, pacification, and search-and-destroy objectives across the region. In 1968 the Tet Offensive sidetracked allied plans, which had called for destruction of enemy bases inside I Corps as well as major gains in the government's control of territory.[105] Despite the previous frustrations, the fourth campaign plan covering 1969 nevertheless aimed for similar goals: rebuffing NVA incursions, neutralizing enemy bases, and extending Saigon's control across all five provinces.[106]

The most important change in both national and I Corps plans for 1969 addressed the role of ARVN. No longer would the South Vietnamese army concentrate on counterinsurgency tasks as it had in 1967 and 1968. Instead ARVN units were ordered to refocus on the big unit war, helping only as required with pacification duties. Territorial security forces would take the regulars' place in battling communist guerrillas and uprooting the shadow government across I Corps.[107] Doubtless the shift in ARVN's role reflected the growing perception that US forces should not and perhaps would not indefinitely shoulder alone the high casualties associated with search-and-destroy tactics. Aside from this directed reversion back to "real soldiering," developing ARVN's capability went nearly unremarked in the region's annual plan. It covered South Vietnamese territorial and paramilitary security forces in more detail, but the task of improving or expanding the region's regular army units hardly earned a mention. Planners ignored perceived deficiencies like ARVN's division- and corps-level planning capacity, insufficient supporting arms, or inadequate communications networks. Neither did they address how many additional South Vietnamese regulars were required to defend in the long term a region then reinforced by the equivalent of five allied divisions.[108]

The plan's coverage of conventional operations emphasized four familiar offensive and defensive objectives. First: regular forces sought to protect allied bases with their vulnerable ports, airfields, supply depots, hospitals, headquarters, and communications nodes. This enduring requirement consumed roughly a division's worth of combat power. Second: allied conventional units were ordered to block NVA incursions across the borders with North Vietnam and Laos. Planners noted that the intensity and frequency of communist attacks within I Corps correlated to enemy infiltration rates, so they could not dampen the level of regional violence without reducing the influx.

Third: ARVN, American, and Korean forces were directed to locate and destroy enemy regular units operating within I Corps. The plan urged allied leaders, once they established contact, to pursue enemy forces aggressively, even across unit boundaries, running them to ground to ensure their complete destruction. And finally: the allies intended to raid communist bases to disrupt the enemy's logistics. The plan identified seven of these sanctuaries within I Corps. For search-and-destroy missions as well as raids on enemy bases, planners recommended that allied units operate together as a way to improve ARVN's proficiency. Unfortunately, they also downplayed the importance of such combined operations by noting how this approach should be employed only "as practicable."[109]

The 1969 plan emphasized pacification operations more than had previous campaign plans. The nationwide Accelerated Pacification Campaign, intended to regain the counterinsurgency initiative following the losses suffered during the Tet onslaughts, was ongoing as the staff crafted the new regional campaign guidance in the fall of 1968. The cities of Da Nang, Hue, and Quang Ngai and their immediate environs received priority of resources for pacification efforts. For the overall small war campaign, I Corps planners identified three primary pillars: population and territory security, an effective political structure, and self-sustaining economic activity. Only the first received emphasis in the plan, which envisioned sustained security as the key to the other two outcomes. The goal was to secure, using Hamlet Evaluation System criteria, 90 percent of I Corps' population in the coming year. Regional forces relieved ARVN units in that role, while Popular Forces augmented by the growing People's Self-Defense Force militia protected the villages and hamlets against local communist guerrillas. In the 1969 plan even support functions like logistics and public affairs emphasized those disciplines' contributions to these pacification security forces.[110]

Under the new guidance, destruction of VCI became a major priority. The plan recognized the significance of the shadow government and the operational role it played in recruiting, supporting, and directing communist military forces. The South Vietnamese Phung Hoang and American Phoenix programs, designed to ferret out and destroy the enemy's political operatives and civilian-military support structure, had begun to gain traction over the second half of 1968. CORDS coordinated this program for the United States, the Ministry of Interior did so for Saigon, and the Vietnamese National Police orchestrated the plan's counter-VCI program. The National Police Field Force and

Provincial Reconnaissance Units assumed roles as the program's primary strike forces. Unfortunately, the plan provided little encouragement to US and Korean military forces to assist the South Vietnamese in this vital initiative, calling it an "as required" task undertaken "as much as possible." A few US military advisers worked with Phoenix in I Corps, but most American forces in 1969 had little awareness of, interest in, or involvement with this pivotal program.[111]

The MAF's participation in I Corps' political activities proved even less vigorous than its support of Phoenix. The combined plan recognized the importance of regional politics, but no Marine or ARVN programs backed up the rhetoric. Planners acknowledged that the people must be won over and that goal was "just as important" as military operations. Yet they were careful to point out that III MAF would not be engaged in military government functions, limiting its activities to civil affairs as opposed to political affairs. In retrospect that caveat seems specious, since the notion of a US military government in South Vietnam was never applicable or considered. American military civic action, by contrast, was widespread. Although well-intentioned, civil affairs operations yielded limited political impact.

Civil affairs programs entailed mostly small-scale ventures intended to improve peoples' lives in practical ways through agricultural, economic, and medical projects. MAF dentists, for example, treated 1,660 Vietnamese in July 1969 alone.[112] The intent was to use social and economic development programs to win citizens' support for their government (the so-called hearts-and-minds approach). The 1969 plan, however, warned military forces to avoid political partisanship. Moreover, planners feared the disruptive influence of urban political disturbances, like those of the Buddhist uprising in 1966, on hard-earned pacification gains. While US military commands eschewed RVN domestic politics, the crucial political contest raged on. It matched South Vietnamese local, district, provincial, and national leaders against the Vietcong's shadow government and united front. In this competition neither III MAF, nor its US civilian agency partners, offered I Corps hamlet and village chiefs, district and province officials, and urban politicians substantive socioeconomic or political support.[113]

Important aspects of the 1969 combined plan nonetheless transpired much as designed. Allied forces conducted aggressive sweeps of enemy bases, clearing with combined operations the three priority base areas near Quang Tri City, Da Nang, and Quang Ngai City (numbered 101, 112, and 121, respectively). In addition, they struck all the other regional bases, rendering two inactive and disrupting the remaining sites hundreds of times by September 1969. Allied search-and-destroy operations produced an estimated thirty thousand enemy casualties and prisoners in I Corps during the year. On the pacification front, both the regional Phoenix and Chieu Hoi programs exceeded their goals. The increased emphasis on pacification programs and battling the enemy's irregulars left the Vietcong in I Corps with just two-thirds of their infrastructure and half their guerrilla fighters by the end of the year. Most important, the area's population and territory security rating increased from 69 percent to 94 percent, exceeding the plan's 90 percent target and expanding Saigon's control over most of the coastal plain—a goal that had eluded III MAF and ARVN's I Corps units since 1965.[114]

Despite such positive outcomes, the plan itself harbored deficiencies that pointed to larger problems undermining the region's future security and development. Every campaign sequences operations and programs to achieve a designated end state. Effective plans delineate clearly how force, space, and time considerations work together to produce desired outcomes. While many of its civil programs ran simultaneously, the 1969 campaign plan did not specify any order to the military operations it described. Instead the MAF and I Corps commanders left that decision to subordinate leaders or provided further execution guidance via separate directives issued throughout the coming year. This failure to prioritize intended actions rendered the document aspirational rather than making it a firm outline for future operations.[115]

Establishing appropriate objectives is one of the most challenging aspects of writing effective plans. The 1969 edition proved problematic in its specified aims. Effective plans specify quantitative goals that can be assessed. The aim to protect 90 percent of the region's people was an example of a worthy objective. No such goal supported the two other major lines of operation. With respect to defeating the NVA/VC, the stated goal was to kill or capture more than the communists could replace. For the development of ARVN's capacity, the objective was modernization to "achieve a maximum state of combat effectiveness."[116] The former objective was measurable (indirectly), though it ceded the initiative to an enemy who controlled the intensity of combat because that enemy could withdraw into inviolable sanctuaries. Gauging progress on the latter goal was even more subjective.

Other plan objectives—reduce enemy attacks; deny the maximum number of enemy bases; enhance Regional Forces/Popular Forces capability; restore "to the greatest extent possible" lines of communication; neutralize infrastructure; increase the number of ralliers; and

maximize intelligence collection—were similarly fuzzy.[117] The combined campaign plans, said MACV intelligence chief Major General
Phillip B. Davidson after the war, were "vague and nonbinding. In fact,
neither the Americans nor the South Vietnamese paid much attention to them."[118] The South Vietnamese Joint General Staff drafted
the 1969 national campaign plan with MACV's help. American staff
officers had authored previous annual editions, with ARVN assistance,
and the earlier documents incorporated more quantifiable goals.[119] The
allied planners in I Corps, following the lead of their higher headquarters, chose to minimize measurable objectives in the new version of the
regional plan. That decision was not an improvement.

The plan's tasks were as hazy as its goals. Partly because they were
grouped by type (e.g., generic divisions and geographic sectors), the
tasks did not include detail specific to each individual unit or locale.
Thus divisions were instructed to conduct "large-scale mobile operations to destroy NVA/VC forces" while sectors were enjoined to
"conduct an active defense." Some units received eighteen tasks while
others, such as the Force Logistics Command, received but one: "Provide support as required." A surfeit of assignments, with no indication
of relative priority or metrics to measure their accomplishment, was
as unhelpful as the admonition to "just do your job." Interestingly,
CORDS, a major subordinate command of III MAF on par with a
Marine division or air wing, received no tasking at all, though several
of the programs it supervised were included in the annexes. The campaign guidance merely instructed the MAF's Advisory Command to
help I Corps' Vietnamese security forces perform their own assigned
tasks, but the plan included no vision of how those units should grow
or modernize despite the fact that ARVN's development constituted
the first of ten goals listed in the assessment annex.[120]

The most damning deficiency of the new combined plan was its
failure to identify an effective way to stop the ongoing invasion of
North Vietnamese troops into I Corps. Instead the 1969 instruction
contained traces of fatal resignation and a disturbing recognition that
the allies, after three and a half years of war, remained surrounded by
enemy units that operated with frustrating freedom. The plan's assumptions noted that even a negotiated settlement would not change
that reality. It predicted that the enemy would remain capable in the
coming year of widespread regional attacks because the allies could not
stop communist encroachment. The plan proposed more interdiction
operations, but bombing, barriers, and a mobile defense had yet to stop
NVA infiltration.[121]

The coming year did nothing to reverse the previous failures to protect MR 1. At the beginning of 1969 the allies faced seventy-one battalions (an estimated 49,200 NVA/VC regulars) *inside* I Corps, more than the number of soldiers ARVN maintained within the zone. A year later, although the number of guerrillas had declined significantly, an additional six thousand NVA/VC troops occupied the five provinces.[122] The plan accurately identified the invasion problem but proffered no operational solution. Successful plans, like the strategies they advance, must attain their designated ends using available means and feasible ways. The allies' combined plan lacked a "way" to achieve its most pressing objective. A WWII Marine planning directive provides a fitting epitaph for the 1969 plan: "Regardless of how well conceived the senior Commander's plan may be, it can be nullified if his front line platoons are incapable of carrying out the mission assigned."[123]

Conclusion

In Aesop's fable, the mice determined that the best way to prevent the murderous cat from sneaking up was to hang a warning bell around its neck. Their plan was suitable (accomplished the mission) but not feasible (possible with the resources available). No individual mouse was willing to install the bell. The moral of the story? No matter how clever or hopeful a plan, it must work in the real world or it is useless. In this chapter I have examined several promising proposals Marine planners developed for I Corps. The 1966 Force Plan projected the number of troops and amount of time necessary to pacify I Corps. It failed because its assumption that NVA infiltration could be minimized proved unfounded. The 1967 barrier project, intended to block a portion of that infiltration, foundered because III MAF commanders wanted to use their units for other purposes and thus slow-rolled the plan's execution until they convinced MACV to give up on the project. The 1969 campaign plan worked only in part. Pacification gradually progressed against local guerrillas and Vietcong infrastructure, but continued incursions of North Vietnamese regulars prevented establishment of lasting security across I Corps. The plans III MAF produced for I Corps envisioned a desired future but failed to devise the actions required to achieve it. The Marines found no way to bell the communist cat.

The Marine Corps had no previous operational experience devising plans for a hybrid war such as III MAF encountered in I Corps.

Neither did prewar education and training equip Marine planners to develop ways that would defeat simultaneously an embedded insurgency and a potent external conventional threat. The pace and scope of planning required to confront these evolving dual perils forced MAF staff officers and commanders to expand their capacity to quickly generate a variety of contingency plans. Their ability to plan in the new environment grew with experience. The MAF's 1970–1971 withdrawal plans, for example, were models of effectiveness under demanding time constraints and ever-changing political and military guidance. But throughout the conflict III MAF tended to subcontract operational plans to subordinate divisions and task forces.

In the end neither the corps-level planners nor their subordinate unit counterparts found an effective method to defend I Corps. American policy prevented ground offensives against Hanoi or its forces' sanctuaries just beyond I Corps' borders. Neither was a barrier defended by ground forces authorized to block the Ho Chi Minh Trail. Marine commanders and their staffs, like their MACV counterparts in Saigon, were therefore constrained to plan and wage a tactical offensive within a defensive operational construct. Under these circumstances, planners found it easier to identify appropriate objectives (e.g., stop infiltration) than to achieve them. The foremost conundrum their proposed operations and programs never solved was how to prevent fresh NVA units from entering I Corps where and when they willed. On this failure—one of both plans and execution—the outcome of the war in I Corps turned.

7

III MAF's Hybrid War

Although circumstances in I Corps were unique, events there illustrate why the allies failed to establish an independent, noncommunist South Vietnam. To gain a full understanding of the regional war, one must appreciate the role played by the sector's senior American headquarters as it translated strategic guidance into tactical actions. What III Marine Amphibious Force did not do is as instructive as what it did. In this chapter I summarize the findings developed in previous chapters. I recap the MAF's campaign in I Corps, analyze how the corps-level Marine headquarters executed its five primary warfighting functions, and highlight the shortfalls that contributed to its failure.

The I Corps Campaign

Marine staff and commanders were not well prepared for the war they encountered in I Corps. Although inheriting a small wars doctrine based on their experience fighting guerrillas in the Philippines and the Caribbean, Marines had never faced an organizationally and ideologically sophisticated people's war akin to the one they encountered in Vietnam. Their experience in WWII and Korea entailed mostly conventional operations, and it had been twenty years since the service had fielded corps-level commands in combat. In the interim between 1945 and 1965, the Marine Corps developed MAGTF doctrine, designed to fuse air and ground elements into a single cohesive team. The new warfighting concept envisioned four scalable organizations—officially designated as Marine Expeditionary Units, Brigades, Forces, and Corps—built around ground combat elements of battalion, regiment, division, and multi-division size. During this period neither WWII-era amphibious corps nor their successor Marine Expeditionary Forces received emphasis in service schools. Similarly, in field exercises and staff wargames the largest MAGTFs rarely played a role beyond establishing amphibious beachheads limited in depth and duration. Thus the III MAF headquarters that deployed to Vietnam in May 1965 had not planned, organized, or trained its forces for sustained operations ashore. From the beginning the MAF command element was in reaction mode as it struggled to master its new environment, a host of joint and combined command challenges, and an enemy employing both a conventional light infantry army and a Maoist civil-military insurgency.

The MAF's tenure in I Corps can be divided into two major phases, delineated by the enemy's 1968 Tet Offensive. During the first thirty-six months III MAF established three primary enclaves, trying but failing to extend them to cover the region's entire populated coastal plain. Initial operations in 1965 against conventional and irregular foes set back the communist cause but did not destroy entire regular units or uproot the insurgents' shadow government. Those tactical outcomes foreshadowed what became a frustrating norm. In the spring of 1966 political protests in I Corps disrupted the allies' programs for several months. Meanwhile the MAF lost control of the strategic A Shau Valley, never to be fully regained. Even when reinforced by the 1st Marine Division, III MAF still faced long odds. It turned back multiple division-size NVA thrusts across the DMZ in the second half of the year while simultaneously battling another NVA division in the region between Chu Lai and Da Nang. The US Army added a brigade task force in 1967, soon expanded to a division, to augment III MAF in I Corps' southern two provinces. The NVA countered with increased assaults across the DMZ from Khe Sanh to the coast. By the end of 1967 a tactical stalemate prevailed, with twenty-seven thousand NVA regulars operating inside I Corps against the equivalent of six allied divisions and forty-six thousand territorial forces.

The second phase of III MAF's war lasted from the Tet Offensive through the command's withdrawal in April 1971. This period comprised three substages. In the first, the communists seized the tactical initiative with the Tet and mini-Tet assaults in January, May, and August 1968. Although the enemy offensives failed militarily, they succeeded in redirecting American goals from victory to an "honorable exit." The second stage, lasting from October 1968 through the fall of 1969, featured a vigorous allied counterattack on both the conventional and pacification fronts. A gradual drawdown and redeployment of American forces characterized the final stage, which covered the MAF's last eighteen months in Vietnam. The Vietcong suffered a serious decline throughout the second phase, especially in their casualty-intensive Tet assaults, exacerbated by the slow grind of continuous small unit actions through 1971. At the division level and below, ARVN's tactical capability gradually improved throughout both phases, although the disappointing results of the Laos incursion just before III MAF departed in 1971 highlighted deficiencies in I Corps' ability to command, maneuver, sustain, and coordinate fires for multi-division operations.

I dubbed the conflict's first phase "the Marine war." Generals Lew Walt and Robert Cushman operated under General William Westmoreland's direction, but III MAF enjoyed considerable latitude in how it structured its campaign. The war in I Corps was always joint and combined in nature, but the first phase was primarily a Marine show on the American side. The second, post-Tet phase entailed far more joint warfighting and less MAF control of operations. This phase introduced two additional US Army divisions into the zone in 1968, inserted a MACV (Forward) command post followed by an army corps subordinate to III MAF, expanded the Seventh Air Force's role in controlling Marine airplanes, and finally subordinated III MAF under XXIV Corps command in 1970.

In both phases of the regional conflict III MAF employed a balanced "big war/small war" approach. The MAF, against the design of Westmoreland's initial attrition strategy but anticipating Abrams's later One War policy, simultaneously emphasized conventional and pacification operations. Some historians suggest that Abrams initiated his comprehensive approach too late to matter. But III MAF's experience in I Corps undermines that interpretation. The MAF applied a One War methodology from the beginning, yet it was not enough to win the regional war.

Fighting the Corps

Command and control—the most important of the five warfighting functions—coordinated the other functions and thus determined III MAF's success in I Corps. The MAF staff entered the war without the numbers and expertise needed to control a multi-division corps. The initial suitcase staff expanded to a thousand Marines by 1968, learning by trial and error what was required to orchestrate civil-military operations across the region. Marine tradition emphasized battalion and regimental actions but downplayed critical corps-level command responsibilities. The MAF's staff officers and commanders viewed their headquarters as an administrative rather than a tactical command. They relied on subordinate divisions and task forces to do most operational planning, rarely moved large units across the region in response to fleeting opportunities, and normally pushed force-level troop units down to divisions rather than using them to control and conduct corps-wide functions.

Corps-level leadership mattered. In the battle for Hue, for example, Cushman failed to provide sound tactical command of three allied divisions, was slow to block NVA reinforcement, and then neglected to pursue the beaten enemy. Cushman's lack of drive and judgment as a corps commander inspired Westmoreland to backstop the III MAF headquarters with MACV (Forward) and then XXIV Corps, an army command that controlled the ground war in I Corps' most vulnerable sector for the rest of the war. At the same time, the MACV commander removed the MAF's direct control of Marine fixed-wing strike and reconnaissance aircraft, turning them over to Seventh Air Force to manage in the name of increased efficiency. Cushman, who went on to become Commandant in 1972, never suffered the professional blame that his poor performance in I Corps warranted. His troubles, and the institutional black eye his actions earned, underscore the important roles that doctrine, education, organization, training, and strong staff support play in equipping senior leaders for effective corps-level command.

The hybrid war in I Corps placed a premium on both conventional and irregular intelligence coverage. The III MAF G-2 section tracked its conventional foes more effectively than it did its insurgent enemies. It methodically followed the composition, movements, and phoenix-like resurgence of main force VC units such as the 1st VC Regiment. Similarly, NVA commands like the 324B Division operating across the DMZ received lavish attention in the MAF intelligence section's order of battle summaries. The ability to anticipate conventional assaults paid off in 1968 when the Tet Offensive surprised III MAF's intelligence analysts less than it did some of their allied counterparts in other parts of Vietnam. Da Nang, as a result, suffered little of the damage Saigon endured because its defenses were stronger and fully alerted for the communists' holiday assault.

By contrast, analyzing the insurgency, as opposed to conventional forces, proved more difficult for the Marines' intelligence apparatus. The MAF's monthly pacification assessment, along with the subsequent Hamlet Evaluation System the CIA developed for MACV based on the Marine model, highlighted useful counterinsurgency trends. The MAF's ability to trace the organizational intricacies of the shadow government, the Vietcong's operational center of gravity, improved over time, but its analysts never devoted as much energy to that task as they did the conventional order of battle. Accordingly, their understanding of that threat paled in comparison to their assessments of the enemy's regular forces. Limited intelligence made it harder to destroy the insurgency's primary strength: its shadow government.

At the macro level, Marine commanders' assessments of their operational challenges foundered on two points. First, they became conditioned to the presence of large NVA and main force Vietcong formations inside I Corps, dismissing the actions of several divisions of communist regulars as routine activities. Accepting their presence and attacks as normal discouraged Marine staff and commanders from reconsidering the efficacy of their mobile defense and its ability to protect I Corps from NVA depredations. While the G-2 section tracked the influxes of NVA, it did not connect the dots and conclude that the regional strategy to protect I Corps was failing. In other words, the information was present, but the analysis was lacking.

Second, III MAF's commanders believed that the insurgency represented the greater long-term threat because they thought NVA units could not operate inside South Vietnam without the VC shadow government's assistance. Concluding that the NVA was, and would remain, dependent on the insurgency for its operational mobility reinforced the idea that ARVN would face a diminished conventional threat so long as the Vietcong stayed dormant. That judgment later proved deadly. Soon after the MAF withdrew, the NVA built up its conventional combined arms and logistic capacity for the offensives they unleased, largely without VC assistance, in 1972 and 1975.

The MAF's threat assessment drove its balanced operational response. Among the three mission-essential tasks, Marine leaders gave primacy to pacification, followed by the big unit war and then development of South Vietnamese security forces. Perhaps inspired by the Marine Corps' institutional memories of fighting guerrillas in Latin America, III MAF dedicated more effort to a sustained and comprehensive small wars program compared to its Army Field Force counterparts. While not as visible or dramatic as large search-and-destroy operations, both civil and military counterinsurgency actions continued at a relentless pace throughout the six-year duration of III MAF's tenure in I Corps. The greatest strength of the Marine small wars program was its emphasis on territorial security forces, especially its Combined Action Program partnership with Popular Forces defending villages. Its biggest pacification failures were the absence of a strong political warfare component and the delay in initiating, coupled with the lack of strong command support for, a counter-VCI program like Phoenix and a citizen's militia.

In waging conventional warfare III MAF's preferred mobile defense blocked major NVA incursions, but this generated high allied casualties and permitted severe damage to I Corps' territory. Meanwhile the US Army–led Advisory Command helped ARVN develop capable companies and battalions, although ARVN I Corps still lacked adequate logistic support, combined arms expertise, and large unit command and staff proficiency. Marine aviation contributed significant mobility, logistic, reconnaissance, communications, and fire support to all three major missions, but III MAF discovered that even a wing twice its normal size could not cope with the demands placed on it by two Marine divisions as well as its US Army, Korean, and South Vietnamese allies. In short, the MAF's operational response—the first wartime test of MAGTF doctrine—proved capable of winning expensive battles but not securing a lasting peace.

In the logistic field, III MAF faced manpower, capability, and capacity challenges in Vietnam. Personnel remained the most troublesome problem throughout the conflict. The force that deployed in 1965 was far too small to meet the growing demands of the war in I Corps. To assist the MAF the Marine Corps reinforced it with another Marine division, deployed two additional regiments of the newly re-created 5th Marine Division, doubled the size of the air wing, and tripled the size of its logistic force. In addition to the demands of rapid expansion, growing casualties further stressed the service's personnel system as it sought to field and replace sufficient qualified Marines in Vietnam. Yet the expanding conflict required three more army divisions and a Korean brigade, extensive aviation support from the navy and air force, and massive logistic augmentation from the navy, the army, and civilian contractors.

The US Navy was the unsung hero supporting logistics in I Corps. It filled several critical gaps: developing and running ports and regional supply facilities and transportation networks, providing medical support from battlefield corpsmen to advanced trauma care in naval hospitals ashore and afloat, and deploying a dozen engineer battalions to augment Marine construction capabilities. The Marine Logistics Command deployed an odd mishmash of units with no habitual supported/supporting relationships, but the arrangements worked well enough once the command expanded and sufficient hubs were established to support front-line forces across the sector. In the end, the ad hoc naval system of logistics kept III MAF going. Despite inevitable growing pains and some self-induced organizational chaos, no operation failed for lack of supplies, equipment, or personnel.

Planning was not a III MAF strength. Its plans shop, something of an orphan within the staff, increased in size and capability but never exerted decisive influence on operations. The 1966 manpower plan foundered on the unfounded assumption that the allies would slash NVA infiltration. The 1967 DMZ barrier plan failed because senior MAF leaders thought it a waste of Marine resources, which they preferred to devote to mobile defense schemes that had already proven inadequate. The 1969 I Corps campaign plan parroted its MACV parent document, generated a litany of vague tasks without viable metrics to measure their completion, and garnered little attention from those tasked to execute it. In the end III MAF's plans reflected the frustrations of the war itself. They identified sound objectives—stop infiltration and destroy the VCI, to name two—but developed no feasible ways to accomplish them.

Assessing III MAF's Performance

One can define "military effectiveness" as the degree to which armed forces achieve political aims through combat or combat readiness.[1] By that standard III MAF, along with its Army Field Force counterparts and MACV higher command, was not effective. Allied military action did not achieve the political goal of an enduring, independent, non-communist South Vietnam. Hanoi was not deterred, coerced, or prohibited from pursuing its mission to conquer Saigon and reunite the two Vietnams. The insurgency was curbed but not destroyed. ARVN was left unprepared to keep both internal and external threats at bay simultaneously. Several aspects of III MAF's regional war help explain these outcomes.

A corps must accurately assess its primary operational problems and then develop and employ effective responses. In this book I have identified shortcomings in III MAF's assessment of its operational environment, weaknesses in its tactical responses to the primary problems it faced, and some missed opportunities. The operational responses failed to adequately remedy the two primary problems: the VC shadow government and NVA infiltration. While these two problems festered, the allies' other accomplishments diminished in importance and impact.

The senior Marine commanders in I Corps wrongly conceptualized the insurgency as the biggest threat while still minimizing the effort to identify and uproot its operational core, the Vietcong infrastructure. Planners and commanders recognized the importance of the shadow government but lacked a way to attack it precisely until the Phoenix program began to hit its stride in late 1968. For the next several years the MAF kept this potentially critical initiative at arm's length rather than reinforcing its constituent parts, especially the critical district operational centers that coordinated the program's actions. Although III MAF enthusiastically assumed the small war mantle in I Corps, its tactical success with counterguerrilla techniques such as the Combined Action Platoons paled in comparison to the disappointing effects of its operational (counter-VCI) and strategic (political warfare) failures.

On the conventional side of the enemy's hybrid threat, the MAF grew desensitized to a large communist army operating inside I Corps. Marine leaders thought that repeatedly repelling NVA incursions would eventually cause Hanoi to give up. Washington withdrew American forces first. Tactically, the MAF knew by the end of 1967 that its mobile defense was not preventing routine NVA incursions that generated high casualties and extreme destruction inside I Corps. But it developed no alternative approach to defend the region. Instead it added troops until the equivalent of nine allied divisions guarded the area, but still the NVA crossed the borders. Like a loyal lemming, III MAF followed MACV over the conceptual cliff of an attrition strategy based on search-and-destroy tactics. Neither headquarters, nor set of commanders, found a way to bar the continuous influx of NVA combat units.

As a regional command, III MAF had a responsibility to help MACV develop an effective theater strategy. Marine generals missed two opportunities—one in the conventional war and another in the pacification campaign—to influence the larger strategic dialogue. Located as it was on the North Vietnamese border, I Corps served as the proving ground for blocking NVA infiltration. Although Walt reluctantly complied with Westmoreland's emphasis on attrition, he and his successor squandered a chance to test a key component of a prevention strategy by emplacing and aggressively defending the DMZ barrier. Senior Marine leaders did not advocate use of a positional defense to block enemy invasions of South Vietnam. The MAF had a direct order in 1967 to test the barrier concept along the northern border, but neither Walt nor Cushman did so because they judged the project a waste of time and resources. Had they completed the assignment either before or after the Tet Offensive, they would have been able to make informed recommendations on the more ambitious proposal to block with allied ground forces the Ho Chi Minh Trail through Laos. While political considerations may have prevented the adoption of such a strategy, III MAF failed to recognize, evaluate, and champion an alternate approach to stemming NVA incursions.

The MAF missed a second chance in the small wars arena to influence the larger strategy. Walt and Victor Krulak pushed Westmoreland for more emphasis on pacification, but no III MAF commander saw the need to help the RVN craft a political/social strategy as a component of the regional counterinsurgency campaign. The ideas outlined in the MAF G-5's 1969 I Corps development study deserved earlier consideration and application. Marine commanders should have heeded the study's insistence that political development must not wait for the establishment of perfect security conditions. Its authors argued that, while socioeconomic development and protection of the population were necessary, the motivation to support both programs flowed from a "rice roots" battle of ideas. Local politics, in other words, drove social, economic, and military outcomes. Forging the policies, programs, and organizational structure to mobilize the people politically thus represented the foremost regional pacification task. Yet III MAF recoiled from these radical recommendations. Except for election support, American units in I Corps seldom rendered direct assistance to political work despite its centrality in a successful counterinsurgency campaign.

Because each region faced similar difficulties under different circumstances, American corps-level headquarters in Vietnam enjoyed leeway to pursue assigned goals in their own way and validate novel operational approaches. After the war Krulak claimed Marines specialized in improvisation and that "adaptability is where victory will be found."[2] In the ways most important to victory, however, III MAF failed to adapt. To be sure, it generated many useful organizational, tactical, and technical innovations. These included the Combined Action Program, the Joint Coordinating Council used to prioritize American and South Vietnamese development projects, the Personnel Reliability Program designed to teach Marines cultural sensitivity, Kit Carson Scouts, Sting Ray patrols that enabled small recon teams to wreak havoc on enemy forces with air and artillery fires, Golden Fleece rice harvest protection operations, expeditionary airfields, the first pacification evaluation criteria, radar terminal guidance of aircraft, bombing based on ground-based beacons, "Super Gaggle" aircraft packages for pinpoint delivery of supplies to beleaguered garrisons, early use of radio direction-finding equipment using ground and air sensors, heavy-lift helicopters dropping napalm in drums carried in cargo nets, surgical suites delivered by helicopter to jungle landing zones, and cutting-edge frozen plasma techniques for trauma care. While impressive, these initiatives paled in comparison to two adaptations that III MAF neglected to make. Put simply, the Marines' creative streak of tactical innovations did not unravel the Gordian knots of resurgent VC infrastructure and unfettered NVA infiltration.

The MAF invested little time or energy in analyzing the campaign-level deficiencies its operations revealed. Its after-action reports, internal studies, and reports to higher headquarters revealed no meaningful reflection on how its programs and operations were achieving its regional campaign goals. Neither did III MAF's principal staff or commanders question their own organizational culture and processes. While corps have a variety of administrative, logistic, and even political roles to play in a hybrid war, they must still exercise standard tactical command responsibilities. These include basic measures such as maintaining a reserve, organizing aggressive pursuit of beaten foes, massing combat power at key points, organizing for success by mandating unit integrity among subordinate commands, establishing force-level counterfire and engineer headquarters, and ensuring lower echelons have direct support such as organic or assigned logistic capabilities. The MAF struggled with balancing the inherent tension between centralized and decentralized control of corps-level forces. In keeping with Marine tradition that emphasized battalion and regimental actions but downplayed critical corps-level functions, III MAF delegated most tactical responsibilities to its subordinate commands. In doing so it forfeited its obligation to identify and weight a main effort. The rudderless battle at Hue and the lack of coherence to DMZ barrier and counterfire efforts followed.

The MAF did not hesitate to challenge its higher headquarters on what it viewed as wrongheaded directives. It enthusiastically opposed MACV on the importance of pacification, the supposed foolishness of the DMZ barrier, the value of naval command of amphibious units landing in sectors already controlled by allied ground headquarters ashore, and, most fervently, the reputed ineffectiveness of a single regional manager for allied aviation. Although not reluctant to contest MACV guidance, MAF leaders did not do so when it came to finding better ways to attack the VCI, identifying an alternative to mobile defense operations, disrupting cross-border sanctuaries, or strengthening

ARVN in I Corps so that it could independently handle both internal and external threats.

The new MAGTF doctrine proved more a hindrance than a help. Senior Marine leaders in I Corps followed closely its tenets, which emphasized the indivisibility of Marine air and ground units. As a corps headquarters, however, III MAF had two more important responsibilities. The first was to ensure that organic assets, including Marine aircraft, supported all subordinate commands, including joint and allied forces, to best accomplish the mission. Westmoreland's dissatisfaction with III MAF's management of that trust prompted the single management controversy. Second: the MAF had an obligation to exercise traditional corps-level ground warfighting doctrine, including the responsibility to maneuver subordinate divisions and brigades as well as employ force-level assets directly when required. Concern with the subtleties of MAGTF doctrine deserved a distant third-place emphasis. The MAF lost control of critical portions of its air and ground wars because its doctrinal priorities were upside down.

Conclusion

In one of his many criticisms of MACV, Krulak cited Marshal Maurice de Saxe's definition of mediocre leaders: "In default of doing what should be done, they do what they know."[3] The same critique could be made of the III MAF headquarters. This naval corps-level command directed field army–size forces in sustained operations for which it was not designed. It encountered, but did not overcome, daunting military and political problems in a hybrid war environment. The MAF followed service doctrine, employed offensive tactics, focused on small unit combat, applied its amphibious and aviation prowess, coordinated combined arms, deployed an ad hoc naval logistic structure, and demonstrated exceptional organizational flexibility (to the brink of operational dysfunction). Nonetheless, III MAF faltered on what had to be accomplished in I Corps. It gravely damaged but could not eliminate the enemy's Maoist infrastructure or the guerrillas who protected it. Similarly, the Marines battered but could not destroy communist conventional formations operating in the area. Most important, the MAF could not prevent the NVA from entering and exiting the region when and where it chose.

Vietnam was a small unit war. Most of its fighting occurred below the battalion level.[4] This fact did not obviate the importance of corps headquarters. Effectiveness at small and large unit operations were not mutually exclusive. Indeed, operations and programs developed, conducted, and supported at the corps level often gave coherence and significance to the myriad skirmishes, engagements, and battles that represented the lion's share of the war. And sometimes, as the fight for Hue illustrated, the situation required a traditional corps-level command post directing multiple divisions. III MAF was not a proficient corps-level headquarters because the Marine Corps had limited experience in that role and paid little attention to studying operations at that level. This deficiency was not solely responsible for III MAF's failure to craft a winning campaign in I Corps. But corps command difficulties ran like a scarlet thread through the MAF's major operational shortfalls.

In their study of military effectiveness between 1914 and 1945, Williamson Murray and Allan Millett concluded that "mistakes in operations and tactics can be corrected [admittedly at a cost]. But political and strategic mistakes live forever."[5] No finer requiem exists for III MAF's experience in Vietnam. Despite corps-level miscues and a steep learning curve, Marines on the sharp end won every engagement of battalion size or larger during the six years that III MAF remained in I Corps. Yet their victories did not matter. Lacking a strategy of prevention, America succumbed politically to its own attrition strategy. Its people tired of the war's high cost and seeming lack of progress. Marine shortcomings contributed to that outcome. In I Corps III MAF did not prepare ARVN to stand alone, did not destroy the shadow government, and did not dissuade or prevent the NVA from continuing its attacks. The rest was detail.

Marine Corps history, claimed Krulak, marked the triumphs not of individual heroes but of a successful institution.[6] The record of III MAF's command element in Vietnam, however, was sorely checkered. It prevented the NVA and VC from conquering I Corps while the MAF defended the region. Its forces helped develop the best ARVN corps, consistently defeated the NVA in battle, and whittled down the region's Vietcong. But III MAF failed to set the security conditions that allowed I Corps to survive for more than a few short years after US forces withdrew. The MAF's story is the saga of a headquarters stacking up costly tactical victories but achieving only a bitter operational stalemate that delayed but did not prevent South Vietnam's ultimate defeat. It is a tale with a trove of corps-level lessons. In the epilogue that follows I will examine how many of them the Marine Corps absorbed before its next major war.

Epilogue

Lessons and Legacies, 1971–1991

What did the Marine Corps learn from III Marine Amphibious Force's experience as a corps-level headquarters in Vietnam? According to its Commandant: not much. As the Marines withdrew in 1971, General Leonard F. Chapman observed "we got defeated and thrown out, [and] the best thing we can do is forget it."[1] With such views espoused by its senior leaders, it is not surprising that in the two decades between the withdrawal from I Corps and its next opportunity for corps-level command in Operation DESERT STORM, the service addressed few of the problems the MAF had encountered. Instead the Marine Corps, like the US Army, turned away from its searing experience in Vietnam to concentrate on new challenges. The army turned back to the Soviet threat in Europe, while the Marines refocused on small unit naval expeditionary missions.[2] This understandable shift need not have prevented a more complete consideration of what happened in I Corps. Effective military organizations learn from their failures as well their successes. The record of the German army between the world wars, when it studied in detail its performance in World War I, illustrates the value of frank assessments.[3] The Marine Corps conducted no such reflective analysis in the aftermath of Vietnam. In this epilogue I detail some of the shortfalls that carried over to the next time Marines fielded a corps-level command.

The generals who commanded III MAF in I Corps had little to say after the war about corps-level command or its doctrinal, organizational, training, and equipment underpinnings. General Walt went on to become assistant Commandant of the Marine Corps. Neither his command memoir nor his available oral history interviews addressed corps-level considerations. General Cushman served as the deputy CIA director, then became Commandant in 1972 even though III MAF had foundered most profoundly under his watch. In his postwar interviews

224

he indicated his preference to push corps troop units like the 1st Force Reconnaissance Company down to divisions for employment but said nothing about what the Marine Corps should learn from its longest experience of corps-level command. General Nickerson likewise left no indication that the ways and means of fighting a MAF was a subject worthy of study or reflection.[4] General McCutcheon, one of the Marine Corps' most intelligent, charismatic, and influential senior leaders, had little time to ponder the war's lessons before his tragic death by cancer in July 1971. It is remarkable that these senior leaders exhibited so little interest in how best to fight a corps from a C2 perspective or what the MAF headquarters did right and wrong during its six-year tenure in I Corps.

After the war, no Marine Corps study evaluated III MAF's performance as a corps-level headquarters in Vietnam. It was as if the command's role in directing advisory, pacification, and conventional operations did not happen or matter. The army contracted the BDM Corporation to evaluate strategic lessons of the war. But that 1980 study, beyond praising single management of airpower, castigating the enclave strategy as an unsuitable alternative to attrition, and noting the defense of Khe Sanh represented energy best spent elsewhere, paid little attention to operations inside "Marine Land."[5] The Marine Corps did not commission a similar study assessing III MAF's actions. Service historical records from 1971 to 1991 reveal studies that addressed aspects of MAF and corps troop doctrine, organization, training, and equipment but no report that examines specifically the senior MAGTF headquarters' composite requirements to effectively command and support a multi-division corps in sustained operations ashore.[6] The studies that were done did not lead to changes that beefed up the MAF's capacity to employ a traditional multi-division corps in combat.

The Marine Corps addressed, reluctantly, one doctrinal issue after the war. Having fought so hard to regain control of Marine fixed-wing aircraft in I Corps, HQMC was not inclined to see the single management arrangement imposed in 1968 as anything other than a doctrinal aberration to be avoided at all costs in future wars. Yet in the 1986 Omnibus Agreement the Commandant acceded to the authority of the senior theater air commander (usually a US Air Force officer) to direct the aviation element of joint campaigns, including how much effort went toward strategic, interdiction, and close air support missions.[7] Stasis prevailed in other doctrinal lanes. Both III MAF and HQMC had conducted studies on decentralizing control of Marine aircraft in

1969, but the working groups concluded no doctrinal adjustments or long-term organizational changes were required. In the postwar period helicopters remained under the purview of the Marine air wings, with all ground requests for support adjudicated by a central scheduling and tasking authority within the MAW.[8] Neither was amphibious doctrine tweaked, even though inserting naval forces inside sectors managed by friendly ground forces ashore had generated confusion in Vietnam, especially concerning airspace control. Most important, senior Marine leaders paid no attention to integrating the doctrine for US Army corps and force-level MAGTFs so that future MAFs might fight multiple divisions and outsized air wings more effectively.

In the two decades between Vietnam and the Gulf War, the Marine Corps enacted few organizational modifications for the MAF. The force-level headquarters switched its name from "amphibious" back to "expeditionary" in 1988, but it added no corps troop units to better support multiple divisions. Force Logistics Command, renamed the Force Service Support Group, remained a brigade-size rather than the division-size force required in Vietnam. No Force Advisory Command emerged in the postwar period despite several decades of experience training its Vietnamese Marine counterpart. Neither did the Marine Corps evaluate the Phoenix program's performance in I Corps to prepare for future struggles against Maoist insurgent infrastructure. Finally, the concept of a Marine Expeditionary Corps organized, trained, and equipped to direct multiple divisions and air wings quietly disappeared from the menu of organizational options. By default, MAFs remained at the pinnacle of the MAGTF structural hierarchy, but they still lacked enough organic artillery, communications, engineering, intelligence, logistics, and military police capacity to support multiple divisions and wings operating across a corps-size zone.

After Vietnam, Marine Corps schools placed little emphasis on corps-level command, force organizational imperatives, or how standard warfighting functions applied at the MAF level. The Quantico Staff College quickly resumed its prewar emphasis on the MAF's role in brief amphibious operations rather than sustained campaigns ashore. Within a year of III MAF's departure from Da Nang, the college's director remarked that "we have deemphasized instruction based on our Vietnam experience. In effect, we have taken our heads out of the jungle. We are resharpening our skills in the amphibious business and again firing up the great Navy-Marine team." Instruction on counterinsurgency disappeared in the 1970s curriculum and returned

only in a very limited way in the 1980s.[9] Student course papers written between Vietnam and DESERT STORM seldom examined MAF/
corps-level topics.[10] Articles in the service's professional journal during this period also reflected a dearth of interest, or even an awareness,
of issues associated with how to fight a naval expeditionary corps.[11]
Civilian scholars matched Marine schools in looking past corps-level
command in Vietnam. No academic monograph written prior to the
Gulf War (or since, until this one) focused on III MAF or Army Field
Force headquarters' performance in Southeast Asia.

    After III MAF's withdrawal from I Corps, the Marine Corps ex-
perienced a decade of recovery followed by a decade of revitalization. During the 1970s the service increased education requirements
for enlisted Marines and reduced widespread substance abuse and
misconduct problems. In the 1980s the Marine Corps improved its
equipment to match upgraded personnel standards. The Fleet Marine
Force fielded new infantry weapons, trucks, artillery, antitank missiles, tanks, light armored vehicles, helicopters, jets, and amphibious
vessels. Fleet training expanded to winter exercises in Scandinavia, a
full range of global amphibious drills, combined arms live-fire maneuvers in the California desert, and rapid response rehearsals to link up
with equipment prepositioned in Norway or aboard ships at sea. The
Marine Corps inculcated maneuver warfare tenets and developed new
special operations capabilities for forward-deployed MEUs.[12] These
manpower, training, and equipment developments enhanced service
capabilities, but few developed corps-level competencies. Each MAF
headquarters conducted occasional command-post or field exercises,
but actual contingencies never required a MAF/MEF–level response.[13]
Combat actions during this period were limited in number and small
in scale: the ill-fated *Mayaguez* rescue in Cambodia (1975); the tragic
"presence" mission in Beirut (1982–1984); the six-day Grenada incursion (1983); and the swift removal of Manual Noriega in Panama (1989).
None of these minor joint operations employed more than one Marine
infantry battalion.

    The next time the Marine Corps employed a corps-level headquar-
ters in combat was in the 1990–1991 Gulf War. General Walter Boomer
commanded I MEF, the California-based headquarters that directed
Marine operations in Operations DESERT SHIELD and DESERT
STORM. The Marine contingent that deployed to Saudi Arabia and
fought Saddam Hussein's Iraqi army in Kuwait totaled eight-four thousand Marines, nearly as many as III MAF commanded at its peak in

Vietnam. Only sixty-six thousand of these troops reported to I MEF. Fifth Fleet commanded the other eighteen thousand Marines, who remained afloat in two brigades and a separate Marine Expeditionary Unit to threaten the Iraqi army from the sea.[14]

The MEF ashore incorporated the standard MAGTF mix of subordinate ground, aviation, and logistic commands plus various corps-level troop units. Two Marine divisions, the 1st and 2nd, provided offensive punch. A US Army armor brigade reinforced the 2nd Marine Division, representing its third maneuver element. The 3rd Marine Wing controlled two fixed-wing and two rotary-wing groups totaling thirty-one squadrons. The sixteen fixed-wing and fifteen rotary-wing squadrons employed a total of 467 aircraft. The logistics element, 1st Force Service Support Group, deployed two General Support Groups and two Direct Support Groups. At the corps troops level, a reserve Marine infantry regiment provided rear-area security and handled prisoners, while a separate regiment stood ready to provide casualty replacements. Additional corps-level troops included a provisional navy Seabee regiment with six construction battalions, two civil affairs groups, a radio reconnaissance battalion, and a ground reconnaissance and intelligence group.[15]

The Gulf War's brevity and intensity did not stress I MEF's capacity for corps-level command. Only limited combat accompanied the MEF's mobile defense of Saudi Arabia during DESERT SHIELD. While the force buildup and defensive phase lasted six months, the offensive fighting that followed remained mercifully brief. The air-centric shaping component of the campaign continued for thirty-eight days, while the ground combat to liberate Kuwait lasted a mere one hundred hours. Both Marine divisions penetrated the Iraqi army's dual border barrier lines and drove swiftly to their objectives just outside Kuwait City. At a cost of twenty-four killed and ninety-two wounded in action, Marine forces shattered eighteen Iraqi divisions, destroying more than a thousand tanks, six hundred armored personnel carriers, and four hundred artillery pieces while killing fifteen hundred Iraqi soldiers and capturing 22,308 more. The rapidity of I MEF's burst through the Iraqi defenses disrupted Central Command's choreographed timeline for US Army VII Corps' assault to envelop the fixed enemy.[16] As a supporting attack in a short campaign, I MEF had no important command decisions to make once the drive commenced. Neither did the conflict entail any unconventional challenges. The quick and decisive outcome, however, obscured some of the challenges I MEF experienced as a corps-level headquarters.

The I MEF organization for combat in Kuwait reveals that the Marine approach to corps-level operations had evolved little since Vietnam. A small headquarters, designed to fight a single division–wing team, needed significant augmentation to command a multi-division corps. The entire Marine Corps, by pooling its global resources, generated a single ad hoc corps. Units from II MEF (North Carolina), III MEF (Okinawa and Hawaii), and the reserve component reinforced I MEF. Army and navy forces augmented it as well. The MEF structure fielded no organic corps-level Marine engineer command (provided by the navy) or artillery headquarters to coordinate counterfire or reinforce division artillery fires. By comparison, US Army VII Corps employed four artillery brigades in addition to its division-level guns, while XVIII Corps commanded two corps-level artillery brigades. The I MEF logistic command, like III MAF's in Vietnam, cobbled together units from outside the MEF to provide the capacity needed to support a corps of sixty-six thousand Marines. The I MEF logisticians of 1st Force Service Support provided the general support functions that the Naval Support Activity had provided in Vietnam. A Direct Support Command, led by II MEF's service support headquarters and comprising logistics units from across the Marine Corps, shuttled supplies forward and performed maintenance for the two divisions' regimental task forces. Like its 1st MAW counterpart in Vietnam, 3rd MAW in the Persian Gulf grew to twice the size of a normal air wing. Many of the wing's aircraft and much of its airfield support capability came from Marine aviation commands outside 3rd MAW.[17]

As it had in Vietnam, the MEF headquarters developed its war plans in a joint and combined environment. The staff did not employ a separate plans directorate during the Gulf War. Instead officers from the G-3 Operations section led development of the staff's tactical plans. A host of Marine liaison officers deployed to army, navy, air force, Central Command, and allied headquarters to coordinate the MEF's preparations with adjacent and senior headquarters. As with the I Corps predecessor, tension existed between Marine airmen and their air force counterparts. This time the argument was not over single management tenets, which had been codified under joint doctrine in 1986, but over how much of the air effort was directed at enemy tactical forces versus strategic or interdiction targets. General Norman Schwarzkopf, Central Command's US Army commander, employed graduates of the army's Fort Leavenworth School of Advanced Military Studies to help develop the outline plan for the war. The Marine Corps set up a similar school in Quantico in 1990 to develop its own campaign planners for future conflicts. Meanwhile, HQMC established the MAGTF Staff Training Program to improve the MEFs' planning and execution of operations.[18]

In the midst of DESERT STORM, the Marine Corps History Division recommended renaming I MEF an "Expeditionary Corps."[19] It is not clear if the Commandant inspired this proposal, a doctrinal concept that had lain dormant since the early 1960s, but a name-change alone would not have altered the MEF's capability or performance. Structural enhancements—including more artillery, engineering, logistics, military police, reconnaissance, and communications capacity—were required to field a naval corps capable of fighting and maintaining multiple divisions. The MEF of 1990, like its counterpart a quarter-century earlier, was an anemic headquarters with insufficient organic air, ground, logistic, and corps troop capacity to support sustained operations ashore. In Vietnam and the Persian Gulf, the Marine Corps addressed some of those shortfalls by borrowing resources from other commands and services. To this day, senior Marine leaders have elected not to develop and maintain the corps-level capabilities that they continually borrow, reinstitute, or simply go without when multi-division MEFs are employed.

After the Gulf War, triumphalism prevailed. President George H. W. Bush voiced a common sentiment when he declared: "The ghosts of Vietnam have been laid to rest beneath the sands of the Arabian desert."[20] If only. Senior army and Marine Corps leaders, most of them veterans of Vietnam, felt vindicated by the Gulf War's outcome, which they attributed to the changes their services had initiated since 1973.[21] For the Marines, those changes did not include development of corps-level command capabilities. Since 1941 the Marine Corps has engaged in four conflicts requiring corps-level headquarters, most recently in the 2003 invasion of Iraq. This study has underscored the value of examining those episodes, together totaling a dozen years of combat, for the insights they offer on organizing, training, and equipping a MAGTF for effective corps-level command. The story of III MAF in Vietnam illustrates what can happen when a corps headquarters is not ready for the conflict it encounters and then fights the war it wants to rather than the one it must.

Notes

Abbreviations Used in Notes

ALMAR	All Marine Corps Activities (messages released to all Marines)
ANGLICO	Air-Naval Gunfire Liaison Company
CC	Command Chronology
CCP	Combined Campaign Plan
CHECO	Contemporary Historical Evaluation of Current Operations (US Air Force)
CINCPAC	Commander in Chief, Pacific
CINCPACFLT	Commander in Chief, Pacific Fleet
CJCS	Chairman, Joint Chiefs of Staff
CMC	Commandant of the Marine Corps
COMCBPAC	Commander, Construction Battalion, Pacific
COMUSMACV	Commander, US Military Assistance Command, Vietnam
CSA	Chief of Staff of the Army
CTZ	Corps Tactical Zone
CY	Calendar Year
DOD	Department of Defense
EWTG	Expeditionary Warfare Training Group
FM	Field Manual
FMF	Fleet Marine Force
FWMAF	Free World Military Assistance Forces
JCS	Joint Chiefs of Staff
LBJL	Lyndon B. Johnson Presidential Library, University of Texas at Austin
LBJP	Lyndon B. Johnson Papers
MCDP	Marine Corps Doctrinal Publication
MCHD	Marine Corps History Division
MCO	Marine Corps Order
MSTP	Marine Air-Ground Task Force Staff Training Program
NARA II	National Archives 2 at College Park, Maryland
PCV	Provisional Corps, Vietnam
RD	Revolutionary Development
RG	Record Group
SPECAT	Special Category (highly sensitive message traffic)

UNCL	Unclassified
VDA	Vietnam Digital Archive (Marine Corps History Division)
VSSG	Vietnam Special Studies Group
WCWP	William C. Westmoreland's Papers

Shortened Citations

1962 MAGTF Order
"The Organization of Marine Air-Ground Task Forces," 27 December 1962, Enclosure 1 "Organizational Structure of Marine Air-Ground Task Forces," Historians' Files, History Division, Marine Corps University, Quantico, VA

1963 FM 100-15
Field Manual 100-15, *Field Service Regulations—Larger Units* (Washington, DC: Headquarters, Department of the Army, 1963)

1969 III MAF G-5 Development Study
III MAF G-5, *Development's Role in Pacification*, 194, Folders 1–4, Box 18, Vietnam War Collection, MCHD

I Corps 1969 CCP
I ARVN Corps/Free World Military Assistance Forces, ICTZ Combined Campaign Plan 1969, 26 December 1968

"III MAF 1968 Military Posture Study"
III MAF Staff Study 2–68, "Military Posture, Northern I Corps," 1 September 1968, Annex D page 9, Folder "18) III MAF: Staff Study 2–68 31 Mar 1968," Box 156 (III MAF), Entry "Records of Units and Other Commands, 1953–1993," RG 127, NARA II

III MAF G-2 1968 Tet Intelligence Study
III MAF G-2, "Development of the Enemy Situation Prior to the 1968 Tet Offensive, Decentralization of Collection Assets in SVN, and Intelligence Support and Services Rendered to III MAF by COMUSMACV Intelligence Agencies," no date—circa 1968, Folder "Vietnam III MAF," Box 8, Vietnam War Collection, MCHD

III MAF Oplan 121–66
III MAF Operation Plan 121–66 (PRACTICE NINE), Annex B pages 1–4, Box 156 (III MAF), Entry "Records of Units and Other Commands, 1953–1993," RG 127, NARA II

CC
III MAF Command Chronology

Chapman Oral History
Leonard F. Chapman, Jr., interviewer not listed, 1979/1981, transcript, 18–21, Oral History Collection, MCHD

CINCPACFLT Amphib Ops Conference Report
Report of Amphibious Operations Conference Held at Direction of CINCPACFLT,

25 February–1 March 1966, Folder 5/2, Box 145, Entry "Records of Units and Other Commands, 1953–1993, FMFPAC," RG 127, NARA II

Combined Staff Barrier Inspection Report, 1–2 January 1968
Message, COMUSMACV to CG III MAF, "Report of Trip to III MAF, 1–2 Jan 68," 151229Z January 1968, Folder "COMUSMACV 1968, Secret Outgoing Message File [2 of 2]," Box 42, WCWP, LBJL

Corson CAP paper
William R. Corson, "Marine Combined Action Program in Vietnam," no date, 24, Folder 20, Box 1, Entry A1 1045 ("Records of or Related to General Officers, 1944–1975"), RG 127, NARA II

"CSA Confirmation Fact Sheet 46"
"Increased Proportion of NVA Troops," Fact Sheet 46, 17 May 1968, Folder "Fact Book, COMUSMACV, Vol. 1 [1 of 5] [CSA Confirmation Hearings]," Box 70, WCWP, LBJL

"CSA Confirmation Fact Sheet 64"
"Personnel Infiltration (DMZ vs Laos)," Fact Sheet 64, 18 May 1968, Folder "Fact Book, COMUSMACV, Vol. 1 [1 of 5] [CSA Confirmation Hearings]," Box 70, WCWP, LBJL

DOUBLE EAGLE Op Order
III MAF Operation Order 307–66 (Operation Double Eagle), 15 January 1966, Folder 9/11, Box 154, Entry "Records of Units and Other Commands, 1953–1993, G-3, III MAF," RG 127, NARA II

DYE MARKER Status Report, 10 August 1967
III MAF/3rd Marine Division DYE MARKER Status Report for CMC, 10 August 1967, Folder "7 (94–0068 CMC Trip Report West Pac, August 3–12, 1967 Part 1 of 3)," Box 11 (1966–1967), Entry 1059, RG 127, NARA II

EWTGC
Collection "Expeditionary Warfare Training Group Collection"

FMFPAC, *Historical Summary, 1965–1967*
FMFPAC, *Historical Summary, U.S. Marine Corps Forces in Vietnam, March 1965–September 1967*, Volume 1, 8–4, Folder "FMFPAC," Box 13, Vietnam War Collection, MCHD

"FMFPAC Force Estimate"
Letter, Lieutenant General Victor H. Krulak to General Wallace M. Greene, Jr., 28 September 1966, encl: "Determination of Force Requirements, I Corps," Folder 12, Box 142, Entry "Records of Units and Other Commands, 1953–1993, FMFPAC," RG 127, NARA II

FMFPAC's Recommended MEC/MEF HQ Organization
Letter, CG FMFPAC to CMC, 25 January 1965, "Concepts for Marine Expeditionary Corps and Marine Expeditionary Force Headquarters," Folder 4 ("(1) FMFPAC: Organization of HQ MEC & MEF"), Box 141, Entry "Records of Units and Other Commands, 1953–1993, FMFPAC," RG 127, NARA II

History of Naval Support Activity
"The History of Naval Support Activity," Folder "Vietnam Da Nang," Box 7 (Combat-L), Collection "Historians' Reference Files, Vietnam," Archives Branch, Naval History and Heritage Command, Washington Navy Yard, Washington, DC

"HQMC Force Estimate"
Letter, General Wallace M. Greene, Jr., to Walt W. Rostow, 2 December 1966, encl. "Force Requirements and Long Range Estimate for I Corp RVN," Folder "Vietnam, Long Range Estimate and Force Requirement for the Successful Prosecution of the War in I Corps, RVN"

"JGS/FWMAF 1968 CCP"
I ARVN Corps/III MAF Combined Campaign Plan 1–68, no date, Folder 5 ["(8) III MAF: I ARVN Corps/III MAF Combined Campaign plan 1–68 1967 part 2 of 3"], Box 157 ["III MAF"], Entry "Records of Units and Other Commands, 1953–1993," RG 127, NARA II

LBJP
Lyndon B. Johnson papers

LBJPL
Lyndon Baines Johnson Presidential Library

"MACV PRACTICE NINE Plan"
"MACV PRACTICE NINE Requirements Plan," 26 November 1966, 25–26, Folder "206-02 Historians Background Material (1966) Files Barrier/Starbird Part 1 of 3," Box 31, Entry A1 52 "HQ MACV," RG 472, NARA II

MCDP 6
Marine Corps Doctrinal Publication (MCDP) 6, *Command and Control* (Washington, DC: Headquarters Marine Corps, 1996)

MCHD
Marine Corps History Division, Quantico, VA

The Marines in Vietnam, 1954–1973
The Marines in Vietnam, 1954–1973: An Anthology and Annotated Bibliography (Washington, DC: HQMC History and Museums Division, 1985)

NARA II
National Archives 2, College Park, MD

VDA
Vietnam Digital Archive, MCHD

WCWP
Collection "Papers of William Westmoreland"

Wilson Oral History
Almon C. Wilson, interviewed by Paul Stillwell, 2002, transcript, 110, Oral History Collection, History Division, US Naval Institute, Annapolis, MD

Introduction: Waging War in I Corps

1. III MAF served as the senior American tactical headquarters in I Corps from 1965 to 1970, when it switched roles with the US Army's XXIV Corps, which had served under III MAF for the previous two years. This study examines III MAF until it departed Vietnam in 1971 because it still served as a corps-level headquarters, though one much diminished in size and responsibility during its final year in country.

2. His words: "It is the singularly unfair peculiarity of war that the credit of success is claimed by all, while a disaster is attributed to one alone." Cornelius Tacitus, "The Life of Cnæus Julius Agricola," ed. Alfred John Church and William Jackson Brodribb, in *Complete Works of Tacitus*, ed. Sara Bryant (New York: Random House, 1876; repr., 1942), www.perseus.tufts.edu/hopper/text?doc=Perseus%3Atext%3A1999.02.0081%3Achapter%3D27.

3. Jeffrey Race, *War Comes to Long An: Revolutionary Conflict in a Vietnamese Province* (Berkeley: University of California Press, 1972).

4. T. H. E. Travers, *How the War Was Won: Command and Technology in the British Army on the Western Front: 1917–1918* (London: Routledge, 1992); Robin Prior and Trevor Wilson, *Command on the Western Front: The Military Career of Sir Henry Rawlinson, 1914–1918* (Oxford, UK: Blackwell, 1992); Simon Robbins, *British Generalship on the Western Front, 1914–1918: Defeat into Victory* (London: Frank Cass, 2004); Andy Simpson, *Directing Operations: British Corps Command on the Western Front, 1914–1918* (Stroud, UK: Spellmount, 2006).

5. Harold R. Winton, *Corps Commanders of the Bulge: Six American Generals and Victory in the Ardennes* (Lawrence: University Press of Kansas, 2007); Douglas E. Delaney, *Corps Commanders: Five Generals at War, 1939–1945* (Vancouver: UBC Press, 2011); Nathan N. Prefer, *Patton's Ghost Corps: Cracking the Siegfried Line* (Novato, CA: Presidio Press, 2000); Michael Reynolds, *Steel Inferno: 1st SS Panzer Corps in Normandy* (New York: Dell Publishing, 1997); Michael Reynolds, *Men of Steel: I SS Panzer Corps The Ardennes and Eastern Front, 1944–45* (Staplehurst, UK: Spellmount, 1999).

6. Bernard Law Montgomery, *The Memoirs of Field Marshal Montgomery* (1958; repr., Barnsley, UK: Pen & Sword Books, 2007); William J. Slim, *Defeat Into Victory* (1961; repr., New York: David McKay Company, 1965); Hermann Balck, *Order in Chaos: The Memoirs of General of Panzer Troops Hermann Balck*, ed. David T. Zabecki and Dieter J. Biedekarken, trans. David T. Zabecki and Dieter J. Biedekarken (1981; repr., Lexington: University Press of Kentucky, 2015); Erich von Manstein, *Lost Victories*, ed. Anthony G. Powell, trans. Anthony G. Powell (1955; repr., Novato, CA: Presidio Press, 1994); F. W. von Mellenthin, *Panzer Battles: A Study of the Employment of Armor in the Second World War*, ed. L. C. F. Turner, trans. H. Betzler (1956; repr., New York: Ballantine Books, 1990); Erhard Raus, *Panzer Operations: The Eastern Front Memoir of General Raus, 1941–1945*, trans. Steven H. Newton (Cambridge, MA: Da Capo Press, 2003); J. Lawton Collins, *Lightning Joe: An Autobiography* (Novato, CA: Presidio Press, 1994); L. K. Truscott, Jr., *Command Missions: A Personal Story* (1954; repr., New York: Random House Publishing, 1990); Matthew B. Ridgway, *Soldier: The Memoirs of Matthew B. Ridgway* (New York: Harper & Brothers, 1956).

7. Shelby L. Stanton, *America's Tenth Legion: X Corps in Korea, 1950* (Novato, CA: Presidio Press, 1989); Roy E. Appleman, *Escaping the Trap: The U.S. Army X Corps in Northeastern Korea* (College Station: Texas A&M University Press, 1990); Richard W. Stewart, *Staff Operations: The X Corps in Korea, December 1950* (Fort Leavenworth, KS: Combat Studies Institute, 1991).

8. Only a few works touch on the topic at all. See, for example, Michael A. Hennessy, *Strategy in Vietnam: The Marines and Revolutionary Warfare in I Corps, 1965–1972* (Westport, CT: Praeger, 1997); Arrigo Velicogna, "Victory and Strategic Culture: The Marines, the Army and Vietnam; First Corps Tactical Zone 1965–1971"(doctoral dissertation, King's College London, 2013), https://kclpure .kcl.ac.uk/portal/en/theses/victory-and-strategic-culture(1fe6e6b0-a7a7-47a5-8f 85-1cb50f299876).html; Edward Thomas Nevgloski, "Understanding the United States Marines' strategy and approach to the conventional war in South Vietnam's Northern provinces, March 1965–December 1967" (doctoral dissertation, King's College London, 2019), https://kclpure.kcl.ac.uk/portal/en/theses/understanding -the-united-states-marines-strategy-and-approach-to-the-conventional-war-in -south-vietnams-northern-provinces-march-1965-december-1967(f220ac6c-d9a8 -4d60-9136-a49c1df40659).html. Several good province-level studies have been produced, but no regional counterparts exist. See, e.g., Eric M. Bergerud, *The Dynamics of Defeat: The Vietnam War in Hau Nghia Province* (Boulder: Westview Press, 1991); Kevin M. Boylan, *Losing Binh Dinh: The Failure of Pacification and Vietnamization, 1969–1971* (Lawrence: University Press of Kansas, 2016).

9. FM 100-15, *Larger Units: Theater Army—Corps* (Washington, DC: Headquarters, Department of the Army, 1968), 822. These developments, which shifted support structure from army to corps level, generated professional debate within the army. For an interesting exchange of views on the prospect of abolishing the corps level of command in the US Army, see Letter, COMUSMACV to CG, US Army Combat Development Command, 27 January 1968, Folder "COMUSMACV Signature File—January 1968 [1 of 2]," Box 40 [2 of 2], Collection "Papers of William Westmoreland" (hereafter WCWP), Lyndon Baines Johnson Presidential Library (hereafter LBJPL), Austin, TX. Westmoreland was not a fan of the proposal to eliminate corps. He thought that administrative and logistical concerns would overwhelm an army commander trying to direct tactically up to eight divisions without subordinate corps echelons of command.

10. This work uses the terms "conventional" and "regular" as synonyms. These terms refer to armed forces that are organized, trained, equipped, and employed to conduct combined arms warfare using standard military formations. It uses the terms "unconventional" and "irregular" as synonyms to convey armed forces that are not similarly organized, trained, equipped, and employed. In this usage, NVA units as well as VC main force units are considered regulars or conventional in nature. Vietcong village or hamlet guerrillas are characterized as unconventional or irregular troops.

11. For an overview of the two schools' positions and the literature associated with each, see Gary R. Hess, *Vietnam: Explaining America's Lost War* (West Sussex, UK: John Wiley & Sons, 2015).

12. Harry G. Summers, Jr., *On Strategy: A Critical Analysis of the Vietnam War* (New York: Dell Publishing, 1984).

13. Andrew F. Krepinevich, Jr., *The Army and Vietnam* (Baltimore: Johns Hopkins University Press, 1986).

14. Lewis Sorley, *A Better War: The Unexamined Victories and Final Tragedy of America's Last Years in Vietnam* (New York: Harcourt Brace, 1999).

15. Andrew J. Birtle, "PROVN, Westmoreland, and the Historians: A Reappraisal," *Journal of Military History* 72 (October 2008): 1213–1247; Gregory A. Daddis, *Westmoreland's War: Reassessing American Strategy in Vietnam* (Oxford, UK: Oxford University Press, 2015).

Prologue: Marines and Corps-Level Command, 1941–1965

1. For comprehensive treatments of the pre–World War II US Marine Corps, see Edwin H. Simmons, *The United States Marines: The First Two Hundred Years, 1775–1975* (New York: Viking Press, 1974); Merrill L. Bartlett and Jack Sweetman, *The U.S. Marine Corps: An Illustrated History* (Annapolis, MD: Naval Institute Press, 2001); Robert Debs Heinl, Jr., *Soldiers of the Sea: The United States Marine Corps, 1775–1962* (Baltimore: Nautical & Aviation Publishing Company of America, 1991); Allan R. Millett, *Semper Fidelis: The History of the United States Marine Corps* (New York: Free Press, 1991); J. Robert Moskin, *The U.S. Marine Corps Story*, 3rd ed. (Boston: Little, Brown, 1992); Annette D. Amerman, *United States Marine Corps in the First World War: Anthology, Selected Bibliography, and Annotated Order of Battle* (Quantico, VA: Marine Corps University History Division, 2016).

2. Millett, *Semper Fidelis*, 336, 438.

3. In WWII, the US Navy defined an amphibious corps as "a task organization of two or more Army or Marine divisions, with headquarters and supporting troops, trained and equipped for amphibious assault operations. It is normally commanded by an officer of the Marine Corps." Chester Nimitz, undated directive titled "Command Relationships in Amphibious Operations in Pacific Ocean Areas," Folder "Index of Basic Directives on Establishment of Theaters of Operation and Commands, WWII and Directives for Joint Amphibious Operations, 1942–44," Box 2, Collection "Expeditionary Warfare Training Group Collection" (# 3805) (hereafter EWTGC, Archives Branch, Marine Corps History Division, Quantico, VA (hereafter MCHD).

4. Louis Caporale, "Corps-level Commands of the USMC," *Marine Corps Gazette* 62, no. 11 (November 1978): 74–77; Gordon Rottman, *The Marine Corps Pacific Theater of Operations, 1941–43* (Oxford, UK: Osprey Publishing, 2004), 33–34; Gordon Rottman, *US Marine Corps Pacific Theater of Operations, 1943–44* (Oxford, UK: Osprey Publishing, 2004), 30–32; Gordon Rottman, *US Marine Corps Pacific Theater of Operations, 1944–45* (Oxford, UK: Osprey Publishing, 2004), 20–21.

5. Charles R. Smith, *Securing the Surrender: Marines in the Occupation of Japan* (Washington, DC: Marine Corps Historical Center, 1997); Rottman, *US Marine Corps Pacific Theater of Operations, 1944–45*, 91–93.

6. Millett, *Semper Fidelis*, 475–517.

7. For the Lebanon intervention, 5,790 Marines went ashore under Marine Brigadier General Sidney S. Wade, commanding the 2nd Provisional Marine Force. Jack Shulimson, *Marines in Lebanon, 1958* (Washington, DC: HQMC History and Museums Division, 1983), 37.

8. Millett, *Semper Fidelis*, 555–558.

9. Two WWII-era army doctrinal publications addressed large unit operations.

FM 100-5, *Field Service Regulations—Operations* (1941), addressed techniques of command and combined arms integration. FM 100-15, *Field Service Regulations—Larger Units* (1942), covered strategic precepts, campaign planning, corps-level and above maneuvers, organizational models, and considerations for air force and armor employment. *Larger Units* emphasized the flexibility inherent in corps' composition based on terrain, enemy, and mission factors, with the expectation that their assigned divisions and corps-level troop units would frequently change as missions altered. In effect through the end of the war, the 1942 manual also reinforced the imperative of early and thorough planning given the expanded dimensions of force, space, and time in large unit operations.

10. MCO 3120.3, "The Organization of Marine Air-Ground Task Forces," 27 December 1962, Enclosure 1 "Organizational Structure of Marine Air-Ground Task Forces," Historians' Files, History Division, Marine Corps University, Quantico, VA (hereafter 1962 MAGTF Order). This directive replaced CMC letter AO3H-jeb of 31 May 1960, "Air-Ground Task Force Command Relationships and Structure, NOTAL."

11. MCO 3340.3, "Employment of Marine Air-Ground Task Forces in Amphibious Operations," 20 April 1962, Historians' Files, History Division, Marine Corps University, Quantico, VA; 1962 MAGTF Order.

12. FMFM 3-1, *Command and Staff Action* (Quantico, VA: Marine Corps Landing Force Development Activities, 1965).

13. In the Okinawa campaign, the only time prior to Vietnam when Marine and army corps fought side by side, only minor differences existed in corps structure. Roy E. Appleman et al., *Okinawa: The Last Battle* (Washington, DC: US Army Center of Military History, 1991), 476–478. Appendix A depicts the Tenth Army task organization. III Amphibious Corp's organizational descendent (III MAF) and the army's XXIV Corps served together again in Vietnam.

14. FM 100-15, *Field Service Regulations—Larger Units* (Washington, DC: Headquarters, Department of the Army, 1963), 61.

15. 1962 MAGTF Order.

16. 1962 MAGTF Order. Plans called for one or more Fleet Marine Force headquarters, normally an administrative rather than a tactical staff, to form the MEC staff. In essence, the 1962 order envisioned the MEC providing a naval corps-level headquarters akin to those fielded in World War II.

17. Donald F. Bittner, *Curriculum Evolution: Marine Corps Command and Staff College, 1920–1988* (Washington, DC: HQMC History and Museums Division, 1988), 30–35; "Program and Schedule Amphibious Warfare School, Senior Course 1947–48, 8 September 1947–28 May 1948," Folder 7 ("Amphibious Warfare School Program and Schedule—Senior Course 1947–48"), Box 7620 ("Amphibious Warfare School Senior Course Syllabi, Programs and Master Schedules, 1947–1951"), Collection "Amphibious Warfare School 1933–2003" (# 3954), MCHD. The total for corps-level topics was eighty-three hours in the 1951 curriculum. "Syllabus and Schedule Amphibious Warfare Senior Course, 1950–51, 6 September 1950–29 May 1951," Folder 15 ("Amphibious Warfare School Syllabus and Schedule Senior Course 1950–51"), Box 7620 ("Amphibious Warfare School Senior Course Syllabi, Programs and Master Schedules, 1947–1951"), Collection "Amphibious Warfare School 1933–2003" [# 3954], MCHD. In contrast to the limited Marine coverage of

higher-level operations, between WWII and Vietnam the US Army's Command and General Staff College focused its instruction on operations at the division, corps, army, and army group levels. See Boyd L. Dastrup, *The US Army Command and General Staff College: A Centennial History* (Manhattan, KS: Sunflower University Press, 1982), 90–105. The German Kriegsakademie circa 1880 devoted its entire third year of tactical instruction to problems at the corps level. Spenser Wilkinson, *The Brain of an Army: A Popular Account of the German General Staff*, 2nd ed. (London: Constable, 1913), 164.

18. Refinements included adding instruction on aviation, atomic warfare, and counterguerrilla operations. But amphibious topics still reigned supreme. In academic year 1951, for example, 603 of 1,232 Command and Staff College curriculum hours (49 percent) were devoted to amphibious instruction. "Syllabus and Schedule Amphibious Warfare Senior Course, 1950–51, 6 September 1950–29 May 1951," Folder 15 ("Amphibious Warfare School Syllabus and Schedule Senior Course 1950–51"), Box 7620 ("Amphibious Warfare School Senior Course Syllabi, Programs and Master Schedules, 1947–1951"), Collection "Amphibious Warfare School, 1933–2003" (# 3954), MCHD. The amphibious emphasis made sense because that role represented the Corps' primary contribution to joint warfighting during World War II and Korea. With respect to the type of operations conducted once ashore, the scenario for the culminating field exercise from 1947 to 1965, Operation PACKARD, often featured a two-division amphibious corps or MEF seizing a lodgment up to twenty miles deep. The plans and student products for this nineteen-year-long series of staff college amphibious exercises are in Boxes 32–101, Collection "Exercises" (# 4118), MCHD.

19. In the same period the *Marine Corps Gazette*, the service's professional journal, printed a single article on corps-level warfighting, cited above in note 4. This fact is based on a survey of the journal's annual indexes for the thirty-five-year period. Every year it published a compilation of each issue's article titles and authors. A three-volume *Marine Corps Gazette* article master index is located in Gray Research Library, Marine Corps Base, Quantico, VA.

20. See Dastrup, *The US Army Command and General Staff College*, 90–105.

21. Marine archival records for the period between WWII and Vietnam reflect numerous examples of smaller landing forces of company to division size conducting exercises in standard US training venues such as Norfolk, Virginia; Camp Lejeune, North Carolina; Vieques, Puerto Rico; and Camp Pendleton and San Clemente Island, California. Adding these routine rehearsals to the count boosts the training total to more than a hundred practice amphibious assaults. Globally deployed navy amphibious groups and their associated Marine battalion landing teams conducted hundreds more amphibious exercises during this twenty-year period. When all these operations are added to the tally, US amphibious forces collectively averaged one training exercise every other week for two decades. Plans, directives, and orders reflecting this "culture of amphibiousity" are found in Boxes 23–101, Collection "Exercises" (# 4118), MCHD. The EWTGC also illustrates the US Navy and Marine Corps' emphasis on amphibious training. The number of corps-level exercises is derived from a survey of the EWTGC exercise files. EWTGs (one in Little Creek, Virginia, and another in Coronado, California) are joint navy–Marine schools that teach amphibious operations, staff planning, and

fire support delivery and coordination skills. Today the Norfolk area school is commanded by a Marine colonel, while the San Diego school is led by a navy captain. The author commanded the Atlantic EWTG from 2009 to 2011. Before the services combined their amphibious training under a single schoolhouse on each coast, the navy and Marines ran independent training commands at both locales. This collection of exercise records captures a sample of the amphibious training conducted by army, navy, and Marine units during the period from 1942 to 1997. The eighty-three-box collection is strongest in its coverage of 1950s and 1960s training, the period of most interest for this study of pre-Vietnam corps-level training and operations. Unlike the Staff College student problems, these fleet training scenarios occasionally incorporated distant exploitations by Marine armor and heliborne forces, objectives up to two hundred miles inland, and insurgent opposition. For details on these 1953–1963 exercises, see boxes 10, 14, 29, 33–34, 42, 48–50, 55–57, and 64 in EWTGC, MCHD.

22. Commander Amphibious Group Two, Operation Order 510–64, 15 September 1964, Folder 3 ("Steel Pike I"), Box 65 ("Steel Pike I 1964"), EWTGC, MCHD; II MEF Operation Order 503–64, September 1964, Folder 3 ("Steel Pike I"), Box 66 ("Steel Pike I[] 1964"), EWTGC, MCHD; Commander, Amphibious Force, Atlantic—Report, 23 December 1963, Folder 7 ("Steel Pike I"); Box 69 ("Steel Pike I 1964"), EWTGC, MCHD; Exercise Overview Publication, February 1965, Folder 7 ("Steel Pike I"), Box 70 ("Steel Pike I 1964"), EWTGC, MCHD; James B. Soper, "Observations: STEEL PIKE and SILVER LANCE," *U.S. Naval Institute Proceedings* 91, no. 11 (November 1965): 46–58.

23. Commander Amphibious Force Pacific, Operation Order 302–65, 1 December 1964, Folder 1 ("Silver Lance"), Box 75 ("Silver Lance, 1965"), EWTGC, MCHD; Post Exercise Report, Part II, May 1965, Folder 9 ("Silver Lance"), Box 92 ("Exercises—Silver Lance, 1965"), Collection "Exercises" [# 4118], MCHD; Soper, "Observations: STEEL PIKE and SILVER LANCE," 46–58.

24. Jack Shulimson and Charles M. Johnson, *U.S. Marines in Vietnam: The Landing and the Buildup, 1965* (Washington, DC: USMC History and Museums Division, 1978), 23–24.

25. Millett, *Semper Fidelis*, 543–558.

Chapter 1. Corps-Level Command in Vietnam

1. Robert Moskin, *The U.S. Marine Corps Story*, 3rd ed. (Boston: Little, Brown, 1992), 649–650.

2. Unless otherwise cited, material for this subsection is drawn from Jack Shulimson and Charles M. Johnson, *U.S. Marines in Vietnam: The Landing and the Buildup, 1965* (Washington, DC: USMC History and Museums Division, 1978).

3. Allan R. Millett, *Semper Fidelis: The History of the United States Marine Corps* (New York: Free Press, 1991), 560–563.

4. Douglas Pike, *Viet Cong: The Organization and Techniques of the National Liberation Front of South Vietnam* (Cambridge, MA: M.I.T. Press, 1966), 217–240; Millett, *Semper Fidelis*, 561; Rod Andrew, Jr., *The First Fight: U.S. Marines in Operation STARLITE, August 1965* (Quantico, VA: Marine Corps University History

Division, 2015), 5–7. This book uses the terms Vietcong and North Vietnamese Army rather than National Liberation Front and People's Army of Vietnam when referencing communist forces because the former terms were more commonly used by allied forces during the conflict.

5. III MAF Command Chronology (hereafter CC), May 1965, 6, Entry "III MAF," Vietnam Digital Archive, MCHD (hereafter VDA); Message, CG, FMFPAC to III MAF, "Establishment of III Marine Amphibious Force," 062057Z May 1965, III MAF CC, May 1965, 12, VDA.

6. III MAF CC, September 1965, 11–12, VDA; III MAF CC, August 1965, 41–51, VDA.

7. Ronald E. Hays II, *Combined Action: U.S. Marines Fighting a Different War, August 1965 to September 1970*). For a depiction of CAP by the officer commanding the program in 1967, see William R. Corson, *The Betrayal* (New York: W. W. Norton, 1968), 174–198. The best portrayal of what life was like in these small, isolated CAP detachments is found in F. J. West, Jr., *The Village* (New York: Bantam Books, 1992).

8. Andrew, *The First Fight*; Nicholas J. Schlosser, *In Persistent Battle: U.S. Marines in Operation Harvest Moon, 8 December to 20 December 1965* (Quantico, VA: Marine Corps University History Division, 2017).

9. Unless otherwise cited, material for this subsection is drawn from Jack Shulimson, *U.S. Marines in Vietnam: An Expanding War, 1966* (Washington, DC: USMC History and Museums Division, 1982).

10. The 1st Marine Division was nearly eighteen thousand strong. 1st Marine Division CC, June 1966, 5, VDA. The division's 7th Regiment had arrived in 1965 to reinforce 3rd Marine Division. The 7th Marines' regimental headquarters planned and conducted Operation STARLITE in August 1965.

11. At the end of 1966 MAF strength stood at 71,582 personnel, an increase of 27,264 since January. III MAF CC, December 1966, 7, VDA; III MAF CC, December 1965, 6, VDA.

12. For his own account of this dramatic period, see Lewis W. Walt, *Strange War, Strange Strategy: A General's Report on Vietnam* (New York: Funk & Wagnalls, 1970), 113–136.

13. III MAF CC; February 1967, 161, VDA.

14. William D. Parker, *Civil Affairs in I Corps, Republic of South Vietnam, April 1996–April 1967* (Washington, DC: HQMC Historical Division, 1970), 93–94.

15. William C. Westmoreland, *A Soldier Reports*, 4th ed. (New York: Dell Publishing, 1984), 216. Walt replied to COMUSMACV's urging: "We will hit VC forces, within the limits of our capability, wherever and whenever they can be located within the I Corps Tactical Zone." Message, CG III MAF to COMUSMACV, "Operations in I Corps," 191400Z November 1965, 13–16, Folder "III MAF Outgoing Messages, November 1965," Entry "1965," Box "III MAF," VDA.

16. Marine forces executed 104,762 operations of squad to company size in 1966. These included 91,700 squad patrols and ambushes plus 10,863 platoon-level reconnaissance, security, and ambush operations. Marine companies conducted 2,199 clearance and search/destroy actions. Records reflect 9,290 VC killed, wounded, captured (including suspects), and surrendered as a result of security operations conducted by Marines units of company size or smaller in 1966. FMFPAC, *Operations of U.S. Marine Forces, Vietnam*, December 1966, 6, 8–13, VDA.

17. Unless otherwise cited, material for this subsection is drawn from Gary L. Telfer, Lane Rogers, and Keith Fleming, Jr., *U.S. Marines in Vietnam: Fighting the North Vietnamese, 1967* (Washington, DC: USMC History and Museums Division, 1984).

18. The MAF fielded eighteen Marine infantry battalions and twenty-one aircraft squadrons. III MAF CC, June 1967, 14, VDA.

19. III MAF CC, January 1967, 21–22, VDA.

20. III MAF CC, February 1966, 98–103 (Enclosure 18: Presentation for Lieutenant General Krulak, 5 February 1966), VDA.

21. Joseph C. Long, *Hill of Angels: U.S. Marines and the Battle for Con Thien, 1967–1968* (Quantico, VA: Marine Corps University History Division, 2016), 1–15.

22. Rod Andrew, Jr., *Hill Fights: The First Battle of Khe Sanh, 1967* (Quantico, VA: Marine Corps University History Division, 2016).

23. FMFPAC, *Operations of U.S. Marine Forces, Vietnam*, July 1967, 9–13, VDA. In Operation BUFFALO, 9th Marine Regiment counterattacked the forces that had assaulted Con Thien, killing 1,290 enemy with battalion sweeps aided by more than one thousand tons of bombs and forty thousand rounds of artillery. For details of that representative DMZ battle, see the USMC History Division archival files (55 pages) in Folder "Operations File, Operation BUFFALO, 2–14 July 1967," Entry "1967 Named Operations," Box "Miscellaneous Archive Data," VDA.

24. Enemy artillery fire destroyed an ammunition dump, wrecked a fuel farm, damaged seventeen helicopters, and forced III MAF to shift an air base and supply dumps out of range of the enemy's cannons. FMFPAC, *Operations of U.S. Marine Forces, Vietnam*, October 1967, 26–27, VDA. The 3rd Marine Division attempted to preempt and then responded to the September attack on Con Thien with Operation KINGFISHER (16 July to 31 October), accounting for 1,100 enemy dead but costing 340 Marines killed and 1,461 wounded. Marine Corps History Division archival files contain 347 pages of material on that three-and-a-half-month operation in Folder "Operations File, Operation KINGFISHER I and II, 16 July–31 October 1967," Entry "1967 Named Operations," Box "Miscellaneous Archive Data," VDA.

25. By way of comparison, Marine forces fighting along the DMZ suffered 564 killed and 5,183 wounded between June and September. These figures reflect only casualties in the 1st and 3rd Marine Divisions, not other US, Korean, or RVN units. MACV, *1967 Command History, Volume 1*, 362, from James W. Willbanks, in author's possession. Subsequent citations of all MACV command histories reference the digital collection of these documents that Professor Willbanks shared.

26. III MAF CC, July 1967, 12–3, 70, VDA; FMFPAC, *Operations of U.S. Marine Forces, Vietnam*, July 1967, 59–64, VDA.

27. Unless otherwise cited, material for this subsection is drawn from Jack Shulimson et al., *U.S. Marines in Vietnam: The Defining Year, 1968* (Washington, DC: HQMC History and Museums Division, 1997).

28. Westmoreland, *A Soldier Reports*, 412–13, 418; U.S. Grant Sharp, Jr., and William C. Westmoreland, *Report on the War in Vietnam* (Washington, DC: US Government Printing Office, 1968), 157, 160, 182.

29. Robert Pisor, *The End of the Line: The Siege of Khe Sanh* (New York: Ballantine Books, 1982).

30. Keith William Nolan, *Battle for Hue, Tet 1968* (New York: Dell Publishing, 1983).

31. Two regiment-size Marine spoiling attacks west (Operation MAMELUKE THRUST) and south (Operation ALLEN BROOK) of Da Nang prevented the second communist offensive in May from achieving success beyond the loss of two remote Special Forces camps. FMFPAC, *Operations of U.S. Marine Forces, Vietnam*, May 1968, 20–27, VDA.

32. FMFPAC, *Operations of U.S. Marine Forces, Vietnam*, February 1968, 53, VDA.

33. In 1968 the forces controlled by XXIV Corps included the 3rd Marine Division and the Army's 1st Cavalry Division (until October), 101st Airborne Division, and 1st Brigade, 5th Mechanized Division. Shelby L. Stanton, *Vietnam Order of Battle* (Washington, DC: U.S. News Books, 1981), 71–72, 77, 83–84, 371–374.

34. III MAF CC, August 1968, 11, VDA.

35. III MAF included a subordinate US Army corps of two divisions (one army and one Marine) and a separate army brigade, two additional infantry divisions (one army and one Marine) reporting directly to the MAF headquarters, a reinforced air wing of six groups (258 fixed-wing aircraft and 270 helicopters), and a ten-thousand-man-strong logistics command. Unless otherwise cited, material for this subsection is drawn from Charles R. Smith, *U.S. Marines in Vietnam: High Mobility and Standdown, 1969* (Washington, DC: USMC History and Museums Division, 1988).

36. After Action Report, Ninth Marine Regiment, Operation DEWEY CANYON, 8 April 1969, VDA, from Ross Phillips, in author's possession; FMFPAC, *Operations of U.S. Marine Forces, Vietnam*, March 1969, 10, VDA.

37. The 101st Division lost 104 dead and more than 400 wounded at Hamburger Hill. III MAF CC, May 1969, 20–23, VDA.

38. Though not as famous as Operation DEWEY CANYON, TAYLOR COMMON employed three times as many helicopter sorties to lift seven times as many troops and hopscotched artillery among thirteen fire bases. FMFPAC, *Operations of U.S. Marine Forces, Vietnam*, December 1968, 11–12, 18, January 1969, 6–12, February 1969, 17–19, and March 1969, 12–13, VDA.

39. This number excludes army and USMC CAP patrols.

40. In October III MAF began assigning Marine battalions to pacification as a primary duty. The new combined initiatives, termed the Infantry Company Intensive Pacification Program and later the Combined Unit Pacification Program, merged elements of US rifle companies with Regional and Popular Forces platoons to improve their efficiency.

41. "Briefing to General Chapman, Commandant of the Marine Corps, by Brigadier General (unreadable)," 10 January 1969, Folder 501–04, Box 11, Entry P-454 (General Records 1969–1973), RG (Record Group) 472 (U.S. Forces in Southeast Asia, 1950–1975), National Archives 2, College Park, MD (hereafter NARA II).

42. Unless otherwise cited, material for this subsection is drawn from Graham A. Cosmas and Terrence P. Murray, *U.S. Marines in Vietnam: Vietnamization and Redeployment, 1970–1971* (Washington, DC: USMC History and Museums Division, 1986).

43. Fighting alongside the MAF in Quang Nam were an ARVN regiment, fourteen thousand territorial troops, 4,500 national police, fifty Revolutionary Development Cadre teams, and 73,000 part-time village militia.

44. Each of these brigades included ground, air, and logistics units. The first to depart in March numbered 12,900 Marines, representing an infantry regiment, an air group, and associated logistics units. Between July and October another fifteen thousand Marines, including an air group, another infantry regiment (7th Marines), and additional logistics elements and corps-level troops redeployed.

45. Gary D. Solis, *Son Thang: An American War Crime* (Annapolis, MD: Naval Institute Press, 1997).

46. Gary D. Solis, *Marines and Military Law in Vietnam: Trial by Fire* (Washington, DC: HQMC History and Museums Division, 1989), 171.

47. Gerald H. Turley, the Marine adviser who took charge of the defense of I Corps in 1972, tells the story in *The Easter Offensive: Vietnam, 1972* (Novato, CA: Presidio Press, 1985).

48. Fact Sheet "Increased Proportion of NVA Troops," Tab I, Folder "Fact Book, COMUSMACV, Vol. 1 [2 of 5] CSA Confirmation Hearings," Box 70, WCWP, LBJPL; Thomas C. Thayer, *War Without Fronts: The American Experience in Vietnam* (1985, Annapolis, MD: Naval Institute Press, 2016), 32.

49. FMFPAC, *Operations of the III MAF*, March-September 1965, 18, VDA.

50. FMFPAC, *Historical Summary, U.S. Marine Corps Forces in Vietnam, March 1965–September 1967, Volume 1: Narrative*, 5–49, 5–50, Folder 1/13, Box 13, Vietnam War Collection (# 3808), MCHD.

51. FMFPAC, *Operations of U.S. Marine Forces, Vietnam*, October 1969, 13, VDA.

52. For a discussion of troop requirements in counterinsurgency, see James T. Quinlivan, "Force Requirements in Stability Operations," *Parameters* 25, no. 4 (Winter 1995): 59–69. For a critique of the "tie-down ratio" of security forces to insurgents (often cited in the 10–20:1 range), see Larry E. Cable, *Conflict of Myths: The Development of Counterinsurgency Doctrine and the Vietnam War* (New York: New York University Press, 1986), 81–83.

53. In a 1968 interview General Vo Nguyen Giap acknowledged the loss of five hundred thousand communist troops since 1965. US estimates for enemy losses at that point were 360,000. US estimates for the period 1965 to 1972 were 851,000 communists killed in action, dead of wounds, or lost to disease. No one, then or now, including the Vietnamese government, precisely knew the extent of the communist losses. Thayer, *War Without Fronts*, 101–104.

54. The South Vietnamese government renamed the four regions (I–IV Corps) as Military Regions (MRs) 1–4 in July 1970. This work uses the titles interchangeably.

55. The American casualty figures are also somewhat misleading because of the way wounds were counted. Any wound requiring treatment was included in the US casualty figures. But as indicated in Table 1.4, 42 percent of the Americans wounded were so lightly hurt that they were treated in the field and returned to immediate action. Westmoreland, concerned by the political impact the casualty numbers were having on the home front, directed late in his tenure to list casualties by category: those treated in the field and returned to duty, and those evacuated for higher-echelon medical care. Charles B. MacDonald's notes from interviews

of William C. Westmoreland, Folder "24 April 1973," Box 30, and Folder "8 July 1973," Box 31, WCWP, LBJPL.

56. US forces suffered five wounded for every one combatant killed in Vietnam. Thayer, *War Without Fronts*, 110. MACV, however, for unknown reasons applied a lesser ratio of 1.5:1 for wounded-to-killed in estimating NVA/VC losses. Phillip B. Davidson, *Secrets of the Vietnam War* (Novato, CA: Presidio Press, 1990), 81.

57. Thayer, *War Without Fronts*, 11–13.

58. MAF casualties in 1967 amounted to 80.6 percent of the 1968 toll. In 1969 the tally equaled 73.4 percent of the 1968 losses.

59. "After Action Report, Operation Harvest Moon," Enclosure 2, III MAF CC, December 1965, 31–47, VDA; Schlosser, *In Persistent Battle*, 8–10, 14–17, 38, 48–49; Shulimson and Johnson, *U.S. Marines in Vietnam, 1965*, 98–111. III MAF carried the 1st VC Regiment at half-strength in its order of battle assessments after HARVEST MOON. III MAF CC, December 1965, 8, VDA.

60. Da Nang was guarded by a substantial garrison, including Marine, ROK, and ARVN infantry regiments, augmented by two additional Marine battalions, a tank battalion, 120 artillery pieces, and ample aviation.

61. COMUSMACV Historical Notes, February 1968, 4, Folder 29, Box 16, WCWP, LBJPL; Shulimson et al., *U.S. Marines in Vietnam, 1968*, 141–163. Westmoreland conveyed to his biographer that "Da Nang was threatened. I had to take command of the northern region personally. Cushman wasn't taking charge. The Marines were reluctant to control and actually command those Army troops I put under them. I kept insisting the Army troops belonged to them, use them!" Charles B. MacDonald's notes from interviews of William C. Westmoreland, Folder "28 January 1973," Box 30, WCWP, LBJPL.

62. Shulimson et al., *U.S. Marines in Vietnam, 1968*, 164–194, 216, 219. General LaHue's 117-page after-action report does not mention a need for additional forces. "Task Force Xray Combat After Action Report, Operation HUE CITY," 14 April 1968, Folder "Task Force X-Ray," Box "1968," VDA. LaHue's ninety-six-minute oral history tape, much of which covered the Hue battle, noted the enemy's ability throughout the battle to move forces and supplies into Hue while evacuating wounded, but he did not comment on why he or other commanders did not call for more allied forces to shut off these lines of communication sooner. Foster C. LaHue Oral History (#2932), MCHD. Cushman did chastise LaHue in a 21 February 1968 message, which read in part: "There is an apparent lack of offensive momentum in the push to open Route 1 from Da Nang to Phu Bai. This task is of overriding importance. . . . As far as I can tell no progress has been made for days. This must be changed and forward progress made immediately." Message, CG III MAF to CG Task Force XRAY, 211320Z February 1968, 81, Folder "III MAF Outgoing Messages–February 1968 #2," Entry "1968," Box "III MAF," VDA.

63. Message, COMUSMACV to CINCPAC, 26 January 1968, Tab 46, Folder 28, Box 14, WCWP, LBJPL.

64. Message, COMUSMACV to CINCPAC, 21 February 1968, Tab 70, Folder 29, Box 16, WCWP, LBJPL.

65. Shulimson et al., *U.S. Marines in Vietnam, 1968*, 192–194.

66. Message, DEPCOMUSMACV to CG, III MAF, 161609Z February 1968, 141, Folder "III MAF Incoming Messages—February 1968," Entry "1968," Box

"III MAF," VDA; Message, DEPCOMUSMACV to CG, III MAF, 201411Z February 1968, 179, Folder "III MAF Incoming Messages—February 1968," Entry "1968," Box "III MAF," VDA; Shulimson et al., *U.S. Marines in Vietnam, 1968,* 205. For Cushman's response, which focused on III MAF logistic assistance to 1st ARVN Division inside Hue, see Message, CG III MAF to Deputy COMUS-MACV FWD, 202332Z February 1968, 82–85, Folder "III MAF Outgoing Messages—February 1968 #2," Entry "1968," Box "III MAF," VDA.

67. Shulimson et al., *U.S. Marines in Vietnam, 1968,* 207, 210–211, 216.

68. Shulimson et al., *U.S. Marines in Vietnam, 1968,* 211, 213, 223.

69. Westmoreland, *A Soldier Reports,* 198.

70. For a summary of the application of Cold War nuclear warfighting theory to the Vietnam conflict, see Fred Kaplan, *The Wizards of Armageddon,* 2nd ed. (Stanford, CA: Stanford University Press, 1991), 328–342. The theory upon which these ideas were based originated in two books by Thomas C. Schelling: *The Strategy of Conflict* (Cambridge, MA: Harvard University Press, 1960), and *Arms and Influence* (New Haven, CT: Yale University Press, 1966). Thankfully, the nuclear application of the punishment strategy has not yet been tested.

71. Political strategy is not in the US military's doctrinal lexicon today either. Political strategy is sometimes rendered in military writing as "political warfare," but neither phrase is found in the DOD-approved list of military terms. *DOD Dictionary of Military and Associated Terms,* https://jdeis.js.mil/jdeis/new_pubs/dictionary.pdf.

72. III MAF G-5, *Development's Role in Pacification,* 194, Folders 1–4, Box 18, Vietnam War Collection, MCHD (hereafter 1969 III MAF G-5 Development Study). This study has received no attention in the scholarly literature on the war. Like the army's more extensive 1966 PROVN study, it offered a different way to approach counterinsurgency.

73. 1969 III MAF G-5 Development Study, 131–132, 134, 195.

74. Pike, in *Viet Cong* chapters 5, 6, and 9, details the social, political, and military phases the South Vietnamese communists employed and the process of organization-building used to consolidate control of the rural villages.

75. Little has been written on South Vietnam's political warfare program or the role the Republic of China (Taiwan) played in establishing and advising it. Based on Republic of China input, Saigon established the Political Warfare Institute in Dalat on 27 May 1961. For a glimpse into this important topic, see Thomas A. Marks, *Counterrevolution in China: Wang Sheng and the Kuomintang* (London: Frank Cass, 1998), 198–210. Thirty Republic of China (Taiwanese) Political Warfare advisers served in South Vietnam, with several assigned to ARVN's I Corps in Da Nang. MACV, *Command History 1970,* Vol. 2, VII-77.

76. 1969 III MAF G-5 Development Study, 4, 143–148, 193–199.

77. Even under CORDS the number of US civilians was limited. In MR 1 in 1970 there were 148 civilians from the US Agency for International Development, six from the Department of Defense, and two from the US Information Agency. All but four of those civilians worked at province or regional headquarters; none served at district level. By contrast, 777 military personnel (83 percent of the total CORDS contingent in the region) were assigned to CORDS in I Corps. MACV, *Command History 1970,* Vol. 2, VII-66.

78. The Vietcong's governing apparatus promised and sometimes delivered such redistributive policies. Communist political agents made their promises contingent on the people's support. In other words, only by paying taxes, providing fathers and sons to fight for the VC, and otherwise assisting the movement, would the practical benefits of landownership or political power be granted. The fact that landownership, in both North and South Vietnam, was an incentive that the communist ideal of communal ownership would take away once a communist government was installed was one of many deceptions Hanoi foisted on its gullible Southern supporters. Nonetheless the enticement of a system that promised tangible increases in personal wealth, status, and power motivated many Southern citizens to support the Vietcong. The practical and theoretical implications of such political policies at the province level are detailed in chapters four through six in Jeffrey Race, *War Comes to Long An: Revolutionary Conflict in a Vietnamese Province* (Berkeley: University of California Press, 1972).

79. 1969 III MAF G-5 Development Study, 136.

80. Race, *War Comes to Long An*, 148–155.

81. The purpose of the study was to recommend policies that would bring the III MAF civic action program into full support of the pacification campaign. The authors were to identify development programs, determine objectives and priorities for them, and develop policy guidance for the programs and objectives. In a cover letter to the study addressed to General Nickerson, the MAF G-5 said the team was not able to identify programs in enough detail to determine objectives, priorities, and guidance. "The study, does not, in any sense of the word, recommend specific detailed programs that can be implemented immediately upon approval. Rather it provides a basis upon which it may be possible to establish the recommended programs if they are deemed suitable, feasible and acceptable." Thus did a promising study disappear down the wormhole of staff action. Memorandum, A/CS G-5 to CG, III MAF, 26 November 1969, 1969 III MAF G-5 Development Study.

Chapter 2. III MAF Command and Control

1. Marine Corps Doctrinal Publication (MCDP) 6, *Command and Control* (Washington, DC: Headquarters Marine Corps, 1996), 35 (hereafter MCDP 6).

2. Letter, CG FMFPAC to CMC, 25 January 1965, "Concepts for Marine Expeditionary Corps and Marine Expeditionary Force Headquarters," Folder 4 ("(1) FMFPAC: Organization of HQ MEC & MEF"), Box 141, Entry "Records of Units and Other Commands, 1953–1993, FMFPAC," RG 127, NARA II (hereafter FMFPAC's Recommended MEC/MEF HQ Organization). The reasons why Krulak recommended against expanding the III MAF headquarters from a part-time cadre to a full-time, fully manned staff are unclear.

3. MCDP 6, 47–52.

4. Official service biographical sketch of General Lewis W. Walt, History Division, Marine Corps University, Quantico, VA, www.usmcu.edu/Research /Marine-Corps-History-Division/People/Whos-Who-in-Marine-Corps-History /Vandegrift-Worley/General-Lewis-W-Walt.

248 Notes to Pages 57–60

5. Lewis W. Walt, *Strange War, Strange Strategy: A General's Report on Vietnam* (New York: Funk & Wagnalls, 1970), 7.

6. Letter, John R. Chaisson to his wife, 6 July 1966, Folder "Correspondence July 1966," Box 2, John R. Chaisson Papers (# 601), MCHD.

7. III MAF Operations Order 201-(Yr), 18 January 1969, 2, Folder "1969," Box "III MAF," VDA, captures this language in a standard administrative order spelling out the MAF's responsibilities.

8. Victor H. Krulak, *First to Fight: An Inside View of the U.S. Marine Corps* (Annapolis, MD: Naval Institute Press, 1984), 182. In his book General Krulak explained his view on why the United States needed a Marine Corps and why it was organized the way it was and operated the way it did.

9. Jack Shulimson, *U.S. Marines in Vietnam: An Expanding War, 1966* (Washington, DC: USMC History and Museums Division, 1982), 81–91; Walt, *Strange War, Strange Strategy*, 113–136. The historian Nicholas J. Schlosser argues that the Walt–Thi relationship was "less than harmonious" because the III MAF commander, along with many other senior Marines in I Corps, deemed the ARVN corps and its divisions poor fighters as well as infiltrated by VC agents. Nicholas J. Schlosser, *In Persistent Battle: U.S. Marines in Operation Harvest Moon, 8 December to 20 December 1965* (Quantico, VA: Marine Corps University History Division, 2017), 15.

10. Schlosser, *In Persistent Battle*, 14.

11. Walt, *Strange War, Strange Strategy*, 33.

12. Official service biographical sketch of General Robert E. Cushman, Jr., History Division, Marine Corps University, Quantico, VA, www.usmcu.edu/Resear ch/Marine-Corps-History-Division/People/Whos-Who-in-Marine-Corps-Histo ry/Abrell-Cushman/General-Robert-E-Cushman-Jr.

13. Allan R. Millett, *Semper Fidelis: The History of the United States Marine Corps* (New York: Free Press, 1991), 611.

14. Jack Shulimson et al., *U.S. Marines in Vietnam: The Defining Year, 1968* (Washington, DC: HQMC History and Museums Division, 1997), 14–15; Millett, *Semper Fidelis*, 612–613. When Cushman was later Commandant and Anderson served with him again, this time as his Assistant Commandant, fellow Marine generals, both active and retired, disliked them both. Their peers quietly lobbied politicians to ensure that Anderson would not serve, as Cushman desired, as the next (twenty-sixth) Commandant.

15. Each of these instances will be examined later in the manuscript.

16. James S. Olson and Randy Roberts, *My Lai: A Brief History with Documents* (Boston: Bedford/St. Martin's, 1998); William C. Westmoreland, *A Soldier Reports*, 4th ed. (New York: Dell Publishing, 1984), 494–501.

17. Figures for this eight-month period were taken from III MAF 1968 CCs, Entry "III MAF," VDA—March, 17; April, 17; May, 22; June, 15; July, 16; August, 19; September, 18; and October, 14. III MAF's records aggregated the two Marine divisions' numbers. Total counts of "innocent civilian deaths" for each unit during this period: 1st/3rd Marine Divisions—1,553; Americal Division—3,711; 1st Cavalry Division—2,615; 101st Division—1,995. Total for all five divisions: 9,874.

18. Official service biographical sketch of Lieutenant General Herman Nickerson, Jr., History Division, Marine Corps University, Quantico, VA, www.usmcu

.edu/Research/Marine-Corps-History-Division/People/Whos-Who-in-Marine
-Corps-History/Mackie-Ozbourn/Lieutenant-General-Herman-Nickerson-Jr.

19. Charles R. Smith, *U.S. Marines in Vietnam: High Mobility and Standdown, 1969* (Washington, DC: USMC History and Museums Division, 1988), 152–158. Ormond R. Simpson, CG of 1st Marine Division, claimed racial conflict was his division's number-one problem in 1969. Gary D. Solis, *Marines and Military Law in Vietnam: Trial by Fire* (Washington, DC: HQMC History and Museums Division, 1989), 131.

20. For instance, in the 18 July 1969 issue of III MAF's newspaper, *Sea Tiger*, Nickerson explained the importance of pacification. All forty of Nickerson's columns for the III MAF weekly newspaper, which ran from June 1969 to March 1970, are contained in Herman Nickerson, Jr., *Leadership Lessons and Remembrances from Vietnam* (Washington, DC: US Marine Corps History and Museums Division, 1988).

21. Smith, *U.S. Marines in Vietnam, 1969*, 223–226.

22. Official service biographical sketch of General Keith B. McCutcheon, History Division, Marine Corps University, Quantico, VA, www.usmcu.edu/Research/Marine-Corps-History-Division/People/Whos-Who-in-Marine-Corps-History/Mackie-Ozbourn/General-Keith-B-McCutcheon. He earned a master's degree in aeronautical engineering degree from the Naval Postgraduate School and the Massachusetts Institute of Technology. McCutcheon earned two master's degrees—one from the NPS and the other from MIT.

23. Graham A. Cosmas and Terrence P. Murray, *U.S. Marines in Vietnam: Vietnamization and Redeployment, 1970–1971* (Washington, DC: USMC History and Museums Division, 1986), 191, 273–279, 344, 352–365, 369.

24. III MAF CC, November 1965, 8, VDA.

25. III MAF CC, June 1966, 20, VDA.

26. III MAF CC, March 1970, 8, VDA; Cosmas and Murray, *U.S. Marines in Vietnam, 1970–1971*, 18. The 1970 transfer of regional command between the services went smoothly, with only minor frictions associated with real-estate issues, communications handoffs, and administrative procedures. Both staffs, following the lead of their commanding generals, resolved such issues quickly and professionally. XXIV Corps soon learned that the increased scope and scale of its new responsibilities required additional personnel to cover its now greatly expanded duties.

27. III MAF CC, August 1969, 4–6, VDA.

28. Letter, CG FMFPAC to CMC, "Concepts for Marine Expeditionary Corps and Marine Expeditionary Force Headquarters," 25 January 1965, Folder 1/4, Box 141, Entry "Records of Units and Other Commands, 1953–1993, FMFPAC," RG 127, NARA II. Ironically, Krulak recommended against standing up a full-time MEF staff just four months before he would need one in Vietnam.

29. Colonel Leo J. Dulacki, the III MAF G-2 in 1965, noted that the suitcase staff "concept lacks vitality *especially in a commitment of forces of long duration.*" Emphasis in original. Jack Shulimson and Charles M. Johnson, *U.S. Marines in Vietnam: The Landing and the Buildup, 1965* (Washington, DC: USMC History and Museums Division, 1978), 44.

30. III MAF point paper, "Formation of permanent MAF headquarters during peacetime situations, prepared to deploy as fully operational MAF headquarters," April 1967, Folder 25, Box 144, Entry "Records of Units and Other Commands, 1953–1993, FMFPAC," RG 127, NARA II. In 1965 only a small III MEF cadre existed. The point paper, delivered at a FMFPAC lessons-learned conference two years later, acknowledged the mistake of not maintaining a fully functioning MEF headquarters during peacetime.

31. Cosmas and Murray, *U.S. Marines in Vietnam, 1970–1971*, 16, 21.

32. III MAF CC, March 1966, 4, VDA; Shulimson, *U.S. Marines in Vietnam, 1966*, 357.

33. Data for the deputy commanding general and army staff billets on the III MAF staff are derived from the Marine Corps official histories, 1965–1971, Appendix A, Marine Command and Staff Lists.

34. III MAF CC, December 1965, Enclosure 3, 1, VDA. The MEF's prescribed table of organization strength in January 1965 was 141 personnel. The December strength represented an increase of 76 percent in the first year alone over its authorized numbers. FMFPAC's Recommended MEC/MEF HQ Organization, Enclosure 2, page 10.

35. III MAF CC, August 1967, 6, VDA.

36. III MAF CC, August 1968, 7, VDA. The command element represented 0.6 percent of the MAF's strength that month.

37. Graham A. Cosmas, *MACV: The Joint Command in the Years of Escalation, 1962–1967* (Washington, DC: US Army Center of Military History, 2006), 331.

38. Shulimson and Johnson, *U.S. Marines in Vietnam, 1965*, 106.

39. Schlosser, *In Persistent Battle*, 33–35; III MAF Board of Investigation, "Investigation to inquire into the circumstances surrounding the landing of Battalion Landing Team 2/1 in the vicinity of BT 074216 and BT 045298 on or about 1030, 10 December 1965," 21 December 1965. Historian Bruce Gudmundsson provided the author a copy of this declassified document, originally obtained from NARA II.

40. Data for these primary staff officer billets on the III MAF staff are derived from the Marine Corps official histories, 1965–1971, Appendix A, Marine Command and Staff Lists.

41. Letters, John R. Chaisson to his wife, 2 March, 19 April, 4 May 1966, Folders "Correspondence March/April /May 1966," Box 2, John R. Chaisson Papers, MCHD. Cushman's chief of staff, Brigadier General Earl E. Anderson, later claimed the III MAF staff had some problems stemming from personnel who were not up to the challenge. Shulimson et al., *U.S. Marines in Vietnam, 1968*, 15.

42. Schlosser, *In Persistent Battle*, 14. Cushman held monthly commanders' conferences to pass guidance in person and share effective techniques. Most practitioners agree it is better for higher-level commanders to visit subordinates rather than frequently summon them to the senior headquarters. In this the MAF commanders agreed with General Westmoreland, who also held commanders' conferences monthly but constantly traveled around Vietnam in the interim to visit subordinates.

43. Gary B. Griffin, *The Directed Telescope: A Traditional Element of Effective Command* (Fort Leavenworth, KS: Combat Studies Institute, 1991), 20–32.

44. Force Order 3124.4B, "Standing Operating Procedure for the Combined

Action Program," 22 June 1968, Folder 25, Box 7, Vietnam War Collection, MCHD.

45. III MAF CC, November 1965, Enclosure 2, 23–28, VDA; III MAF CC, January 1969, 8, VDA; III MAF CC, May 1969, 8, VDA; III MAF CC, January 1971, 7, VDA.

46. III MAF Operation Order 307–66 (Operation Double Eagle), 15 January 1966, Folder 9/11, Box 154, Entry "Records of Units and Other Commands, 1953–1993, G-3, III MAF," RG 127, NARA II (hereafter DOUBLE EAGLE Op Order); Shulimson, *U.S. Marines in Vietnam, 1966*, 22. Tasking two levels down was a common technique of the German army in WWII. For a discussion of this method, see Richard E. Simpkin, *Race to the Swift: Thoughts on Twenty-First Century Warfare* (London: Brassey's, 2000), 233. In this technique, the corps assigns the task to the Task Force/brigade/regiment while the division supervises and assists its subordinate command that was assigned to carry out the task. This procedure, though uncommon in modern practice, is authorized in contemporary Marine doctrine, even under normal circumstances when an officer is not dual-hatted as commander of both the tasking and executing units. See MCDP 6, 134.

47. III MAF/SA ICTZ Letter of Instruction 26–68, 1 November 1968, 2–3, Folder 20/6, Box 161, Entry "Records of Units and Other Commands, 1953–1993," RG 127, NARA II.

48. Shulimson et al., *U.S. Marines in Vietnam, 1968*, 84.

49. Cosmas, *MACV: The Joint Command in the Years of Escalation, 1962–1967*, 361. Unlike the advisory command, CORDS did not report in the monthly III MAF command chronologies. Even though CORDS maintained primary responsibility for pacification and development operations, the MAF G-5 continued to report civil affairs operations.

50. MCDP 6, 77–81, 110, 124.

51. DOUBLE EAGLE Op Order, 2.

52. III MAF CC, February 1966, 5, VDA; Jack Shulimson, *U.S. Marines in Vietnam, 1966*, 19–36. General Krulak was critical of DOUBLE EAGLE I and II because the allied forces withdrew after the operations concluded, allowing enemy forces to return and regain control over the area's population.

53. The South Vietnamese army generals commanding the four military regions served simultaneously in both military and political capacities as Saigon's senior representative. They commanded the ARVN corps assigned to each region, which also bore the same name as the sector. Thus "I Corps" referred to both the northern five provinces of South Vietnam as a region as well as the ARVN military corps-level command that defended the area.

54. III MAF CC, November 1965, Encl 2 (MACV LOI-4), 27, VDA; Cosmas, *MACV: The Joint Command in the Years of Escalation, 1962–1967*, 331. Colonel Edwin H. Simmons, III MAF G-3 in 1965 and 1966, noted that the Special Forces "resisted this authority." Shulimson, *U.S. Marines in Vietnam, 1966*, 58.

55. General Walt commanded all navy forces ashore in I Corps during the same period that he was serving as both commanding general of both 3rd Marine Division and III MAF. Shulimson and Johnson, *U.S. Marines in Vietnam, 1965*, 44, 182–184; Shulimson, *U.S. Marines in Vietnam, 1966*, 6–8, 44, 75, 182–184, 286, 297–300; Shulimson et al., *U.S. Marines in Vietnam, 1968*, 4.

56. Francis Fox Parry, *Three-War Marine: The Pacific–Korea–Vietnam*, 2nd ed. (New York: Jove Books, 1989), 274–276; FMFPAC Staff Study, *Application of Amphibious Doctrine in Vietnam*, 22 April 1966, Folder 6/4, Box 4, Vietnam War Collection, MCHD; *Report of Amphibious Operations Conference Held at Direction of CINCPACFLT*, 25 February–1 March 1966, Folder 5/2, Box 145, Entry "Records of Units and Other Commands, 1953–1993, FMFPAC," RG 127, NARA II (hereafter CINCPACFLT Amphib Ops Conference Report); Shulimson, *U.S. Marines in Vietnam, 1966*, 297–306.

57. Shulimson and Johnson, *U.S. Marines in Vietnam, 1965*, 120; Shulimson, *U.S. Marines in Vietnam, 1966*, 7; Cosmas and Murray, *U.S. Marines in Vietnam, 1970–1971*, 24, 27.

58. III MAF CC, August 1966, 16, VDA; Shulimson, *U.S. Marines in Vietnam, 1966*, 222–223; Shulimson et al., *U.S. Marines in Vietnam, 1968*, 84. Extract of General Cushman's Oral History transcript, 475–76, Folder "Cushman Debrief," Box A-24-E-7-1, Ronald H. Spector Papers, MCHD.

59. Rottman, *US Marine Corps Pacific Theater of Operations, 1944–45*, 58–76.

60. Shulimson and Johnson, *U.S. Marines in Vietnam, 1965*, 229–231; Smith, *U.S. Marines in Vietnam, 1969*, 220, 260, 341–344.

61. III MAF Fact Sheet on the Combined Action Force, 31 March 1970, Folder 9, Box 11, Vietnam War Collection, MCHD. In early 1970 General Nickerson established a Combined Action Force headquarters, under a Marine Colonel, to oversee the four groups. The Combined Action Force reported directly to III MAF.

62. Telfer, Rogers, and Fleming, *U.S. Marines in Vietnam, 1967*, 184–185; Smith, *U.S. Marines in Vietnam, 1969*, 2. Prior to CORDS, the Marines coordinated regional civil development actions through the Joint Coordination Council, the first of its kind in Vietnam. The I Corps Joint Coordinating Council was established on 6 September 1965 with III MAF Deputy Commanding General McCutcheon as General Walt's representative. "Statement of Mission, Composition, and Functions I Corps Joint Coordinating Council," 24 January 1967, Folder 1, Box 16, Vietnam War Collection, MCHD; Shulimson and Johnson, *U.S. Marines in Vietnam, 1965*, 143–144.

63. III MAF CC, August 1965, 11, VDA.

64. Westmoreland, *A Soldier Reports*, 170–172. Proposals for combined command continued throughout the war. Westmoreland explained his rationale opposing the concept to Admiral Sharp, CINCPAC, in a message in the midst of the Tet Offensive. Message, COMUSMACV to CINCPAC, "Command Relationships," 191132Z February 1968, Folder "COMUSMACV 1968, Secret Outgoing Msg File [2 of 2]," Box 42, WCWP, LBJPL.

65. MCDP 6, 91.

66. The eight subordinate commands did not include three corps troop units: 29th Civil Affairs Company (USA); 7th Psychological Operations Battalion (USA); and 1st Radio Battalion (USMC). III MAF CC, December 1967, 3, VDA.

67. A Vietnam-era field army comprised three corps of three divisions along with the customary assortment of combat, combat support, and combat service support units in general support of all the army's forces. FM 100-15, *Larger Units: Theater Army—Corps* (1968), 7-2. One US Army Field Force commander claimed his "span of control was unmanageable," leaving him to concentrate on crises only.

Douglas Kinnard, *The War Managers: American Generals Reflect on Vietnam*, rev. ed (1977; repr., Boston: Da Capo Press, 1991), 58.

68. A Marine commander later observed that mixing combat units "demonstrated the interchangeable nature of Marine battalions and gave the division commanding generals great flexibility" while noting that commanders much preferred to fight with their organic units. Edwin H. Simmons, "Marine Corps Operations in Vietnam, 1968," in *The Marines in Vietnam, 1954–1973: An Anthology and Annotated Bibliography* (Washington, DC: HQMC History and Museums Division, 1985), 103 (hereafter *The Marines in Vietnam, 1954–1973*).

69. Shulimson, *U.S. Marines in Vietnam, 1966*, 19–23.

70. Shulimson et al., *U.S. Marine in Vietnam, 1968*, 330.

71. Most commanders objected to the mixing of units, noting that it decreased efficiency and effectiveness. Leon N. Utter, the commanding officer of 2nd Battalion, 7th Marines commented after the war: "Platoons, companies and battalions are not interchangeable parts of identical machines." Utter's regimental commander, Colonel Oscar F. Peatross, noted his command fought as an integral unit more frequently than the other regiments, which provided a significant tactical advantage. Shulimson, *U.S. Marines in Vietnam, 1966*, 128.

72. Shulimson et al., *U.S. Marine in Vietnam, 1968*, 353.

73. Message, CG III MAF to subordinate commanders, 130136Z April 1968, 92, File "III MAF Outgoing Messages, April 1968," VDA.

74. Wilkinson, *The Brain of an Army*, 112–113.

75. FM 100-15, *Larger Units: Theater Army—Corps* (1968), 8–2.

76. Westmoreland prompted III MAF to use the US Army Field Artillery Group headquarters in I Corps to assume a tactical role along the DMZ. This did not occur until the decision was in the hands of XXIV Corps. Message, COMUSMACV to CG, III MAF, "108th Arty Grp," 191125Z October 1967, Folder "COMUSMACV Signature File—Secret 1967 [1 of 2]," Box 40 [1 of 2], WCWP, LBJPL.

77. This engineering C2 issued is further examined in chapter 5 in the section on navy construction support.

78. MCDP 6, 134.

79. Early concerns about splitting up the MAGTF, including both its air and ground components, appeared in an information paper dated 4 January 1966. At the time these risks were deemed manageable, and the authors acknowledged that MACV possessed the authority to do what it needed to do organizationally to improve military effectiveness. III MAF CC, January 1966, Encl 12 "Fragmentation of Marine Air-Ground Team," 63–64, VDA. In 1967 Krulak told his fellow generals: "Today we have what we longed for in Korea. It is no accident. We have CINCPAC to thank for putting his foot down and saying, 'no, the Marines fight as a team. I will not see them broken up.' We have him to thank, plus the stubborn persuasion on him by a few Marines. Today we have our [air-ground] team in its classic sense and for the first time really in combat history." Ironically, this independent status lasted only another few months. Cosmas, *MACV: The Joint Command in the Years of Escalation, 1962–1967*, 330.

80. In 1967 CORDS was authorized eighty-seven civilians in I Corps. "Joint Table of Distribution, MACV CORDS," 15 October 1967, Folder 6-4-10A, Box

III, Entry A1 52, RG 472 (Records of United States Forces in Southeast Asia), NARA II. In 1969, the Naval Support Activity employed 6,700 civilians. Smith, *U.S. Marines in Vietnam, 1969*, 264.

81. In General Wallace Greene's first visit to Vietnam, his handwritten trip report notes included a line reading: "Eventually, depending on VC actions, at least a MEC may be required in combined operations with South Vietnamese forces." His prediction proved necessary, but the MEC was never employed in South Vietnam. CMC working notes, PAC trip 1965, Folder 2, Box 21, Entry "Records Relating to Military Operations, Programs and Organization, 1947–1976, ROK [Republic of Korea] Forces Vietnam, Correspondence, 1968 to Historical Information Command & General Staff College," RG 127, NARA II.

82. Westmoreland, *A Soldier Reports*, 214–216; Cosmas, *MACV: The Joint Command in the Years of Escalation, 1962–1967*, 333–334; Charles B. MacDonald interview notes, Folder "17 June 1973," Box 31, WCWP, LBJPL.

83. Charles B. MacDonald's notes from his interviews of William C. Westmoreland are full of Westmoreland's references to III MAF's lax supervision, unwillingness to conduct search-and-destroy operations, tendency to compartmentalize assets by service, reluctance to request reinforcements when required, and lack of initiative. Boxes 30 and 31, WCWP, LBJPL; Shulimson et al., *U.S. Marines in Vietnam: The Defining Year, 1968*, 12–15.

84. Cosmas, *MACV: The Joint Command in the Years of Escalation, 1962–1967*, 334.

85. Messages, COMUSMACV to CINCPAC, 251350Z and 260445Z January 1968, Folder "Eyes Only Message File 1-31 January 1968 [1 of 2]," Box 38, WCWP, LBJPL; Message, COMUSMACV to CG, I FFORCEV, 280352Z January 1968, "Contingency Plan," Folder "PCV Oplan 1-68 'Northern Cross,'" Box 1, Entry 43425, RG 472, NARA II; Letter of Instruction, COMUSMACV to Deputy Commander, COMUSMACV, 16 February 1968, Folder "Personal Correspondence of Sensitive Nature," Box 62, WCWP, LBJPL; Shulimson et al., *U.S. Marines in Vietnam, 1968*, 110–111.

86. Messages, COMUSMACV to CINCPAC, 171013Z and 211229Z February 1968, Folder "Eyes Only Message File 1-29 February 1968 [2 of 2]," Box 38, WCWP, LBJPL; Message, COMUSMACV to CG, III MAF, "Activation of Provisional Corps Vietnam," 091215Z March 1968, Folder "COMUSMACV 1968, Secret Outgoing Msg File [1 of 2]," Box 42, WCWP, LBJPL; Shulimson et al., *U.S. Marines in Vietnam, 1968*, 236–240.

87. MACV Letter of Instructions—Role and Missions of Provisional Corps Vietnam (PROV CORPS V), 3 March 1968, Folder "COMUSMACV Secret Correspondence for 1967 & 1968 [1 of 2]," Box 42, WCWP, LBJPL; Shulimson et al., *U.S. Marines in Vietnam, 1968*, 240.

88. Erik B. Villard, *Combat Operations: Staying the Course, October 1967 to September 1968* (Washington, DC: US Army Center of Military History, 2017), 599; Shulimson et al., *U.S. Marines in Vietnam: The Defining Year, 1968*, 361.

89. XXIV Corps Operations Order 2-C-70 (CAVALIER BEACH), 1400H February 1970, Folder 203–01, Box 80, Entry 43244, RG 472, NARA II; III MAF CC March 1970, 8, VDA; Cosmas and Murray, *U.S. Marines in Vietnam, 1970–1971*, 17.

90. Shulimson et al., *U.S. Marines in Vietnam, 1968*, 240.

91. Cosmas and Murray, *U.S. Marines in Vietnam, 1970–1971*, 16–17.

92. The only twentieth-century case the author has found of a corps commanding a corps occurred in the British Eighth Army in North Africa in 1943 at the battle to penetrate the German Mareth Line. Lieutenant General Sir Brian Horrocks's (British) X Corps took Lieutenant General Bernard Freyberg's New Zealand Corps under command for the operation. The NZ Corps HQ had a division-size command element for what was also a division-size force with no corps troops assigned. Horrocks's larger corps headquarters and its full staff were needed to help command and control the breakthrough battle. The battle, and its awkward command arrangement on the line's southern flank, lasted just a week. Douglas E. Delaney, *Corps Commanders: Five British and Canadian Generals at War, 1939–45* (Vancouver, BC: UBC Press, 2011), 33–34.

93. Graham A. Cosmas, cited in Shulimson et al., *U.S. Marines in Vietnam, 1968*, 240.

94. Peter Brush, "Uncommon Ground: Interservice Rivalry in I Corps," *Vietnam*, October 1999, 23.

95. Westmoreland, *A Soldier Reports*, 453–454. Westmoreland put out a press release on 6 March 1968 refuting press speculation that the new command arrangements reflected dissatisfaction with III MAF's performance: "Contrary to these speculative news stories, I wish to make it absolutely clear that these arrangements are based on tactical and management considerations and have nothing to do with the performance of the Marines, which is, and always has been, excellent." Statement by General William C. Westmoreland, 6 March 1968, Folder "#30 History File [I] 1-31 March 1968," Box 16, WCWP, LBJPL.

96. The "Smith versus Smith" controversy refers to an incident that occurred during the battle for Saipan in World War II. Marine Lieutenant General Holland M. Smith, commanding V Amphibious Corps, relieved army Major General Ralph Smith, commanding 27th (USA) Infantry Division, for cause. The case generated a firestorm of accusations and long-lasting bad relations between the two services. For the Marine defense of the decision, see Norman V. Cooper, *A Fighting General: The Biography of Gen Holland M. "Howlin Mad" Smith* (Quantico, VA: Marine Corps Association, 1987). Harry A. Galiley argues that the relief was unjustified in *"Howlin' Mad" vs. the Army: Conflict in Command Saipan, 1944* (Novato, CA: Presidio Press, 1986).

97. Shulimson et al., *U.S. Marines in Vietnam, 1968*, 236–240.

98. Cosmas, *MACV: The Joint Command in the Years of Escalation, 1962–1967*, 314–320; Bruce Palmer, Jr., *The 25-Year War: America's Military Role in Vietnam* (Lexington: University Press of Kentucky, 1984), 73, 193–194.

99. Westmoreland, *A Soldier Reports*, 452; Robert M. Burch, *Command and Control, 1968–1968* (Honolulu, HI: Headquarters Pacific Air Force, CHECO Division, 1969), 11–19; Kenneth J. Clifford, *Progress and Purpose: A Developmental History of the U.S. Marine Corps, 1900–1970* (Washington, DC: HQMC History Division 1973), 109–112; Shulimson et al., *U.S. Marines in Vietnam, 1968*, 465–466, 472.

100. Westmoreland, *A Soldier Reports*, 450; Charles B. MacDonald's notes from interviews of William C. Westmoreland, Folder "4-5 February 1979," Box 30, WCWP, LBJPL; Shulimson et al., *U.S. Marines in Vietnam, 1968*, 474, 487, 490–493.

101. Letters, COMUSMACV to CG III MAF and MACV Deputy Commander

for Air Operations (CG Seventh Air Force), "Single Management of Strike and Reconnaissance Air Assets," 7/8 March 1968, Folder "#30 History File [I] 1-31 March 1968," Box 16, WCWP, LBJPL; Shulimson et al., *U.S. Marines in Vietnam, 1968*, 466, 471–475, 491–492. For Seventh Air Force's views on how the new system worked, see its briefing to MACV: "Single Management of Strike and Reconnaissance Air Assets," no date, Folder 1401, Box 0018, Sam Johnson Collection, Vietnam Center and Archive, Texas Tech University, Lubbock, TX, www.vietnam.ttu .edu/Virtualarchive/items.php?item=F031100018140; Project CHECO Southeast Asia Report #210, *Single Manager for Air in South Vietnam—1967 to April 1968*, 1 July 1968, Folder 0896, Box 0005, Sam Johnson Collection, Vietnam Center and Archive, Texas Tech University, Lubbock, TX, www.vietnam.ttu.edu/virtualarch ive/items.php?item=F031100050896.

102. CINCPAC noted that in April 1968 the US Air Force wing at Da Nang flew 1,404 missions over North Vietnam and Laos rather than supporting US Army divisions in I Corps. The Air Force, in effect, redirected Marine sorties to army units to free up its own aircraft for deep and interdiction strikes. Shulimson et al., *U.S. Marines in Vietnam, 1968*, 503, 505, 515; Smith, *U.S. Marines in Vietnam, 1969*, 224–225; Cosmas and Murray, *U.S. Marines in Vietnam, 1970–1971*, 274. Westmoreland's defense of the single-manager policy is best conveyed in two late March 1968 cables to the JCS. Messages, COMUSMACV to CJCS, "Single Management of Strike and Reconnaissance Air Assets," 290712Z March 1968 and untitled, 311320Z March 1968, Folder "Eyes Only Message File 1-31 March 1968 [2 of 2]," Box 39 [1 of 2], WCWP, LBJPL. While the army, navy, and Marine Corps opposed the policy, the Chairman of the Joint Chiefs agreed with the air force and MACV. General Wheeler stated his position in Message, CJCS to COMUS-MACV, "Operational Control of III MAF Aviation Assets," 271722Z April 1968, Folder "Eyes Only Message File 1-30 April 1968 [2 of 2]," Box 39 (1 of 2), WCWP, LBJPL.

103. FMFPAC, *Operations of U.S. Marine Forces, Vietnam*, December 1968, 81–85; Shulimson et al., *U.S. Marines in Vietnam, 1968*, 505, 507; Smith, *U.S. Marines in Vietnam, 1969*, 225–226.

104. Keith B. McCutcheon, "Marine Aviation in Vietnam, 1962–1970," in *The Marines in Vietnam, 1953–1973: An Anthology and Annotated Bibliography*, ed. Jack Shulimson (Washington, DC: Headquarters Marine Corps History and Museums Division, 1985), 274–276; Cosmas and Murray, *U.S. Marines in Vietnam, 1970–1971*, 273–279.

105. Shulimson et al., *U.S. Marine in Vietnam, 1968*, 476, 491, 495. A Marine Expeditionary Corps, which III MAF was in all but name, was authorized to contain two Marine aircraft wings. MCO 3120.3, "The Organization of Marine Air-Ground Task Forces," 27 December 1962. Copy provided to author by Annette Amerman, historian at the History Division, Marine Corps University, Quantico, VA. Westmoreland said he "did not want AF in the position of controlling the helicopters; I could not live with that." Charles B. MacDonald's notes from interviews of William C. Westmoreland, Folder "19–20 March 1973," Box 30, WCWP, LBJPL.

106. Message, CG FMFPAC to CG III MAF, 110141Z October 1967, File "III MAF Incoming Messages October 1967," 21–25, Box "1967," Entry "III MAF," VDA; CINCPACFLT Amphib Ops Conference Report; FMFPAC staff study,

Application of Amphibious Doctrine in Vietnam, 22 April 1966, Folder 6/4, Box 4, Vietnam War Collection, MCHD; Letter, CINCPAC to CG III MAF, Operation DECKHOUSE III After Action, 19 September 1966, Folder 4/5, Box 31, Entry A1 1022, RG 127, NARA II; P. L. Hilgartner, "Amphibious Doctrine in Vietnam," in *The Marines in Vietnam, 1954–1973*, 294–297.

107. Dennis J. Murphy, "Let's Practice What We Preach About Helicopter Operations," *Marine Corps Gazette* 53, no. 8 (August 1969):18–24; Palmer, *The 25-Year War*, 160; Shulimson et al., *U.S. Marines in Vietnam, 1968*, 515–522, 526–532. General Davis sketched the more aggressive regimental air assault techniques he employed in I Corps in Raymond G. Davis and Richard O. Camp, "Marines in Assault by Helicopter," *Marine Corps Gazette* 52, no. 9 (September 1968): 22–28.

108. "Board Report for Utilization, Command and Control of III MAF Helo Assets," 17 May 1969, Folder 7/1, Box 160, Entry "Records of Units and Other Commands III MAF," RG 127, NARA II; HQMC Operations Analysis Group study, *Comparison of U.S. Army and U.S. Marine Corps Helicopter Assets*, 8 September 1969, Folder 8/10, Box 10, Vietnam War Collection, MCHD; III MAF Operations Analysis Section study, *Helicopter Utilization Capability, First Marine Air Wing*, 11 June 1969, Folder 17/9, Box 9, Vietnam War Collection, MCHD; III MAF Operations Analysis Section study, *Interim Report on Effective Management of III MAF Helicopter Operations*, 15 July 1969, Folder 6/8, Box 8, Vietnam War Collection, MCHD; Shulimson et al., *U.S. Marines in Vietnam, 1968*, 531–532; Smith, *U.S. Marines in Vietnam, 1969*, 239–241; Cosmas and Murray, *U.S. Marines in Vietnam, 1970–1971*, 288.

109. The Vietnam verdict was further validated by subsequent joint doctrine. In 1986 DOD introduced the Joint Forces Air Component Commander concept, which appeared in Joint Pub 3-01.2 *Joint Doctrine for Theater Counterair Operations*, 1 April 1986, http://edocs.nps.edu/dodpubs/topic/jointpubs/JP3/JP3_01.2_8 6040I.pdf. The 1991 Gulf War was the first major test of the new, now doctrinally sanctioned, single-manager application. The Marine Corps opposed the Joint Forces Air Component Commander concept as another threat to the integrity of its MAGTFs but lost the argument for the same reasons the single-management system prevailed in Vietnam.

Chapter 3. III MAF Intelligence

1. MCDP 2, *Intelligence* (Washington, DC: Headquarters, United States Marine Corps, 1997), 5–7, 42–44, 55–57, 59–64.

2. Military History Institute of Vietnam, *Victory in Vietnam: The Official History of the People's Army of Vietnam, 1954–1975*, trans. Merle L. Pribbenow (1988, 1994, Lawrence: University Press of Kansas, 2002), xvi, 67, 124–128; Bui Tin, *From Enemy to Friend: A North Vietnamese Perspective on the War* (Annapolis, MD: Naval Institute Press, 2002), 10–11, 44–45. Orthodox scholars disputed this link long after the war, arguing that South Vietnamese insurgents were not under the control of their political masters in the North. Even communist sources now admit that the insurgency was merely another tool employed by Hanoi to overthrow the Southern regime.

3. The Vietnamese politician and theorist Truong Chinh (actual name Dang Xuan Khu) described the "war of interlocking" in his book *Primer for Revolt* (reprint, New York: Frederick A. Praeger, 1963), 139–145. For a superb analysis of how Truong Chinh's approach to war confounded the Americans, not just the Marines, in Vietnam, see Wray R. Johonson, *Vietnam and American Doctrine for Small Wars* (Bangkok: White Lotus Press, 2001), 47–86. Giap's insight on the primacy of politics, quoted on page 33 of Johnson's work, is found in Giap's book *People's War, People's Army: The Viet Cong Insurrection Manual for Underdeveloped Countries* (1961, reprint, New York: Frederick A. Praeger, 1962), 79.

4. Douglas Pike, *Viet Cong: The Organization and Techniques of the National Liberation Front of South Vietnam* (Cambridge, MA: MIT Press, 1966); U.S. Grant Sharp, Jr., and William C. Westmoreland, *Report on the War in Vietnam* (Washington, DC: US Government Printing Office, 1968), 203–208; MACV, *Command History 1968*, Vol. 1, 59–67; William R. Andrews, *The Village War, Vietnamese Communist Revolutionary Activities in Dinh Tuong Province, 1960–1964* (Columbia: University of Missouri Press, 1973); Jeffrey Race, *War Comes to Long An: Revolutionary conflict in a Vietnamese Province* (Berkeley: University of California Press, 1972); James Trullinger, *Village at War: An Account of Revolution in Vietnam* (New York: Longman, 1980); David W. P. Elliot, *The Vietnamese War and Social Change in the Mekong Delta, 1930–1975*, 2 vols. (Armonk, NW: M. E. Sharpe, 2003); David Hunt, *Vietnam's Southern Revolution: From Peasant Insurrection to Total War* (Amherst: University of Massachusetts Press, 2008).

5. Phillip B. Davidson, *Secrets of the Vietnam War* (Novato, CA: Presidio Press, 1990), 21.

6. Leon Cohan, Jr., "Intelligence and Viet-Nam," *Marine Corps Gazette* 50, no. 2 (February 1966): 47–49. The Marine Corps intelligence community did not acquire a coherent educational and operational path for its officer corps until the mid-1990s. Major General Paul K. Van Riper, Director of Intelligence, initiated a new officer Military Occupational Specialty pipeline in 1995 based on perceived problems in DESERT STORM. ALMAR 100/95, *Program to Improve Marine Corps Intelligence* (Washington, DC: Headquarters Marine Corps, 1995). The MAF's fifth G-2 (in three months), Colonel Leo J. Dulacki, was an exception to the rule of G-2 leaders with limited intelligence experience. He had commanded a battalion in Korea and served two tours with the Defense Intelligence Agency. Jack Shulimson and Charles M. Johnson, *U.S. Marines in Vietnam: The Landing and the Buildup, 1965* (Washington, DC: USMC History and Museums Division, 1978), 69.

7. Figures derived from primary staff officer rosters contained in USMC official histories of the Vietnam War.

8. Davidson, *Secrets of the Vietnam War*, 8–9. Davidson claimed that Robert Komer was allowed to set up a separate intelligence organization for CORDS because General Westmoreland didn't want him to blame MACV if pacification failed.

9. FM 30-9, *Military Intelligence Battalion Field Army* (Washington, DC: Headquarters, Department of the Army, 1958), 61–66.

10. See, for example, III MAF CC, December 1965, 4–9, VDA; Shulimson and Johnson, *U.S. Marines in Vietnam, 1965*, 246–247.

11. III MAF CC, January 1967, 134–135, VDA. The G-1 (Administration) section contained only four officers, the G-4 (Logistics) section nine, and the G-5 (Civil Affairs) section six. The G-3 (Operations) section was the largest, boasting forty-three, including four colonels and eleven lieutenant colonels.

12. III MAF G-2, "Development of the Enemy Situation Prior to the 1968 Tet Offensive, Decentralization of Collection Assets in SVN, and Intelligence Support and Services Rendered to III MAF by COMUSMACV Intelligence Agencies," no date—circa 1968 (hereafter III MAF G-2 1968 Tet Intelligence Study), VII-6 to VII-9, Folder "Vietnam III MAF," Box 8, Vietnam War Collection, MCHD; MACV, *Command History 1968*, Vol. 2, 569–570.

13. MCHD holds 179 III MAF weekly intelligence summaries from 1966 to 1970. Examples are cited throughout this chapter.

14. Pike, *Viet Cong*, 234–239; Michael Lee Lanning and Dan Cragg, *Inside the VC and the NVA: The Real Story of North Vietnam's Armed Forces* (1992, College Station: Texas A&M University Press, 2008), 81–82.

15. III MAF Periodic Intelligence Report #42, 20 November 1966, Annex A pages 2–3, Folder "III MAF—Periodic Intelligence Reports #37-48—9 October–31 December 1966," Box "1966," Entry "III MAF," VDA.

16. Otto J. Lehrack, *The First Battle: Operation Starlite and the Beginning of the Blood Debt in Vietnam* (2004, New York: Presidio Press, 2006), 47–54; Shulimson and Johnson, *U.S. Marines in Vietnam, 1965*, 51, 69. The May and July victories also foreshadowed future Pyrrhic clashes. The regiment's 40th Battalion lost an entire company in the first fight, leaving only one unwounded survivor. The rebuilt VC battalion was similarly damaged in the second engagement, where one company lost all but two soldiers dead or wounded.

17. Sources for these reports included local Vietnamese agents, National Police, District Headquarters, RVN Military Security Services, ARVN I Corps, and ARVN 2nd Division. III MAF CC, August 1965, 12, VDA.

18. Shulimson and Johnson, *U.S. Marines in Vietnam, 1965*, 69–70. What the official history called "corroborative information from another source" was in fact signals intelligence from III MAF's 1st Radio Battalion (a signals intelligence collection unit) and national-level National Security Agency assets working for MACV. Rod Andrew, Jr., *The First Fight: U.S. Marines in Operation STARLITE, August 1965* (Quantico, VA: Marine Corps University History Division, 2015), 9–10. The MACV J-2, army Major General Joseph A. McChristian, claimed credit for locating the 1st VC headquarters in his book on MACV intelligence operations. Joseph A. McChristian, *The Role of Military Intelligence, 1965–1967* (Washington, DC: Department of the Army, 1974), 9.

19. Prebattle Marine intelligence indicated the 40th and 60th VC Battalions and the regimental command post were present along with parts of the 90th Battalion and 45th Weapons Battalion. The regimental command post was actually located ten miles south of the battlefield, along with the rest of the Weapons Battalion and the 90th Battalion. Lehrack, *The First Battle*, 64; Andrew, *The First Fight*, 10–17; Shulimson and Johnson, *U.S. Marines in Vietnam, 1965*, 70–72, 80.

20. Contemporary US military doctrine regards unit casualties of 30 percent as destruction criteria. See U.S. Army Field Manual 6-30, *Tactics, Techniques, and*

Procedures for Observed Fire (Washington, DC: Department of the Army, 1991), Annex E page 4, and U.S. Army Field Manual 3-09, *Field Artillery Operations and Fire Support* (Washington, DC: Department of the Army, 2014), 1–3.

21. Shulimson and Johnson, *U.S. Marines in Vietnam, 1965*, 101–111; Nicholas J. Schlosser, *In Persistent Battle: U.S. Marines in Operation Harvest Moon, 8 December to 20 December 1965* (Quantico, VA: Marine Corps University History Division, 2017), 10, 38–47. III MAF carried the 1st VC Regiment at half-strength in its order of battle assessments after HARVEST MOON. III MAF CC, December 1965, 8, VDA.

22. It is, of course, possible that the MAF's assessments of casualties suffered by the 1st VC Regiment were grossly inflated and that the enemy unit was resilient because it was never badly damaged. Westmoreland had several studies done that validated the accuracy of MACV's casualty reports, concluding that they erred on the conservative side. William C. Westmoreland, *A Soldier Reports*, 4th ed. (New York: Dell Publishing, 1984), 358–359; Charles B. MacDonald interview notes, Folder "12–14 March 1973," Box 30, WCWP, LBJPL. Guenter Lewy's survey of the Vietnam body count controversy provides evidence supporting both the US estimates' accuracy and their inflation. Clearly some US leaders exaggerated body counts, submitted numbers without physical evidence, or simply lied. Some evidence indicates that, while counts were sometimes (or even often) exaggerated, in aggregate they reflected accurate assessments because factors influencing "over" and "under" estimates tended to cancel each other out. Aggregate counts were also validated against other sources to include captured enemy documents, radio intercepts, wounded prisoners, communist recruiting and infiltration data, and of course physical remains. Other evaluations reached opposite conclusions. "Worst case" studies Lewy cited determined that nationwide the number of enemy killed in action was overstated by as much as 30 percent to 50 percent. Lewy concluded that estimates of enemy wounded were likely more accurate. In 1966 the US Intelligence Board concluded that, for every hundred enemy killed, fifty more likely died of their wounds or were permanently disabled. Guenter Lewy, *America in Vietnam* (New York: Oxford University Press, 1980), 78–82, 471. Even after deducting for a 30–50 percent body count inflation factor, the 1st VC Regiment was still destroyed on average once per year during the 1965–1967 period. Adding the "died of wounds/disabled" category to the 1st VC Regiment's projected losses suggests that each year 45 percent of its fighters died or were too injured to fight again. Less seriously wounded casualties further swelled that toll. In short, even large disparities in the number of enemy killed does not obviate the essential point: the regiment was able to recoup serious battle losses.

23. See, for example, III MAF Periodic Intelligence Report #13, 03 May 1966, 6, Folder "III MAF—Periodic Intelligence Reports #1-20—30 January–18 June 1966," Box "1966," Entry "III MAF," VDA; III MAF Periodic Intelligence Report #28, 16 August 1966, Annex A page 8, Folder "III MAF—Periodic Intelligence Reports #21-36—19 June–8 October 1966," Box "1966," Entry "III MAF," VDA; III MAF Periodic Intelligence Report #39, 30 October 1966, Annex A pages 6 and 13, Folder "III MAF—Periodic Intelligence Reports #37-48—9 October–31 December 1966," Box "1966," Entry "III MAF," VDA; III MAF Periodic Intelligence Report #42, 20 November 1966, Annex A pages 2–4, Folder "III MAF—Periodic

Intelligence Reports #37-48—9 October–31 December 1966," Box "1966," Entry "III MAF," VDA; III MAF Periodic Intelligence Report #13–67, 2 April 1967, A-24, A-25, Annex B page 2, Folder "III MAF—Periodic Intelligence Reports #9-67 thru 16-67—26 February–22 April 1967," Box "1967," Entry "III MAF," VDA.

24. III MAF Periodic Intelligence Report #22–67, 4 June 1967, Annex C page 2, Folder "III MAF—Periodic Intelligence Reports #17-67 thru 22-67—23 April–3 June 1967," Box "1967," Entry "III MAF," VDA; III MAF Periodic Intelligence Report #27-67, 9 July 1967, Annex B page 3, Folder "III MAF—Periodic Intelligence Reports #23-67 thru 27-67—4 June–8 July 1967," Box "1967," Entry "III MAF," VDA.

25. See, for example, III MAF Periodic Intelligence Report #44, 4 December 1966, Annex B pages 2–3, Folder "III MAF—Periodic Intelligence Reports #37-48—9 October–31 December 1966," Box "1966," Entry "III MAF," VDA; III MAF Periodic Intelligence Report #45, 11 December 1966, Annex B pages 1–2, Folder "III MAF—Periodic Intelligence Reports #37-48—9 October–31 December 1966," Box "1966," Entry "III MAF," VDA; III MAF Periodic Intelligence Report #3-67, 22 January 1967, Annex B page 1, Folder "III MAF—Periodic Intelligence Reports #1-67 thru 8-67—1 January–25 February 1967," Box "1967," Entry "III MAF," VDA; III MAF Periodic Intelligence Report #9-67, 5 March 1967, Annex C pages 1–2, Folder "III MAF—Periodic Intelligence Reports #9-67 thru 16-67—26 February–22 April 1967," Box "1967," Entry "III MAF," VDA.

26. Lien-hang T. Nguyen, *Hanoi's War: An International History of the War for Peace in Vietnam* (Chapel Hill: University of North Carolina Press, 2012), 59–60, 64–65. Hanoi's leaders made the decision to commit NVA units to South Vietnam at the Ninth Plenum in December 1963. This timeline, confirmed by North Vietnamese sources, undermines the once-favored historical narrative that only American air strikes in August 1964 or the introduction of US ground forces in March 1965 forced Hanoi to dispatch troops to the South.

27. Jack Shulimson, *U.S. Marines in Vietnam: An Expanding War, 1966* (Washington, DC: USMC History and Museums Division, 1982), 51, 177.

28. III MAF CC, July 1966, 14, 17, VDA; Shulimson, *U.S. Marines in Vietnam, 1966*, 139–140, 145, 158.

29. III MAF Periodic Intelligence Report #15-67, 16 April 1967, Annex A page 29, Folder "III MAF—Periodic Intelligence Reports #9-67 thru 16-67—26 February–22 April 1967," Box "1967," Entry "III MAF," VDA.

30. III MAF CC, August 1966, 13–16, VDA; III MAF CC, September 1966, 14–17, VDA; III MAF CC, July 1967, 11, 26–28, 30–31, VDA; III MAF CC, September 1967, 11, 19–21, VDA.

31. Shulimson, *U.S. Marines in Vietnam, 1966*, 181–184; Gary L. Telfer, Lane Rogers, and Keith Fleming, Jr., *U.S. Marines in Vietnam: Fighting the North Vietnamese, 1967* (Washington, DC: USMC History and Museums Division, 1984), 39, 42, 104; III MAF Periodic Intelligence Report #21-67, 28 May 1967, Annex E pages 3–5, Folder "III MAF—Periodic Intelligence Reports #17-67 thru 22-67—23 April–3 June 1967," Box "1967," Entry "III MAF," VDA.

32. III MAF Periodic Intelligence Report #8-67, 26 February 1967, 1, Annex A pages 2–3, Folder "III MAF—Periodic Intelligence Reports #1-67 thru 8-67—1 January–25 February 1967," Box "1967," Entry "III MAF," VDA.

33. The III MAF G-2 estimated 27,935 NVA/VC conventional troops in I Corps in September 1967. The MAF reported 96,511 army, navy, air force, and Marine personnel that month—about 3.5 times more conventional troops than the communists fielded. III MAF CC, September 1967, 10, 21–22, VDA.

34. III MAF CC, September 1967, 11, 19–21, VDA. The most recent official Marine history of the period concluded that the 10 September 1967 battle four miles southwest of Con Thien against "the entire *812th NVA Regiment*. . . . spoiled a major enemy attack in the making." Joseph C. Long, *Hill of Angels: U.S. Marines and the Battle for Con Thien, 1967–1968* (Quantico, VA: Marine Corps University History Division, 2016), 34–36. Marine analysts at the time assessed the May attack on the same base as a raid designed to capture artillery pieces but concluded that the failed autumn assault was intended to seize and hold the commanding high ground. In both cases III MAF intelligence officers deemed the enemy's primary goal not physical destruction of the base but rather the morale impact such a tactical victory would have on domestic North and South Vietnamese audiences as well as its influence on the international community. III MAF Periodic Intelligence Report #19-67, 14 May 1967, 1, 7–8, Folder "III MAF—Periodic Intelligence Reports #17-67 thru 22-67—23 April–3 June 1967," Box "1967," Entry "III MAF," VDA; III MAF CC, May 1967, 29, VDA; III MAF CC, September 1967, 11, VDA.

35. III MAF Periodic Intelligence Report #15-67, 16 April 1967, Annex B page 2, Folder "III MAF—Periodic Intelligence Reports #9-67 thru 16-67—26 February–22 April 1967," Box "1967," Entry "III MAF," VDA; III MAF Periodic Intelligence Report #19-67, 14 May 1967, Annex A page 2, Annex D page 2, Folder "III MAF—Periodic Intelligence Reports #17-67 thru 22-67—23 April–3 June 1967," Box "1967," Entry "III MAF," VDA. Sample calculation factors: sixteen thousand NVA in Quang Tri Province; one pound of food per man per day (less than a 1.5 pound per day planning factor for US forces); and sixteen thousand pounds food per day required for the entire force. An average backpack load of fifty pounds of food per bearer would require 320 porters per day. One bearer supported each ten-man squad, delivering at least one hundred pounds of food for each ten-day period. Thus, each porter had to make the trip into South Vietnam two or three times every ten days. Porter detachments could make a night journey southward, remain with the resupplied unit during the day, and then return across the DMZ into North Vietnam in the next cycle of darkness. Some of the NVA units, such as those clustered around Con Thien, were close enough for foot-mobile resupply columns to make the round trip on the same night.

36. At longer distances human (or animal) transport must consume part of the load they carry, thus diminishing the amount of food or fodder delivered at the destination. This "feed to speed" ratio has been a factor in expeditionary military logistics since armies first marched. See Donald W. Engels, *Alexander the Great and the Logistics of the Macedonian Army* (1978, Berkeley: University of California Press, 1980), for a complete exposition on this practical constraint. Similar limitations apply to military transport (trucks, trains, ships) powered by fossil fuels today.

37. Approximate NVA casualty figures were derived from USMC official history summaries of 1966–1967 operations in Quang Tri Province.

38. III MAF G-2 estimated enemy regular (NVA, main force VC, local force VC) strength in Quang Tri Province at 15,590 on 14 January 1968—the date closest

to the end of 1967 for which figures are available. III MAF Periodic Intelligence Report #2-68, 14 January 1968, Annex A page 2, Folder "III MAF—Periodic Intelligence Reports #2-68 [thru] 18–68—7 January–5 May 1968," Box "1968," Entry "III MAF," VDA. Estimates for 8 July 1967, the last estimate in the records for 1967, was 26,060. III MAF Periodic Intelligence Report #27-67, 9 July 1967, Annex A page 1, Folder "III MAF—Periodic Intelligence Reports #23-67 [thru] 27-67—4 June–8 July 1967," Box "1967," Entry "III MAF," VDA. The estimate for 7 January 1967 was 28, 564. III MAF Periodic Intelligence Report #1-67, 8 January 1967, Annex A page 1, Folder "III MAF—Periodic Intelligence Reports #1-67 [thru] 8-67—1 January–25 February 1967," Box "1967," Entry "III MAF," VDA. The average of those estimates is 23,404 communist regulars. An NVA/VC KIA total of eight thousand for Quang Tri Province in 1967 means that roughly 35 percent of the average enemy strength in the province died. For the 324B Division (9,600 men), that ratio equals 3,360 KIA. Estimates for wounded, calculated by the formula used in the III MAF G-2, added 1,109 wounded soldiers for the 324B Division. This equals 4,469 dead or wounded soldiers for the year—a casualty rate of approximately 46 percent. The Marine wounded in action formula was more conservative than that applied by MACV. The MACV G-2 estimated 1.5 wounded for each dead enemy combatant. That formula produces an estimate of 87 percent killed or wounded for the division over the course of 1967. Marine analysts estimated enemy unit strengths by subtracting confirmed KIA from a unit's table of organization strength. Then they subtracted one-third of the KIA numbers from the unit strength to account for wounded who would not return. The rest of the estimated wounded were expected to return to action. Unit strengths were upgraded again as reports of newly arrived levies appeared via a range of collection sources. III MAF Periodic Intelligence Report #19-67, 14 May 1967, Annex A page 12, Folder "III MAF—Periodic Intelligence Reports #17-67 thru 22-67—23 April–3 June 1967," Box "1967," Entry "III MAF," VDA. A medical rallier (the term used to describe communist troops and cadre who surrendered) from 5th VC Division (a unit outside I Corps, but the III MAF G-2 deemed his insights valid for the III MAF sector also) reported that communist medical planning estimated four to six civilians were required to carry off each wounded soldier. Enemy medical planners also anticipated four wounded for each killed soldier (more in line with traditional estimates than the conservative MACV estimate). The rallier noted that in his experience the wounded-to-killed ratio had hovered in the 1:1 range. III MAF Periodic Intelligence Report #2-67, 15 January 1967, Annex B pages 1–2, Folder "III MAF—Periodic Intelligence Reports #1-67 thru 8-67—1 January–25 February 1967," Box "1967," Entry "III MAF," VDA.

39. III MAF Periodic Intelligence Report #1-67, 8 January 1967, Annex A pages 2 and 8, Folder "III MAF—Periodic Intelligence Reports #1-67 thru 8-67—1 January–25 February 1967," Box "1967," Entry "III MAF," VDA; III MAF Periodic Intelligence Report #2-68, 14 January 1968, Annex A page 4, Folder "III MAF—Periodic Intelligence Reports #2-68—7 January–5 May 1968," Box "1968," Entry "III MAF," VDA.

40. The consensus interpretation is that the communist offensive achieved a partial surprise. Stanley Karnow cites a postwar West Point textbook characterizing it as an "intelligence failure ranking with Pearl Harbor." Stanley Karnow,

Vietnam: A History, 2nd ed. (New York: Penguin Books, 1997), 556. Dave Palmer refers to the same source, agreeing that "the North Vietnamese gained complete surprise." Dave Richard Palmer, *Summons of the Trumpet: U.S.-Vietnam in Perspective* (Novato, CA: Presidio Press, 1982), 179. George Herring claims the United States and South Vietnam were caught "off guard." George C. Herring, *America's Longest War: The United States and Vietnam, 1950–1975*, 5th ed. (New York: McGraw-Hill Education, 2014), 237. For views of CIA and MACV intelligence officers at the time, see George W. Allen, *None So Blind: A Personal Account of the Intelligence Failure in Vietnam* (Chicago: Ivan R. Dee, 2001), 255–260, and Bruce E. Jones, *War Without Windows: A True Account of a Young Army Officer Trapped in an Intelligence Cover-Up in Vietnam* (New York: Vanguard Press, 1987), 88, 116, 125, 127, 134–135, 141, 144–145, 158–160, 284. For the account of the MACV commander and his G-2, see Westmoreland, *A Soldier Reports*, 313–314, 411–423. The MACV G-2 admitted tactical but not strategic surprise. He declared that the enemy's assault into "the heart of Allied Strength—the cities" entailed rashness that, to have anticipated, would have required intelligence officers to credit the enemy with folly. Davidson, *Secrets of the Vietnam War*, 429–433. The most extensive academic assessment of the Tet Offensive from an intelligence perspective notes multiple indications and warnings in the months prior to the assault. It also acknowledges that allied intelligence analysis failed to synthesize those indications into a comprehensive evaluation that prepared commanders more fully for the onslaught. James J. Wirtz, *The Tet Offensive: Intelligence Failure in War* (Ithaca, NY: Cornell University Press, 1991). In a more recent assessment, a historian of the Tet Offensive concludes: "The Americans and the RVN knew something was coming but did not understand how big it would be, or how widespread, and in most areas, they were not sure when it would occur." Edwin E. Moise, *The Myths of TET: The Most Misunderstood Event of the Vietnam War* (Lawrence: University Press of Kansas, 2017), 129.

41. Gary L. Telfer, Lane Rogers, and Keith Fleming, Jr., *U.S. Marines in Vietnam: Fighting the North Vietnamese, 1967* (Washington, DC: USMC History and Museums Division, 1984), 259.

42. Westmoreland, *A Soldier Reports*, 411, 416, 421; Sharp and Westmoreland, *Report on the War in Vietnam*, 157–160; Jack Shulimson et al., *U.S. Marines in Vietnam: The Defining Year, 1968* (Washington, DC: HQMC History and Museums Division, 1997), 17.

43. These three CIA assessments were dated 21 November, 8 December, and 19 December 1967. Harold P. Ford, *CIA and the Vietnam Policymakers: Three Episodes, 1962–1968* (Washington, DC: CIA Center for the Study of Intelligence, 1998), 119–123.

44. Westmoreland, *A Soldier Reports*, 421.

45. Davidson, *Secrets of the Vietnam War*, 104; MACV, *Command History 1968*, Vol. 2, 881.

46. Pribbenow, trans., *Victory in Vietnam*, 207.

47. Pribbenow, trans., *Victory in Vietnam*, 214–216.

48. Pribbenow, trans., Victory in Vietnam, 216.

49. FMFPAC, *Operations of U.S. Marine Forces, Vietnam*, November 1967.

50. Message, CG III MAF to COMUSMACV, 120550Z January 1968, "CY 67

Assessment," 65–75, Folder "III MAF—Outgoing Messages—January 1968 (part 2)," Box "1968," Entry "III MAF," VDA.

51. MACV, *Command History 1968*, Vol. 2, 883–884.

52. III MAF Periodic Intelligence Report #2-68, 15 January 1968, 2–3, 7, Folder "III MAF—Periodic Intelligence Reports #2-68—7 January–5 May 1968," Box "1968," Entry "III MAF," VDA.

53. MACV, *Command History 1968*, Vol. 2, 883.

54. Westmoreland, *A Soldier Reports*, 415; Jack Shulimson et al., *U.S. Marines in Vietnam, 1968*, 17.

55. Message, CG III MAF to CG, 3rd Marine Division, 130252Z January 1968, 20, Folder "III MAF—Outgoing Messages—January 1968 (part 1)," Box "1968," Entry "III MAF," VDA.

56. Message, CG FMFPAC to CG, III MAF, 121957Z January 1968, 31, and Message, CG FMFPAC to CMC and CG, III MAF, 132035Z January 1968, 33–37, Folder "III MAF—Incoming Messages—January 1968," Box "1968," Entry "III MAF," VDA. In this exchange General Krulak endorsed the MACV commander's decision to defend the remote base and advised against the other options considered by Washington politicians—either withdrawing or counterattacking into Laos.

57. Sharp and Westmoreland, *Report on the War in Vietnam*, 157; Westmoreland, *A Soldier Reports*, 417–418, 420.

58. Davidson, *Secrets of the Vietnam War*, 114; Sharp and Westmoreland, *Report on the War in Vietnam*, 158; Ford, *CIA and the Vietnam Policymakers*, 113.

59. Ford, *CIA and the Vietnam Policymakers*, 115.

60. MACV, *Command History 1968*, Vol. 2, 883–884.

61. Foreign Intelligence Advisory Board Report, "Warning of the Tet Offensive," Folder "Tet: Warning & Surprise," Box 43, Wallace M. Greene Papers (# 3093), MCHD.

62. III MAF G-2 1968 Tet Intelligence Study, VII-1 to VII-6.

63. Merle L. Pribbenow, trans., *Victory in Vietnam*, 218.

64. MACV, *Command History 1968*, Vol. 2, 1026.

65. III MAF G-2 1968 Tet Intelligence Study, VII-1 to VII-6.

66. Michael Warner, "'US Intelligence and Vietnam': The Official Version(s)," *Intelligence and National Security* 25, no. 5 (October 2010): 625–630.

67. The US Army 9th Infantry Division, operating in the Mekong Delta, determined in a two-month study of its intelligence resources that personnel-based sources (agents, POWs, ralliers, tips resulting from civic action engagements, etc.) proved twice as reliable as information derived by machines (aerial sensors, ground-based radar, signals intelligence, etc.). Julian J. Ewell and Ira A. Hunt, Jr., *Sharpening the Combat Edge: The Use of Analysis to Reinforce Military Judgment* (Washington, DC: Department of the Army, 1995), 102–104.

68. Westmoreland, *A Soldier Reports*, 422.

69. Russel H. Stolfi, *U.S. Marine Corps Civic Action Efforts in Vietnam, March 1965—March 1966* (Washington, DC: Headquarters Marine Corps G-3 Division Historical Branch, 1968), 76–77; Shulimson, *U.S. Marines in Vietnam, 1966*, 257.

70. Davidson, *Secrets of the Vietnam War*, 8–9.

71. In February 1968, President Nguyen Van Thieu established the Central

Recovery Committee to coordinate the government's pacification response to the Tet crisis. Led initially by Vice President Nguyen Cao Ky, and then Prime Minister Nguyen Van Loc, the early RVN response proved lackadaisical. Saigon's Central Revolutionary Development Council, an underresourced counterpart to CORDS, also proved ineffective. It was not until November 1968 that Thieu set up the Central Pacification and Development Council, reporting to the prime minister, to manage the Accelerated Pacification Campaign. Richard A. Hunt, *Pacification: The American Struggle for Vietnam's Hearts and Minds* (Boulder: Westview Press, 1995), 144–147, 196; Charles R. Smith, *U.S. Marines in Vietnam: High Mobility and Standdown, 1969* (Washington, DC: USMC History and Museums Division, 1988), 281–284.

72. For an insightful analysis of the role and function of communist infrastructure in four post-Vietnam Maoist insurgencies, see Thomas A. Marks, *Maoist Insurgency Since Vietnam* (London: Frank Cass, 1996).

73. Pike, *Viet Cong*, 111.

74. III MAF Special Intelligence Study 2-68, *Military Region 5—ICTZ VC Political Infrastructure*, August 1968 and Special Intelligence Study 3-68, *Tri Thien Hue Military Region VC Political Infrastructure*, September 1968, Folder 12/8, Box 160, Entry "Records of Units and Other Commands, 1953–1993, III MAF," RG 127, NARA II. A year later, more than half of the VCI cadre nationwide had been identified by name. CINCPAC, *Measurement of Progress in Southeast Asia*, 30 September 1969, 46, Folder "011645-UNCL [unclassified]," Box 12, Entry UD 46-E, RG 127, NARA II.

75. Smith, *U.S. Marines in Vietnam, 1969*, 283.

76. Hunt, *Pacification*, 194–198.

77. Message, COMUSMACV to CINCPAC, "Phung Hoang Operational Results: December 1969," 271035Z January 1970, Folder "5-3-2-D," Box 181, Entry A1 52, RG 472, NARA II; Smith, *U.S. Marines in Vietnam, 1969*, 294–295. The 5,363 VCI claimed included 1,680 killed, 2,340 captured, and 1,343 surrendered.

78. Thomas C. Thayer, *War Without Fronts: The American Experience in Vietnam* (1985, Annapolis, MD: Naval Institute Press, 2016), 207.

79. CINCPAC, *Measurement of Progress in Southeast Asia*, 30 September 1969, 45–47, Folder "011645-UNCL [unclassified]," Box 12, Entry UD 46-E, RG 127, NARA II; III MAF G-2 (Chief, Phoenix Division, DEPCORDS), "BIG MACK Report—Fact Sheet on Refinement in VCI Strength Accounting," 5, Folder 204–57 (BIG MACK), Box 1, Entry 33104, RG 472, NARA II.

80. III MAF G-2, "Special Intelligence Study 2-68, Military Region 5—ICTZ VC Political Infrastructure," 20 August 1968, cover letter, Folder 8, Box 160, Entry "Records of Units and Other Commands, 1953–1993 (III MAF)," RG 127, NARA II.

81. Letter, Alexander Firfer to William E. Colby, 31 December 1969, Folder "1619-01: Civic Action Meeting Files—Phoenix Committee Meetings, 1970," Box 25, Entry 33100, RG 472, NARA II.

82. Letter, W. E. Burmester (Public Safety Directorate, Da Nang) to Carl Fritz (I Corps Deputy CORDS Director), 20 November 1969 and Letter, ICTZ PHOENIX Coordinator to III MAF DEPCORDS, with draft study on "Revitalization of PHOENIX Program in ICTZ," 24 October 1969, Folder "1603-034,

DIOCC Background Info, 1970," Box 9, Entry 33104, RG 472, NARA II; Letter, III MAF Deputy for CORDS to III MAF CG, 26 August 1969, Folder "1603-03A: PHOENIX/PHUNG HOANG Activity Files, 1969," Box 14, Entry 33100, RG 472, NARA II.

83. Hunt, *Pacification*, 95, 194–198, 204, 248, 260–261.

84. III MAF CC, December 1969, 39, VDA.

85. Smith, *U.S. Marines in Vietnam, 1969*, 285, 294–295.

86. The III MAF order of battle report carried 12,055 guerrillas (not NVA, VC main force, or VC local force units) in I Corps at the end of 1969. III MAF Periodic Intelligence Report #51-69, 23 December 1969, Annex A page 4, Folder "III MAF—Periodic Intelligence Reports #46-69 thru 51–69—9 November–23 December 1969," Box "1969," Entry "III MAF," VDA.

87. Vietnam Special Studies Group (VSSG), *Study on the Situation in the Countryside*, 11 June 1970, Folder "1601-11A: Civil Affairs Advisory Files—Study on the Situation in the Countryside, 1970 [1 of 2]," Box 21, Entry 33100, RG 472, NARA II.

88. Message, III MAF CORDS Deputy to COMUSMACV CORDS, 041400 February 1970, "VSSG Project," Folder "228-07: Command Reporting Files—VSSG Report, 1970," Box 20, Entry 33100, RG 472, NARA II.

89. XXIV Corps Fact Sheet, "Progress and Problems, Phoenix Division," 14 August 1970, Folder "1603-03A, Correspondence—PHX, Hq ICTZ, Outgoing (Folder 1 of 2) 1970," Box 9, Entry 33104, RG 472, NARA II.

90. Because systems analysis had become the rage at the Pentagon, subordinate headquarters also added this capability to their repertoire, if only in self-defense. In 1966 III MAF established a small operations research cell that began to analyze topics such as helicopter utilization, counterfire techniques, and ammunition management. Based on their rotation dates, the first two officers qualified in the field of operations research arrived in the summer of 1966. III MAF CC, December 1966, 60, VDA. Five of the III MAF operations research studies mentioned are in Boxes 8–10, Vietnam War Collection, MCHD. It remains unclear how much influence, if any, this small section's analyses exerted on the III MAF staff or its commanders.

91. The army's field manual for staff officers (also used by Marines) said of assessments: "The preparation of estimates is a continuous process. The development of new information and considerations necessitates revisions of estimates so that recommendations or decisions based on the estimates will be more accurate." FM 101-5 *Staff Organization and Procedure* (Washington, DC: Headquarters, Department of the Army, 1970), 2–5.

92. III MAF CC, July 1969, 23, VDA.

93. The outcome of the bitter fight across northern I Corps during the 1972 Easter Offensive does not disprove this assessment. While a stalemate resulted from the see-saw battle, ARVN suffered an infantry division destroyed, lost territory in Quang Tri Province that it never recovered, and survived thanks to extensive naval gunfire and aviation fires controlled by American advisers and fire support teams. For firsthand accounts of this near-run affair, see Gerald H. Turley, *The Easter Offensive: Vietnam, 1972* (Novato, CA: Presidio Press, 1985) and John Grider Miller, *The Bridge at Dong Ha* (Annapolis, MD: Naval Institute Press, 1989).

94. Westmoreland, *A Soldier Reports*, 186–187; Allan R. Millett, "Wallace M. Greene Jr., 1964–1968," in *Commandants of the Marine Corps*, ed. Allan R. Millett and Jack Shulimson (Annapolis, MD: Naval Institute Press, 2004), 395–397; Michael A. Hennessy, *Strategy in Vietnam: The Marines and Revolutionary Warfare in I Corps, 1965–1972* (Westport, CT: Praeger, 1997), 75.

95. Victor H. Krulak, *First to Fight: An Inside View of the U.S. Marine Corps* (Annapolis, MD: Naval Institute Press, 1984), 180, 186, 198; Shulimson, *U.S. Marines in Vietnam, 1966*, 13.

96. Krulak, *First to Fight*, 195–200, 207–208; Shulimson, *U.S. Marines in Vietnam, 1966*, 13–14.

97. Lewis W. Walt, *Strange War, Strange Strategy: A General's Report on Vietnam* (New York: Funk & Wagnalls, 1970), 29. Walt devoted a brief chapter (one of seventeen) of just seven pages to the NVA, while the bulk of his story concentrated on the insurgent threat.

98. CG III MAF to HQMC Chief of Staff, 29 December 1966, in III MAF Operation Plan 121-66 (PRACTICE NINE), Box 156, Entry "Records of Units and Other Commands, 1953–1993," RG 127 (Records of the U.S. Marine Corps), NARA II.

99. Jack Shulimson et al., *U.S. Marines in Vietnam: The Defining Year, 1968* (Washington, DC: HQMC History and Museums Division, 1997), 608.

100. Message, CG III MAF to CMC and FMFPAC, 011450Z December 1967, 13–16, Folder "7/4) III MAF: 'Dye Marker' Exclusive Messages, 20 October 1966–13 March 1967," Box 157, Entry "Records of Units and Other Commands, 1953–1993," RG 127, NARA II.

101. Smith, *U.S. Marines in Vietnam, 1969*, 52.

102. III MAF CC, April 1969, 23, 27, VDA.

103. Krulak, *First to Fight*, 199. By Krulak's 1965 estimate, the 25 percent reduction in enemy manpower achieved by 1972 would cost 218,750 allied fatalities. His projection, when adjusted for the change from 20 percent to 25 percent of enemy manpower lost, had been off by just 1,250 friendly deaths.

104. Krulak, *First to Fight*, 199.

Chapter 4. III MAF Operations

1. China supplied weapons, engineering equipment, and logistic units to North Vietnam during the war. More than 320,000 Chinese troops served in North Vietnam between 1965 and 1968. Chinese troop presence peaked in 1967 at 170,000. Qiang Zhai, *China and the Vietnam Wars: 1950–1975* (Chapel Hill: University of North Carolina Press, 2000), 135. Russia furnished fighter jets, surface-to-air missiles, tanks, and other sophisticated weapons. It also sent three thousand troops to assist in operating the equipment, especially the air defense systems. George C. Herring, *America's Longest War: The United States and Vietnam, 1950–1975*, 5th ed. (New York: McGraw-Hill Education, 2014), 182–183.

2. Ngo Quang Truong, *RVNAF and US Operational Cooperation and Coordination* (Washington, DC: US Army Center of Military History, 1980), 172.

3. Willard Pearson, *The War in the Northern Provinces, 1966–1968* (Washington, DC: Department of the Army, 1975), 105.

4. Walt devoted two of his book's seventeen chapters to how he handled this crisis. Lewis W. Walt, *Strange War, Strange Strategy: A General's Report on Vietnam* (New York: Funk & Wagnalls, 1970), 113–136. Westmoreland said he did "good work." Charles B. MacDonald's notes from interviews of William C. Westmoreland, Folder "20 May 1973," Box 30, WCWP, LBJPL.

5. For a comprehensive overview of the ARVN generals' penchant for playing politics, see the chapter on this subject in Jeffrey J. Clarke, *Advice and Support: The Final Years, 1965–1973* (Washington, DC: US Army Center of Military History, 1988), 255–269.

6. III MAF CC, August 1966, 7, VDA.

7. Cau Van Vien et al., *The U.S. Adviser* (Washington, DC: US Army Center of Military History, 1980), 47, 57.

8. Jack Shulimson and Charles M. Johnson, *U.S. Marines in Vietnam: The Landing and the Buildup, 1965* (Washington, DC: USMC History and Museums Division, 1978), 208. For more on US Marine training and advising of South Vietnamese Marines, see Charles D. Melson and Wanda J. Renfrow, ed., *Marine Advisors with the Vietnamese Marine Corps* (Quantico, VA: Marine Corps University History Division, 2009). Each of the Marine Corps' official histories of the Vietnam War also contains a section on the US Marine Corps' RVN Marine advisory command as well as the activities of the ANGLICO detachments. ANGLICO Marines provided fire support expertise (planning, coordinating, and controlling aviation, naval gunfire, and artillery fires) to allied and joint partners.

9. Clarke, *Advice and Support: The Final Years, 1965–1973*, 56–57, 373.

10. Truong, *RVNAF and US Operational Cooperation and Coordination*, 157–159.

11. Truong, *RVNAF and US Operational Cooperation and Coordination*, 157. Westmoreland claimed the MAF was "not using the Vietnamese as partners. . . . Marines had [a] tendency to run everything as a U.S. show." Charles B. MacDonald interview notes, Folder "24 April 1973," Box 30, WCWP, LBJPL.

12. "OP File—Op STARLITE—18 Aug-18 Sep," Box "1965 Named Operations," Entry "Miscellaneous Archive Data," VDA; Rod Andrew, Jr., *The First Fight: U.S. Marines in Operation STARLITE, August 1965* (Quantico, VA: Marine Corps University History Division, 2015); Nicholas J. Schlosser, *In Persistent Battle: U.S. Marines in Operation Harvest Moon, 8 December to 20 December 1965* (Quantico, VA: Marine Corps University History Division, 2017); Jack Shulimson, *U.S. Marines in Vietnam: An Expanding War, 1966* (Washington, DC: USMC History and Museums Division, 1982), 159–176; Gary L. Telfer, Lane Rogers, and Keith Fleming, Jr., *U.S. Marines in Vietnam: Fighting the North Vietnamese, 1967* (Washington, DC: USMC History and Museums Division, 1984), 24–30; John J. Tolson, *Airmobility, 1961–1971* (1973, Washington, DC: Department of the Army, 1999), 205–209. Vinh Loc was a district a few miles southeast of Hue on the coast of Thua Thien Province. A combined task force consisting of ARVN, US Army, and US Navy forces swept the island in September 1968, killing 154 and capturing 370 VC. CORDS considered it a model operation. Richard A. Hunt, *Pacification: The American Struggle for Vietnam's Hearts and Minds* (Boulder: Westview Press, 1995),

172–175. In September General Cushman and his chief of staff acknowledged the success and wondered why 1st Marine Division's Task Force X-Ray had never previously achieved a similar outcome. Message, CG XXIV Corps to COMUS-MACV and CG, III MAF, 132024Z, 40–42, File "III MAF Incoming Messages September 1968 (1)," Box "1968," Entry "III MAF," VDA.

13. Truong, *RVNAF and US Operational Cooperation and Coordination*, 68, 117.

14. MACV's SEER (System for Evaluating the Effectiveness of RVNAF) reports for the third quarter of 1969 listed I Corps' 1st and 2nd Divisions as the two most effective among the ten regular ARVN infantry divisions in the country. "MACV SEER Report, 3d Qtr CY 69," no date, 31, Folder 221–07, Box 36, Entry P 465 (General Records 1968–1973), RG 472, NARA II. Six months later the 2nd Division had slipped in its evaluation of combat effectiveness, but I Corps still held the strongest assessments of the four ARVN corps commands. Its scores in March 1970 even exceeded the collective average for the ARVN rangers, armored cavalry, airborne, and Marines who were considered the elite commands in the South Vietnamese defense forces. "MACV SEER Report, 1st Qtr CY 70," no date, 32, Folder 223–07, Box 37, Entry "P 465, #33530 (General Records 1968–1973)," RG 472, NARA II.

15. Clarke, *Advice and Support: The Final Years, 1965–1973*, 183.

16. "Senior Officer Debriefing Report: COL [Colonel] John J. Beeson, Deputy Senior Advisor, I Corps Tactical Zone, Period 1 July 1967 to 19 August 1968," 29 January 1969, 14–15, 21, US Army Heritage & Education Center, Carlisle, PA.

17. "Senior Officer Debriefing Report: BG Henry J. Muller Jr., Deputy Senior Advisor, I Corps Tactical Zone, Period 12 Sep 69 to 15 Jun 70," 8 September 1970, 2, US Army Heritage & Education Center, Carlisle, PA.

18. FMFPAC, *Operations of U.S. Marine Forces, Vietnam*, December 1969, 89, VDA; Charles R. Smith, *U.S. Marines in Vietnam: High Mobility and Standdown, 1969* (Washington, DC: USMC History and Museums Division, 1988), 2–3.

19. "MACV SEER Report, 3d Qtr CY 69," 27 November 1969, 15, 23, 25–27, 31, 34–39, Folder 228–27, Box 36, Entry P 465, RG 472, NARA II.

20. Robert K. Brigham, *ARVN: Life and Death in the South Vietnamese Army* (Lawrence: University Press of Kansas, 2006); Andrew Wiest, *Vietnam's Forgotten Army: Heroism and Betrayal in the ARVN* (New York: New York University Press, 2008); James H. Willbanks, *Abandoning Vietnam: How America Left and South Vietnam Lost Its War* (Lawrence: University Press of Kansas, 2004).

21. Ronald H. Spector, *Advice and Support: The Early Years, 1941–1960* (Washington, DC: US Army Center of Military History, 1985), 164–165; Clarke, *Advice and Support: The Final Years, 1965–1973*, 500–505, 521.

22. ARVN's planning skills were a problem at every level from company to corps, but the latter, being the most complex and least practiced, proved the most damaging deficiency. Truong, *RVNAF and US Operational Cooperation and Coordination*, 69–72, 182–183; Vien et al., *The U.S. Adviser*, 58, 75.

23. Truong, *RVNAF and US Operational Cooperation and Coordination*, 17. General Truong was widely considered ARVN's finest general. He commanded the 1st ARVN division in I Corps from 1966 to 1970, then was promoted to command ARVN's IV Corps in the Mekong Delta. After the early retreats during the 1972 Easter Offensive, Truong was brought back to take charge of ARVN's I Corps. He

directed the RVN counteroffensive that recaptured Quang Tri City. He was still in command of I Corps during the NVA's 1975 final offensive. His corps' collapse was due more to the incompetent guidance emanating from President Thieu in Saigon than any tactical miscue Truong committed. He and his family escaped Vietnam in 1975 and settled in Virginia.

24. James H. Willbanks, *A Raid Too Far: Operation Lam Son 719 and Vietnamization in Laos* (College Station: Texas A&M University Press, 2014); Turley, *The Easter Offensive: Vietnam, 1972*; Cao Van Vien, *The Final Collapse* (Washington, DC: US Army Center of Military History, 1985). General Nickerson admitted that III MAF did not train the I Corps staff to conduct corps-level combat operations. Herman Nickerson, Jr., interview by Martin Russ, 10 July 1976, #6312 (tape 3-2A), Oral History Collection, MCHD.

25. Shulimson, *U.S. Marines in Vietnam, 1966*, 11–14.

26. Victor H. Krulak, interview by Benis M. Frank, 22 June 1970, interview Session V, Side 1, Tape 1, transcript, 244, Oral History Collection, MCHD.

27. Data on landings derived from material on the Special Landing Forces in the Marine Corps official histories of the war, 1965–1969; "History of Amphibious Operations in South Vietnam, March 1965–December 1966," Folder "VN Amhib Com Phibfor 7th Flt Ops Mar 65-Dec 66," Box 344, Vietnam Command File (#372), Archives Branch, Naval History and Heritage Command, Washington Navy Yard, Washington, DC.

28. There were fifty named operations of battalion size or above in 1965, ninety in 1966, 110 in 1967, seventy-nine in 1968, sixty-two in 1969, seventeen in 1970, and three in the first few months of 1971. Data derived from end-of-year FMFPAC operations reports for 1965–1966 and 1968–1970; Edwin H. Simmons, "Marine Corps Operations in Vietnam, 1967," in *The Marines in Vietnam, 1954–1973: An Anthology and Annotated Bibliography* (Washington, DC: HQMC History and Museums Division, 1985), 96; Graham A. Cosmas and Terrence P. Murray, *U.S. Marines in Vietnam: Vietnamization and Redeployment, 1970–1971* (Washington, DC: USMC History and Museums Division, 1986), 215–216, 234–235. The March–April 1971 FMFPAC operations report indicated III MAF conducted "approximately 400" major operations between March 1965 and April 1971. FMFPAC, *Operations of U.S. Marine Forces, Vietnam*, March and April 1971, 2, VDA.

29. Statistics from just the first phase of this one operation: 1,073 battalion days in the field; 14,228 helicopter sorties; 5,190 tactical air sorties; 33,330 artillery missions; 223 naval gunfire missions; USMC: 225 KIA and 1,159 wounded in action; NVA/VC: 1,397 KIA, 27 POWs, and 248 weapons captured. III MAF CC, January 1967, 8, VDA.

30. For a sense of the sustained commitment required to defend large air bases, see Alan Vick, *Snakes in the Eagle's Nest: A History of Ground Attacks on Air Bases* (Santa Monica, CA: RAND, 1995), chapter 5 (covering the defense of air bases in Vietnam).

31. General Walt initially assessed the enclaves' security force requirements as follows: one battalion at Phu Bai, five battalions at Da Nang, and four battalions at Chu Lai. Message, CG III MAF to COMUSMACV, "Operations in I Corps," 191400Z November 1965, 13–16, File "Outgoing Messages November 1965," Box "1965," Entry "III MAF," VDA.

32. William C. Westmoreland, *A Soldier Reports*, 4th ed. (New York: Dell Publishing, 1984), 214–216.

33. Jack Shulimson et al., *U.S. Marines in Vietnam: The Defining Year, 1968* (Washington, DC: HQMC History and Museums Division, 1997), 13–14, 69, 576.

34. Colonel John C. Studt, Operations Officer of 9th Marines during the time Westmoreland was criticizing Marine defenses, agreed with the MACV commander: "As humiliating as this was for Marines, Gen Westmoreland was absolutely right: Marines didn't have a clue how to construct good bunkers. We taught hasty field fortification and that was it." Peter Baestrup, the *Washington Post* correspondent who had served as a Marine officer in Korea and visited Khe Sanh at the end of January 1968, remarked "Marines don't like to dig." Shulimson et al., *U.S. Marines in Vietnam, 1968*, 13–14, 41, 46, 69, 256.

35. Field Manual 100-15, *Field Service Regulations—Larger Units* (Washington, DC: Headquarters, Department of the Army, 1963) (hereafter 1963 FM 100-15), 51–54. The MAF, as a naval corps-level headquarters, used US Army doctrine for large unit ground operations during Vietnam. The MAF's amphibious corps predecessors had done the same during WWII. Positional/area and mobile defenses remain the two primary forms of defense in contemporary military doctrine.

36. Operation HASTINGS was the largest (at reinforced brigade level) operation of the war to that date. It involved seven USMC infantry battalions and one reinforced (five-battery) artillery battalion under the command of 3rd Marine Division's Task Force Delta. A parallel 1st ARVN Division operation, LAM SON 289, included three thousand troops from 1st ARVN Division and a contingent of airborne troops. The operation employed 1,180 tactical air strikes; 1,170 tons of bombs and rockets; 34,500 rounds of artillery; and 10,000 helicopter sorties. Casualties—USMC: 126 KIA, 448 wounded in action; NVA/VC: 783 KIA, 14 POWs. The allies recovered 226 enemy weapons and 300,000 rounds of ammunition. III MAF CC, July 1966, 6, VDA; Shulimson, *U.S. Marines in Vietnam, 1966*, 159–176.

37. It is not clear where the phrase "high mobility operations" originated, but Marines used it rather than the more common army term "air assault." The terms will be used interchangeably in this manuscript. Note that the Marine term was considered so seminal that the service's official history volume for the war in Vietnam in 1969 was titled *High Mobility and Standdown*. Decades later Marines still avoided calling rotary-wing assaults by the army vernacular, opting instead to refer to them as "heliborne operations."

38. For complete coverage of the army's air assault doctrine in action in Vietnam, see Tolson, *Airmobility*. General Davis's enthusiasm for the superiority of heliborne assaults comes through clearly in his 1990 memoir: Ray G. Davis with Bill Davis, "Protector of Freedom: The Story of Ray Davis, M.O.H. Lessons Learned in Combat and Life" (unpublished manuscript, 11 June 2018), Box A-11-J-7-3, Raymond G. Davis Papers (# 2079), MCHD.

39. Telfer, Rogers, and Fleming, *U.S. Marines in Vietnam, 1967*, 182–183.

40. Andrew F. Krepinevich, Jr., *The Army and Vietnam* (Baltimore: Johns Hopkins University Press, 1986).

41. Shulimson, *U.S. Marines in Vietnam, 1966*, 13–14.

42. United States Marine Corps, *Small Wars Manual* (Washington, DC: USMC, 1940; Manhattan, KS: Sunflower University Press, 1996), 32. Citations refer to the Sunflower edition. Marine Colonel John E. Greenwood, a MAF staff officer in 1965 and later an infantry battalion and Combined Action Group commanding officer, noted that his generation was more influenced by contemporary doctrine, service school curriculums, and academic scholarship than by 1930s-era small wars experiences handed down by older Marines. Shulimson and Johnson, *U.S. Marines in Vietnam, 1965*, 133.

43. Andrew J. Birtle, *US Army Counterinsurgency and Contingency Operations Doctrine, 1942–1976* (Washington, DC: US Army Center of Military History, 2007), 435–445, 486–495.

44. FMFPAC, *Operations of U.S. Marine Forces, Vietnam*, April 1967, 86, VDA.

45. FMFPAC, *Operations of U.S. Marine Forces, Vietnam*, January 1968, 28, VDA.

46. Telfer, Rogers, and Fleming, *U.S. Marines in Vietnam, 1967*, 192.

47. III MAF CC, December 1967, 31, VDA.

48. Russel H. Stolfi, *U.S. Marine Corps Civic Action Efforts in Vietnam, March 1965—March 1966* (Washington, DC: Headquarters Marine Corps G-3 Division Historical Branch, 1968), 13–14.

49. Phillip B. Davidson, *Vietnam at War, The History, 1946–1975* (Novato, CA: Presidio Press, 1988), 386; Shulimson et al., *U.S. Marines in Vietnam, 1968*, 608.

50. I Corps CORDS Field Overview, December 1969, Folder "I CTZ CORDS Field Overviews, Jan-Dec 69," Box 1, Entry 33102, RG 472, NARA II.

51. FMFPAC, *Operations of U.S. Marine Forces, Vietnam*, December 1969, v, 24–32, VDA.

52. Smith, *U.S. Marines in Vietnam, 1969*, 619–620, 625.

53. Thomas C. Thayer, *War Without Fronts: The American Experience in Vietnam* (1985, Annapolis, MD: Naval Institute Press, 2016), 155–167.

54. The program started with 3rd Battalion, 4th Marines, under Lieutenant Colonel William Taylor. Taylor got the idea from his adjutant and civil affairs officer, Captain John H. Mullen, Jr. FMFPAC Staff Study, "The Marine Combined Action Program Vietnam," no date, 3, Folder 14/6, Box 146, Entry "Records of Units and Other Command 1953–1993," RG 127, NARA II; Ronald E. Hays II, *Combined Action: U.S. Marines Fighting a Different War, August 1965 to September 1970*), 12–13; Shulimson and Johnson, *U.S. Marines in Vietnam, 1965*, 133.

55. FMFPAC, *Operations of U.S. Marine Forces, Vietnam*, December 1969, 32–34, VDA. CAP claims of 1,938 dead NVA/VC amounted to 6.4 percent of the 30,803 KIA reported by III MAF in 1969. This damage was done by a CAP force that represented just under 2 percent of III MAF's 117,173 personnel in December 1969. III MAF CC, December 1969, 10, VDA.

56. For example, between April and September of 1968 only 17.5 percent of Popular Forces platoons had CAPs assigned. They conducted 45.5 percent of all Popular Forces actions in I Corps, caused 39 percent of the enemy's casualties caused by Popular Forces, and absorbed 23 percent of the Popular Forces' casualties. FMFPAC, *Operations of U.S. Marine Forces, Vietnam*, December 1968, 68, VDA. Between 1 August and 31 December 1966, 39,840 Popular Forces soldiers, one-fourth of the total nationwide, deserted. During that same period, no CAP

Popular Forces platoon recorded a single desertion. William R. Corson, "Marine Combined Action Program in Vietnam," no date, 24, Folder 20, Box 1, Entry A1 1045 ("Records of or Related to General Officers, 1944–1975"), RG 127, NARA II (hereafter Corson CAP paper).

57. Telfer, Rogers, and Fleming, *U.S. Marines in Vietnam, 1967*, 190; Jack Shulimson et al., *U.S. Marines in Vietnam*, 619–620, 625; Smith, *U.S. Marines in Vietnam, 1969*, 292; Cosmas and Murray, *U.S. Marines in Vietnam, 1970–1971*, 147.

58. Jack Shulimson et al., *U.S. Marines in Vietnam, 1968*, 621; FMFPAC, *Operations of U.S. Marine Forces, Vietnam*, December 1968, 69, VDA.

59. Smith, *U.S. Marines in Vietnam, 1969*, 290.

60. Cosmas and Murray, *U.S. Marines in Vietnam, 1970–1971*, 182. The region-wide "secure" rating (villages rated either A or B on the HES scale) for I Corps on 31 January 1971 stood at 75.6 percent. CORDS MR 1 Field Overview, February 1971, Folder "MR 1 CORDS Field Overviews, Jan–Dec 71," Box 1, Entry 33102 (MACV Office of CORDS MR 1 Plans, Programs and Reports Division), RG 472, NARA II.

61. CORDS MR 1 Field Overview, March 1971, Folder "MR 1 CORDS Field Overviews, Jan-Dec 71," Box 1, Entry 33102 (MACV Office of CORDS MR 1 Plans, Programs and Reports Division), RG 472, NARA II.

62. General Lam assumed command of ARVN's I Corps in May 1966. The MAF turned over command of US forces in I Corps to the army's XXIV Corps on 9 March 1970. Four III MAF commanding generals worked with ARVN I Corps' staff and commanders during that interim. General Lam commanded ARVN's Laotian incursion from February to April 1971 and was later relieved for poor performance during the 1972 NVA Easter Offensive.

63. Wiest, *Vietnam's Forgotten Army*, 129–137.

64. Cosmas and Murray, *U.S. Marines in Vietnam, 1970–1971*, 132. This range of refugees represented 21–31 percent of I Corps' 1970 population of 2.9 million people.

65. 1963 FM 100-15, 51–54.

66. The March 1966 battle outside Quang Ngai City was code-named Operation UTAH. III MAF's records from that engagement (fifty-three pages) are found in Folder "Operations File, Operation UTAH, 5–8 March 1966," Box "1966 Named Operations," Entry "Miscellaneous Archive Data," VDA; Shulimson, *U.S. Marines in Vietnam, 1966*, 56–65, 109–119.

67. III MAF CC, July 1966, 10, VDA; Shulimson, *U.S. Marines in Vietnam, 1966*, 159–176.

68. MACV, *Command History 1967*, Vol. 1, 356–359; Telfer, Rogers, and Fleming, *U.S. Marines in Vietnam, 1967*, 9–30.

69. Tarawa was a November 1943 battle in the Marines' Central Pacific campaign in WWII. The 2nd Marine Division lost 1,009 dead and 2,101 wounded in a brutal, seventy-six-hour fight against 4,500 Japanese defending a heavily fortified island bastion. Jeter A. Isely and Philip A. Crowl, *The U.S. Marines and Amphibious War: Its Theory, and Its Practice in the Pacific* (Princeton, NJ: Princeton University Press, 1951), 192–252.

70. Marines suffered 29,190 wounded during the 1965–1967 period. Indirect fire caused 31 percent of those wounds. Mines and booby traps produced 28 percent

of the casualties, while bullets were responsible for 27 percent. Lawrence A. Palinkas and Patricia Coben, *Combat Casualties Among U.S. Marine Corps Personnel in Vietnam, 1964–1972* (San Diego, CA: Naval Health Research Center, 1985), 6, 9. In Vietnam the Marine Corps lost 508 dead in 1965, 1,862 in 1966, and 3,786 in 1967. The bloodiest year was 1968, with 5,047 dead. "Marine Vietnam Casualties" (from the DOD Combat Area Casualty File), www.marzone.com/7thMarines/usmc_cas _stats.pdf. These numbers do not reflect ARVN, US Army, or Korean Marine casualties that occurred in I Corps.

71. Shulimson, *U.S. Marines in Vietnam, 1966*, 271. These numbers do not include ARVN, US Army, US Navy, and US Air Force aviation losses in I Corps.

72. Message, CG FMFPAC to CMC, 230948Z September 1967, 68–80, Folder "FMFPAC—SPECAT Exclusive—In and Out—Sep—Nov 1967," Box "1967," Entry "FMFPAC," VDA.

73. US combat deaths in Vietnam totaled 5,000 in 1966, 9,300 in 1967, 14,500 in 1968, 9,400 in 1969, 4,200 in 1970, 1,300 in 1971, and 300 in 1972. The year 1968 was 50 percent more deadly than any other single year. Thayer, *War Without Fronts*, 116, 119.

74. MACV, *Command History 1971*, Volume 1, III-12.

75. FMFPAC published a monthly operations report for III MAF's activities in Vietnam. Two of the nine sections focused specifically on small wars actions: (4) Small Unit Counterguerrilla Operations and (5) Revolutionary Development and Pacification. In 1968, for example, III MAF conducted more than 208,000 patrols, ambushes, and sweeps of company size or smaller. It averaged 570 such operations per day across I Corps. These actions accounted for 8,100 NVA/VC reported killed during the year. FMFPAC, *Operations of U.S. Marine Forces, Vietnam*, December 1968 and 1968 Summary, 4, 42, VDA. US Army divisions and Field Forces did not report their tactical actions below the battalion level, which suggests how few of these smaller unit counterguerrilla operations they were conducting.

76. Shulimson et al., *U.S. Marines in Vietnam, 1968*, 628; Smith, *U.S. Marines in Vietnam, 1969*, 290.

77. Lieutenant General Nickerson claimed seventy-five CAP squads had moved to new villages by 5 December 1969. Herman Nickerson, Jr., *Leadership Lessons and Remembrances from Vietnam* (Washington, DC: US Marine Corps History and Museums Division, 1988), 59; Cosmas and Murray, *U.S. Marines in Vietnam, 1970–1971*, 149.

78. Bruce C. Allnutt, *Marine Combined Action Capabilities: The Vietnam Experience* (McLean, VA: Human Sciences Research, 1969), 56, 63–64, Appendix B pages 4–6, Appendix G. This field study was conducted for Headquarters Marine Corps and funded by the Office of Naval Research.

79. A review of 103 Combined Action Group and Force monthly command chronologies from 1968 through 1971 reveals little about CAP's focus or progress on eliminating the Vietcong infrastructure. Some reports included VCI as categories of POWs or Hoi Chanh (ralliers), but they seldom recorded numbers in those categories. The CAPs did turn over to the District Operations/Intelligence Centers a significant number of suspected VC detainees (1,707 across all four Combined Action Groups in 1969 for instance) but there is no record of how many of those detained were determined to be part of the VCI. "Fact Sheet on

the Combined Action Force," 31 March 1970, 16, Folder "2d CAG—Fact Sheet—March 1970," Box "2d Combined Action Group, 1970," Entry "III MAF Major Subordinate Commands," VDA.

80. The author is indebted to Professor Tom Marks of National Defense University for this insight. For the implications of this assessment in postwar insurgencies, see Thomas A. Marks, *Maoist Insurgency Since Vietnam* (London: Frank Cass, 1996).

81. For example, Douglas Pike published in 1966 his seminal study on the Vietcong, still unsurpassed in its detailed analysis of the movement's political and military branches. It was available to III MAF planners, staff officers, and commanders. Douglas Pike, *Viet Cong: The Organization and Techniques of the National Liberation Front of South Vietnam* (Cambridge, MA: M.I.T. Press, 1966).

82. Another example of the fact the CAPs did not directly attack the VCI is illustrated by the analysis of an early CAP commander, Lieutenant Colonel W. R. Corson. Corson claimed that CAPs hurt the shadow government in three ways: making it harder for the VC to recruit in the villages; making it harder for the VC to gather supplies, especially food, from the villagers; and killing VC in combat actions. He did not distinguish between guerrillas and political cadre and other noncombatant VCI in his explanation. Corson CAP paper, 13–17.

83. Shulimson et al., *U.S. Marines in Vietnam, 1968*, 60; Thayer, *War Without Fronts*, 210–211. For an account of a young Marine lieutenant advising a Phoenix Provincial Reconnaissance Unit in the 1968–1970 period, see Andrew R. Finlayson, *Rice Paddy Recon: A Marine Officer's Second Tour in Vietnam, 1968–1970* (Jefferson, NC: McFarland, 2014).

84. Mark Moyar, *Phoenix and the Birds of Prey: Counterinsurgency and Counterterrorism in Vietnam* (1997, Lincoln: University of Nebraska Press, 2007), 381–391. Statistics from DOD's systems analysis office indicate that territorial forces accounted for the largest share of VCI killed or captured in 1970 (50 percent) and 1971 (39 percent). If this is true, it is interesting that CAPs had so little visibility on the VCI personnel that their operations captured or killed. Thayer, *War Without Fronts*, 210.

85. Cosmas and Murray, *U.S. Marines in Vietnam, 1970–1971*, 136. Only 19 percent of the security forces in I Corps were with the People's Self-Defense Force in early 1970, but this number still equaled the total number of Regional Forces/Popular Forces troops in the region.

86. U.S. Grant Sharp, Jr., and William C. Westmoreland, *Report on the War in Vietnam* (Washington, DC: US Government Printing Office, 1968), 284, 287–288.

87. Lewis Sorley held that only after Abrams took over from Westmoreland in 1968 did the "Other War" receive the attention and resources that pacification deserved. Lewis Sorley, *A Better War: The Unexamined Victories and Final Tragedy of America's Last Years in Vietnam* (New York: Harcourt Brace, 1999). Andrew Birtle and Greg Daddis found more evidence of a balanced MACV approach from the beginning and credit Abrams with less originality in his emphasis on pacification. Andrew J. Birtle, "PROVN, Westmoreland, and the Historians: A Reappraisal," *The Journal of Military History* 72 (October 2008): 1213–1247; Gregory A. Daddis, *Westmoreland's War: Reassessing American Strategy in Vietnam* (Oxford, UK: Oxford

University Press, 2015). While scholars disagree on MACV's early emphasis on pacification, III MAF's balanced big war/small war approach remained consistent throughout its I Corps tenure.

88. While two or three subordinate maneuver divisions were the doctrinal norm for a corps, larger formations were not unprecedented. At Anzio in 1944, US VI Corps controlled seven divisions. Christopher Hibbert, *Anzio: The Bid for Rome* (New York: Ballantine Books, 1970), 127, 130, 146; Steven J. Zaloga, *Anzio 1944: The Beleaguered Beachhead* (Oxford, UK: Osprey Publishing, 2005), 78.

Chapter 5. III MAF Personnel and Logistics

1. Jack Shulimson and Charles M. Johnson, *U.S. Marines in Vietnam: The Landing and the Buildup, 1965* (Washington, DC: USMC History and Museums Division, 1978), 116–117. Walt took command on 4 June 1965. On 30 May the MAF reported a strength of 17,567, of which about 10 percent were sailors. III MAF CCs: May 1965, 4; July 1965, 5, VDA. The June command chronology did not report a unit strength. Overall allied troop strength in I Corps also grew significantly by the summer of 1968. In 1965 3rd Marine Division was the only US division in MR 1. Three years later it was reinforced by the equivalent of five more divisions. These included one US Marine division plus two additional regiments from a newly formed Marine division, three US Army divisions, and the Korean Marine brigade.

2. Jack Shulimson et al., *U.S. Marines in Vietnam: The Defining Year, 1968* (Washington, DC: HQMC History and Museums Division, 1997), 557, 581.

3. III MAF CC, August 1968, 10, VDA; 1st Marine Division CC, Mar 1968, 6, VDA; 3rd Marine Division CC, Mar 1968, 6, VDA; Edwin H. Simmons, "Marine Corps Operations in Vietnam, 1965–1966," in *The Marines in Vietnam, 1954–1973*, 66–67; Shulimson et al., *U.S. Marines in Vietnam, 1968*, 557, 576.

4. Shulimson et al., *U.S. Marines in Vietnam, 1968*, 569. The official history concluded that unit rotation would have required tripling the Corps' 1968 strength of 307,352 Marines. This calculation would dictate a nearly one-million-man Marine Corps. (WWII max strength for the Corps totaled only 485,053 in 1945.) Tripling the deployed force in 1968 required 267,000 troops. When one considers that it took 307,000 Marines to keep eighty-nine thousand in Vietnam that year (2.5 Marines outside the country for every Marine in the RVN), a total force of at least at least half a million troops seems a minimum to support a rotation of III MAF units, replace casualties, and still maintain other operational, training, and logistic commitments.

5. Leonard F. Chapman, Jr., interviewer not listed, 1979/1981, transcript, 18–21, Oral History Collection, MCHD (hereafter Chapman Oral History); Shulimson and Johnson, *U.S. Marines in Vietnam, 1965*, 116–117; Jack Shulimson, *U.S. Marines in Vietnam: An Expanding War, 1966* (Washington, DC: USMC History and Museums Division, 1982), 283.

6. Allan R. Millett, "Wallace M. Greene Jr., 1964–1968," in *Commandants of the Marine Corps*, ed. Allan R. Millett and Jack Shulimson (Annapolis, MD: Naval

Institute Press, 2004), 394; Walter S. Poole, *The Joint Chiefs of Staff and National Policy, 1965–1968* (Washington, DC: Joint Chiefs of Staff Office of Joint History, 2012), 48; Shulimson, *U.S. Marines in Vietnam, 1966*, 283. One reason for not calling up the Marine Reserve in 1965 was that a partial mobilization would destroy the Organized Reserve's 4th Marine Division/Team's ability to furnish a ready combat force for larger contingencies. Public Affairs Unit 4-1, *The Marine Corps Reserve: A History* (Washington, DC: Division of Reserve, Headquarters US Marine Corps, 1966), 252.

7. Stanley Karnow, *Vietnam: A History*, 2nd ed. (New York: Penguin Books, 1997), 511–512; George C. Herring, *America's Longest War: The United States and Vietnam, 1950–1975*, 5th ed. (New York: McGraw-Hill Education, 2014), 213–231; Guenter Lewy, *America in Vietnam* (New York: Oxford University Press, 1980), 50, 74, 129–132; Larry Berman, *Planning a Tragedy: The Americanization of the War in Vietnam* (New York: W. W. Norton, 1982), 100–105, 119–128, 146–149.

8. Ronald H. Spector, "The Vietnam War and the Army's Self-Image," in *The Second Indochina War*, ed. John Schlight (Washington, DC: US Army Center of Military History, 1986), 174–179; Bruce Palmer, Jr., *The 25-Year War: America's Military Role in Vietnam* (Lexington: University Press of Kentucky, 1984), 169–170.

9. Chapman Oral History, 22–26; "Evolution of the War, U.S. Grand Strategy and Force Deployments, 1965–1967," *Pentagon Papers*, Part IV.C.6.c., Vol. 3, Program 6, 71–79, https://nara-media-001.s3.amazonaws.com/arcmedia/research/pentagon-papers/Pentagon-Papers-Part-IV-C-6-c.pdf; Shulimson et al., *U.S. Marines in Vietnam, 1968*, 574–575. In 1962 HQMC recast the Organized Reserve into a force that fielded 4th Marine Division and 4th Marine Aircraft Wing, essentially mirroring the structure of active-duty MEFs rather than serving as a diverse pool of small units that would furnish individual replacements in time of war. Public Affairs Unit 4-1, *The Marine Corps Reserve: A History*, 229–230; Millett, *Semper Fidelis*, 552.

10. Shulimson, *U.S. Marines in Vietnam, 1966*, 284; Shulimson et al., *U.S. Marines in Vietnam, 1968*, 557–558, 560, 579–580; Edwin H. Simmons, "Marine Corps Operations in Vietnam, 1969–1972," in *The Marines in Vietnam Anthology, 1954–1973*, 157.

11. Shulimson et al., *U.S. Marines in Vietnam, 1968*, 557–559, 580–581.

12. David Anthony Dawson, *The Impact of Project 100,000 on the Marine Corps* (Washington, DC: HQMC History and Museums Division, 1995); Shulimson et al., *U.S. Marines in Vietnam, 1968*, 559–560. A 2014 study noted that this cohort of service members came from the bottom of America's socioeconomic stratum and most New Standards Men (as the Project 100,000 personnel were called) could not read at a sixth-grade level. They experienced twice the failure rate in the training pipeline, twice the rate of discipline problems in their units, and 15 percent lower promotion rates. Yet 75–95 percent of the Class IV enlistees succeeded in their basic and advanced training, did not cause even minor disciplinary problems, and were rated by supervisors as good or highly effective in their job performance. This analysis concluded that "most New Standards Men performed their duties in a satisfactory manner. The *1971 Project 100,000 Final Report* categorized performance of New Standards men in relation to other service members by service and reported that they performed only slightly below personnel not in the program." Kirklin J. Bateman, "Project 100,000: New Standards Men and the U.S. Military

in Vietnam" (PhD diss., George Mason University, 2014), 103–138, 195, http://ma
rs.gmu.edu/jspui/bitstream/handle/1920/8959/Bateman_gmu_0883E_10679.pdf
?sequence=1. For the countervailing view, arguing that Class IV Marines "had an
immediate negative effect on discipline," see Gary D. Solis, *Marines and Military
Law in Vietnam: Trial by Fire* (Washington, DC: HQMC History and Museums
Division, 1989), 73–74. He cites the HQMC G-1, Brigadier General Jonas Platt,
Major General Rathvon McC. Tompkins, CG of 3rd Marine Division, Captain W.
Hays Parks, the 1st Marine Division's chief trial counsel, and General Westmore-
land to buttress the claim.

13. Shulimson et al., *U.S. Marines in Vietnam, 1968,* 561–562.

14. Shulimson et al., *U.S. Marines in Vietnam, 1968,* 562–563.

15. Allan R. Millett, *Semper Fidelis: The History of the United States Marine Corps*
(New York: Free Press, 1991), 579.

16. Shulimson et al., *U.S. Marines in Vietnam, 1968,* 564–565.

17. Bernard C. Nalty and Ralph F. Moody, *A Brief History of U.S. Marine Corps
Officer Procurement, 1775–1969* (Washington, DC: HQMC Historical Division,
1970), 20–25; Shulimson et al., *U.S. Marines in Vietnam, 1968,* 562–563.

18. Shulimson et al., *U.S. Marines in Vietnam, 1968,* 562–564. The Marine Corps
had experienced similar junior officer and NCO/SNCO leadership challenges following three years of combat in the Pacific and again in Korea. Millett, *Semper
Fidelis,* 522–523.

19. William R. Fails, *Marines and Helicopters, 1962–1973* (Washington, DC:
HQMC History and Museums Division, 1978), 129–148; Millett, *Semper Fidelis,*
578–579; Shulimson et al., *U.S. Marines in Vietnam, 1968,* 569–571. Aviation ground
crew shortages resulted not from a failure to send enough mechanics to Vietnam
but from men who were wounded, sick, on rest and recreation, or detailed to functions such as security and base support billets.

20. The 1st Marine Aircraft Wing lost 119 aircraft (fixed- and rotary-wing
combined) in 1969. Noncombat losses accounted for 38 percent of the planes and
helicopters lost for the year. Seventy-four were lost in combat. The other forty-
five losses resulted from accidents, weather, and other noncombat causes. Figures
derived from 1st MAW 1969 command chronologies, VDA: January, 14; February,
13; March, 13; April, 14; May, 13; June, 13; July, 13; August, 15–16; September, 38;
October, 43; November, 13; December, 12.

21. Millett, *Semper Fidelis,* 569; Shulimson and Johnson, *U.S. Marines in Vietnam,
1965,* 117; Charles R. Smith, *U.S. Marines in Vietnam: High Mobility and Standdown,
1969* (Washington, DC: USMC History and Museums Division, 1988), 275; Graham A. Cosmas and Terrence P. Murray, *U.S. Marines in Vietnam: Vietnamization
and Redeployment, 1970–1971* (Washington, DC: USMC History and Museums Division, 1986), 333–334.

22. RLT-27 CC, Feb 1968, 4–5, VDA; 1st Bn, 27th Marine Regiment CC, Feb
1968, 5–6, VDA; 2d Bn, 27th Mar Regt CC, Feb 1968, 9, VDA; Shulimson et al.,
U.S. Marines in Vietnam, 1968, 572–574. Third Battalion, 27th Marines transferred
in or out 1,700 men in just four days prior to the unit's deployment to Vietnam. 3d
Bn, 27th Mar Regiment CC, Feb 1968, 4–5, VDA.

23. Shulimson et al., *U.S. Marines in Vietnam, 1968,* 574, 578–579. RLT-27 was
supposed to stay in Vietnam for only three months to reinforce III MAF for the

Tet crisis. It stayed until September 1968 because the army brigade slated to relieve it was slow to deploy (including thirteen weeks of refresher training in the United States) and then required an additional month of training in Vietnam before it was allowed to operate independently.

24. Shulimson, *U.S. Marines in Vietnam, 1966*, 285; Edwin H. Simmons, "Marine Corps Operations in Vietnam, 1967," in *The Marines in Vietnam Anthology, 1954–1973*, 75; Millett, *Semper Fidelis*, 568.

25. Shulimson, *U.S. Marines in Vietnam, 1966*, 284; Shulimson et al., *U.S. Marines in Vietnam, 1968*, 577–579.

26. Frank C. Collins, Jr., "Maritime Support in I Corps," in *The Marines in Vietnam, 1954–1973 An Anthology and Annotated Bibliography*, ed. Jack Shulimson (Washington, DC: HQMC History and Museum Division, 1985), 344.

27. At the field army and theater levels, US Army doctrine in 1965 prescribed task-organized logistic support based on the mission assigned. Typical services provided included supply, maintenance, construction, medical care, transportation, communication, salvage, laundry, and graves registration. FM 100-15, *Field Service Regulations—Larger Units* (Washington, DC: Headquarters, Department of the Army, 1963), 13, 37–38.

28. III MAF CC, October 1965, 15, VDA; III MAF CC, April 1966, 8, VDA. Prior to NSA's activation in October, the MAF had managed its responsibilities through a small Naval Component Command staff, drawn from the MAF's own small staff, led by a Marine colonel. Task Group 76.4, Seventh Fleet's amphibious logistics support group, provided harbor services similar to those required by an unopposed amphibious landing. After NSA stood up, the Marine staff serving as the Naval Component Command under III MAF comprised just eighteen men. III MAF CC, July 1965, 10, 63–65, VDA; K. P. Huff, "Building the Advanced Base at Da Nang," in *Vietnam: The Naval Story*, ed. Frank Uhlig, Jr. (Annapolis, MD: Naval Institute Press, 1986), 178–181; III MAF CC, February 1966, 14, VDA.

29. For the story of Service Force Pacific Fleet in WWII, see Samuel Eliot Morison, *History of United States Naval Operations in World War II* (1951, Annapolis, MD: Naval Institute Press, 2011), vol. 7, 100–113, vol. 8, 341–350, vol. 12, 74–85, and vol. 14, 156–169.

30. Collins, "Maritime Support in I Corps," in *The Marines in Vietnam Anthology, 1954–1973*, 325.

31. Huff, "Building the Advanced Base at Da Nang," 175, 185–187, 195–197, 201; Collins, "Maritime Support in I Corps," in *The Marines in Vietnam Anthology, 1954–1973*, 329–332; FMFPAC, *Operations of the III Marine Amphibious Force, Vietnam*, February 1966, 46, VDA.

32. FMFPAC, *Operations of the III Marine Amphibious Force, Vietnam*, November 1965, 25–26, VDA; III MAF CC, February 1966, 19, 21, VDA; Shulimson, *U.S. Marines in Vietnam, 1966*, 285–287.

33. Collins, "Maritime Support in I Corps," in *The Marines in Vietnam Anthology, 1954–1973*, 329; Thomas R. Weschler, interviewed by Paul Stillwell, 1995, transcript, 37, Oral History Collection, History Division, US Naval Institute, Annapolis, MD.

34. "The History of Naval Support Activity," Folder "Vietnam Da Nang,"

Box 7 (Combat-L), Collection "Historians' Reference Files, Vietnam," Archives Branch, Naval History and Heritage Command, Washington Navy Yard, Washington, DC (hereafter History of Naval Support Activity).

35. Collins, "Maritime Support in I Corps," 332.

36. Edwin B. Hooper, *Mobility, Support, Endurance: A Story of Naval Operational Logistics in the Vietnam War, 1965–1968* (Washington, DC: US Navy Naval History Division, 1972), 113.

37. James B. Soper, "A View from the FMFPac of Logistics in the Western Pacific, 1965–1971," in *The Marines in Vietnam Anthology, 1954–1973*, 303.

38. Hooper, *Mobility, Support, Endurance*, 192–195; Collins, "Maritime Support in I Corps,"325–328, 332–337.

39. Smith, *U.S. Marines in Vietnam, 1969*, 15, 264.

40. Collins, "Maritime Support in I Corps," 332, 335–336.

41. Shulimson and Johnson, *U.S. Marines in Vietnam, 1965*, 184.

42. Collins, "Maritime Support in I Corps," 334.

43. Hooper, *Mobility, Support, Endurance*, 255.

44. Collins, "Maritime Support in I Corps," 345.

45. Hooper, *Mobility, Support, Endurance*, 46, 240–241.

46. Collins, "Maritime Support in I Corps," 328.

47. Hooper, *Mobility, Support, Endurance*, 95.

48. "History of Naval Support Activity."

49. Hooper, *Mobility, Support, Endurance*, 97, 100; Huff, "Building the Advanced Base at Da Nang," 200.

50. "History of Naval Support Activity."

51. Shulimson et al., *U.S. Marines in Vietnam, 1968*, 582–586; Smith, *U.S. Marines in Vietnam, 1969*, 265–267; Cosmas and Murray, *U.S. Marines in Vietnam, 1970–1971*, 320–324.

52. William F. Simlik, undated, oral history transcript, 17, 19, Folder 4 (Withdrawal of USMC Logistics Organizations from Vietnam), Box 21, Vietnam War Collection, MCHD.

53. During the war, navy training for corpsmen lasted twice as long as that given army medics. Jerome Greer Chandler, "Their Brothers' Keepers: Medics and Corpsmen in Vietnam," in *VFW Magazine*, 11 January 2018, www.airforcemedicine.af.mil/News/Display/Article/1413458/their-brothers-keepers-medics-corpsmen-in-vietnam; Ronald C. Mosbaugh, "Corpsman Up!," https://libertyyes.homestead.com/Doc-Ron-Mosbaugh.html. Corpsman Pyle was killed in action five months later, on 28 May 1969. He was one of 638 corpsmen who died in combat in Vietnam. Another 4,563 were wounded. Four Vietnam War corpsmen earned the Medal of Honor, thirty received the Navy Cross, 127 won Silver Stars, and 290 were recognized with Bronze Stars. Mark T. Hacala, "The U.S. Navy Hospital Corps: A Century of Tradition, Valor, and Sacrifice," www.corpsman.com/history/history-of-the-hospital-corps. Jan K. Herman, *Navy Medicine in Vietnam: Passage to Freedom to the Fall of Saigon* (Washington, DC: Naval History and Heritage Command, 2010), 36.

54. Almon C. Wilson, interviewed by Paul Stillwell, 2002, transcript, 110, Oral History Collection, History Division, US Naval Institute, Annapolis, MD

(hereafter Wilson Oral History). When he was a captain, Rear Admiral Wilson, USN, served as the commander of 3rd Medical Battalion in Da Nang from July 1965 to June 1966.

55. Lawrence A. Palinkas and Patricia Coben, *Combat Casualties Among U.S. Marine Corps Personnel in Vietnam, 1964–1972* (San Diego, CA: Naval Health Research Center, 1985), 11.

56. Frank O. McClendon, Jr., "Doctors and Dentists, Nurses and Corpsmen in Vietnam," in *The Marines in Vietnam Anthology, 1954–1973*, 354.

57. Wilson Oral History, 78, 80–81, 88; Herman, *Navy Medicine in Vietnam*, 15–19.

58. Ninth Marine Regiment After Action Report, Operation DEWEY CANYON, 8 April 1969, 44, VDA, from Ross Phillips, in author's possession.

59. Shulimson, *U.S. Marines in Vietnam, 1966*, 290; Smith, *U.S. Marines in Vietnam, 1969*, 272. Three dental companies, one organic to each division plus one reinforcing company, also augmented III MAF's medical capabilities. Shulimson et al., *U.S. Marines in Vietnam, 1968*, 587.

60. McClendon, "Doctors and Dentists, Nurses and Corpsmen in Vietnam," 348–349.

61. Henry Ward Trueblood, *A Surgeon's War: My Year in Vietnam* (San Francisco, CA: Astor & Lenox, 2015), 139–144; Herman, *Navy Medicine in Vietnam*, 26.

62. FMFPAC, *Operations of U.S. Marine Forces, Vietnam*, May 1970, 37–38, VDA.

63. FMFPAC, *Operations of U.S. Marine Forces, Vietnam*, March 1970, 36, VDA; FMFPAC, *Operations of U.S. Marine Forces, Vietnam*, December 1970, 79–80, VDA; Wilson Oral History, 105; McClendon, "Doctors and Dentists, Nurses and Corpsmen in Vietnam," 350–351, 353; Herman, *Navy Medicine in Vietnam*, 29–33.

64. McClendon, "Doctors and Dentists, Nurses and Corpsmen in Vietnam," 350, 353.

65. III MAF CC, May 1969, 49, VDA.

66. Palinkas and Coben, *Combat Casualties Among U.S. Marine Corps Personnel in Vietnam: 1964–1972*, 2, 9.

67. Shulimson et al., *U.S. Marines in Vietnam, 1968*, 583.

68. McClendon, "Doctors and Dentists, Nurses and Corpsmen in Vietnam," 355.

69. Palinkas and Coben, *Combat Casualties Among U.S. Marine Corps Personnel in Vietnam: 1964–1972*, 11.

70. Charles J. Merdinger, "Civil Engineers, Seabees, and Bases in Vietnam," in *Vietnam: The Naval Story*, ed. Frank Uhlig, Jr. (Annapolis, MD: Naval Institute Press, 1986), 230, 240, 249—250. For the story of the Seabees' exploits in WWII, see the two-volume history by William Bradford Huie: *Can Do! The Story of the Seabees*, rev. ed. (New York: E. P. Dutton, 1944; Annapolis, MD: Naval Institute Press, 1997), and *From Omaha to Okinawa*, 2nd ed. (1945; repr., New York: E. P. Dutton, 2014). One of those KIA was Carpenter's Mate (Aviation) Petty Officer Third Class Marvin G. Shields, US Navy, the first Seabee Medal of Honor winner. Shields earned the award at the Battle of Dong Xoai, a Civilian Irregular Defense Group (Special Forces) camp located fifty-five miles north of Saigon, in June 1965. His story is found in "The Navy Civil Engineer Corps Historical Vignettes," 81–83; US Navy Seabee Museum website, online reading room, "Publications, History

of Civil Engineer Corps Vignettes," www.history.navy.mil/content/history/mu
seums/seabee/explore/online-reading-room/Publications.html.

71. For an overview of Seabee civic action team deployments worldwide, including Vietnam, see COMCBPAC Reports special edition labeled "Helping Others Help Themselves" but titled "Seabee Teams, October 1959—July 1968." For
the details of the teams' actions in Vietnam, see the after-action report issued by
Commander Naval Construction Battalions, US Pacific Fleet Detachment, Republic of Vietnam, "U.S. Pacific Fleet Detachment Republic of Vietnam, Completion Report, 1963–1972," 30 May 1972. Both documents are available at the Seabee
Museum website's online reading room under the heading "Publications, COM-
CBPAC Reports," www.history.navy.mil/content/history/museums/seabee/explo
re/online-reading-room/Publications/commander-construction-battalion-pacific
-reports.html.

72. Merdinger, "Civil Engineers, Seabees, and Bases in Vietnam," 230.

73. Hooper, *Mobility, Support, Endurance*, 187–188; Huff, "Building the Advanced
Base at Da Nang," 186, 199–200; Charles J. Merdinger, interviewed by John T.
Mason, Jr., 1971–72, transcript, 240–246, 250–274, Oral History Collection, History Division, US Naval Institute, Annapolis, MD. Captain Merdinger, US Navy,
ran the Public Works Department for NSA Da Nang in 1967–1968.

74. Merdinger, "Civil Engineers, Seabees, and Bases in Vietnam," 247–248.
For the official history of Seabee performance in Vietnam, see Richard Tregaskis, *Southeast Asia: Building the Bases*. Available on the US Navy Seabee Museum's website, under "Research," "Online Reading Room," "Publications," at
www.history.navy.mil/content/history/museums/seabee/explore/online-reading
-room/ Publications.html. Additional details (two hundred pages of battalion-level
overviews as well as commandwide reports by functional area) are found in the
three COMCBPAC Reports for 1966, 1967, and 1968 located at the same URL
under "Commander Construction Battalions Pacific Reports."

75. Merdinger, "Civil Engineers, Seabees, and Bases in Vietnam," 242, 245.

76. Victor H. Krulak, *First to Fight: An Inside View of the U.S. Marine Corps* (An-
napolis, MD: Naval Institute Press, 1984), 192–193; Keith B. McCutcheon, "Marine Aviation in Vietnam, 1962–1970," in *The Marines in Vietnam, 1953–1973: An
Anthology and Annotated Bibliography*, ed. Jack Shulimson (Washington, DC: Headquarters Marine Corps History and Museums Division, 1985), 266–268; Tregaskis,
Southeast Asia: Building the Bases, 109–115; Shulimson and Johnson, *U.S. Marines in
Vietnam, 1965*, 39–42, 186, 190. General Krulak bet, and lost, a case of scotch to
Army Major General Richard G. Stilwell, then MACV's chief of staff. Krulak wa-
gered that a whole squadron would be flying from the Chu Lai field within thirty
days. Only half a Marine A-4 squadron was operational on the appointed day. Mc-
Cutcheon, "Marine Aviation in Vietnam, 1962–1970," 267. Walt's quote was cited
in Tregaskis, *Southeast Asia: Building the Bases*, 115.

77. Hooper, *Mobility, Support, Endurance*, 189–191.

78. Merdinger, "Civil Engineers, Seabees, and Bases in Vietnam," 239–240.

79. Hooper, *Mobility, Support, Endurance*, 71; Merdinger, "Civil Engineers, Seabees, and Bases in Vietnam," 239–240, 242.

80. Smith, *U.S. Marines in Vietnam, 1969*, 267.

81. FMFPAC, *Historical Summary, U.S. Marine Corps Forces in Vietnam, March 1965–September 1967*, Volume 1, 8–4, Folder "FMFPAC," Box 13, Vietnam War Collection, MCHD (hereafter FMFPAC, *Historical Summary, 1965–1967*); Shulimson and Johnson, *U.S. Marines in Vietnam, 1965*, 182–184.

82. MAF CC, July 1968, 27–34, 55–56, VDA.

83. List of MAF G-4s drawn from USMC official histories: Shulimson and Johnson, *U.S. Marines in Vietnam, 1965*, 228; Shulimson, *U.S. Marines in Vietnam, 1966*, 342; Gary L. Telfer, Lane Rogers, and Keith Fleming, Jr., *U.S. Marines in Vietnam: Fighting the North Vietnamese, 1967* (Washington, DC: USMC History and Museums Division, 1984), 273; Shulimson et al., *U.S. Marines in Vietnam, 1968*, 713; Smith, *U.S. Marines in Vietnam, 1969*, 336; Cosmas and Murray, *U.S. Marines in Vietnam, 1970–1971*, 428.

84. In the 1945 Okinawa operation, for example, III Amphibious Corps, with three subordinate infantry divisions, fielded just one service regiment, a field supply depot, a motor transport battalion, and three hospital units as corps-level logistics units. Benis M. Frank and Henry I. Shaw, Jr., *Victory and Occupation*, vol. 5, *History of U.S. Marine Corps Operations in World War II* (Washington, DC: HQMC G-3 Division Historical Branch, 1968), 852–853.

85. The Marine Corps had largely ignored logistic concerns after the Korean conflict and fared poorly in managing its supply and fiscal affairs since the late 1950s. Government Accounting Office reports in 1960 and 1964 identified service-wide problems in maintenance, procurement, supply management, and distribution. Except for levels of supply, General Greene assessed most areas of the Corps' peacetime readiness positively early in 1965. One of the shortcomings of the 4th Marine Brigade that intervened in the Dominican Republic in April 1965, just one month after 9th MEB landed in Da Nang, was too few logistic units. Millett, "Wallace M. Greene Jr., 1964–1968," 390, 392–393; Millett, *Semper Fidelis*, 546–547.

86. The Marine logistic element grew in 1965 from 9th MEB's 592 personnel in March to 3,000 men in the MAF's Force Logistics Support Group by the end of the year. FMFPAC, *Historical Summary, 1965–1967*, 8–2 to 8–6; Shulimson and Johnson, *U.S. Marines in Vietnam, 1965*, 185.

87. III MAF CC, March 1966, 19, VDA; Shulimson, *U.S. Marines in Vietnam, 1966*, 288. After the Korean conflict, Marine divisions had organic service regiments, but these were reduced to service battalions by the 1956 Hogaboom Restructuring Board. The removed logistic capacity migrated to an enlarged Service Regiment at the Force level. III MAF deployed to Vietnam with this logistic structure. Millett, *Semper Fidelis*, 527.

88. Force Logistic Command (FLC) CC, February 1967, 8, 19–32, VDA; Telfer, Rogers, and Fleming, *U.S. Marines in Vietnam, 1967*, 225.

89. Initially the Force Logistic Support Groups (FLSGs) at Chu Lai and Phu Bai were called Force Logistic Support Units. The two Force Logistic Support Units expanded and were renamed FLSGs when III MAF's original Force Logistics Support Group became the Force Logistic Command, which activated in March 1966. FMFPAC, *Historical Summary, 1965–1967*, 8–6, 8–8; Shulimson, *U.S. Marines in Vietnam, 1966*, 287–288.

90. FLSG 'A' CC, January 1968, 3, VDA; FLSG 'B' CC, January 1968, 3, VDA; Shulimson et al., *U.S. Marines in Vietnam, 1968*, 582.

91. FLC CC, November 1968, 4, VDA; Smith, *U.S. Marines in Vietnam, 1969*, 260–261.

92. A 15 March 1968 FLC press release, on the occasion of the command's second anniversary, stated: "Basic Marine supply structure provides for supply sections down through company level with companies requesting supplies from battalions, battalions from regiments and regiments from the divisions. The divisions then send their requisitions to supply centers such as Barstow, Calif., or Albany, Ga. However, with two divisions and a part of a third in Vietnam, not to mention an air wing, it became evident and practical to centralize all support and supply functions in one force-level organization. Thus, Force Logistic Command was born—a product of the Vietnam war." This depiction ignored the presence and role of the MAF's service regiment in the supply chain and did not address how taking logistics commands from subordinate units improved the previously existing system. FLC CC, March 1968, 22–23, VDA.

93. Wilson Oral History, 84.

94. General Walt described 1965 as "a critical period—when only exceptional ingenuity, initiative and extremely hard and dedicated labor kept the supplies flowing to the fighting troops." Shulimson, *U.S. Marines in Vietnam, 1966*, 285.

95. FMFPAC, *Operations of the III Marine Amphibious Force, Vietnam*, November 1965, 20–21, VDA; FMFPAC, *Operations of the III Marine Amphibious Force, Vietnam*, December 1965, 42–43, VDA; Shulimson and Johnson, *U.S. Marines in Vietnam, 1965*, 185.

96. Cosmas and Murray, *U.S. Marines in Vietnam, 1970–1971*, 317. During 1967 Brigadier General Louis Metzger, USMC, served as CG, 9th MAB in Okinawa and then assistant division commander, 3rd Marine Division in Vietnam. After the war he observed: "While CG, 9th MAB, I was appalled at the condition of the Marines and their equipment when they arrived on Okinawa [from Vietnam]. My observations in-country [as assistant commander of the 3d Marine Division] did nothing to dispel my opinion." Telfer, Rogers, and Fleming, *U.S. Marines in Vietnam, 1967*, 224.

97. FMFPAC, *Operations of U.S. Marine Forces, Vietnam*, July 1970, 40–43, VDA; Ed Gilbert, *The US Marine Corps in the Vietnam War, III Marine Amphibious Force, 1965–1975* (Oxford, UK: Osprey Publishing, 2006), 39, 50, 52.

98. Smith, *U.S. Marines in Vietnam, 1969*, 260–261.

99. The fuel lost to enemy fire in June represented only 2.2 percent of the fuel that FLSG-B received that month. The loss of ammunition when the Dong Ha supply point blew up that month, however, represented 88 percent of the ammunition FLSG-B received in June 1968. Shulimson et al., *U.S. Marines in Vietnam, 1968*, 583, 592–593; FLSG 'B' CC, January 1968, 6, VDA; FLSG 'B' CC, March 1968, 6–7, VDA; FLSG 'B' CC, April 1968, 6–8, VDA; FLSG 'B' CC, May 1968, 6–8, VDA; FLSG 'B' CC, June 1968, 5–8, 10, VDA. In April 1969 a grass fire of unknown origin consumed thirty-eight tons of ammunition at a supply point near the Da Nang air base. This disaster destroyed 40 percent of the FLC's regional ammo stocks in a single day and kept on-hand accounts below the desired forty-five-day level for the next four months. FLC CC, April 1969, 11, VDA; Smith, *U.S. Marines in Vietnam, 1969*, 263.

100. III MAF CC, August 1968, 31–36, VDA.

101. Dave Winecoff, "Night Ambush!" *Marine Corps Gazette* 68, no. 1 (January 1984): 52.

102. 1st Battalion, Fifth Marines CC, February 1970, 3–7, Item Number 1201048050, U.S. Marine Corps History Division Vietnam War Documents Collection, Vietnam Center and Archive, Texas Tech University, Lubbock, TX.

103. FMFPAC, *Historical Summary, 1965–1967*, 8–14; FLC CC, June 1966, 46, 82–88, VDA; Smith, *U.S. Marines in Vietnam, 1969*, 261.

104. FMFPAC, *Operations of U.S. Marine Forces, Vietnam*, February 1967, 74, VDA; FMFPAC, *Historical Summary, 1965–1967*, 8-15 to 8-16; Soper, "A View from FMFPac of Logistics in the Western Pacific, 1965–1971," 305; Shulimson, *U.S. Marines in Vietnam, 1966*, 290; Telfer, Rogers, and Fleming, *U.S. Marines in Vietnam, 1967*, 227.

105. FMFPAC, *Operations of U.S. Marine Forces, Vietnam*, December 1968, 111–112, VDA; Shulimson et al., *U.S. Marines in Vietnam, 1968*, 523–526.

106. 1st MAW CC, October 1967, 11–12, VDA; FMFPAC, *Operations of U.S. Marine Forces, Vietnam*, October 1967, 68–69, VDA; FMFPAC, *Operations of U.S. Marine Forces, Vietnam*, November 1967, 40, VDA; McCutcheon, "Marine Aviation in Vietnam, 1962–1970," 283; Shulimson et al., *U.S. Marines in Vietnam, 1968*, 522–523.

107. III MAF CC, December 1967, 30, VDA; III MAF CC, November 1968, 35–36, VDA; FLC CC, November 1968, 8, VDA; FLC CC, January 1969, 7, VDA; Telfer, Rogers, and Fleming, *U.S. Marines in Vietnam, 1967*, 229; Shulimson et al., *U.S. Marines in Vietnam, 1968*, 593; Simmons, "Marine Corps Operations in Vietnam, 1967," 93. For a darker view of the fielding of the M-16 than that described in the official sources referenced above, see William H. Hallihan, *Misfire: The History of How America's Small Arms Have Failed Our Military* (New York: Charles Scribner's Sons, 1994), 445–521. Hallihan traces the M-16's troubled early development and cites the results of the investigations conducted in 1967 by a subcommittee of the House Armed Services Committee led by Representative Richard Ichord (a Missouri Democrat). These hearings revealed grave negligence in the fielding of the new rifle, resulting in combat casualties in Vietnam prior to the 1967 modifications noted in the text.

108. FMFPAC, *Operations of U.S. Marine Forces, Vietnam*, December 1970, 83, VDA. In 1968, for example, tonnage of cargo moved by truck exceeded that moved by helicopter by a factor of 6.5. FMFPAC, *Operations of U.S. Marine Forces, Vietnam*, December 1968, 88, 109, VDA.

109. Smith, *U.S. Marines in Vietnam, 1969*, 268, 270–272. For a study of US improvisation in arming and armoring trucks engaged in Vietnam convoy duty, see Timothy J. Kutta, *Gun Trucks* (Carrollton, TX: Squadron/Signal Publications, 1996).

110. 1st Marine Aircraft Wing typically kept a detachment of four C-130s at Da Nang for movement of men, cargo, and fuel. The C-130's primary purpose was in-flight refueling. McCutcheon, "Marine Aviation in Vietnam, 1962–1970," 281; Shulimson et al., *U.S. Marines in Vietnam, 1968*, 463.

111. 1st MAW CC, February 1968, 13, VDA.

112. FMFPAC, *Operations of U.S. Marine Forces, Vietnam*, March 1968, 81–83, VDA; Richard D. Camp and Leonard A. Blasiol, *Ringed by Fire: U.S. Marines and*

the Siege of Khe Sanh, 21 January to 9 July 1968 (Quantico, VA: Marine Corps University History Division, 2019), 45–48; Telfer, Rogers, and Fleming, *U.S. Marines in Vietnam, 1967*, 229; Shulimson et al., *U.S. Marines in Vietnam, 1968*, 481.

113. FMFPAC, *Operations of U.S. Marine Forces, Vietnam*, March-April 1971, 37–38, VDA. "One of our most aggravating problems was that all of the gear, all of the equipment, all of the vehicles that we retrograded to the United States had to pass an agricultural inspection. So consequently, they had to be *spotless*, absolutely spotless." Simlik Oral History, 16. These inspections were (and still are) the bane of deployed units. Designed to prevent unwanted flora and fauna from making their way into the United States, these checks required detailed cleaning of military equipment and vehicles. Troops, just wanting to get home, traditionally saw this necessary preventative measure as another form of harassment.

114. ARVN accepted only 15 percent of the equipment the US Army offered. This contrast underscores the effort III MAF put into the material transfer program and the standards its logisticians achieved. Cosmas and Murray, *U.S. Marines in Vietnam, 1970–1971*, 335–338; FMFPAC, *Operations of U.S. Marine Forces, Vietnam*, in VDA: August 1970, 38–39; September 1970, 31–32; November 1970, 23–25; December 1970, 67–72; January-February 1971, 32–34; March-April 1971, 39–43.

115. Edwin H. Simmons, "Marine Corps Operations in Vietnam, 1969–1972," 150; Cosmas and Murray, *U.S. Marines in Vietnam, 1970–1971*, 336–337; FMFPAC, *Operations of U.S. Marine Forces, Vietnam*, in VDA: June 1970, 40–41; September 1970, 31–32; December 1970, 67–69; January-February 1971, 32–34; March-April 1971, 39–43.

116. Cosmas and Murray, *U.S. Marines in Vietnam, 1970–1971*, 339–342; FMFPAC, *Operations of U.S. Marine Forces, Vietnam*, in VDA: September 1970, 27; December 1970, 65–66, 72–73; January-February 1971, 34–35.

117. Simlik Oral History, 26.

118. This estimate is based on approximately ten thousand logistic Marines under FLC, ten thousand sailors and eleven thousand civilians working for NSA, and eight thousand soldiers under US Army Support Command, Da Nang. Together, in the summer of 1968, they supported 159,000 uniformed personnel under III MAF in I Corps. For the US Army count of its logisticians in I Corps and the way they organized and operated in support of XXIV (USA) Corps, see Brigadier General James W. Gunn, USA, "Senior Officer Debriefing Report: US Army Support Command, Da Nang, Period October 1968–October 1969" (Washington, DC: Department of the Army, 1969), 2, https://apps.dtic.mil/sti/tr/pdf/AD0505836.pdf. Brigadier General Gunn commanded US Army Support Command, Da Nang during this period.

119. FMFPAC, *Operations of U.S. Marine Forces, Vietnam*, December 1970, 63, VDA; FMFPAC, *Operations of U.S. Marine Forces, Vietnam*, March–April 1971, 32–33, VDA.

120. Smith, *U.S. Marines in Vietnam, 1969*, 260–262.

121. WWII doctrine for corps stated: "As a part of the army, the corps has few administrative functions other than those pertaining to corps troops. When the corps is detached from the army for both operations and administration, it must operate the necessary administrative installations for its own supply and evacuation. In such a situation it must be reinforced by the necessary service units."

Field Manual 100-15, *Field Service Regulations—Larger Units* (Washington, DC: Government Printing Office, 1942), 57. Army doctrine for corps and field armies in 1965 did not prescribe combat service support units for either echelon. Instead it noted that support functions would be task organized as required from theater level units. 1963 FM 100-15, 22, 37–38, 40–41. A major change, published in 1966, outlined a robust Field Army Support Command with support brigades for each assigned corps, an army rear support brigade, and separate brigades covering ammunition, medical, military police, and transportation functions. The corps support brigade was reinforced by additional task organized elements from each of the army-level logistic brigades. This doctrine envisioned a division-size logistics command supporting each field army and a reinforced brigade-size command supporting subordinate corps. Field Manual 100-15, *Field Service Regulations—Larger Units* (Washington, DC: Headquarters, Department of the Army, 1966), 5, 9–11, 14. A subsequent intrawar update of the manual maintained the corps' Combat Service Support organization. Field Manual 100-15, *Larger Units: Theater Army—Corps* (Washington, DC: Headquarters, Department of the Army, 1968), 7-2, 7-17 to 7-19, 8-2. An updated version of the same doctrinal manual published in 1973 envisioned a separate corps operating independently, or at least far afield, from its field army headquarters. These independent corps, operating in conditions akin to the situation III MAF faced in Vietnam, received a Corps Support Command that bumped up its battalion-level functional components to brigade- or group-size elements. The task-organized Corps Support Command included a support brigade (or two groups), a medical brigade, a transportation brigade, a military police group, a civil affairs battalion, a field depot, an ammunition group, a fuels group, a finance unit, a movement control unit, a material management company, and a data processing unit. In other words, a corps operating independently or at a distance from army headquarters received a division-size logistic command. Of note, these logistic commands did not draw their personnel and material from subordinate division-level logistic commands or from sister corps. Field Manual 100-15, *Larger Units: Theater Army—Corps* (Washington, DC: Headquarters, Department of the Army, 1973), 7-2, 7-12 to 7-14, 8-2, and 8-25 to 8-27.

122. A participant in the planning for MACV's corps-size incursion into Laos, Operation EL PASO, detailed the geographic and logistic considerations that drove that campaign design in John M. Collins, *Military Geography for Professionals and the Public*, 2nd ed. (Omaha, NE: Potomac Books, 1998), 367–385; William C. Westmoreland, *A Soldier Reports*, 4th ed. (New York: Dell Publishing, 1984), 355–357, 412–413, and 542.

Chapter 6. III MAF Plans

1. John M. Shaw, *The Cambodian Campaign: The 1970 Offensive and America's Vietnam War* (Lawrence: University Press of Kansas, 2005); James H. Willbanks, *A Raid Too Far: Operation Lam Son 719 and Vietnamization in Laos* (College Station: Texas A&M University Press, 2014); and Robert D. Sander, *Invasion of Laos 1971: Lam Son 719* (Norman: University of Oklahoma Press, 2014). Other external incursion proposals, including contingencies to raid deeper into Cambodia and Laos,

permanently block the Ho Chi Minh Trail, and invade North Vietnam, generate less historical interest, since they were not executed. An analysis of the MACV plan to block the Ho Chi Minh Trail appears in John M. Collins, *Military Geography for Professionals and the Public*, 2nd ed. (Omaha, NE: Potomac Books, 1998), 367–385. Scrutiny of MACV, corps, and division-level options for operations inside South Vietnam are also rare in the war's literature.

2. Dwight D. Eisenhower remarks at the National Defense Executive Reserve Conference, 14 November 1957, Public Papers of the Presidents of the United States (1957 Comp.), University of Michigan Digital Library, https://quod.lib.umich.edu/p/ppotpus/4728417.1957.001/858?page=root;rgn=full+text;size=100;view=image. In addition to his role as Supreme Allied Commander in Europe, Eisenhower served early in the war as chief of the US Army's War Plans Division in Washington.

3. Functional plans, subsets of both force design and employment plans, concentrate on specific facets such as administration, intelligence, aviation, logistics, or communications. For a concise but insightful overview of the nature and theory of military planning, see contemporary Marine doctrine on the subject in Marine Corps Doctrinal Publication 5, *Planning* (Washington, DC: Headquarters Marine Corps, 1997). For more extensive coverage from a contemporary joint perspective, see Joint Publication 5-0, *Joint Planning* (Washington, DC: Government Printing Office, 2017), www.jcs.mil/Portals/36/Documents/Doctrine/pubs/jp5_0_20171606.pdf.

4. III MAF CC, August 1965, 6, VDA. Marine Corps staffs from battalion to brigade level had employed a four section executive staff (S/G-1, personnel; S/G-2, intelligence; S/G-3, operations and training; and S/G-4, supply) since 1936. ("S" means the staff officer worked for a unit commanded by an officer below flag rank. "G" designated staff of a unit commanded by a general officer.) The four-section staff was incorporated in the division organization adopted in 1941. The staffs of the amphibious corps during WWII followed the division staff model, including special staff billets addressing functions such as air, artillery, engineer, medical, signal, etc. Kenneth W. Condit, John H. Johnstone, and Ella W. Nargele, *A Brief History of Headquarters Marine Corps Staff Organization* (Washington, DC: HQMC Historical Division, 1970), 14–15, 17–18.

5. III MAF CC, October 1965, 5, 12, VDA. The III MAF G-6 converted from Plans to Communications in February 1968, though the G-6 did not appear as the Communications Directorate in USMC official histories until January 1969. III MAF CC, February 1968, 50; Charles R. Smith, *U.S. Marines in Vietnam: High Mobility and Standdown, 1969* (Washington, DC: USMC History and Museums Division, 1988), 336. There is some confusion as to where the Plans section existed in the III MAF table of organization from October 1965 (when it became the G-6) through early 1968, as note 7 below explains.

6. III MAF CC, February 1966, 48–49, VDA. The rest of the primary staff billets, and many of the special staff positions, were filled by full colonels.

7. While MAF command chronologies listed G-6 Plans as a primary staff billet throughout 1966 and 1967, these planners served as a subsection under the G-3 Operations staff. The Marine Corps' official histories of the war do not show the G-6 as a primary staff code during those two years. Jack Shulimson, *U.S. Marines*

290 Notes to Pages 185–187

in Vietnam: An Expanding War, 1966 (Washington, DC: USMC History and Museums Division, 1982), 342; Gary L. Telfer, Lane Rogers, and Keith Fleming, Jr., *U.S. Marines in Vietnam: Fighting the North Vietnamese, 1967* (Washington, DC: USMC History and Museums Division, 1984), 273.

8. III MAF CC, December 1966, 56, VDA.

9. III MAF CC, June 1967, 8, 676, VDA.

10. III MAF CC, May 1968, 53, VDA.

11. III MAF CC, August 1968, 55, VDA; III MAF CC, September 1968, 60–61, VDA.

12. III MAF CCs in VDA: July 1970, 42; October 1970, 42; November 1970, 41; December 1970, 6; February 1971, 40.

13. In his postwar interviews with biographer Charles MacDonald, Westmoreland frequently referenced his dependence on staff contingency plans and war games. Charles B. MacDonald interview notes, 28 January–17 August 1973, Boxes 30–31, WCWP, LBJPL; Graham A. Cosmas, *MACV: The Joint Command in the Years of Escalation, 1962–1967* (Washington, DC: US Army Center of Military History, 2006), 333–334.

14. The Plans section's turnover pales in comparison, however, to that experienced by the G-5 (Civil Affairs) staff. In 1967 it suffered through ten principal staff officers in a single year. Telfer, Rogers, and Fleming, *U.S. Marines in Vietnam, 1967*, 273.

15. The numbers and composition of the MAF plans shop are derived from III MAF's monthly command chronologies, May 1965 to April 1971, VDA.

16. Bruce Palmer, Jr., *The 25-Year War: America's Military Role in Vietnam* (Lexington: University Press of Kentucky, 1984), 73; Cosmas, *MACV: The Joint Command in the Years of Escalation, 1962–1967*, 316–318. For examples of FMFPAC plans and studies, see, for example: "FMFPAC Outline Concept for Destruction of the Enemy in the DMZ Area, Vietnam (S), 22 May 1967;" Folder 18; Box 143; "FMFPAC Staff Study: Possible Actions in DMZ Area if Enemy Resumes Intense Artillery/Rocket/Mortar Attacks, 31 January 1968," Folder 17, Box 142, both in Entry "Records of Units and Other Commands, 1953–1993, FMFPAC," RG 127, NARA II. Despite these critiques of Marine planning proficiency, it is not clear if or to what degree III MAF lagged its counterpart US Army Field Force headquarters in the development of sound operations plans.

17. The plan is seldom mentioned in the literature on the war. An exception is historian Michael Hennessy, who used its analysis to highlight the challenges III MAF faced in pacifying I Corps. Michael A. Hennessy, *Strategy in Vietnam: The Marines and Revolutionary Warfare in I Corps, 1965–1972* (Westport, CT: Praeger, 1997), 94–97.

18. As part of the Marine chain of command's staff planning cycle, FMFPAC planners submitted a thirty-six-page supporting staff study to HQMC in September 1966. The Honolulu plan cautioned against extrapolating operational projections beyond 1967; highlighted the ARVN I Corps CG's promise to devote twenty-five of his thirty-one infantry battalions to revolutionary development work; judged enemy infiltration/recruitment at two-thirds the monthly level claimed by HQMC; advocated CAP-like programs for both Regional Forces and ARVN units; and envisioned less-contested territory being cleared in the coming

year than their counterparts in Washington forecast. Nevertheless, the FMFPAC estimate came to the same conclusion on the amount of additional allied force required for I Corps. Letter, Lieutenant General Victor H. Krulak to General Wallace M. Greene, Jr., 28 September 1966, encl: "Determination of Force Requirements, I Corps," Folder 12, Box 142, Entry "Records of Units and Other Commands, 1953–1993, FMFPAC," RG 127, NARA II (hereafter FMFPAC Force Estimate).

19. Letter, General Wallace M. Greene, Jr., to Walt W. Rostow, 2 December 1966, encl. "Force Requirements and Long Range Estimate for I Corp RVN," Folder "Vietnam, Long Range Estimate and Force Requirement for the Successful Prosecution of the War in I Corps, RVN" (hereafter HQMC Force Estimate), Box 196, Vietnam Country File, National Security File, Lyndon B. Johnson Papers (hereafter LBJP), LBJPL.

20. Shulimson, *U.S. Marines in Vietnam, 1966*, 284. The division initially activated on 11 November 1943 and stood down on 5 February 1946. It reactivated at Camp Pendleton, California, on 1 March 1966 and deactivated on 26 November 1969.

21. HQMC Force Estimate. General Greene also authorized his staff to prepare a similar product for the IV Corps area in the Mekong Delta (which had no assigned US corps-level headquarters) and advocated US Army headquarters prepare like plans for I and II Corps as well as South Vietnam writ large. Rostow asked General Greene to look at "thresholds of enemy viability once his supporting mechanisms and basic structure have been degraded." Greene promised to do so and indicated that the estimate would be updated periodically. No archival records indicate subsequent iterations of the I Corps Force Plan. Neither do records reveal evidence of a subsequent HQMC plan for IV Corps or similar plans initiated by MACV or US Army I/II Field Forces for other regions of South Vietnam.

22. The estimate included a range of six infiltration/recruitment variables, ranging from a composite of 2,300 to 8,000 NVA/VC. HQMC Force Estimate, Annex B page 5.

23. HQMC Force Estimate, 2–3, 15, 22–23, 27.

24. HQMC Force Estimate, 8–9, 14–15. Planners recognized cross-border sanctuaries presented a problem in defeating communist forces in South Vietnam. They noted that a 10:1 ratio favoring security forces led to success in Malaya and recommended at least an 11:1 ratio in the RVN based on the added difficulty the regional sanctuaries presented. Events proved it was impossible to attain the 11:1 ratio in Vietnam without stopping NVA infiltration.

25. HQMC Force Estimate, 9–14.

26. The plan's model held ARVN strength steady because the South Vietnamese army was not programmed to expand in I Corps, see HQMC Force Estimate, 18.

27. HQMC Force Estimate, 17–18, 27, Annex B pages 1–7.

28. Shulimson, *U.S. Marines in Vietnam, 1966*, 346–348; HQMC Force Estimate, 19, Table B-III, Annex B, Annex D, Annex E. The study noted that the additional squadrons would take the Marine Corps approximately three years to build, train, and deploy. Annex E page 2.

29. HQMC Force Estimate, Annex E Appendix 5 page 2, Annex F, and Annex G pages 7–8 and G-4-A-1.

30. HQMC Force Estimate, 19–20, 22–23, 24–26, 28. The estimate of ten months to expand the Marine enclaves across the entire coastal plain proved overly optimistic. In August 1967, ten months after the Force Plan was published, III MAF pacification statistics listed only 925,221 South Vietnamese in the "secure" classification. The number of South Vietnamese living in secure areas had increased by 403,221 (not quite doubled) in the ten months since the plan was written. But those in secure areas still represented only 39 percent of the 2.4 million civilians living in the populated sector along the sea. HQMC Force Estimate, 22–23, Annex C pages 1–2; FMFPAC Force Estimate, 20; FMFPAC, *Operations of U.S. Marine Forces, Vietnam*, August 1967, 17, VDA.

31. HQMC Force Estimate, 26, 28–29, Annex D page 2; Shulimson, *U.S. Marines in Vietnam, 1966*, 347–348. In 1966 1st MAW fielded three utility/observation light helicopter squadrons and fifteen medium lift squadrons. The estimate recommended five light observation, fifteen medium lift, and three heavy lift squadrons for a total of twenty-three.

32. HQMC Force Estimate, 10–14, 20–23, 25–26; Jack Shulimson et al., *U.S. Marines in Vietnam: The Defining Year, 1968* (Washington, DC: HQMC History and Museums Division, 1997), 516–526; Smith, *U.S. Marines in Vietnam, 1969*, 239–241.

33. Smith, *U.S. Marines in Vietnam, 1969*, 285, 294; MACV, *Command History 1970*, Vol. 1, 3-105, Graham A. Cosmas and Terrence P. Murray, *U.S. Marines in Vietnam: Vietnamization and Redeployment, 1970–1971* (Washington, DC: USMC History and Museums Division, 1986), 4–5. Note that the MACV and USMC official history estimates of conventional enemy forces in I Corps in January 1970 are significantly higher (250k–255k) than the estimate shown in III MAF's January 1970 command chronology (~31k, see Table 1).

34. Planners examined the impact of a slower reduction to the enemy's infiltration rate, including a 50 percent reduction in forty months rather than the same amount in twenty months. They also looked at much higher rates of infiltration, including monthly averages of 6,500 and 8,000. The plan acknowledged that more infiltration would slow the pace of expanding security into contested zones and "create problems for Marine Corps forces in I Corps." HQMC Force Estimate, 19–20, 27, Annex B page 10.

35. "The enemy forces, in mass, will provide a better target for our ground and air forces which, in turn, will rapidly accelerate the enemy attrition rate. While massing NVA forces in I Corps will pose a low order threat to Marine forces, it will, nevertheless, ultimately shorten the war." HQMC Force Estimate, 19–20.

36. HQMC Force Estimate, 18, Annex B pages 5 and 9.

37. Peter Brush, "The Story of the McNamara Line," www.shss.montclair .edu/english/furr/pbmcnamara.html. Brush notes that anonymous soldiers in the field christened the project on the same day McNamara publicly revealed its construction.

38. Alistair Horne, *A Savage War of Peace: Algeria, 1954–1962*, rev. ed. (New York: Penguin Books, 1987), 263–266.

39. Examples include John Prados, *The Blood Road: The Ho Chi Minh Trail and the Vietnam War* (New York: John Wiley & Sons, 1999), 212–220, 376–377; Andrew F. Krepinevich, Jr., *The Army and Vietnam* (Baltimore: Johns Hopkins University

Press, 1986), 184–185, 263, 270–271; Phillip B. Davidson, *Vietnam at War, The History, 1946–1975* (Novato, CA: Presidio Press, 1988), 351–353.

40. For a survey of the military efficacy of walls, see Jeremy Black, *Fortifications and Siegecraft: Defense and Attack Through the Ages* (Lanham, MD: Rowman & Littlefield, 2018). David Frye goes further in *Walls: A History of Civilization in Blood and Brick* (New York: Scribner, 2018), arguing that walls were essential for the development of human civilization across all cultures.

41. Keith W. Taylor, *A History of the Vietnamese* (Cambridge: Cambridge University Press, 2013), 279.

42. Tran Trong Trung, *Supreme Commander Vo Nguyen Giap During the Years of American Imperialist Escalation of the War, 1965–1969* (Hanoi, SRV: National Political-Truth Publishing House, 2015), 38, 43, 93, 106, 137–138, 140, 160–162. Special thanks to independent scholar Merle Pribbenow for sharing this translated source. The historian Robert Brigham cites General Doan Chuong, director of Hanoi's Institute for Strategic Studies: "If the supply route had been truly cut off during the war, this would have been a very serious development. . . . We could not, and in fact did not, allow the trail to be cut off." Robert S. McNamara et al., *Argument Without End: In Search of Answers to the Vietnam Tragedy* (New York: PublicAffairs, 1999), 414–416.

43. "MACV PRACTICE NINE Requirements Plan," 26 November 1966, 25–26, Folder "206-02 Historians Background Material (1966) Files Barrier/Starbird Part 1 of 3," Box 31, Entry A1 52 "HQ MACV," RG 472, NARA II (hereafter MACV PRACTICE NINE Plan).

44. "Increased Proportion of NVA Troops," Fact Sheet 46, 17 May 1968, Folder "Fact Book, COMUSMACV, Vol. 1 [1 of 5] [CSA Confirmation Hearings]," Box 70, WCWP, LBJPL (hereafter CSA Confirmation Fact Sheet 46).

45. "Personnel Infiltration (DMZ vs Laos)," Fact Sheet 64, 18 May 1968, Folder "Fact Book, COMUSMACV, Vol. 1 [1 of 5] [CSA Confirmation Hearings]," Box 70, WCWP, LBJPL (hereafter CSA Confirmation Fact Sheet 64).

46. CSA Confirmation Fact Sheet 46.

47. James S. Robbins, *This Time We Win: Revisiting the Tet Offensive* (New York: Encounter Books, 2012), 82–83.

48. IDA Study 255, "Air Supported Anti-Infiltration Barrier," Folder "Vietnam Barrier 2D 9/66–9/68 [1 of 2]," Box 74, Country File—Vietnam, National Security File, LBJP, LBJPL.

49. Charles B. MacDonald interview notes, Folder "11 February 1973," Box 30, and Folders "8 July 1973" and "15–17 August 1973," Box 31, WCWP, LBJPL; MACV PRACTICE NINE Plan, Annex A, Appendix 5, pages 3–4.

50. Shulimson, *U.S. Marines in Vietnam, 1966*, 317.

51. The company-size strongpoints measured two hundred meters square. III MAF Operation Plan 121–66 (PRACTICE NINE), Annex B pages 1–4, Box 156 (III MAF), Entry "Records of Units and Other Commands, 1953–1993," RG 127, NARA II (hereafter III MAF Oplan 121–66); MACV PRACTICE NINE Plan, Annex G, Appendix 1, Tab B, Enclosure 1 and Annex G, Appendix 1, Tab C, Enclosure 1.

52. Memo, Secretary of Defense McNamara to President Johnson, 11 September 1967, Folder "Vietnam Barrier 2D, 9/66–9/68, 12 of 21," Box 74, Country File—Vietnam, National Security File, LBJP, LBJPL.

53. Krulak did not mention the barrier in his history of the Corps, although he devoted three of the book's fourteen chapters to Vietnam. Victor H. Krulak, *First to Fight: An Inside View of the U.S. Marine Corps* (Annapolis, MD: Naval Institute Press, 1984). Nonetheless, his wartime message traffic made clear his disparaging views of the barrier. See, for example, his concerns about the rising costs of the project in Message, CG FMFPAC to CMC, 302249Z July 1967, Folder 7 ("94–0068 CMC Trip Report West Pac, August 3–12, 1967 Part 1 of 3"), Box 11 (1966–1967), Entry 1059 (Office of the Commandant; Records Relating to Official Trips of the Commandant and Assistant Commandant, 1950–1973), RG 127, NARA II.

54. Telfer, Rogers, and Fleming, *U.S. Marines in Vietnam, 1967*, 87.

55. Message, CG III MAG to CMC, 140250Z Jan 67, Folder "III MAF: DYE MARKER exclusive messages, 20 Oct 1966–13 Mar 1967," Box 157 (III MAF), Entry "Records of Units and Other Commands, 1953–1993," RG 127, NARA II.

56. Shulimson, *U.S. Marines in Vietnam, 1966*, 318.

57. Telfer, Rogers, and Fleming, *U.S. Marines in Vietnam, 1967*, 91.

58. MACV PRACTICE NINE Plan, Annex A, Appendix 5, page 4. In a January 1967 VIP brief, a 3rd Marine Division briefer concluded that "we're not enthusiastic over any barrier defense approach to the infiltration problem—if there is such a problem in our area." Shulimson, *U.S. Marines in Vietnam, 1966*, 318. CINCPAC concurred. In a 6 February 1967 message to the Joint Chiefs, Admiral Sharp wrote: "The level of infiltration in the area in which the obstacle system is to be installed does not justify diversion of the effort required to construct and man such a system. Moreover, there is no indication that present operations are inadequate to cope with what has been an insignificant infiltration problem in this particular area of SVN." Telfer, Rogers, and Fleming, *U.S. Marines in Vietnam, 1967*, 88.

59. Shulimson, *U.S. Marines in Vietnam, 1966*, 318; Telfer, Rogers, and Fleming, *U.S. Marines in Vietnam, 1967*, 88.

60. "Operation Plan 11–67 (I Corps, ARVN-III MAF Defense of Northern Quang Tri Province)," no date, Frames 405–439, Reel 21, Box 4 (Records of the US Marine Corps in the Vietnam War Part III: Divisional Command Histories, 1965–1971), Vietnam Archive Microfilm Collection, Vietnam Center and Archive, Texas Tech University, Lubbock, TX; Telfer, Rogers, and Fleming, *U.S. Marines in Vietnam, 1967*, 91.

61. III MAF/3rd Marine Division DYE MARKER Status Report for CMC, 10 August 1967, Folder "7 (94–0068 CMC Trip Report West Pac, August 3–12, 1967 Part 1 of 3)," Box 11 (1966–1967), Entry 1059, RG 127, NARA II (hereafter DYE MARKER Status Report, 10 August 1967).

62. Message, CG III MAF to COMUSMACV, "Strong Point Obstacle System," 050342Z September 1967, Folder "III MAF: DYE MARKER exclusive messages, 20 Oct 1966–13 Mar 1967," Box 157 (III MAF), Entry "Records of Units and Other Commands, 1953–1993," RG 127, NARA II.

63. Westmoreland History Notes, Thursday 7 September 1967, Folder "# 21 History File: 21 Aug—9 Sep 1967," Box "Westmoreland History files 21, 22, 23, & 24," Library, US Army Center of Military History, Washington, DC; Message, CG III MAF to COMUSMCV, COMUSMACV Visit to III MAF," 080814Z September 67, Folder "# 21 History File: 21 Aug–9 Sep 1967," Box "Westmoreland

History files 21, 22, 23, & 24," Library, US Army Center of Military History, Washington, DC; MACV Memo for Record, "Strong Point/Obstacle System in III MAF," 8 September 1967, Folder "F# 21 History File: 21 Aug–9 Sep 1967," Box "Westmoreland History files 21, 22, 23, & 24," US Army Center of Military History, Washington, DC; Message, CG III MAF to COMUSMACV, "Report of General Westmoreland's Visit to III MAF on 13 September 1967," 141456Z September 1967, Folder "#22 History File 10–30 Sep 67," Box 13, WCWP, LBJPL; Message, COMUSMACV to CINCPAC, 161208Z September 1967, Folder "Miscellaneous Cables, 1964–1967," Box 64, WCWP, LBJPL.

64. III MAF Operation Plan 12–67, 12 September 1967, Folder "12) III MAF Operation Plans (by date) 1967," Box 163 (III MAF), Entry "Records of Units and Other Commands, 1953–1993," RG 127, NARA II; III MAF Operation Plan 13–67, 241800H November 1967, Folder "10) III MAF: Op Order #13-67 24 Nov 1967," Box 163 (III MAF), Entry "Records of Units and Other Commands, 1953–1993," RG 127, NARA II; Telfer, Rogers, and Fleming, *U.S. Marines in Vietnam, 1967*, 93; Shulimson et al., *U.S. Marines in Vietnam, 1968*, 26.

65. Telfer, Rogers, and Fleming, *U.S. Marines in Vietnam, 1967*, 94.

66. III MAF Staff Study 2-68, "Military Posture, Northern I Corps," 1 September 1968, Annex D page 9, Folder "18) III MAF: Staff Study 2-68 31 Mar 1968," Box 156 (III MAF), Entry "Records of Units and Other Commands, 1953–1993," RG 127, NARA II (hereafter III MAF 1968 Military Posture Study).

67. Fact Sheet, "Muscle Shoals," 19 May 1968, Tab 4, Folder "Fact Book, COMUSMACV, Vol. 1 [3 of 5] [CSA Confirmation Hearings]," Box 70, WCWP, LBJPL.

68. National Security Council Memo, Earl J. Young to Bromley Smith, 9 September 1968, with attached article on MUSCLE SHOALS project taken from April 1968 *SE Asia Analysis Report* prepared by OASD(SA) SEA Programs Division, Folder "Vietnam Barrier 2D 9/66–9/88 [1 of 2]," Box 74, Country File—Vietnam, National Security File, LBJP, LBJPL.

69. Brush, "The Story of the McNamara Line," www.shss.montclair.edu/english/furr/pbmcnamara.html. A version of this article appeared in *Vietnam* magazine, February 1996, 18–24.

70. Richard D. Camp and Leonard A. Blasiol, *Ringed by Fire: U.S. Marines and the Siege of Khe Sanh, 21 January to 9 July 1968* (Quantico, VA: Marine Corps University History Division, 2019), 17–18.

71. III MAF 1968 Military Posture Study, 12–13.

72. Operation Plan 405–68 (Dual Blade II), 27 November 1968, Folder "1601-10A: Pacification Study Files—Misc. Plans and Studies, 1968 [1 of 3]," Box 7, Entry 33100 [MACV Office of Civil Operations for Rural Development Support, MR 1 Program Coordination Staff], RG 472, NARA II.

73. Fact sheet 149, "Duck Blind," no date, Tab 6, Folder "Fact Book, COMUSMACV, Vol. 1 [4 of 5] [CSA Confirmation Hearings]," Box 70, WCWP, LBJPL; Smith, *U.S. Marines in Vietnam, 1969*, 259; Cosmas and Murray, *U.S. Marines in Vietnam, 1970–1971*, 258–260.

74. Anthony J. Tambini, *Wiring Vietnam: The Electronic Wall* (Lanham, MD: Scarecrow Press, 2007), 138–142.

75. Message, CG FMFPAC to CG III MAF, 222034Z October 1966, Folder

labeled "7) III MAF: 'DYE MARKER' Exclusive Messages 20 Oct 1966–13 Mar 1969," Box 157 (III MAF), Entry "Records of Units and Other Commands, 1953–1993," RG 127, NARA II.

76. III MAF OPlan 121–66, 3.

77. Message, CG III MAF to COMUSMACV, 261046Z April 1967, Folder "7) III MAF: 'DYE MARKER' Exclusive Messages 20 Oct 1966–13 Mar 1969," Box 157 (III MAF), Entry "Records of Units and Other Commands, 1953–1993," RG 127, NARA II.

78. Message, CG FMFPAC to CMC, 302255Z July 1967, Folder "7) III MAF: 'DYE MARKER' Exclusive Messages 20 Oct 1966–13 Mar 1969," Box 157 (III MAF), Entry "Records of Units and Other Commands, 1953–1993," RG 127, NARA II.

79. Message, CG III MAF to COMUSMACV, 160938Z August 1967 and Message, CG FMFPAC to CG III MAF, 122213Z August 1967, Folder "7) III MAF: 'DYE MARKER' Exclusive Messages 20 Oct 1966–13 Mar 1969," Box 157 (III MAF), Entry "Records of Units and Other Commands, 1953–1993," RG 127, NARA.

80. Westmoreland History Notes, 2 and 12 October 1967, Folder "# 23 History File: 1-15 October 1967," Box "Westmoreland History files 21, 22, 23, & 24," Library, US Army Center of Military History, Washington, DC.

81. Westmoreland History Notes, 19 October 1967, Folder "# 24 History File: 15 Oct—12 Nov 1967," Box "Westmoreland History files 21, 22, 23, & 24," Library, US Army Center of Military History, Washington, DC.

82. Message, COMUSMACV to III MAF, "Project DYE MARKER," 22025Z October 1967, Folder "COMUSMACV Signature File—Secret 1967 [1 of 2]," Box 40 [1 of 2], WCWP, LBJPL.

83. Westmoreland History Notes, 26 December 1967, Folder "# 27 History File: 17–27 Dec 67," Box 14, WCWP, LBJPL.

84. Message, COMUSMACV to CG III MAF, "Report of Trip to III MAF, 1–2 Jan 68," 151229Z January 1968, Folder "COMUSMACV 1968, Secret Outgoing Message File [2 of 2]," Box 42, WCWP, LBJPL (hereafter Combined Staff Barrier Inspection Report, 1–2 January 1968).

85. Shulimson et al., *U.S. Marines in Vietnam, 1968*, 27, 29. For samples of media-fueled US Army criticism of Marine actions along the DMZ, see the long Krulak response (triggered by an August 1967 *New York Times* article) in Message, CG FMFPAC to CMC, 021152Z August 1967, 5–21, Folder "III MAF Incoming Messages August 1967," Box "1967," Entry "III MAF," VDA. In November 1967 a piece in the *Economist* criticizing Marines on the DMZ prompted several long messages from Krulak (one of eighteen pages) as well as responses by the Chairman of the Joint Chiefs and the Commandant. Message, CG FMFPAC to CMC, 060312Z November 1967, 24–32, Folder "FMFPAC—SPECAT exclusive, In and Out, September-November 1967," Box "1967," Entry "FMFPAC," VDA; Message, CG FMFPAC to CG III MAF, 022325Z November 1967, 6–9, Folder "III MAF Incoming Messages, November 1967," Box "1967," Entry "III MAF," VDA. In March 1968 the CG, 3rd Marine Division got upset about a critical *Los Angeles Times* article. Message, CG 3rd Marine Division to CG III MAF, 070513Z, 258–66, Folder "III MAF Incoming Messages, March1968," Box "1968," Entry "III MAF," VDA. In the same folder, the following headquarters also commented via message traffic on this article: MACV, 269, 277; JCS, 275; and FMFPAC, 315–319.

86. Combined Staff Barrier Inspection Report, 1–2 January 1968; Shulimson et al., *U.S. Marines in Vietnam, 1968*, 24, 28–29, 31. The estimated construction timelines were based on doctrinal planning factors for field fortification emplacement.

87. Other battalions provided security for the effort but did not help clear the barrier's trace or build its defensive positions.

88. Message, CG, FMFPAC to CMC, 302249Z July 1967, 22–23, Folder "III MAF Incoming Messages, July 1967," Box "1967," Entry "III MAF," VDA; DYE MARKER Status Report, 10 August 1967, Annex B "Assets Expended 12 April to 10 Aug 1967;" 1st MAW CC, August 1967, 2–3, VDA. By the end of 1967 the cost of equipment destroyed while working on the barrier system reached $1,622,348. Telfer, Rogers, and Fleming, *U.S. Marines in Vietnam, 1967*, 94. This monetary loss still amounted to the approximate cost of just two A-4E jets (approximately $750,000 per aircraft), www.skyhawk.org/article/douglas-a4-skyhawk-production-history#a4e.

89. III MAF Fact Sheet for Assistant Commandant of the Marine Corps visit (28 October–4 November 1968), "Da Nang Barrier," 16 October 1968, Folder 11, Box 27 (3rd MAF to 3rd MEF), Entry "Records of Units and Other Commands, 1953–1993," RG 127, NARA II; Shulimson et al., *U.S. Marines in Vietnam, 1968*, 347, 591.

90. United Press International article, 23 October 1967, copy in Folder "PC#3032 Gen Greene's Position on McNamara's 'Wall' 1968," Box 106, Wallace M. Greene Papers (# 3093), MCHD.

91. Message, COMUSMACV to CINCPAC, 161208Z September 1967, Folder "Miscellaneous Cables, 1964–1967," Box 64, WCWP, LBJPL.

92. III MAF Casualty Estimate Study, 14 July 1967, Folders 7 and 8, Box 152 (III MAF), Entry "Records of Units and Other Commands, 1953–1993," RG 127, NARA II.

93. FMFPAC Staff Study, "Possible Actions in DMZ Area if Enemy Resumes Intense Artillery/Rocket/Mortar Attacks," 31 January 1968, 2, Folder 13 [17) FM-FPAC: Possible Actions in DMZ Area 31 Jan 1965], Box 142 [FMFPAC], Entry "Records of Units and Other Commands, 1953–1993," RG 127, NARA II.

94. Fact Sheet 121, "Background Data for Confirmation Hearings," Tab F, Folder "Fact Book, COMUSMACV, Vol. 1 [3 of 5] [CSA confirmation hearings]," Box 70, WCWP, LBJPL. An August 1967 III MAF study claimed that the barrier was intended to stop small but not large groups of infiltrators. DYE MARKER Status Report, 10 August 1967, Annex B pages 1–3. III MAF reinforced this idea in the command's March 1968 staff estimate. III MAF 1968 Military Posture Study, 6. Cushman made the same case to a congressional delegation visiting I Corps in December 1967. When asked if he thought DYE MARKER was a good way to stop infiltration, he replied: "Yes. Under conditions of infiltration of supplies and replacements, it could be easily built and would be very effective; however, invasion in force is now the threat and the system, once built, would be very effective against this also, but the presence in force of both infantry and artillery may make the system very costly in lives to build. I am keeping a constant assessment of this and if I think it is becoming too costly I will so state and make recommendations." Message, CG III MAF to CMC/FMFPAC, 011450Z December 1967, Folder 4 [(7) III MAF: "DYE MARKER" Exclusive Messages, 20 Oct 1966–13 Mar 1967], Box

157 [III MAF], Entry "Records of Units and Other Commands, 1953–1993," RG 127, NARA II.

95. FMFPAC Estimate of the Situation, DMZ Area, Vietnam, 5 April 1967, 9, Folder 6 [(3) FMFPAC: FMFPAC Estimate of the Situation, CMZ Area, Vietnam 5 Apr 1967], Box 141 [FMFPAC], Entry "Records of Units and Other Commands, 1953–1993," RG 127, NARA II.

96. CSA Confirmation Fact Sheet 64.

97. Message, CG III MAF to CG 3rd Marine Division, 221623Z October 1967, Folder 4 ["(7) III MAF "DYE MARKER" Exclusive Messages, 20 Oct 1966–13 Mar 1967"], Box 157 ["III MAF"], Entry "Records of Units and Other Commands, 1953–1993," RG 127, NARA II.

98. Shulimson et al., *U.S. Marines in Vietnam, 1968*, 28, 31.

99. I ARVN Corps/Free World Military Assistance Forces, ICTZ Combined Campaign Plan 1969, 26 December 1968 (hereafter I Corps 1969 CCP), Folder 6 ["(3) III MAF: III MAF/I ARVN Corps CCP 1969 26 Dec 1968 (part 1 of 3)"], Box 162 ["III MAF"], Entry "Records of Units and Other Commands, 1953–1993," RG 127, NARA II. Three senior officers signed the combined plan: Lieutenant General Hoang Xuan Lam, CG ARVN I Corps; Brigadier General Dong Ho Lee, CG 2nd Korean Marine Brigade; and Lieutenant General R. E. Cushman, CG, III MAF.

100. I Corps 1969 CCP.

101. RVNAF, Joint General Staff and Free World Military Assistance Forces, Vietnam Combined Campaign Plan 1969, 30 September 1968, Folder "Combined Campaign Plan—1969 (part 1 of 2)," Box 2 ["Combined Campaign Plan (Part 1 of 2) 1968 THRU Combined Campaign Plan [Part 2 of 2] 1969"], Entry A1 120 ["Studies, Reports and Plans; 1966–1972"], RG 472, NARA II. The senior commanders of six allied commands in South Vietnam signed this combined plan: South Vietnam, United States, Korea, Thailand, Australia, and New Zealand. It is not clear why the senior officer of the Philippines contingent was not included.

102. I Corps 1969 CCP. The two-page section on CAP (Tab A) was added to Appendix 1 (Concept for the Use of Forces) to Annex B (Military Support for Pacification).

103. Shulimson, *U.S. Marines in Vietnam, 1966*, 15.

104. Telfer, Rogers, and Fleming, *U.S. Marines in Vietnam, 1967*, 6–7.

105. I ARVN Corps/III MAF Combined Campaign Plan 1-68, no date (hereafter JGS/FWMAF 1968 CCP), Folder 5 ["(8) III MAF: I ARVN Corps/III MAF Combined Campaign Plan 1-68 1967 part 2 of 3"], Box 157 ["III MAF"], Entry "Records of Units and Other Commands, 1953–1993," RG 127, NARA II; Shulimson et al., *U.S. Marines in Vietnam, 1968*, 15.

106. I Corps 1969 CCP, 5–7.

107. I Corps 1969 CCP, 7–9, 29. This changed intent was captured best in one of the Coordinating Instructions: "This plan provides for no functional separation of responsibilities between RVNAF and FWMAF [Free World Military Assistance Forces]. To prepare for the time when it must assume the entire responsibility, RVNAF must participate fully, within its capability, in all types of operations necessary to accomplish the mission."

108. The US Army Advisory Group was tasked to "continue the advisory effort to I ARVN Corps and subordinate regular forces to assist in the accomplishment of tasks assigned." The plan did identify required improvements in ARVN's logistics support. I Corps 1969 CCP, 27, Annex N pages 2–3.

109. I Corps 1969 CCP, 3–4, Annex L Appendix 1 page 1, Annex M pages 1, 9–10.

110. I Corps 1969 CCP, 14–15, 32, 69–70, Annex N page 5, Annex P page 1.

111. I Corps 1969 CCP, 26, Annex A Appendix 1 page 14–15, Annex B Appendix 1 page 4, and Annex J (Attack on VC Infrastructure).

112. III MAF CC, July 1969, 32, VDA.

113. I Corps 1969 CCP, 3, Annex B page 2, Annex B Appendix 3.

114. CINCPAC, *CINCPAC Measurement of Progress in Southeast Asia*, 30 September 1969, 78–82, Folder "Pacific Command: Measurement of Progress in S.E. Asia, Sept. 30, 1969 (011645-VNLL)," Box 12 ("Pacific Command 1969 to U.S. Readiness Command 1974"), Entry "UD 46-E (Reference Coll. Of External Military Command Docs, 1948–1978)," RG 127, NARA II; Smith, *U.S. Marines in Vietnam, 1969*, 6, 13, 24–25, 80–95, 126, 319–321; Cosmas and Murray, *U.S. Marines in Vietnam, 1970–1971, 5.*

115. I Corps 1969 CCP, 29.

116. I Corps 1969 CCP, Annex B page 1, Annex Q page 2.

117. I Corps 1969 CCP, Annex Q pages 2–3.

118. Phillip B. Davidson, *Secrets of the Vietnam War* (Novato, CA: Presidio Press, 1990), 9–10.

119. JGS/FWMAF 1968 CCP; Smith, *U.S. Marines in Vietnam, 1969*, 11.

120. I Corps 1969 CCP, 11–28.

121. I Corps 1969 CCP, 3–6.

122. Smith, *U.S. Marines in Vietnam, 1969*, 6–8; Cosmas and Murray, *U.S. Marines in Vietnam, 1970–1971, 5.*

123. *Battle Doctrine for Front Line Leaders* (Quantico, VA: Marine Corps Development and Education Command Education Center, 1981), 1. The 3rd Marine Division developed this reference as a training guide during World War II. Quote cited in *Planning*, MCDP 5 (Washington, DC: Headquarters, United States Marine Corps, 1997), 27.

Chapter 7. III MAF's Hybrid War

1. The historians Allan Millett and Williamson Murray, in their three-volume study of military effectiveness of the armed forces of seven nations between 1914 and 1945, define the concept as the "process by which armed forces convert resources into fighting power." This definition better describes efficiency than effectiveness, so this study adopts a revised definition that stresses purpose over process. Allan R. Millett, Williamson Murray, and Kenneth H. Watman, "The Effectiveness of Military Organizations," in *The First World War*, vol. 1, *Military Effectiveness*, ed. Allan R. Millett and Williamson Murray, 2nd ed. (New York: Cambridge University Press, 2010), 2.

2. Victor H. Krulak, *First to Fight: An Inside View of the U.S. Marine Corps* (Annapolis, MD: Naval Institute Press, 1984), 179.

3. Krulak, *First to Fight*, 208.

4. Thomas C. Thayer, *War Without Fronts: The American Experience in Vietnam* (1985, Annapolis, MD: Naval Institute Press, 2016), 43–53. Units smaller than battalion conducted more than 95 percent of all communist ground attacks between 1965 and 1972.

5. Millett and Murray, introduction to *The First World War*, vol. 1, *Military Effectiveness*, xviii.

6. "Although the Corps contains its share of visible heroes, its triumphs, in an aberration of history, are triumphs of the institution itself and not the attainments of individual Marines." Krulak, *First to Fight*, 223.

Epilogue: Lessons and Legacies, 1971–1991

1. Michael A. Hennessy, *Strategy in Vietnam: The Marines and Revolutionary Warfare in I Corps, 1965–1972* (Westport, CT: Praeger, 1997), 181.

2. Conrad Crane, *Avoiding Vietnam: The U.S. Army's Response to Defeat in Southeast Asia* (Carlisle, PA: US Army War College Strategic Studies Institute, 2002); Robert A. Doughty, *The Evolution of US Army Tactical Doctrine, 1946–76* (Fort Leavenworth, KS: Combat Studies Institute, 1979), 40–46.

3. Williamson Murray, "Armored Warfare: The British, French, and German Experiences," in *Military Innovation in the Interwar Period*, ed. Williamson Murray and Allan R. Millett (Cambridge: Cambridge University Press, 1998), 35–38.

4. See Walt tapes 6006a and 6007; Cushman tapes 3626, 3751, 3892, 4058a, 5046, 6009, 6078, and 6247a; and Nickerson tape 6312. All located in Oral History Collection, MCHD. Cushman's comments on pushing force-level units down to divisions are found on tape # 4058a.

5. *Conduct of the War*, vol. 6, *Study of Strategic Lessons Learned in Vietnam* (Maclean, VA: BDM Corporation, 1980), 3-43 to 3-45, 3-94 to 3-122, and 11-48 to 11-62.

6. Collection "Studies and Reports, 1930–2006," MCHD. The Quantico archive maintains a collection of more than 2,600 studies and reports (334 boxes) conducted by and about the Marine Corps between 1930 and 2006. The lack of focus on the MAF's role and requirements as a corps-level headquarters is particularly interesting because studies examining Marine Corps force structure were in session almost continuously from 1971 through 1990. See, e.g., box 59 (FMF structure, 1972), box 65 (FMF structure, 1971–75), boxes 68–69 (the Haynes Board, 1975–1976), boxes 70–74 (force structure review boards from 1980–1991), box 177 (service structure, 1978), box 199 (MAGTF design, 1986), box 248 (permanent MAGTF HQ, 1985), box 306 (HQ redundancy study, 1986), and box 331 (sustaining a MEF in Southwest Asia for more than 180 days, 1990).

7. Robert M. Bray and Richard C. Murrow, *Marine TACAIR and the 1986 Omnibus Agreement* (Maxwell, AL: US Air Force Air University, 1990). This research report, written as a guide to the subject for the Joint Flag Officer Warfighting Course, surveyed the controversy that ensued following the release of the Joint

Chiefs of Staff doctrinal statement and the White Letter released by the Marine Commandant, General P. X. Kelly, explaining the new joint service agreement.

8. "Aviation: Board Report for Utilization, Command and Control of III MAF Helo Assets, 17 May 1969," Folder 3, Box 3, Collection "Studies and Reports, 1930–2006," MCHD; Graham A. Cosmas and Terrence P. Murray, *U.S. Marines in Vietnam: Vietnamization and Redeployment, 1970–1971* (Washington, DC: USMC History and Museums Division, 1986), 288.

9. Donald F. Bittner, *Curriculum Evolution: Marine Corps Command and Staff College, 1920–1988* (Washington, DC: Headquarters Marine Corps History and Museums Division, 1988), 56–73. The staff college director in 1972 was then–Brigadier General Samuel Jaskilka. He had served on sea duty in the Pacific during WWII, led E Company, 2nd Battalion, 5th Marines ashore at Inchon in 1950, and earned two Silver Stars and a Bronze Star in combat in Korea. During Vietnam he served as the assistant division commander of 1st Marine Division in 1969 and CG, Task Force Yankee before working in MACV's J-3 (Operations) shop. After the war General Jaskilka commanded 2nd Marine Division. He earned four stars and served as assistant Commandant of the Marine Corps from 1975 to 1978.

10. Of more than 1,800 student papers written, twelve addressed a Vietnam topic, while just sixteen (less than 1 percent) analyzed aspects of corps-level warfighting. See boxes 96–121 (within the archive's 1934–1975 set of Marine Corps schools Individual Research Papers) and boxes dated 1976–1991, Collection "Individual Research Papers" (# 3953), MCHD.

11. Based on a survey of hard copy *Marine Corps Gazettes* issues from 1971 to 1991, Al Gray Research Center, Marine Corps University, Quantico, VA. One article traced the history of corps-level commands in the Marine Corps. Louis Caporale, "Corps-level Commands of the USMC," *Marine Corps Gazette* 62, no. 11 (November 1978): 74–77.

12. Allan R. Millett, *Semper Fidelis: The History of the United States Marine Corps* (New York: Free Press, 1991), 607–635.

13. Marine historical records, although not capturing all corps-level exercises in this era, list twelve between 1971 and 1989. Most of these exercises were amphibious in character. Not surprising, the archive's exercise files reveal many more exercises conducted at the Marine Amphibious Brigade or Marine Amphibious Unit level than at the MAF level. Boxes 120, 122, 125, 127, 133, 140, 145, 162, 167–68, 170, Collection "Exercises" (# 4118), MCHD.

14. Robert Moskin, *The U.S. Marine Corps Story*, 3rd ed. (Boston: Little, Brown, 1992), 773, 786.

15. Paul W. Westermeyer, *Liberating Kuwait: U.S. Marines in the Gulf War, 1990–1991* (Quantico, VA: Marine Corps University History Division, 2014), 241–248; Moskin, *The U.S. Marine Corps Story*, 775; Thomas D. Dinackus, *Order of Battle: Allied Ground Forces of Operation Desert Storm* (Central Point, OR: Hellgate Press, 2000), 10, Charts 16 and 17.

16. Westermeyer, *Liberating Kuwait*, 221; Merrill L. Bartlett and Jack Sweetman, *The U.S. Marine Corps: An Illustrated History* (Annapolis, MD: Naval Institute Press, 2001), 280–287; Moskin, *The U.S. Marine Corps Story*, 769–798; Millett, *Semper Fidelis*, 636–640.

17. Westermeyer, *Liberating Kuwait*, 241–248; Dinackus, *Order of Battle*, 4-24

to 4-27. A twenty-nine-page untitled paper written in the period of DESERT STORM assessed the Marine Corps' logistic experience in Vietnam, stating: "This paper is written on the assumption that there are some useful logistics lessons to be learned from our involvement and departure from Vietnam which could be of value to our present efforts to disengage from Operation DESERT SHIELD/DESERT STORM, especially in the area of logistics. . . . Alas logistics lessons learned were never recorded." Attached to the analysis was the final report of the III MAF Force Logistic Command's Commanding General in 1971. Folder 1, "Vietnam: Logistics—Lessons Learned," Box 21, Vietnam War Collection, MCHD.

18. Millett, *Semper Fidelis*, 630–631; Westermeyer, *Liberating Kuwait*, 69–73, 87–89, 145–149; documents describing initiation of Marine Corps University's School of Advanced Warfighting in author's possession; Message, CMC to All Marines (ALMAR 238/93, "Marine Air-Ground Task Force Staff Training Program (MSTP)," 130800Z August 1993; Letter, CMC to All General Officers, "MAGTF Staff Training Program (Green Letter 3–92)," 29 September 1992; MSTP Lineage; James F. Amos, "The MEF is our Mission . . . The MAGTF Staff Training Program (MSTP)," *Marine Corps Gazette* 78, no. 2 (February 1994): 26–27. Copies of MSTP documents provided by MSTP, in possession of author.

19. Westermeyer, *Liberating Kuwait*, 75–76; Marine Corps History Division Point Paper, "Activation of a Marine Expeditionary Corps for Operation Desert Storm," 30 January 1991. The author is grateful to the historian Paul Westermeyer of the Marine Corps History Division for sharing a copy of this document.

20. George C. Herring, *From Colony to Superpower: U.S. Foreign Relations Since 1776* (New York: Oxford University Press, 2008), 912.

21. Robert H. Scales, *Certain Victory: The U.S. Army in the Gulf War* (Dulles, VA: Brassey's, 1994); Colin L. Powell and Joseph E. Persico, *My American Journey* (New York: Random House, 1995), 525–532; Norman Friedman, *Desert Victory: The War for Kuwait* (Annapolis, MD: Naval Institute Press, 1991), 236–260; Rick Atkinson, *Crusade: The Untold Story of the Persian Gulf War* (Boston: Houghton Mifflin, 1993), 113, 61–62, 122–123, 198, 453, 488–500.

Bibliography

Archival Sources

Ike Skelton Combined Arms Research Library, Fort Leavenworth, KS
    Obsolete Manual Collection
Lyndon B. Johnson Presidential Library, Austin, TX
    Vietnam Country File
    William C. Gibbons Papers
    William C. Westmoreland Papers
National Archives 2, College Park, MD
    RG 127   Records of the US Marine Corps
    RG 472   US Forces in Southeast Asia, 1950–1975
Naval History and Heritage Command Archive, Washington Navy Yard, Washington, DC
    Historians' Reference Files
    Vietnam Command File
US Army Center of Military History, Fort McNair, Washington, DC
    Thomas C. Thayer Papers
    Vietnam Interview Tapes
        VNIT 626—Clifford Drake
        VNIT 622—COL (no first name) Glikes
        VNIT 624—Eugene Marder
        VNIT 185—Bruce Palmer
    William C. Westmoreland Papers
US Army Heritage and Education Center, Carlisle, PA
    MACV Command Historian's Collection
    Senior Officer Debrief Collection
        Olinto M. Barsanti
        John J. Beeson III
        Charles A. Corcoran
        Welborn G. Dolvin
        Julian J. Ewell
        George I. Forsythe
        Charles M. Gettys
        James W. Gunn
        John G. Hill
        Robert C. Hixon
        David L. Jones

Samuel W. Koster
Robert V. Lee, Jr.
Henry J. Miller, Jr.
Albert E. Milloy
Henry J. Muller, Jr.
Allan G. Pixton
Rowland H. Renwanz
James W. Sutherland, Jr.
Robert E. Wagner
John M. Wright, Jr.
George H. Young, Jr.
Melvin Zais
US Marine Corps History Division, Archives Branch, Quantico, VA
Command Chronologies, Studies, Messages, Reports (Digital Copies)
Fleet Marine Force, Pacific
Operations of U.S. Marine Forces, Vietnam
III MAF
3rd Marine Division
1st Marine Division
Task Force X-Ray
27th Marine Regiment
1st Marine Aircraft Wing
Force Logistics Command
1st Force Service Regiment
Combined Action Force
1st Combined Action Group
2nd Combined Action Group
3rd Combined Action Group
4th Combined Action Group

Manuscript Collections

US Marine Corps History Division, Archives Branch, Quantico, VA
Amphibious Warfare School Papers
Earl E. Anderson Papers
Norman J. Anderson Papers
William E. Barber Papers
Robert H. Barrow Papers
John R. Chaisson Papers
Command and Staff College Papers
Raymond G. Davis Papers
Leo J. Dulacki Papers
Hugh M. Elwood Papers
Expeditionary Warfare Training Group Papers
Wallace M. Greene Papers
Bruno A. Hochmuth Papers
James R. Jones Papers

William K. Jones Papers
Victor H. Krulak Papers
Marine Corps Schools Papers (Individual Research Projects)
Marine Corps Training Exercise Papers
Keith B. McCutcheon Papers
Thomas H. Miller, Jr. Papers
Raymond L. Murray Papers
Herman Nickerson, Jr. Papers
Jonas M. Platt Papers
Charles J. Quilter Papers
Benjamin S. Read Papers
Donn J. Robertson Papers
Edwin H. Simmons Papers
Ormond R. Simpson Papers
Ronald H. Spector Papers
    Robert E. Cushman, Jr. Oral History Transcript
Rathvon McClure Tompkins Papers
Vietnam War Papers
    William F. Simlik Oral History Transcript
Lewis W. Walt Papers
Oral History Collection
    Leonard F. Chapman, Jr.
    Robert E. Cushman, Jr.
    Victor H. Krulak
    Foster C. LaHue
    Herman Nickerson, Jr.
    Lewis W. Walt
US Naval Institute, Annapolis, MD
    Oral History Collection
    Charles J. Merdinger
    Thomas R. Weschler
    Almon C. Wilson
US Navy Seabee Museum, Port Hueneme, CA
    Vietnam War Collection
Vietnam Center and Archive, Texas Tech University, Lubbock, TX
    Sam Johnson Collection
    US Marine Corps History Division Vietnam War Documents Collection
    Vietnam Archive Microfilm Collection
    Vernon Anderson Papers
    Marion E. Carl Papers
    Robert R. Darron Papers
    John K. Davis Papers
    Raymond G. Davis Papers
    Ross T. Dwyer Papers
    Lowell E. English Papers
    Donald R. Gardner Papers
    Frank E. Garretson Papers

Jefferson D. Howell, Jr. Papers
Frederick J. Karch Papers
Oral History Collection
    John R. Chaisson
    Raymond G. Davis
    Ross T. Dwyer
    Lowell E. English
    Frederick J. Karch
    Oscar F. Peatross
    Lawrence F. Snowden
    William J. Van Ryzin
Oscar F. Peatross Papers
Jonas M. Platt Papers
Donn J. Robertson Papers
Ormond R. Simpson Papers
Lawrence F. Snowden Papers
William J. Van Ryzin Papers
Louis H. Wilson Papers

Government Publications and Documents

Amerman, Annette D. *United States Marine Corps in the First World War: Anthology, Selected Bibliography, and Annotated Order of Battle.* Quantico, VA: Marine Corps University History Division, 2016.

Andrew, Jr., Rod. *The First Fight: U.S. Marines in Operation STARLITE, August 1965.* Quantico, VA: Marine Corps University History Division, 2015.

———. *Hill Fights: The First Battle of Khe Sanh, 1967.* Quantico, VA: Marine Corps University History Division, 2016.

Appleman, Roy E., et al. *Okinawa: The Last Battle.* Washington, DC: US Army Center of Military History, 1991.

Birtle, Andrew J. *US Army Counterinsurgency and Contingency Operations Doctrine, 1942–1976.* Washington, DC: US Army Center of Military History, 2007.

Bittner, Donald F. *Curriculum Evolution: Marine Corps Command and Staff College, 1920–1988.* Washington, DC: Headquarters Marine Corps History and Museums Division, 1988.

Burch, Robert M. *Command and Control, 1966–1968.* Honolulu, HI: Headquarters, Pacific Air Force, CHECO Division, 1969.

Camp, Richard D., and Leonard A. Blasiol. *Ringed by Fire: U.S. Marines and the Siege of Khe Sanh, 21 January to 9 July 1968.* Quantico, VA: Marine Corps University History Division, 2019.

Clarke, Jeffrey J. *Advice and Support: The Final Years, 1965–1973.* Washington, DC: US Army Center of Military History, 1988.

Clifford, Kenneth J. *Progress and Purpose: A Developmental History of the U.S. Marine Corps, 1900–1970.* Washington, DC: Headquarters Marine Corps History Division, 1973.

Collins, Jr., Frank C. "Maritime Support in I Corps." In *The Marines in Vietnam,*

1954–1973: An Anthology and Annotated Bibliography. edited by Jack Shulimson, 322–345. Washington, DC: Headquarters Marine Corps History and Museum Division, 1985.

Condit, Kenneth W., John H. Johnstone, and Ella W. Nargele. *A Brief History of Headquarters Marine Corps Staff Organization.* Washington, DC: Headquarters Marine Corps Historical Division, 1970.

Cosmas, Graham A. *MACV: The Joint Command in the Years of Escalation, 1962–1967.* Washington, DC: US Army Center of Military History, 2006.

———. *MACV: The Joint Command in the Years of Withdrawal, 1968–1973.* Washington, DC: US Army Center of Military History, 2006.

Cosmas, Graham A., and Terrence P. Murray. *U.S. Marines in Vietnam: Vietnamization and Redeployment, 1970–1971.* Washington, DC: USMC History and Museums Division, 1986.

Crane, Conrad. *Avoiding Vietnam: The U.S. Army's Response to Defeat in Southeast Asia.* Carlisle, PA: US Army War College Strategic Studies Institute, 2002.

Dawson, David Anthony. *The Impact of Project 100,000 on the Marine Corps.* Washington, DC: Headquarters Marine Corps History and Museums Division, 1995.

Doughty, Robert A. *The Evolution of US Army Tactical Doctrine, 1946–76.* Fort Leavenworth, KS: Combat Studies Institute, 1979.

Eisenhower, Dwight D. Remarks at the National Defense Executive Reserve Conference, 14 November 1957, *Public Papers of the Presidents of the United States* (1957 Comp.), University of Michigan Digital Library. https://quod.lib.umich.edu/p/ppotpus/4728417.1957.001/858?page=root;rgn=full+text;size=100;view=image.

Ewell, Julian J., and Ira A. Hunt, Jr. *Sharpening the Combat Edge: The Use of Analysis to Reinforce Military Judgment.* Washington, DC: Department of the Army, 1995.

Fails, William R. *Marines and Helicopters, 1962–1973.* Washington, DC: Headquarters Marine Corps History and Museums Division, 1978.

Frank, Benis M., and Henry I. Shaw, Jr. *Victory and Occupation.* Vol. 5, *History of U.S. Marine Corps Operations in World War II.* Washington, DC: Headquarters Marine Corps G-3 Division Historical Branch, 1968.

Griffin, Gary B. *The Directed Telescope: A Traditional Element of Effective Command.* Fort Leavenworth, KS: Combat Studies Institute, 1991.

Gunn, Brigadier General James W., USA. "Senior Officer Debriefing Report: US Army Support Command, Da Nang, Period October 1968–October 1969." Washington, DC: Department of the Army, 1969. https://apps.dtic.mil/sti/tr/pdf/AD0505836.pdf.

Hays, II, Ronald E. *Combined Action: U.S. Marines Fighting a Different War, August 1965 to September 1970.* Quantico, VA: Marine Corps University History Division, 2019.

Headquarters Department of the Army. *Field Artillery Operations and Fire Support.* Field Manual 3-09. Washington, DC: Department of the Army, 2014.

———. *Field Service Regulations—Larger Units.* Field Manual 100-15, Washington, DC: Government Printing Office, 1942.

———. *Field Service Regulations—Larger Units.* Field Manual 100-15. Washington, DC: Department of the Army, 1963.

———. *Field Service Regulations—Larger Units.* Field Manual 100-15. Washington, DC: Department of the Army, 1966.

———. *Larger Units: Theater Army—Corps.* Field Manual 100-15. Washington, DC: Department of the Army, 1968.

———. *Larger Units: Theater Army—Corps.* Field Manual 100-15. Washington, DC: Department of the Army, 1973.

———. *Military Intelligence Battalion, Field Army.* Field Manual 30-9. Washington, DC: Department of the Army, 1958.

———. *Staff Organization and Procedure.* Field Manual 101-5. Washington, DC: Department of the Army, 1970.

———. *Tactics, Techniques, and Procedures for Observed Fire.* Field Manual 6-30. Washington, DC: Department of the Army, 1991.

Headquarters US Marine Corps. ALMAR 100/95. *Program to Improve Marine Corps Intelligence.* Washington, DC: Headquarters US Marine Corps, 1995.

———. *Command and Control.* MCDP 6. Washington, DC: Headquarters US Marine Corps, 1996.

———. *Intelligence.* MCDP 2. Washington, DC: Headquarters US Marine Corps, 1997.

———. *Planning.* MCDP 5. Washington, DC: Headquarters US Marine Corps, 1997.

Herman, Jan K. *Navy Medicine in Vietnam: Passage to Freedom to the Fall of Saigon.* Washington, DC: Naval History and Heritage Command, 2010.

Hooper, Edwin B. *Mobility, Support, Endurance: A Story of Naval Operational Logistics in the Vietnam War, 1965–1968.* Washington, DC: US Navy Naval History Division, 1972.

Marine Corps Landing Force Activities. *Command and Staff Action.* Fleet Marine Force Manual 3-1. Quantico, VA: Marine Corps Landing Force Development Activities, 1965.

McChristian, Joseph A. *The Role of Military Intelligence, 1965–1967.* Washington, DC: Department of the Army, 1974.

McCutcheon, Keith B. "Marine Aviation in Vietnam, 1962–1970." In *The Marines in Vietnam, 1953–1973: An Anthology and Annotated Bibliography,* edited by Jack Shulimson, 260–293. Washington, DC: Headquarters Marine Corps History and Museums Division, 1985.

Military History Institute of Vietnam. *Victory in Vietnam: The Official History of the People's Army of Vietnam, 1954–1975.* Translated by Merle L. Pribbenow. Lawrence: University Press of Kansas, 2002. First published 1988. Page references are to the 2002 edition.

Morison, Samuel Eliot. *History of United States Naval Operations in World War II.* 15 vols. Annapolis, MD: Naval Institute Press, 2011. First published 1951.

Nickerson, Herman, Jr. *Leadership Lessons and Remembrances from Vietnam.* Washington, DC: US Marine Corps History and Museums Division, 1988.

Palinkas, Lawrence A., and Patricia Coben. *Combat Casualties Among U.S. Marine Corps Personnel in Vietnam, 1964–1972.* San Diego, CA: Naval Health Research Center, 1985.

Parker, William D. *Civil Affairs in I Corps, Republic of South Vietnam, April 1966–April 1967.* Washington, DC: Headquarters Marine Corps Historical Division, 1970.

Pearson, Willard. *The War in the Northern Provinces, 1966–1968*. Washington, DC: Department of the Army, 1975.

Poole, Walter S. *The Joint Chiefs of Staff and National Policy, 1965–1968*. Washington, DC: Joint Chiefs of Staff Office of Joint History, 2012.

Public Affairs Unit 4–1. *The Marine Corps Reserve: A History*. Washington, DC: Division of Reserve, Headquarters Marine Corps, 1966.

Schlosser, Nicholas J. *In Persistent Battle: U.S. Marines in Operation Harvest Moon, 8 December to 20 December 1965*. Quantico, VA: Marine Corps University History Division, 2017.

Sharp, U.S. Grant Sharp, Jr., and William Westmoreland. *Report on the War in Vietnam*. Washington, DC: US Government Printing Office, 1968.

Shulimson, Jack. *Marines in Lebanon 1958*. Washington, DC: Headquarters Marine Corps History and Museums Division, 1983.

———. *U.S. Marines in Vietnam: An Expanding War, 1966*. Washington, DC: Headquarters Marine Corps History and Museums Division, 1982.

Shulimson, Jack, and Charles M. Johnson. *U.S. Marines in Vietnam: The Landing and the Buildup, 1965*. Washington, DC: Headquarters Marine Corps History and Museums Division, 1978.

Shulimson, Jack, et al. *U.S. Marines in Vietnam: The Defining Year, 1968*. Washington, DC: Headquarters Marine Corps History and Museums Division, 1997.

Simmons, Edwin H. "Marine Corps Operations in Vietnam, 1965–1966." In *The Marines in Vietnam, 1954–1973: An Anthology and Annotated Bibliography*, edited by Jack Shulimson, 35–68. Washington, DC: Headquarters Marine Corps History and Museums Division, 1985.

———. "Marine Corps Operations in Vietnam, 1967." In *The Marines in Vietnam, 1954–1973: An Anthology and Annotated Bibliography*, edited by Jack Shulimson, 69–98. Washington, DC: Headquarters Marine Corps History and Museums Division, 1985.

———. "Marine Corps Operations in Vietnam, 1968." In *The Marines in Vietnam, 1954–1973: An Anthology and Annotated Bibliography*, edited by Jack Shulimson, 99–129. Washington, DC: Headquarters Marine Corps History and Museums Division, 1985.

Smith, Charles R. *Securing the Surrender: Marines in the Occupation of Japan*. Washington, DC: Marine Corps Historical Center, 1997.

———. *U.S. Marines in Vietnam: High Mobility and Standdown, 1969*. Washington, DC: Headquarters Marine Corps History and Museums Division, 1988.

Solis, Gary D. *Marines and Military Law in Vietnam: Trial by Fire*. Washington, DC: Headquarters Marine Corps History and Museums Division, 1989.

Spector, Ronald H. *Advice and Support: The Early Years, 1941–1960*. Washington, DC: US Army Center of Military History, 1985.

———. "The Vietnam War and the Army's Self-Image." In *Second Indochina War Symposium: Papers and Commentary*, edited by John Schlight, 169–185. Washington, DC: US Army Center of Military History, 1986.

Stewart, Richard W. *Staff Operations: The X Corps in Korea, December 1950*. Fort Leavenworth, KS: Combat Studies Institute, 1991.

Stolfi, Russel H. *U.S. Marine Corps Civic Action Efforts in Vietnam, March 1965–March*

1966. Washington, DC: Headquarters Marine Corps G-3 Division Historical Branch, 1968.

Telfer, Gary L., Lane Rogers, and Keith Fleming, Jr. *U.S. Marines in Vietnam: Fighting the North Vietnamese, 1967*. Washington, DC: Headquarters Marine Corps History and Museums Division, 1984.

Tolson, John J. *Airmobility, 1961–1971*. Washington, DC: Department of the Army, 1999. First published in 1973.

Truong, Ngo Quang. *RVNAF and U.S. Operational Cooperation and Coordination*. Washington, DC: US Army Center of Military History, 1980.

US Department of Defense. *Joint Planning*. Joint Publication 5-0. Washington, DC: Government Printing Office, 2017.

———. *Pentagon Papers* ["Report of the Office of the Secretary of Defense Vietnam Task Force," 15 January 1969.] National Archives 2, College Park, MD. www.archives.gov/research/pentagon-papers.

US Marine Corps. *Battle Doctrine for Front Line Leaders*. Quantico, VA: Marine Corps Development and Education Command Education Center, 1981.

———. *Small Wars Manual*. Manhattan, KS: Sunflower University Press, 1996. First published 1940 by US Marine Corps. Page references are to the 1996 edition.

Vick, Alan. *Snakes in the Eagle's Nest: A History of Ground Attacks on Air Bases*. Santa Monica, CA: RAND, 1995.

Vien, Cao Van. *The Final Collapse*. Washington, DC: US Army Center of Military History, 1985.

Vien, Cao Van, et al. *The U.S. Adviser*. Washington, DC: US Army Center of Military History, 1980.

Villard, Erik B. *Combat Operations: Staying the Course, October 1967 to September 1968*. Washington, DC: US Army Center of Military History, 2017.

Westermeyer, Paul W. *Liberating Kuwait: U.S. Marines in the Gulf War, 1990–1991*. Quantico, VA: Marine Corps University History Division, 2014.

Secondary Sources

Allen, George W. *None So Blind: A Personal Account of the Intelligence Failure in Vietnam*. Chicago: Ivan R. Dee, 2001.

Allnut, Bruce C. *Marine Combined Action Capabilities: The Vietnam Experience*. McLean, VA: Human Sciences Research, 1969.

Amos, James F. "The MEF is our Mission . . . The MAGTF Staff Training Program (MSTP)." *Marine Corps Gazette* 78, no. 2 (February 1994): 26–27.

Andrews, William R. *The Village War, Vietnamese Communist Revolutionary Activities in Dinh Tuong Province, 1960–1964*. Columbia: University of Missouri Press, 1973.

Appleman, Roy E. *Escaping the Trap: The U.S. Army X Corps in Northeastern Korea*. College Station: Texas A&M University Press, 1990.

Atkinson, Rick. *Crusade: The Untold Story of the Persian Gulf War*. Boston: Houghton Mifflin, 1993.

Balck, Hermann. *Order in Chaos: The Memoirs of General of Panzer Troops Hermann*

Black. Edited by David T. Zabecki and Dieter J. Biedekarken. Translated by David T. Zabecki and Dieter J. Biedekarken. Lexington: University Press of Kentucky, 2015.

Bartlett, Merrill L., and Jack Sweetman. *The U.S. Marine Corps: An Illustrated History*. Annapolis, MD: Naval Institute Press, 2001.

Bateman, Kirklin J. "Project 100,000: New Standards Men and the U.S. Military in Vietnam." Doctoral dissertation, George Mason University, 2014.

BDM Corporation. *A Study of Strategic Lessons Learned in Vietnam*. 8 vols. Maclean, VA: BDM Corporation, 1980.

Bergerud, Eric M. *The Dynamics of Defeat: The Vietnam War in Hau Nghia Province*. Boulder: Westview Press, 1991.

Berman, Larry. *Planning a Tragedy: The Americanization of the War in Vietnam*. New York: W. W. Norton, 1982.

Birtle, Andrew J. "PROVN, Westmoreland, and the Historians: A Reappraisal." *The Journal of Military History* 72 (October 2008): 1213–1247.

Black, Jeremy. *Fortifications and Siegecraft: Defense and Attack Through the Ages*. Lanham, MD: Rowman & Littlefield, 2018.

Boylan, Kevin M. *Losing Binh Dinh: The Failure of Pacification and Vietnamization, 1969- 1971*. Lawrence: University Press of Kansas, 2016.

Bray, Robert M., and Richard C. Murrow. *Marine TACAIR and the 1986 Omnibus Agreement*. Maxwell, AL: US Air Force Air University, 1990.

Brigham, Robert K. *ARVN: Life and Death in the South Vietnamese Army*. Lawrence: University Press of Kansas, 2006.

Brush, Peter. "The Story of the McNamara Line." *Vietnam* 9 (February 1996): 18–24.

———. "Uncommon Ground: Interservice Rivalry in I Corps." *Vietnam* 12, no. 3 (October 1999): 22–28.

Cable, Larry E. *Conflict of Myths: The Development of Counterinsurgency Doctrine and the Vietnam War*. New York: New York University Press, 1986.

Caporale, Louis. "Corps-level Commands of the USMC." *Marine Corps Gazette* 62, no. 11 (November 1978): 74–77.

Cohan, Jr., Leon. "Intelligence and Viet-Nam." *Marine Corps Gazette* 50, no. 2 (February 1966): 47–49.

Collins, J. Lawton. *Lightning Joe: An Autobiography*. Baton Rouge: Louisiana State University, 1979.

Collins, John M. *Military Geography for Professionals and the Public*, 2nd ed. Omaha, NE: Potomac Books, 1998.

Cooper, Norman V. *A Fighting General: The Biography of Gen Holland M. "Howlin Mad" Smith*. Quantico, VA: The Marine Corps Association, 1987.

Corson, William R. *The Betrayal*. New York: W. W. Norton, 1968.

Daddis, Gregory A. *Westmoreland's War: Reassessing American Strategy in Vietnam*. Oxford, UK: Oxford University Press, 2015.

Dastrup, Boyd L. *The US Army Command and General Staff College: A Centennial History*. Manhattan, KS: Sunflower University Press, 1982.

Davidson, Phillip B. *Secrets of the Vietnam War*. Novato, CA: Presidio Press, 1990.

———. *Vietnam at War, The History: 1946–1975*. Novato, CA: Presidio Press, 1988.

Davis, Raymond G., and Richard O. Camp. "Marines in Assault by Helicopter." *Marine Corps Gazette* 52, no. 9 (September 1968): 22–28.

Delaney, Douglas E. *Corps Commanders: Five British and Canadian Generals at War, 1939–45.* Vancouver, BC: UBC Press, 2011.

Dinackus, Thomas D. *Order of Battle: Allied Ground Forces of Operation Desert Storm.* Central Point, OR: Hellgate Press, 2000.

Elliot, David W. P. *The Vietnamese War and Social Change in the Mekong Delta, 1930–1975,* 2 vols. Armonk, NY: M. E. Sharpe, 2003.

Engels, Donald W. *Alexander the Great and the Logistics of the Macedonian Army.* Berkeley: University of California Press, 1980.

Finlayson, Andrew R. *Rice Paddy Recon: A Marine Officer's Second Tour in Vietnam, 1968–1970.* Jefferson, NC: McFarland & Company, 2014.

Friedman, Norman. *Desert Victory: The War for Kuwait.* Annapolis, MD: Naval Institute Press, 1991.

Galiley, Harry A. *"Howlin' Mad" vs. the Army: Conflict in Command Saipan, 1944.* Novato, CA: Presidio Press, 1986.

Giap, Vo Nguyen. *People's War, People's Army: The Viet Cong Insurrection Manual for Underdeveloped Countries.* 1961. Reprint. New York: Frederick A. Praeger, 1962.

Gilbert, Ed. *The U.S. Marine Corps in the Vietnam War: III Marine Amphibious Force, 1965–1975.* Oxford, UK: Osprey Publishing, 2006.

Hallihan, William H. *Misfire: The History of How America's Small Arms Have Failed Our Military.* New York: Charles Scribner's Sons, 1994.

Hannah, Norman. *The Key to Failure: Laos and the Vietnam War.* New York: Madison Books, 1987.

Heinl, Jr., Robert Debs. *Soldiers of the Sea: The United States Marine Corps, 1775–1962.* Baltimore, MD: The Nautical & Aviation Publishing Company of America, 1991.

Hennessy, Michael A. *Strategy in Vietnam: The Marines and Revolutionary Warfare in I Corps, 1965–1972.* Westport, CT: Praeger, 1997.

Herring, George C. *America's Longest War: The United States and Vietnam, 1950–1975,* 5th ed. New York: McGraw-Hill Education, 2014.

———. *From Colony to Superpower: U.S. Foreign Relations Since 1776.* New York: Oxford University Press, 2008.

Hess, Gary R. *Vietnam: Explaining America's Lost War.* West Sussex, UK: John Wiley & Sons, 2015.

Hibbert, Christopher. *Anzio: The Bid for Rome.* New York: Ballantine Books, 1970.

Horne, Alistair. *A Savage War of Peace: Algeria, 1954–1962,* rev. ed. New York: Penguin Books, 1987.

Huff, K. P. "Building the Advanced Base at Da Nang." In *Vietnam: The Naval Story,* edited by Frank Uhlig, Jr., 175–201. Annapolis, MD: Naval Institute Press, 1986.

Huie, William Bradford. *Can Do! The Story of the Seabees.* Annapolis, MD: Naval Institute Press, 1997. First published 1944 by E. P. Dutton.

———. *From Omaha to Okinawa.* New York: E. P. Dutton, 2014. First published 1945.

Hunt, David. *Vietnam's Southern Revolution: From Peasant Insurrection to Total War.* Amherst: University of Massachusetts Press, 2008.

Hunt, Richard A. *Pacification: The American Struggle for Vietnam's Hearts and Minds.* Boulder: Westview Press, 1995.

Isely, Jeter A., and Philip A. Crowl. *The U.S. Marines and Amphibious War: Its Theory, and Its Practice in the Pacific.* Princeton, NJ: Princeton University Press, 1951.

Johnson, Wray R. *Vietnam and American Doctrine for Small Wars.* Bangkok: White Lotus Press, 2001.

Jones, Bruce E. *War Without Windows: A True Account of a Young Army Officer Trapped in an Intelligence Cover-Up in Vietnam.* New York: Vanguard Press, 1987.

Karnow, Stanley. *Vietnam: A History,* 2nd ed. New York: Penguin Books, 1997.

Kinnard, Douglas. *The War Managers: American Generals Reflect on Vietnam.* Boston: Da Capo Press, 1991. First published 1977 by University Press of New England. Page references are to the 1991 edition.

Krepinevich, Jr., Andrew F. *The Army and Vietnam.* Baltimore: Johns Hopkins University Press, 1986.

Krulak, Victor H. *First to Fight: An Inside View of the U.S. Marine Corps.* Annapolis, MD: Naval Institute Press, 1984.

Kutta, Timothy J. *Gun Trucks.* Carrollton, TX: Squadron/Signal Publications, 1996.

Lanning, Michael Lee, and Dan Cragg. *Inside the VC and the NVA: The Real Story of North Vietnam's Armed Forces.* College Station: Texas A&M University Press, 2008.

Lehrack, Otto J. *The First Battle: Operation Starlite and the Beginning of the Blood Debt in Vietnam.* 2004, New York: Presidio Press, 2006.

Lewy, Guenter. *America in Vietnam.* New York: Oxford University Press, 1980.

Long, Joseph C. *Hill of Angels: U.S. Marines and the Battle for Con Thien, 1967–1968.* Quantico, VA: Marine Corps University History Division, 2016.

Manstein, Erich von. *Lost Victories.* Edited by Anthony G. Powell. Translated by Anthony G. Powell. Novato, CA: Presidio Press, 1994. First published 1955 by Methuen Publishing.

Marks, Thomas A. *Maoist Insurgency Since Vietnam.* London: Frank Cass, 1996.

McNamara, Robert S., et al. *Argument Without End: In Search of Answers to the Vietnam Tragedy.* New York: PublicAffairs, 1999.

Mellenthin, F. W. von. *Panzer Battles: A Study of the Employment of Armor in the Second World War.* Edited by L. C. F. Turner. Translated by H. Betzler. New York: Ballantine Books, 1990. First published in US 1956 by University of Oklahoma Press.

Melson, Charles D., and Wanda J. Renfrow, ed. *Marine Advisors with the Vietnamese Marine Corps.* Quantico, VA: Marine Corps University History Division, 2009.

Merdinger, Charles J. "Civil Engineers, Seabees, and Bases in Vietnam." In *Vietnam: The Naval Story.* Edited by Frank Uhlig, Jr., 228–253. Annapolis, MD: Naval Institute Press, 1986.

Millett, Allan R. *Semper Fidelis: The History of the United States Marine Corps.* New York: Free Press, 1991.

———. "Wallace M. Greene Jr., 1964–1968." In *Commandants of the Marine Corps,* edited by Allan R. Millett and Jack Shumlison, 381–401. Annapolis, MD: Naval Institute Press, 2004.

Millett, Allan R., Williamson Murray, and Kenneth H. Watman. "The Effectiveness of Military Organizations." In *The First World* War. Vol. 1, *Military*

Effectiveness. 2nd ed. Edited by Allan R. Millett and Williamson Murray, 1–30. New York: Cambridge University Press, 2010.

Moise, Edwin E. *The Myths of Tet: The Most Misunderstood Event of the Vietnam War.* Lawrence: University Press of Kansas, 2017.

Montgomery, Bernard Law. *The Memoirs of Field Marshal Montgomery.* Barnsley, UK: Pen & Sword Books, 2007. First published 1958 by World Publishing. Page references are to the 2007 edition.

Moskin, J. Robert. *The U.S. Marine Corps Story,* 3rd ed. Boston: Little, Brown, 1992.

Moyar, Mark. *Phoenix and the Birds of Prey: Counterinsurgency and Counterterrorism in Vietnam.* Lincoln: University of Nebraska Press, 2007. First published 1997.

Murphy, Dennis J. "Let's Practice What We Preach About Helicopter Operations." *Marine Corps Gazette* 53, no. 8 (August 1969): 18–24.

Nevgloski, Edward Thomas. "Understanding the United States Marines' strategy and approach to the conventional war in South Vietnam's Northern provinces, March 1965–December 1967." Doctoral dissertation, King's College London, 2019.

Nguyen, Lien-hang T. *Hanoi's War: An International History of the War for Peace in Vietnam.* Chapel Hill: University of North Carolina Press, 2012.

Nolan, William Nolan. *Battle for Hue, Tet 1968.* New York: Dell Publishing, 1983.

Olson, James S., and Randy Roberts. *My Lai: A Brief History with Documents.* Boston: Bedford/St. Martin's, 1998.

Palmer, Dave Richard. *Summons of the Trumpet: U.S.-Vietnam in Perspective.* Novato, CA: Presidio Press, 1982.

Palmer, Jr., Bruce. *The 25-Year War: America's Military Role in Vietnam.* Lexington: University Press of Kentucky, 1984.

Parry, Francis Fox. *Three-War Marine: The Pacific–Korea–Vietnam.* New York: Jove Books, 1989. First published 1987 by Pacifica Press. Page references are to the 1989 edition.

Pike, Douglas. *Viet Cong: The Organization and Techniques of the National Liberation Front of South Vietnam.* Cambridge, MA: MIT Press, 1966.

Pisor, Robert. *The End of the Line: The Siege of Khe Sanh.* New York: Ballantine Books, 1982.

Powell, Colin L., and Joseph E. Persico. *My American Journey.* New York: Random House, 1995.

Prados, John. *The Blood Road: The Ho Chi Minh Trail and the Vietnam War.* New York: John Wiley & Sons, 1999.

Prefer, Nathan N. *Patton's Ghost Corps: Cracking the Siegfried Line.* Novato, CA: Presidio Press, 2000.

Quinlivan, James T. "Force Requirements in Stability Operations." *Parameters* 25, no. 4 (Winter 1995): 59–69.

Race, Jeffrey. *War Comes to Long An: Revolutionary Conflict in a Vietnamese Province.* Berkeley: University of California Press, 1973.

Raus, Erhard. *Panzer Operations: The Eastern Front Memoir of General Raus, 1941–1945.* Translated by Steven H. Newton. Cambridge, MA: Da Capo Press, 2003.

Reynolds, Michael. *Men of Steel: I SS Panzer Corps the Ardennes and Eastern Front, 1944–45.* Staplehurst, UK: Spellmount, 1999.

———. *Steel Inferno: 1st SS Panzer Corps in Normandy.* New York: Dell Publishing, 1997.

Ridgway, Matthew B. *Soldier: The Memoirs of Matthew B. Ridgway.* New York: Harper & Brothers, 1956.

Robbins, James S. *This Time We Win: Revisiting the Tet Offensive.* New York: Encounter Books, 2012.

Rottman, Gordon. *The Marine Corps Pacific Theater of Operations, 1941–43.* Oxford, UK: Osprey Publishing, 2004.

———. *U.S. Marine Corps Pacific Theater of Operations, 1943–44.* Oxford, UK: Osprey Publishing, 2004.

———. *U.S. Marine Corps Pacific Theater of Operations, 1944–45.* Oxford, UK: Osprey Publishing, 2004.

Sander, Robert D. *Invasion of Laos 1971: Lam Son 719.* Norman: University of Oklahoma Press, 2014.

Scales, Robert H. *Certain Victory: The U.S. Army in the Gulf War.* Dulles, VA: Brassey's, 1994.

Schelling, Thomas C. *Arms and Influence.* New Haven, CT: Yale University Press, 1966.

———. *The Strategy of Conflict.* Cambridge, MA: Harvard University Press, 1960.

Shaw, John M. *The Cambodian Campaign: The 1970 Offensive and America's Vietnam War.* Lawrence: University Press of Kansas, 2005.

Simmons, Edwin H. *The United States Marines: The First Two Hundred Years, 1775–1975.* New York: Viking Press, 1974.

Simpkin, Richard E. *Race to the Swift: Thoughts on Twenty-First Century Warfare.* London: Brassey's, 2000.

Slim, William J. *Defeat into Victory.* New York: David McKay Company, 1965. First published 1956 by Cassell. Page references are to the 1965 edition.

Solis, Gary D. *Son Thang: An American War Crime.* Annapolis, MD: Naval Institute Press, 1997.

Soper, James B. "Observations: STEEL PIKE and SILVER LANCE," *U.S. Naval Institute Proceedings* 91, no. 11 (November 1965): 46–58.

Sorley, Lewis. *A Better War: The Unexamined Victories and Final Tragedy of America's Last Years in Vietnam.* New York: Harcourt Brace, 1999.

Stanton, Shelby L. *America's Tenth Legion: X Corps in Korea, 1950.* Novato, CA: Presidio Press, 1989.

———. *Vietnam Order of Battle.* Washington, DC: U.S. News Books, 1981.

Summers, Jr., Harry G. *On Strategy: A Critical Analysis of the Vietnam War.* New York: Dell Publishing, 1984.

Tacitus, Cornelius. "The Life of Cnaeus Julius Agricola," edited by Alfred John Church and William Jackson Brodribb. In *Complete Works of Tacitus*, edited by Sara Bryant. New York: Random House, 1876; repr., 1942. www.perseus.tufts .edu/hopper/text?doc=Perseus%3Atext%3A1999.02.0081%3Achapter%3D27.

Tambini, Anthony J. *Wiring Vietnam: The Electronic Wall.* Lanham, MD: Scarecrow Press, 2007.

Taylor, Keith W. *A History of the Vietnamese.* Cambridge: Cambridge University Press, 2013.

Thayer, Thomas C. *War Without Fronts: The American Experience in Vietnam*. Annapolis, MD: Naval Institute Press, 2016. First published 1985 by Westview Press. Page references are to the 2016 edition.

Tin, Bui. *From Enemy to Friend: A North Vietnamese Perspective on the War*. Annapolis, MD: Naval Institute Press, 2002.

Trueblood, Henry Ward. *A Surgeon's War: My Year in Vietnam*. San Francisco, CA: Astor & Lenox, 2015.

Trullinger, James. *Village at War: An Account of Revolution in Vietnam*. New York: Longman, 1980.

Trung, Tran Trong. *Supreme Commander Vo Nguyen Giap During the Years of American Imperialist Escalation of the War, 1965–1969*. Hanoi: National Political-Truth Publishing House, 2015.

Truong Chinh. *Primer for Revolt*. Reprint. New York: Frederick A. Praeger, 1963.

Truscott, Jr., Lucian K. *Command Missions: A Personal Story*. New York: Random House Publishing, 1990. First published 1954 by E. P. Dutton.

Turley, Gerald H. *The Easter Offensive: Vietnam, 1972*. Novato, CA: Presidio Press, 1985.

Velicogna, Arrigo. "Victory and Strategic Culture: The Marines, the Army and Vietnam; First Corps Tactical Zone 1965–1971." Doctoral dissertation, King's College London, 2013.

Walls, David Frye. *Walls: A History of Civilization in Blood and Brick*. New York: Scribner, 2018.

Walt, Lewis W. *Strange War, Strange Strategy: A General's Report on Vietnam*. New York: Funk & Wagnalls, 1970.

West, Jr., F. J. *The Village*. New York: Bantam Books, 1992.

Westmoreland, William C. *A Soldier Reports*, 4th ed. New York: Dell Publishing, 1984.

Wiest, Andrew. *Vietnam's Forgotten Army: Heroism and Betrayal in the ARVN*. New York: New York University Press, 2008.

Wilkinson, Spenser. *The Brain of an Army: A Popular Account of the German General Staff*, 2nd ed. London: Constable, 1913.

Willbanks, James H. *Abandoning Vietnam: How America Left and South Vietnam Lost Its War*. Lawrence: University Press of Kansas, 2004.

———. *A Raid Too Far: Operation Lam Son 719 and Vietnamization in Laos*. College Station: Texas A&M University Press, 2014.

Winecoff, Dave. "Night Ambush!" *Marine Corps Gazette* 68, no. 1 (January 1984): 47–52.

Winton, Harold R. *Corps Commanders of the Bulge: Six American Generals and Victory in the Ardennes*. Lawrence: University Press of Kansas, 2007.

Wirtz, James J. *The Tet Offensive: Intelligence Failure in War*. Ithaca, NY: Cornell University Press, 1991.

Zaloga, Steven J. *Anzio 1944: The Beleaguered Beachhead*. Oxford, UK: Osprey Publishing, 2005.

Zhai, Qiang. *China and the Vietnam Wars: 1950–1975* Chapel Hill: University of North Carolina Press, 2000.

Index

Horrocks, Lt. Gen. Brian, 255n92
hospitals, 167, 168–169, 175
House Armed Services Committee,
286n107
Hue, Battle of, 30, 43–45, 46, 102, 141,
245n62
Hussein, Saddam, 227
hybrid war, 215–216, 219, 221, 222

Inchon, Battle of, 8
Infantry Company Intensive Pacification
Program, 243n40
intelligence operations, 215–216
Iwo Jima, Battle of, 8, 70

Jaskilka, Gen. Samuel, 301n9
Johnson, Gen. Harold K., 201
Johnson, Lyndon B., 28, 46, 98, 101, 156,
157, 187
Joint Coordinating Council, 220, 252n62
Joint Forces Air Component
Commander concept, 257n109

Karnow, Stanley, 263n40
Khe Sanh, Battle of, 77, 178, 225
Khe Sanh airfield, 27, 82, 124
Kit Carson Scouts, 27, 220
Komer, Robert W. "Blowtorch," 28, 67,
104, 129, 258n8
Korean Marine brigade, 26, 70, 184
Korean War, 5, 15
Koster, Maj. Gen. Samuel B., 67
Krepinevich, Andrew F., Jr., 6
The Army and Vietnam, 126
Krulak, Lt. Gen. Victor
on adaptability, 220
on amphibious operations, 122
bet with Army Maj. Gen. Stilwell,
283n76
on casualties, 113
on Chu Lai airfield construction, 171
on conventional war, 113–114
criticism of DOUBLE EAGLE I
and II, 251n52
criticism of MACV, 222
on DMZ barrier plan, 199, 200,
293n53, 296n85
estimate of enemy fatalities, 268n103
on expansion of the III MAF
headquarters, 247n2
on ink-blot strategy, 111

on Marine Corps, 223
on MEF staff, 249n28
military career of, 24, 55, 57, 147
monthly report to Washington, 100
operational advice, 111
on pacification, 111, 126, 220
photograph of, 147
planning effort, 196
RLT-27 case, 161
Walt and, 57–58
Ky, Maj. Gen. Nguyen Cao, 26, 58,
266n71
Kyle, Gen. Wood B., 196

LaHue, Brig. Gen. Foster C., 44, 245n62
Laos
NVA sanctuaries in, 133, 220
raids along the border of, 27, 28, 30,
101, 132, 176, 195, 288n122
Larsen, Lt. Gen. Stanley R., 76
Lewy, Guenter, 260n22
Loc, Nguyen Van, 266n71

M-16 rifle, 177, 286n107
MacDonald, Charles B., 254n83
MAGTF Staff Training Program, 230
Manstein, Gen. Erich von, 5
Marine Air-Ground Task Force
(MAGTF) doctrine
air and ground components, 253n79
criticism of, 142
development of, 10, 14, 19, 23, 212–213
effectiveness of, 13
flaws of, 222
as operational standard, 16, 62, 116, 122
organizational design of, 173
test of, 142, 217
Marine Corps Gazette, 239n19
Marine enlisted training, 158
Marine Expeditionary Corps (MEC), 10,
17, 19, 70, 76, 238n16, 254n81
Marine Expeditionary Force (MEF), 10,
17, 23, 86, 173, 250n34
Marine Logistics Command, 217
Marine Reserve, 156, 278n6, 278n9
Marine schools, 238–239n17, 239n18,
239n21
Marine sergeants, 158
Mayaguez rescue in Cambodia, 227
McCutcheon, Lt. Gen. Keith B.
death of, 225

Printed in the USA
CPSIA information can be obtained
at www.ICGtesting.com
CBHW031930290824
13830CB00004B/15/J

9 780700 636938